MRS. RESTINO'S
COUNTRY KITCHEN

Mrs. Restino's Country Kitchen

written & illustrated by
Susan Restino

Shelter Publications Inc.   Bolinas   California

Distributed in the United States by Random House, Inc., New York, N.Y. and in Canada by Random House of Canada, Limited, Toronto

Library of Congress Cataloging in Publication Data
Restino, Susan.
  (Country kitchen)
  Mrs. Restino's Country Kitchen.
  p.   cm.
  Includes bibliographical references and index.
  ISBN 0-936070-18-8 (Shelter)
  ISBN 0-679-76946-3 (Random House)
  1. Cookery.   2. Stoves, Wood.
TX652.R469   1996
469—dc20   95-23432
                             CIP

Canadian Cataloguing in Publication Data
Restino, Susan.
  Mrs. Restino's Country Kitchen
Includes index.
ISBN 0-679-30792-3
1. Cookery, Canadian – Nova Scotia style.
2. Cookery – Nova Scotia 1. Title.
TX715.6.R47   1996
641.59716   C95-932890-4

We are grateful to Frances Moore Lappé for permission to reprint the chart on p. 88 from *Diet for a Small Planet*, Ballantine Books, Random House, © 1991 by Frances Moore Lappé.

1 2 3 4 5 6 — 01 00 99 98 97 96
Lowest numbers indicate number and year of this printing.

First Printing: April 1996

Printed in Canada

NOTE: This book has special Repkover "lay-flat" binding.
(Note how the spine is constructed.)

Additional copies of this book may be purchased for $16 plus $3 shipping and handling from:

    Shelter Publications, Inc.
    P.O. Box 279
    Bolinas, California 94924 USA

Or write for a free catalog of books.

Introduction

This is a cookbook for people who want to learn more about how to use healthy ingredients to whip up delicious meals without too much fuss. It's also full of stories about our life on the farm and how we learned to do things on our own.

I am not a professional cook. I do not spend large chunks of my life perfecting my mousse technique or getting better at piecrusts. The things I put time into are mass recipes, things like whole wheat bread, potluck casseroles, or pots of jam. I picked up a wealth of French cooking techniques working as an au pair (mother's helper) in Europe in the '60s. Then I fell in love with Asian stir-fry and hummus from the Middle East. But by far the most important influence came from cooking on our farm in Nova Scotia, for my husband, who has an Italian appetite, and for our two children. That was where I learned to make the most of what was available, and to pay close attention to nutrition, as well as making delicious things to eat.

There are recipes in this book from around the world and right next door, and there are recipes both traditional and experimental. Chicken with Chanterelles. Rice dry-roasted instead of fried. Salads and stir-fries appropriate to the season of the year. Desserts that are good endings to meals, not meals in themselves.

There are also sections about how to brew wines and beer, bake your own bread, make cheese out of milk, dry herbs, and operate a wood-burning cook stove. It seems to me that such capacities engender a kind of independence, a way of beating the system and doing things on your own.

We live tucked back in a steep little valley in the Cape Breton highlands of Nova Scotia, Canada, surrounded by trees and hills and streams. Once there were maybe a dozen little farms out here. Now and again you come across a pile of stones or an ancient, gnarled apple tree, but there is remarkably little trace of the community that lived here a hundred years ago.

My husband and I came from away, as they say in Cape Breton. We emigrated from New England to Canada in the early 1970s. We spent several years on a borrowed farm, but we lusted after land and a compost pile of our own. We found the right place, and with the help of our neighbors hastily assembled a 10 x 20 foot cabin for ourselves and our two small children, Samantha (aged 7) and Carey (aged 1). That first summer we also raised a barn in which to house our goats, horses and chickens. I began writing all this in a tent under an apple tree, just as a way of keeping track of recipes from season to season.

Looking back, I am amazed at how much energy we had. We cleared pastures, pulled stumps, established gardens and survived with very little money. In the winter we ate potatoes, carrots, cabbages, apples and beets, from a hillside root cellar, deep under the snow. We kept a freezer at a farm of a neighbor who had electricity three miles away, packed with greens, fruits, fish and meats. We bought whole grains and legumes by the 50-pound sack. We travelled, when necessary, by bicycle or horse and wagon. At that time we had no telephone or electricity, no television or radio, and no motor vehicle. We didn't, for the most part, miss them. We were focused on the land, the turning of the seasons, the growing of the children, and our own survival.

It seemed to us of value that the children participated in that struggle. They helped us till the garden, tend the animals, fuel the stove, and build additions to the farm: a chicken house, a wood shed, a kitchen. We had time to wander with them and gather things in season: fiddleheads and brook trout in the spring, chanterelles and berries in the summer, apples and game in the fall. We made endless batches of cookies. In the winter we skied and snowshoed and went sliding. I remember the two of them sitting in the back of the sleigh, drawing lines with sticks in the snow as the big black horse trotted silently home in the magical winter night.

✧

Nothing stays the same. The children grew. Samantha liked home schooling, but Carey wanted to ride the big yellow bus. We bought a half-ton truck and had a telephone installed in the kitchen, so we could keep after the highway department about the road, which, in the spring, was a mire.

When we needed a bigger house, Charley and I went to work in the woods, cutting and planting for the forest industry, supplying the paper mills in Nova Scotia. With the money we built a wood frame house, well insulated, with deep water lines and woodstove heat. Through all of this, we kept the farm running, and continued to cook terrific meals for each other.

Our daughters grew up and moved out on their own. Both now live in Alaska, which they say is like Cape Breton in some ways, but with "real" mountains. Samantha and her husband, Scott, now work as paramedics in isolated communities in the far north. Carey serves in restaurants. Both like to garden, bake bread and cook. They also paint, draw and write terrific letters. I write to them, send the occasional package, and welcome them home once in a while. It's a great thing for young people to get out and explore the world, to get a sense of the planet as a living entity. We are not only citizens of one valley, one town, one country or climate.

After the kids were gone, Charley and I began to take farming more seriously. We planted gourmet crops such as asparagus and strawberries. We set up a large greenhouse for tomatoes, melons, peppers, and basil. We joined an organic farming movement that brings young people to our farm to help with the harvest work. I wrote magazine articles about the sorts of things we do around here: hunt fiddleheads, can tomatoes, recycle everything. I have always illustrated my own cookbooks, but after the kids were gone I began to draw and paint more for the sheer pleasure of it.

⊷

We're not trying to turn back the clock. There are a great many things about the times we live in now which I'm grateful for. But that doesn't mean we have to buy the whole package, or pay the price thereof. We like to do things for ourselves, to cook with foods that are very near their source. Some we grow and some we buy. We try to know what we're eating and where it comes from, to be sure that it's not laced with sprays, preservatives and artificial who-knows-what-all. And it feels good to do something to slow down our personal consumption of the earth's limited resources.

It's not, however, just that I like the philosophy of our lifestyle; it's also fun. Country cooks have to do a lot of

improvising, experimenting, and inventing in the kitchen. You have to, since the store may be far away. But after the initial shock wears off (A birthday cake? Without eggs?) you begin to enjoy getting into the essentials of cooking. It becomes less like something out of a package or a book and more something you just feel like eating. I've tried to get enough fundamentals into this book so that maybe when you get through reading it, you won't need cookbooks any more.

If so, be sure to pass it along.

Susan Restino
Baddeck, Nova Scotia

CONTENTS

Herbs & Condiments 57

fines herbes: celery, parsley, thyme, shallots & tarragon.

Sauces & Marinades 74

Vegetarian Dishes   85

Special Cooking   108

Fish & Shellfish   113

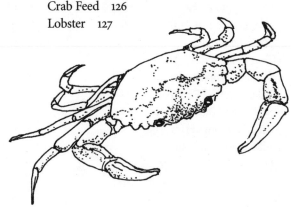

Quickbreads   192

Desserts   198

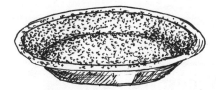

Dairy   226

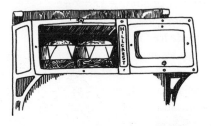

*This book is dedicated to necessity,
the mother of all our best efforts.*

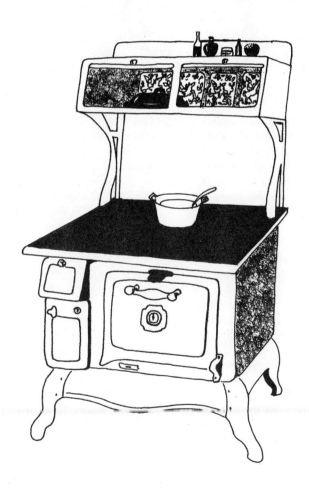

Hors d'Oeuvres

When a bunch of people get together for a common meal, it's usually quite a while before they get around to eating. Everybody is so excited to see one another. There is much talk about the weather, gardens and projects, and for those of us who still have them around, how are the kids?

At a time like this, simple, straightforward hors d'oeuvres are in order. Nothing difficult or complicated. I remember once, long ago, spending all afternoon making 24 popovers stuffed with tuna fish salad, all of which were eaten at once by the first two ten-year-olds who hit the food table. Nor am I greatly excited by boxes of expensive crackers, so costly, so dry, so unimaginative. What I want on the table is something healthy and attractive, easy to munch on, with a few exotic flavors to mark the special occasion.

Fresh, tender, uncooked vegetables on a tray or dish accompanied by tasty pots of dip are some of the most attractive things a host can set out.

How do I decide what to serve? I go out into my garden the morning before the party and see what's available. If that isn't an option for you, select vegetables in the market with care. Only small fresh vegetables will be tasty and tender served raw. Wash them well!

No matter how carefully arranged, a vegetable platter will begin to look messy when half of them are eaten up. If it's to be a long party, with people coming and going, rearrange the vegetable tray from time to time, or add more from bags of vegetables pre-chopped and stashed in the fridge. For pots of dip, read on.

Favorite vegetables include:

tiny cherry tomatoes
snow peas
sliced mushrooms
strips and slivers of green, red, and
 yellow peppers
broccoli florets
cauliflower
tiny whole carrots
wedges of turnip
celeriac and kohlrabi
strips of celery
cucumbers
small, fresh beans
radishes
Jerusalem artichokes
green onions
sliced asparagus
daylily buds

Spring Dip

Mix a day in advance for best results.
Terrific stuff for a party, with crackers or
vegetables.
½ cup sour cream
½ cup plain yogurt
½ Tbsp lemon juice
1 clove crushed garlic
1 Tbsp chopped mint
pinch of salt
Cover tightly; refrigerate overnight.

Blue Cheese Dip

Wake up your palate; serve with freshly cut
slices of crisp apple and turnip.

Mash:
¼ cup blue cheese
Add and mix in gradually:
½ cup sour cream
Spoon into a clean bowl before serving.

Hot Salsa

When the tomatoes are ripe and fresh,
that's the moment to make a pot of fresh
salsa. It works as a dip with hot pita bread
or corn chips, or as a sauce with Mexican
dishes or any bland food — rice, beans,
fish, even tofu.

Chop, then mince fine:
2 cups fresh tomatoes
1 medium onion
2 Tbsp seeded jalapeño peppers
Toss in a bowl with:
1 Tbsp red wine or **2 tsp wine vinegar**
1 tsp ground cumin
dash of salt
To serve as a dip, toast pita bread, then cut
into 8 or 10 wedges.

Hummus

A pungent, eye-watering spread used often
in the Middle East and adored by
passionate garlic lovers everywhere. Tahini
is a sesame butter (like peanut butter),
available in health food stores.

Soak overnight, rinse, and cook *(see p. 89):*
garbanzo beans (chickpeas)
3 times as much water as peas
1 onion
Grind softened chickpeas to a fine paste
with a food mill, food processor, or
blender. To 1 cup mashed chickpeas add:
2 to 4 cloves crushed or smashed garlic
¼ cup olive oil
½ cup tahini
juice of 1 good-sized lemon
salt to taste (about 2 pinches)
1 to 2 Tbsp fresh chopped parsley
Add water as needed to make a smooth
texture.

Guacamole

Avocados are so good that many people just mash them up, plain, to use as a sauce or sandwich filling. I like to add things to liven up the flavor.

Slice, skin, remove pits, and mash with a fork:
2 avocados
Add:
2 Tbsp minced onion
juice of ½ lemon
dash of cayenne pepper
dash of salt
Cover and keep cool for an hour or two. Serve with corn chips or crisp, unsalted crackers.

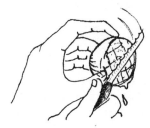

Onion Dip

This is a mild, pleasant dip. My mother used to serve it on special occasions with potato chips, which were a rare treat. It's also tasty with celery sticks, cherry tomatoes, and small cucumbers.

Mash in a small bowl:
¼ cup cream cheese
Gradually mix in:
½ cup sour cream
The clean, bright flavor is **onion juice,** which is extracted by first cutting the onion in half through the equator, cutting a shallow grid into each half, then scraping the onion halves with a serrated knife. Let the juice drip into the sour cream mixture. Stir well and refrigerate, covered, for 1 to 3 hours.

Garnish this with **fresh, chopped chives.**

Tofu Dip

Tofu, or Japanese bean curd, has almost no flavor of its own. It needs a lot of help. On the other hand, it's very good for you and very tasty when mixed with the following.

Press through a sieve or mash thoroughly:
1 cup (8 oz) tofu
3 Tbsp safflower oil
3 Tbsp tamari soy sauce
2 Tbsp lemon juice
½ tsp salt
1 clove crushed garlic
Cover and refrigerate for 1 hour or longer. Serve with crackers and raw or marinated vegetables.

Antipasto Grill

Broiled vegetables are a good first course for a long dinner party. Serve on platters with an assortment of vegetable dips and corn chips.

Chop and slice into handy pieces:
1 small eggplant
1 small zucchini
1 large yellow pepper
1 large red pepper
Add:
10 whole mushrooms
In a small bowl combine:
¼ cup olive oil
3 Tbsp wine vinegar
1 clove crushed garlic
1 Tbsp grated Parmesan cheese
1 tsp Dijon mustard
Beat these ingredients together.

Preheat the grill and lightly oil the grill pan. Lightly paint or dip the vegetables in the marinade mixture, and broil 3 to 5 minutes.

Turn all vegetables once during broiling and re-coat as necessary.

SERVES 4

Tempura

The making of tempura is a cooking adventure, to be undertaken when you want to do something great in the kitchen. Various combinations are famous in their own right, such as corn and onion fritters, and fried daylily buds. Tempura cannot be prepared much ahead of time. It is a creature of the moment, served as hors d'oeuvres or with snowy mounds of rice, and perhaps a little fish cooked in the same batter and hot oil as the tender garden vegetables.

Batter: Break into a shallow bowl and briefly beat:
1 egg
Using half the eggshell as a measuring cup, add to the beaten egg:
2 half-shells of white flour
3 half-shells of water
Mix as needed. Expand in these proportions as you go.

Oil: Fill a heavy, deep pan half-full of light vegetable oil; heat slowly to 375°F. When it is ready, you can drop a cube of bread into it and count slowly to 60; it should be brown.

Making Tempura: Have ready before you start: a slotted spoon, brown paper on a tray to drain the finished vegetables, plenty of potholders, and, just in case of fire, a lid for the pan and a big box of baking soda or salt.

Vegetables will cook best if chilled. Some people like to dip them in batter, chill for 30 minutes, then fry; it makes a neater job.

Fry pieces a few at a time. How many depends on your pot, but too many will lower the temperature of the oil too much. From time to time, skim bits of batter out of your pot. Don't let the oil smoke.

Vegetables you may use:

Raw and Whole
asparagus tips
green beans
mushrooms
watercress
daylily flowers and buds
Japanese knotweed shoots
tiny onions

Raw and Sliced
broccoli florets
cauliflower florets
eggplant
summer squash
onions
bamboo shoots
green peppers
celery

Grated or Chopped Fine
To cook these, add more flour to the batter so the shreds will hang together in small clumps.
corn cut from the cob
onions
carrots
cabbages

Sliced and Parboiled 2 Minutes
carrots
winter squash
Jerusalem artichokes

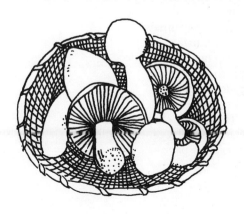

CHILDREN'S HORS D'OEUVRES

Hors d'oeuvres serve a whole different purpose for growing children. They are often very hungry when they arrive at the party. If you set out chips or crackers they will whip right through them, and then eat little else until dessert comes along. However, I have found that, if offered, they will accept:

dry-roasted sunflower seeds *(see below)*
popcorn *(see below)*
stuffed eggs *(see below)*
sesame crackers*(see p. 186)*
mild cheese, cut in chunks or strips
roasted peanuts
fresh or frozen fruit, cut in manageable
    pieces

Stuffed Eggs

Eggs are easier to shell if they are not too fresh. If you grow or buy fresh eggs, store them for at least 3 days before hard-boiling.

Start in a pan of cold water:
4 eggs
Bring the pan to a rapid boil, and cook 10 to 12 minutes. Shell eggs and cut in half vertically with a very sharp knife. Slice off a little of the curved base so they will sit upright. Take out the yolks and mash them up. Then stuff the eggs with this mixture:
4 mashed yolks
3 Tbsp mayonnaise
½ tsp mustard
½ tsp tamari soy sauce
pinch of paprika
pinch of pepper
½ tsp salt
1 Tbsp finely chopped parsley
Garnish each egg with a pinch of chopped parsley or paprika.

Dry-Roasted Sunflower Seeds

Put a handful of
shelled plain sunflower seeds
in a heavy skillet. Shake or stir over moderate heat as the seeds brown slightly, 5 to 7 minutes. Cool before serving.

Popcorn

In a 4-quart pot with a heavy bottom and tight lid, heat:
¼ cup safflower oil
1 cup popcorn kernels
Cover the pan and cook over high heat, shaking it slightly every few seconds to keep the kernels from burning on one side. When the popcorn begins to pop, turn the heat down until it just keeps popping; stay with the pot. When the popping slows down, remove from heat. It is traditional to shake melted butter and salt over the popcorn, but you need not do so every time you make it.

Soups & Stocks

Homemade soups are an important part of my kitchen. They make good lunches and snacks, and keep people from eating up all the bread in the house as they come foraging through the kitchen. You can also run a cup of soup through the food mill or the blender and have an instant supply of baby food. And when unexpected guests arrive at dinnertime, you can stretch a meal by tacking a soup course on at the beginning.

STOCKS

Most soups taste better when made with stock, although you can make soups without it. Stock is water in which vegetables and/or bones have been cooked to extract the flavor and nutrition. It's easy to make, store, and use up. A pressure cooker, crockpot, or an ordinary pot can be used.

Vegetable Stock

In a deep, heavy Dutch oven or pressure cooker, heat:
2 Tbsp oil
Add, for every quart of soup stock you want to make:
2 sliced carrots
2 chopped onions
1 chopped stalk celery or **about ¼ cup celery tops**
2 or 3 sprigs parsley
1 bay leaf
1 tsp salt
a couple of peppercorns
Sauté all of this lightly for a few minutes, not long enough to brown anything; then pour in:
2 quarts water
Bring to a boil, then simmer, covered, for about 2 hours. It will cook down to about 1 quart. Strain it through a sieve (be sure to get those peppercorns out). This is now soup stock, to be used in gravy, sauce, or soup. Keep refrigerated or freeze.

1 QUART STOCK

Chicken Stock

Chicken makes wonderful stock, a base for superb soups and sauces. You may use chicken backs or the bones left over from any chicken dish. Boiling will sterilize them, even if they've been to the table. Avoid necks of commercial birds, as they may contain drug residues.

bones from 1 chicken
2 qts water
2 to 3 celery tops
1 chopped onion
2 to 3 sprigs parsley
1 diced carrot
1 bay leaf
4 peppercorns
2 Tbsp marjoram
1 tsp salt

Cover bones with water and add all other ingredients. Bring to a rapid boil for 15 minutes, then reduce heat and simmer, covered, for about 1 hour.

Chicken stock can also be made in a pressure cooker. Fill cooker no more than ⅔ full of water, bones and vegetables. Bring to 15 pounds pressure and lower heat according to pressure cooker instructions. Pressure-cook for 30 minutes. Cool stock completely before removing lid.

Strain and cool. Refrigerate up to 3 days. To keep it longer, freeze it.

1 QUART STOCK

Beef Stock

You can make a similar stock using venison instead of beef.

2 cloves
1 onion
2 lb beef shank or **flank**
2 lb beef or **venison bones**
2 qts water
1 chopped carrot
2 to 3 sprigs parsley
2 tsp salt

Stick the cloves into the onion. Combine all ingredients in a pressure cooker or large pot and cover with water. Cook at 15 pounds pressure for 1 hour or simmer 6 hours over low heat. Strain broth into containers and cover tightly when cool. Refrigerate for up to 1 week or freeze.

1 QUART STOCK

Fish Stock

Fish makes the most delicate of all stocks. Put heads, tails, skin, and bones in a good-sized pot. Add:

2 qts water

And for every quart of water:

1 whole onion with a clove stuck in it
1 bay leaf
⅓ cup white wine (optional)
1 stalk celery
3 white peppercorns
1 tsp coriander seeds
1 tsp salt

Bring this almost to a boil (don't let it boil at any point if you can help it, since it will smell up the house and discourage you from making it again) and simmer gently over very low heat, covered, for about 1 hour. Strain, being careful to get the peppercorns and coriander seeds out. This is a finished stock, for fish soups or sauces, and needs no additional cooking. If you are not going to use it within a couple of days, freeze it.

1 QUART STOCK

MISO

Miso, like soy sauce, is a product of fermented soybeans. It comes in a thick black paste and smells a little like cheese. It is very high in protein, keeps well without refrigeration and it makes delicious instant soups.

There are three kinds of miso.

Hatcho miso: Made from fermented soybeans. A very dark, firm miso with a strong, almost musky Cheddar-like flavor from long aging.

Use **1 heaping tsp hatcho miso** to **1 cup water**.

Kome miso: Made from fermented soybeans and rice, kome miso is lighter in color and texture. The flavor is more acidic, less heavy.

Use **1 heaping Tbsp kome miso** to **1 cup water**.

Mugi miso: Made from fermented soybeans and barley, mugi miso is very thick and pasty.

Use **1 heaping Tbsp mugi miso** to **1 cup water**.

Of course, these are general guidelines; you may add or subtract as you see fit. There are, however, several things to remember about miso. It is very salty, so do not add salt until after you have the soup all made; then do so only with great care and restraint. Miso (like soy sauce and yogurt) contains enzymes that are helpful to digestion but that are destroyed by too much heat. The method of cooking for miso soups is to add the miso at the end, being careful not to boil it. Finally, all miso, and hatcho miso in particular, is hard to mix directly with hot water.

Measure your miso into a cup and work a little warm water into it with a spoon; then add more liquid, and finally empty it all into the simmering soup.

Miso soups are traditionally composed of sliced, simmered root vegetables, nuts, and seafoods that float around in the clear dark broth.

Miso Soup

In a soup pot, heat:
2 tsp light oil
and sauté lightly:
1 sliced onion (cut like thin wedges of a pie)
2 sliced carrots (cut in thick diagonals)
After 5 minutes, add 3 cups water and simmer, lid on, for 15 minutes. Mash **miso** (**3 tsp hatcho miso** or **3 Tbsp** either **kome** or **mugi miso**) in a cup with a little water; add to soup and serve.

SERVES 2

Clear Onion Soup

This is the quickest, easiest, most rewarding soup on earth.

Heat in a heavy soup pot:
2 or 3 Tbsp corn oil or **butter**
Slice very thin and add:
2 or 3 onions
Sauté these carefully, so they don't burn, until they are good and brown. Then add:
3 Tbsp white flour
Stir and cook gently for a couple of minutes. Then add:
1 qt stock *(see pp. 13–14)*
Cover the pot and let it simmer for around 30 minutes over medium heat. Serve with croutons, or you may slice and toast:
1 piece of bread per serving
Sprinkle the bread with:
grated Parmesan, Swiss, or **Cheddar cheese**
Float the bread in the soup pot and put the pot under a broiler for 2 minutes, or until the cheese melts.

Variation
If you make this with vegetable stock *(see p. 13)* and are dissatisfied with the pale color and lack of flavor, you may add:
¼ cup tamari soy sauce
Serve at once.

SERVES 3 TO 4

Borscht

"Borscht!" sounds more like something you're supposed to yell to lagging sled dogs than the name of an exotic, red sweet-and-sour soup. Borscht is, basically, beet soup; tomatoes and perhaps a dash of lemon or vinegar are added to cut the sweetness. It's a good autumn/fall soup, best served with its traditional accompaniments.

Combine:
3 cups stock
1 qt stewed fresh or canned tomatoes
½ cup chopped leeks, scallions, or **onion tops**
Bring to a simmering point; add:
2 cups grated raw beets
Simmer, covered, 30 minutes to 1 hour, until beets are tender. Mash up tomatoes, using a fork or potato masher. Meanwhile, set out:
sour cream, garnished with **chopped dill** and/or **chives**
rye bread
dill pickles
pickled herring *(see Solomon Gundy, p. 119)*
lemon wedges

SERVES 4

Homemade Chicken Soup

There's no substitute for the real thing. Cures colds, broken hearts and wild beasts.

Bring to a full rolling boil:
6 cups chicken stock *(see p. 14)*
Add and boil for 5 minutes:
1 cup sliced carrot
1 cup small shell pasta
Add and boil for 5 minutes longer:
1 cup cooked, chopped chicken
½ cup frozen peas
¼ cup chopped parsley
salt and pepper to taste

SERVES 4

Golden Soup

In this farmhouse version of instant food, you can use squash or pumpkin for an easy gourmet meal. Serve with muffins or brown bread.

Wash, clean, and chop into large chunks:
1 winter squash or **pumpkin**
Place these in a large pot with an inch or so of water. Cover and bring to a boil; then turn down heat and simmer for 30 minutes or until the squash is tender. Meanwhile, heat in a heavy skillet:
1 Tbsp safflower oil
1 chopped onion
Add sautéed onions to the squash as it cooks. When the squash is soft, purée onions and squash in a food mill, blender or food processor. Return to pot.
For 3 cups of squash, add:
3 cups milk
You may substitute all or part of the milk with:
double-strength reconstituted dried milk
Season to taste with:
¼ tsp smashed rosemary
salt, pepper, cumin or **coriander,** and **a dash of nutmeg**
finely chopped parsley
Add more milk as needed. Don't let it boil.

SERVES 4

Split Pea Soup

There are various ways to get a rich ham flavor into split pea soup. One is to sauté the onions in bacon fat. Another is to float a hunk of bacon or ham fat in the pot. Or you can simmer a ham bone. The main thing is that rich, smoky flavor.

In a deep, heavy soup pot, heat:
3 Tbsp sesame oil
Add and sauté until golden:
1 sliced onion

Add and bring to a boil:
4 cups water
1 ham bone (if you've got it)
3 chopped carrots
1 cup green or yellow split peas
½ tsp salt
1 bay leaf
Cover and cook over moderate heat for 2 to 3 hours. Add more water as needed. Serve with cornbread *(see p. 197)* or hoecakes *(see p. 194)*, or croutons fried in bacon fat. Some people slice hard-boiled eggs on top, or crumble them on as a garnish.

SERVES 4

Broccoli Soup

A sophisticated, delicate Japanese soup, very quickly made. It's a good use for a small amount of broccoli. You may substitute other vegetables.

Cut into wedges:
1 small onion (3 Tbsp)
Cut into ¼-inch slices:
1 carrot
1 cup broccoli stems
Bring to a boil:
5 cups water
Immerse the vegetables, turn down to a simmer, cover, and cook 15 minutes. Break up and add:
1 or 2 cups broccoli florets
Simmer, covered, for 5 minutes. Add:
2 Tbsp tamari soy sauce
Don't allow the soup to boil after you add the soy sauce. Serve hot.

SERVES 2 TO 3

BISQUES

Cream soups can be made very quickly and are always impressive, warming, and nutritious. They are not necessarily made with cream. Their thick, smooth texture may come from milk, canned milk, dried skim milk, flour, or mashed potatoes. Their delicate flavors come from onions, steamed seafood, or the carefully hoarded water from cooking a strong vegetables (such as broccoli or asparagus). It's a nice touch to garnish the soup with a little chopped, cooked food — whatever flavor is in the broth. For example, you might have a feed of steamed lobster or asparagus once in a blue moon. Keep the cooking water (put it away as soon as you finish cooking, so nobody throws it out) and save out a little lobster meat or some asparagus tips. Make the soup a day later, and garnish with the bits you saved.

Potato Bisque

An important item in any cook's arsenal is a fabulous dish that uses nothing special and takes less than half an hour to prepare. This soup base is marvelously versatile and pleases everyone, even fussy little kids.

In a heavy soup pot, heat:
4 Tbsp butter or **safflower oil**
Carefully sauté:
1 chopped onion or **½ cup sliced green onions**
When they look limp, sprinkle over them:
4 Tbsp unbleached white flour or **whole wheat flour**
Cook for a minute or two, then stir and add:
4 cups water or **stock** *(see Stocks, p. 13–14)*
3 cups cubed raw potatoes
1 tsp salt
ground pepper
Bring to a boil, reduce heat, and simmer, covered, for 15 minutes, or until the potatoes become soft. Mash the potatoes in the pot with a fork or masher, or, if you prefer, in a food mill or blender. Return them to the soup and add:
3 cups milk
Heat gently for a few minutes, being careful not to boil. Served hot, it can be garnished with chopped chives and a pat of butter floating on top. Served cold, as vichysoisse, it is good sprinkled with paprika on top.

SERVES 4

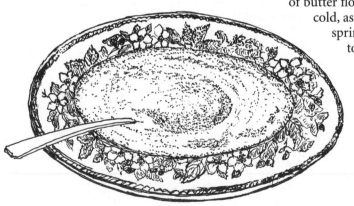

Asparagus Bisque

1 recipe Potato Bisque *(see p. 18)*
12 fresh asparagus spears
1 cup water
½ tsp salt

Cut the spears in half, reserving the green tops. Peel the lower stems and chop into ½-inch pieces. Add to Potato Bisque, along with the potatoes. Boil the tops separately in a small pan with ½ cup salted water for 6 to 10 minutes. Remove tops and chop into ¼-inch pieces; they should be very small. Add their cooking water to the soup. When the soup is almost ready to serve, garnish with chopped asparagus tops. Simmer 3 to 4 minutes before serving.

SERVES 4

Mushroom Bisque

1 recipe Potato Bisque *(see p. 18)*
24 fresh mushrooms
3 Tbsp butter

Begin with the basic recipe for Potato Bisque. Remove mushroom stems, chop fine, and add them to Potato Bisque, along with the potatoes. Meanwhile, heat butter in a small skillet, slice mushroom caps vertically, and sauté until golden over medium heat. Add them to the soup along with the milk. Serve hot with toast.

SERVES 4

Cream of Chicken Soup

Dark meat has more flavor; light meat is more tender. A mixture is good.

1 recipe Potato Bisque *(see p. 18)*
1 cup cooked, chopped chicken
2 cups Chicken Stock *(see p. 14)*
chopped parsley

Add chopped chicken to Potato Bisque, along with the potatoes. Use chicken stock instead of water. Garnish with parsley instead of chives.

SERVES 4

Corn Chowder

1 recipe Potato Bisque *(see p. 18)*
Add to Potato Bisque, along with the potatoes:
1 cup corn, fresh, frozen, or **canned**
¼ cup diced green peppers

SERVES 4

Fish Chowder

The most popular fish for this is haddock, but you can use any fresh or cooked fish, or leftovers. Salmon has wonderful color.

1 recipe Potato Bisque *(see p. 18)*
1 cup fish
2 cups Fish Stock *(see p. 14)*
½ tsp celery salt
white wine

Add fish to Potato Bisque, along with the potatoes. Use fish stock (or substitute water). Flake the fish when you mash the potatoes, and season with celery salt and wine.

SERVES 4

Clam Chowder

You may use fresh or canned clams, or even mussels, provided they are well washed. If using fresh shellfish, clean thoroughly *(see pp. 122–23)* and separate into two dishes, one of soft parts and another of tough necks. Reserve juice by opening shellfish over a bowl.

1 recipe Potato Bisque *(see p. 18)*
1 rib chopped celery
1 cup chopped clam necks
1 cup chopped clam soft parts
1 cup clam juice

Sauté celery along with onion in Potato Bisque and add clam necks to soup along with potatoes. Use clam juice as part of the water. Add the soft clam parts when you add the milk. Serve with soda biscuits.

SERVES 4

Bean Soups

You can make bean soup out of any kind of dried beans or peas, keeping in mind that some varieties take longer to cook than others. In general, the larger, the longer, ranging from 2 to 6 hours (see Dried Beans, p. 89). All legumes cook faster if soaked overnight.

Sort through and pick over:
1 cup dried legumes
Soak overnight in:
2 cups cold water
In the morning, empty them (and their water) into a heavy cooking pot and add:
6 cups boiling water
1 large onion stuck with 3 cloves
1 clove garlic
3 stalks celery, with leaves, or **2 Tbsp dried celery leaves**
1 carrot
1 ham bone, or **piece of bacon** or **ham fat** (optional)
1 bay leaf
ground pepper
½ tsp salt
Boil rapidly, covered, for 30 minutes, then simmer, covered, until the beans soften, from 2 to 4 hours. Take out ½ cup of cooked beans and put the rest of them, plus anything else that will go, through a food mill, or mash them with a fork. Return the puréed and the whole beans to the pot and adjust the salt.

SERVES 4

Variations
U.S. Senate Bean Soup: Use marrow beans or yellow-eye beans; add a potato and mash it along with the beans.

Tomato Bean Soup: In place of 1 cup boiling water, add 1 cup stewed canned tomatoes and their water.

Whole Bean Soup: Chop the vegetables and sauté them in bacon or ham fat before adding the beans and water. Use ground pepper; mince the garlic and omit the cloves. Do not put through a food mill, but mash some of the beans with a potato masher or spoon against the side of the pot.

Black Bean Soup: Omit the carrot; use black beans. Serve with wedges of lemon and hard-boiled eggs.

Stone Soup

A tramp came by, looking for a meal. "Go away with you," said the old woman, but the tramp insisted he'd show her how to make a rich, delicious soup out of only water and a stone. So the story goes. . . . But of course it does taste better with a few other ingredients. Add water as needed toward the end if evaporation makes it too thick.

In a large pot, combine:
1 clean stone
10 cups water or **stock** (see pp. 13–14)
2 sliced carrots
1 chopped onion
1 stalk chopped celery
1 cup barley
½ cup haricot or white beans
½ tsp thyme
1 bay leaf
1 tsp salt
ground pepper
Bring to a boil, cover, lower heat and simmer for a couple of hours or until the beans are soft through. Ten minutes before you serve, remove stone and add:
½ cup fresh or **frozen peas**

SERVES 4 TO 6

Mrs. Restino's Minestrone Soup

Definitely our favorite soup, this combines beans and grain to complete the missing amino acids in both. Thus, a bowl or two makes a big change in the middle of your day. A flexible soup — I've never made it quite the same way twice. Add water as needed toward the end if evaporation makes it too thick.

In a deep, heavy pot, heat:
1 Tbsp safflower oil or **pork fat**
Add:
1 chopped onion
2 stalks chopped celery (with leaves)
When the onions are limp, you may add, if you like:
1 clove crushed garlic
Sauté one minute longer; then add:
2 quarts hot water or **stock** (see pp. 13–14)
1 tsp salt
Bring to a rapid boil over high heat; add slowly, so it keeps boiling:
½ to 1 cup navy, white, or **speckled beans**
Boil for 60 minutes, covered. Then add:
1 to 2 cups cooked or **canned tomatoes** (with liquid)

4 cups water or **stock**
1 tsp oregano
a pinch of pepper
1 tsp basil
Cook slowly, covered, for 60 minutes or longer. In the last 15 minutes, add 1½ cups fresh vegetables, such as:
corn (frozen is OK), **green peas** or **beans, mushrooms, chopped summer squash, chopped greens,** or **parsley**
You may also add:
½ cup uncooked egg noodles (any shape, as long as they're small)
Boil 10 minutes or until noodles are tender. This soup is even better the second day, with last night's vegetable leftovers added.

SERVES 4 TO 6

Vegetables in Season

GROWING YOUR OWN VEGETABLES

Gardening is one of the great joys of living in the country. No matter how much or how little you have done, it is always something of a success, and there is always more to learn. Through the garden, you become much more aware of the soil beneath your feet, the climate you live in, and the weather. The seasons pass; you turn the earth, plant seeds, mulch, weed, prune and harvest. And I like the finality of winter snow — covering it all for a few months; it's like wiping clean the slate. Next spring you can start another new and different garden.

If you haven't gardened before, go at it gradually. Seeds are so inexpensive, and the catalogs have such marvelous promises of what will come of them — but they don't have your soil, your weather, your schedule, or your back. A few reliable vegetables will do to start: lettuce, chard or spinach, radishes, peas, beans, and summer squash. Talk to your neighbors about what they grow; gardeners are always happy to give advice.

This year we have worked harder than ever at our garden. The strawberries we set out last fall are mulched two inches deep with hardwood chips. The onions, planted in a place that was untilled grass last year, are surrounded completely by black plastic: Charley folded the plastic like an accordion, and drilled holes so that when unfolded there were literally hundreds of closely set holes in a grid. An onion set went in each hole. The onions are now large and green and weedless. The corn, potatoes, sunflowers, beans and peas are all huge crops; the tomatoes, peppers, melons, and basil are growing inside a 12 x 35-foot greenhouse, protected from wind, hail and black flies; the tomatoes and peppers are already setting fruit, and it is not yet the first of August. We have had tons of lettuce and a few good feeds of asparagus, and I have already frozen a dozen or more bags of chard. Gardening in Cape Breton.

Even if you don't have a garden at all, it makes sense to eat locally grown vegetables in season. Out of season means that somebody had to drive a truck or fly a plane, consuming gasoline and spewing fumes all the way.

The seasons of this chapter are New England and Canadian Maritime seasons.

SPRING
asparagus
fiddleheads
greens
Jerusalem artichokes
parsnips
peas
snow peas
sugar snaps

SUMMER
beans
cattail cobs
corn
purslane
wild mushrooms
summer squash and zucchini
tomatoes
peppers
salad and dressings
cucumbers

FALL
broccoli
Chinese and Savoy cabbages
Brussels sprouts
cauliflower

WINTER
beets
cabbage
carrots
winter squash
potatoes
alfalfa sprouts

PREPARING VEGETABLES

The Potato Exercise

First of all, choose a large, straight-bladed knife. The French chef's knife, with a triangular blade, is designed for this sort of thing, but any good slicing knife will do. It need not be very sharp. You should also

have a wooden chopping surface on a counter low enough for good leverage.

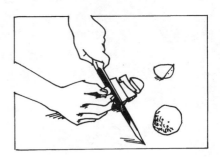

Keeping the knife tip on the chopping board, swing the blade up and down, without lifting the tip of the knife off the board. Observe the degree of control you have: the blade goes exactly where you want it, enabling you to push vegetables around safely with your other hand.

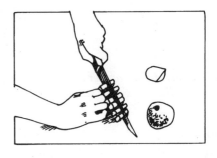

Wash a potato and hold it on the board. Keeping the knife tip firmly in place, swing the handle up and down as you push the potato into the guillotine. The thickness of the slices is controlled by the hand pushing the potato. As you reach the end, curl your fingers so that the blade is pressed against your knuckles, cutting only the potato.

To further chop the potato, place the tip of the knife just beyond the rough pile of sliced pieces. Swing the blade up and down without lifting the tip, but moving the handle over a little after each cut. Soon your potato will be in matchstick pieces. Now place the knife at a right angle to the previous cut, or push the pile around with the side of the knife and your other hand, and cut the pile into cubes — still keeping the tip of the knife securely on the board. For tough cuts, press top of blade with the other hand.

Carrots

Carrots and other tapered roots are sliced in the same way, the tip of the knife held to the board and the other hand, fingers curled, pushing the root into the swinging blade. To achieve even-sized pieces, you may start by cutting diagonally rather than straight up and down. As the cuts progress up the root, allow the angle to become smaller and smaller until at the top you are cutting vertically.

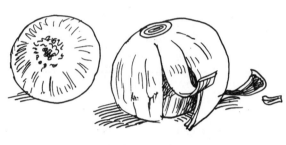

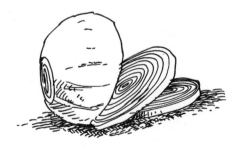

Broccoli, Cauliflower

With a paring knife, remove the florets first in large clumps. If the stem has a very thick skin, pare it off. Cut into even-sized chunks. Cook stem pieces 3 to 4 minutes longer than florets.

Onions

Onions are more slippery than many other vegetables, thus requiring a sharper knife so the blade won't slip. It's important to work quickly with onions. The marvelous aroma that makes onions an essential part of cookery also, alas, makes the eyes sting and water. The trick is to be fast.

Peeling: Slice a little piece off one side of the onion, just enough to provide a secure base on one side. Cut off the top and bottom and quickly peel away the brown skin with your fingertips.

Slicing: Holding the onion lightly in your fingertips, put the tip of the knife on the board for the guillotine effect. Raise and lower the blade as you move the onion into it, keeping your fingers curled back. The last slice will be thick; simply chop it.

Chopping: If the onion is small, first divide it through the equator. If it's large, slice through the Tropics of Cancer and Capricorn as well. Lay the pieces, broadside down, and chop first one way and then the other with the tip firmly on the board. If need be, hold the tip down with your other hand.

SPRING VEGETABLES

In the spring I always seem to develop a tremendous appetite for fresh greens. Maybe that's because green leaves are so tender and delicious as they first appear and grow in the pale sunlight and cool nights of May and June. So are fern tips, such as fiddleheads and asparagus. In spring there are also crisp sweet over-wintered roots such as Jerusalem artichokes and parsnips. And, while the weather is still cool, the peas begin to ripen.

Most of the work of gardening takes place in spring. That's when you plow or till, dig in manure and compost, set up fences, trellises and greenhouses, plant seeds, and do the first spring weeding. It's quite a workout after the soft living of winter. Perhaps that's why spring vegetables and foragables taste so terrific. Appetite is, after all, the best sauce.

ASPARAGUS

If you've never tasted freshly picked and carefully cooked asparagus, you're in for a surprise. It melts in your mouth and tastes sublime. Asparagus can even be eaten raw. Shortly after picking, the sugars begin to turn to starch and the stalks begin to dry and lose flavor. You can slow this process by (a) keeping asparagus cool, and (b) re-cutting the cut ends and submerging them in cold water during storage. Think of them as flowers. Serve as soon as possible.

Growing Asparagus

To grow asparagus, according to legendary tales of gardening, you dig a pit big enough to bury yourself and fill it with manure. Then you plant asparagus and weed it for three years without remuneration. After that, you get to pick fresh, free asparagus every spring for about twenty years.

The first stems to appear in early spring are the thickest and most tender. You may go on cutting stems until they start coming up thin. This is a sign that the rootstock has taken as much as it can take. Let these last, thin stalks become a forest of cloudy fronds to feed the roots over the summer.

Steamed Asparagus

Generally, I cut up asparagus stalks before cooking and divide them into two or three categories, since the tougher white bottoms require more cooking time than the tender green tips. The really woody bits I set aside for soup. The rest I cook as follows.

In a deep saucepan with a tight lid, bring to a boil:
1 cup water
Place a vegetable steamer or rack in the pan and put in:
the bottom halves of asparagus stalks
Steam these 4 to 6 minutes, then add:
asparagus tips
Steam 4 to 6 minutes longer. Test them with a fork from time to time to get an idea of what's happening; within minutes of being done, the tips will turn to mush, so watch it. If you are not serving them right away, let them cool. Cold asparagus is no failure. Serve with:
Holiday Sauce *(see p. 80)*
or with melted butter and a squeeze of lemon.

Other Asparagus Recipes
Asparagus Bisque *(see p. 19)*
Asparagus Quiche *(see p. 98)*

FIDDLEHEADS

Fiddleheads, the tightly curled heads of emerging ostrich ferns, can be gathered in the early spring. They're a wonderful excuse to go traipsing up and down rivers and streams; all you need is a pair of rubber boots and a couple of plastic bags in your pockets. The tan, papery covering on each new fiddlehead is easy to pick off (not fuzzy) and should be removed as soon as you get home, before cooking or storing, as it's quite bitter. Fiddleheads may be refrigerated for up to 4 days in a perforated plastic bag or open container. They also freeze quite nicely (*see p. 286*).

Boiled Fiddleheads

It is possible to steam a small amount (say, a cup) of fiddleheads, but to cook up a larger amount, boiling water must surround each fiddlehead. If any husks have been left on, they will fall off in the water.

Put:
2 to 4 cups clean fiddleheads
in:
2 qts boiling water
1 tsp salt
1 Tbsp vinegar
Cook at a full rolling boil for 7 minutes. Drain at once, and serve with butter or Holiday Sauce (*see p. 80*).

SERVES 4

GREENS

The young and tender leaves of greens are the very first vegetables to appear in the spring. Wild edible greens such as mustard and dandelions send out tender shoots long before anything has sprouted from a seed, because their roots are already established.

Greens, especially wild ones with slightly peppery flavors, make wonderful stuffings for pies, pastries and noodle dishes. Sometimes these are combined with soft cheeses such as cottage cheese or feta, or even tofu, which is very similar to soft cheese in texture and flavor (*see Lasagne Blanco à la Eleanor, p. 96*).

One pound of uncooked greens equals one cup of cooked greens. Allow ½ cup of cooked greens per serving. Greens should never be cooked in aluminum pans; they pick up a metallic taste, not to mention some questionable qualities. Among the many kinds of greens are:

Beet Tops: If planted from seed, it will be a month or more before you can find enough greens in the beet patch to make a meal. One spring, however, I noticed a whole crop of them growing out of the compost heap where we had thrown beets over the winter. Since beets are biennials, they had promptly taken root and sent up a leafy flower stalk. This year we simply left some beets, well mulched, in the garden. Beet tops are cooked like spinach or chard if young, a little longer when full grown.

Lamb's Quarters: A delicious spring green, lamb's quarters (also known as pigweed) are delicate and tender when young, and have a flavor like broccoli as they get older. We like them so much that I make a special effort to leave two or three plants to mature in the garden (they get quite tall) and seed next year's crop. When lamb's quarters are about 7 or 8 inches tall, we harvest and freeze them.

Lettuce: There are many different kinds of lettuce and they all come up fast in the early spring. Lettuce can be cooked or used in salad; because of its delicacy, it is ready to eat in minutes.

Mustard Greens: As you might expect, mustard greens are a little peppery; they are best young, cooked with milk or salt pork, or mixed in with other cooked greens. Wild mustard is a little stronger than the cultivated variety.

Dandelion: Some do and some don't mind the slightly bitter flavor of wild dandelion greens. The younger you pick them, the milder they are. You can greatly reduce the edge by cooking them together with a complete protein, such as milk or salt pork. There is a cultivated, broad-leafed variety that produces a larger plant and is less bitter.

Radish and Turnip Greens: These are strong, as greens go, and should be picked when very young. They're a little tough for salad but very tasty when cooked with a complete protein, such as milk, fresh cheeses, or salt pork.

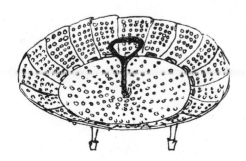

Spinach,
New Zealand
Spinach, and Chard: As
a gardener, I prefer chard;
it's hardier and doesn't go to
seed until the second year
because it's a biennial. As a cook, I prefer
spinach as it keeps longer in the fridge; it's
also a little more tender and doesn't have
the heavy central stalk even when full
grown. All three are fine salad material,
good to cook, and easy to freeze.

Young Broccoli, Cauliflower, Brussels
Sprouts, and Cabbage Leaves: As these
grow, they produce many extra lower
leaves, which will eventually wilt and fall
off; might as well pick them and make
some early slaw or add them to sautéed
vegetables. Or use them as creamed greens.

Washing and Preparing Greens

Unless grown hydroponically, greens
should always be washed. No amount of
fancy cooking will make anybody want to
eat sand.

The best way to wash greens is to
submerge them in a basin or bucket of
cold water for a few minutes, then stir
them around. The grit will fall to the
bottom. They may then be dried,
either by whirling them in a centrifugal spinner, by wrapping them in a clean
dishtowel or by taking them outside and
whirling them in a wire basket.

After you wash them, consider the stems. If
you can nip them off with your fingernail,
they're tender; if not, they will take much
longer than the greens to cook. Fold the
leaf lengthwise, underside out, and tear out
the stems and any tendrils that come with
it. If the leaves are very large, you may
want to tear them into smaller pieces.

Steaming Greens

Once upon a time, the universal Western
method of cooking greens was to submerge them in a huge pot of boiling water.
This cooks out much of the vitamin C, so
it makes more sense to steam them.

There are two ways to steam greens. One,
put the wet greens in a lidded pan, with or
without oil, and cook until the greens are
wilted and tender. Two, use a vegetable
steamer. This device has adjustable sides to
allow it to fit into almost any sized pan
and it can be lifted out easily, enabling one
to remove all the contents at once as soon
as they are done.

Cheese Patties

There are many uses for a combination of fresh cottage cheese and chopped cooked greens: it can be a layer between lasagne noodles, a pastry stuffing or this simple sautéed burger.

In a mixing bowl, beat together:
2 eggs
Mix in:
½ cup bread crumbs
Allow this to sit for a few minutes. Then mix in:
1 cup cottage cheese
1 cup cooked, chopped spinach or **other greens**
2 Tbsp minced onion
1 tsp dried basil or **1 Tbsp fresh chopped basil**
Add 2 to 3 Tbsp flour as needed to make the mixture thick enough to shape. Shape into 8 patties.

Heat in a heavy frying pan:
1 Tbsp safflower oil
Sauté burgers over medium heat until browned on both sides. Serve hot.

SERVES 4

Greens with Onions

Use a mild-flavored green, such as spinach, chard, lettuce, or lamb's quarters.

Wash carefully:
1 lb greens
Heat in a heavy frying pan:
2 Tbsp light oil or **butter** or **drippings**
Slice or chop and add:
1 or 2 onions
Sauté the onions until transparent. Add the wet greens and cover the pan closely; simmer about 5 minutes, until wilted and tender.

SERVES 4

Variation
Cook as above, but add **1 cup milk** when you put in the greens. This is especially good for peppery greens such as mustard, dandelion, turnip tops, and radish greens. Cover and simmer over low heat so that the milk does not boil.

Aemono

This is an authentic Japanese dish, except that they serve it cold, and I like it better hot. Use a tender green, such as spinach, young chard, lamb's quarters, or lettuce.

Wash carefully:
1 lb greens
In a heavy frying pan, heat:
2 Tbsp dark sesame oil
Add the greens, cover, and simmer over low heat until the leaves wilt — about 5 minutes. Meanwhile, in another pan, roast until brown *(see p. 175):*
¼ cup sesame seeds
When the greens are cooked, add the seeds and:
2 Tbsp tamari soy sauce

SERVES 4

JERUSALEM ARTICHOKES

Many an old house has by it a big patch of stalky-looking plants — Jerusalem artichokes. They have a tangle of tiny tubers at their base, which are thin and wasted in the summer, fat in the winter, and delicious in the early spring, before

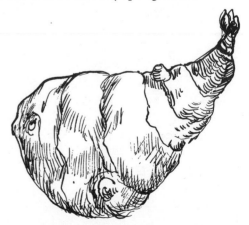

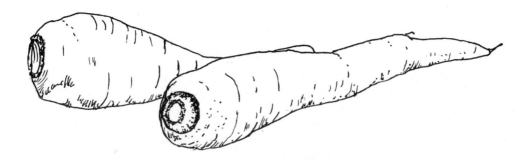

they start to grow above ground again. In spring, go after them at midday, when the ground has thawed, and you will find them 2 to 4 inches below ground, scattered within a foot of each stalk. Eat them soon after you dig them, since they won't keep but a week or two. Old, withered roots may be planted someplace new, such as your own backyard, where you will soon have a crop of your own.

Jerusalem artichokes taste a little like parsnips, only they're more delicate and tender, and less sweet. They shouldn't be cooked very long.

Raw Jerusalem Artichokes

Scrub well:
a handful of Jerusalem artichokes
Trim off tops and rootlets. Slice and serve as hors d'oeuvres with a bowl of:
Suzy's Vinaigrette *(see p. 44)*

SERVES 4

Sautéed Jerusalem Artichokes

Scrub well:
a handful of Jerusalem artichokes
Heat in a heavy skillet:
3 Tbsp clarified butter or **vegetable oil**
Add:
1 chopped onion
and the Jerusalem artichokes, sliced. When they have browned a bit, add:
½ cup water
Cover tightly and steam 5 to 10 minutes (check with a fork after 5).

SERVES 2

PARSNIPS

Parsnips are technically a fall or winter vegetable, since they take a whole summer to mature — at least 4 months. However, since they're so soft, they don't really keep very well in a root cellar. You will find after a month or so that the flesh begins to shrink and get tough. Parsnips are better kept in the garden until spring, well mulched with wood chips, sawdust, or lots of hay.

As soon as the ground thaws enough to get at them, start digging them up. Use them within a week of harvest for maximum freshness.

Sautéed Parsnips

Wash and slice ¼-inch thick on a diagonal:
5 or **6 parsnips**
Heat in a heavy frying pan :
2 Tbsp oil
Sauté the parsnips, stirring every few minutes to brown as many surfaces as you can — about 10 minutes. Then add:
½ cup water or **stock**
You may add at this point:
½ to 1 cup frozen or **raw peas**
Steam for about 5 minutes (or until the peas are done). You may add at the end:
a sprinkling of brown sugar
2 Tbsp chopped parsley
2 Tbsp butter

SERVES 2 TO 4

PEAS

You can never plant enough peas. Like sweet corn, they should be picked just before cooking. If this isn't possible, at least keep them cool; their sweetness will quickly turn to starch at room temperature. You can add ½ tsp sugar to old peas to improve them, but nothing will recapture the indescribable flavor of the fresh young ones.

Steamed Peas

Fresh peas take about 5 minutes to steam in a tightly lidded pot. You may also try simmering them in ¼ to ½ cup milk or cream sauce from 5 to 10 minutes. I would not use any seasoning at all on fresh peas, but old or frozen ones are nice with a little fresh basil, mint, or parsley chopped into the pot.

If you never have enough for a serving all round, combine them with other vegetables, such as parsnips, carrots, celery, leeks or onions.

SNOW PEAS

Snow peas are a variety of pea that is used only when the pods are flat and have not yet filled out with peas. They are most often used in combination stir-fries, but may also be found in soups and salads. Freshly picked, they are crisp and sweet.

SUGAR SNAPS

Seldom does a completely new vegetable come along that is as successful and delicious as the sugar snap pea, which fills out within an edible pod, and does not have to be shelled. This saves gardening cooks hours of labor, especially in households where peas are frozen. Pea-shelling day, an annual event in many homes, becomes sugar-snap-freezing morning. *(To freeze sugar snaps, see p. 287.)* The afternoon can be spent doing something else.

Sugar snap peas are tasty by themselves, steamed for 5 to 7 minutes and served with a pat of butter, or they can be made into this festive dish.

Sweet-and-Sour Sugar Snaps

Mix together:
¼ cup water
2 Tbsp vinegar
3 Tbsp brown sugar
1 Tbsp cornstarch or **arrowroot**
Set this to one side. Chop:
1 onion
1 green pepper (optional)
In a heavy skillet, heat:
2 to 3 Tbsp safflower oil
Sauté the onions a bit, then add the green peppers and:
2 to 3 cups whole sugar snap peas
Keep the heat high; shake the pan and stir to keep the bottom from scorching. When they are all nicely heated, add:
½ cup water
Cover and steam over fairly rapid heat for 3 minutes. Remove lid only to add the cornstarch mixture; give it a quick stir and return the lid. Turn off heat and let sit 5 minutes. Then stir again as you serve. The edible-podded peas will be coated with a glossy sweet-and-sour sauce.

SERVES 4

SUMMER VEGETABLES

Summer is outdoors. Everything is so different — in smells, in looks, in sounds, and in the way you think, and eat, and work — that it might as well be a different place altogether from the one it was in the winter. The green everywhere splashed with color; the slamming of the screen doors; the pounding of bare feet through the house; the flapping of sheets on the line. And, most of all, the garden, the endless overlapping flow of vegetables and fruits — so many, so wonderful, so delicious.

It isn't all free, of course, and much of the quality of summer living has to do with the long hours spent over the rows, amid the black flies and mosquitoes, weeding, pruning and gathering. When people visit, they tend to gather in the garden, talking of success and failure, of mulches and insect problems and the effect of the weather this year. It is always the rainiest, or the driest, or the least or most buggy summer.

Meals are in large part shaped by vegetables in season. And, too, by the fact that nobody wants to stand around the stove, cooking, for any longer than absolutely necessary. It's too hot inside, and too glorious outside. Fortunately, vegetables cook quickly, and you don't have to run the oven if you don't want to. Simmer a pot of grains while you chop and stir-fry some vegetables. Add eggs, or fresh-caught fish, or a mound of cottage cheese. Once a week or so, when it rains, bake bread, cook beans, simmer a soup. Otherwise, let the garden cook for you.

BEANS

Snap beans, string beans, pole beans, bush beans, green beans, yellow beans: dozens of names, endless varieties. The real division is between slender, young, fresh beans and large, old, or wilted beans. The only way to get them young and tender is fresh from the garden. We have had the best success with a French filet bean now available in many North American seed catalogs. Fortunately, they grow very easily in almost any soil or climate. Young beans are so delicate and delicious that I can never bring myself to do anything fancy to them. Sometimes we even eat them raw. But there are lots of things that can be done with older, larger, tougher, or frozen beans.

Young Fresh Beans

Nip off the ends; rinse quickly under cold water if dirty. A handful will do for a serving; you may chop them or not, as you please. Steam over boiling water for 5 to 7 minutes, or until tender. If you must hold them before serving, remove the water and keep them barely warm.

Large Beans

Chop or nip off the ends; if necessary, string them. Slice them into 2-inch pieces, straight or diagonally; or, if you have time, they may be "Frenched" into long thin strips. Do your cutting just before cooking to preserve the vitamins. Steam over boiling water, tightly lidded, for 10 to 15 minutes, or until tender. Before serving, you may season them with:

1 chopped leek or **a few chopped chives**
2 Tbsp chopped parsley
freshly ground pepper
a pinch of celery seeds or **thyme**
½ cup sautéed sliced mushrooms, or
½ cup slivered almonds

Beans and Tomatoes

A light and easy dish. In a heavy skillet, heat:
2 Tbsp light oil (olive oil, if you have it)
Add:
1 chopped onion
1 chopped green pepper (optional)
When the onions are limp, add:
1 clove crushed garlic
Sauté a minute; then add:
2 cups fresh or canned chopped tomatoes, drained
1 tsp oregano
½ tsp salt
½ tsp freshly ground pepper
Simmer gently for 10 minutes, then add:
1 or 2 qts fresh or frozen beans
Simmer, covered, 5 to 10 minutes, until beans are just done.

SERVES 4 TO 6

Bean Sandwiches

Cooked leftover green beans a make terrific sandwich filling. Chop the beans a bit, then add mayonnaise, a dash of savory, or whatever you wish.

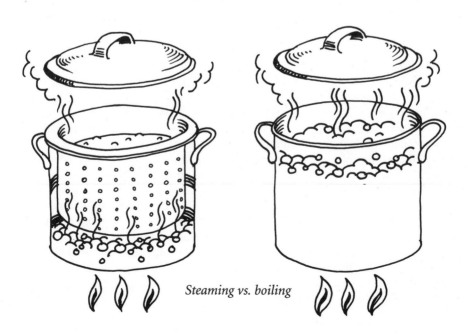

Steaming vs. boiling

Corn on the Cob

In my father's house, one first brought to a boil:

a large pot of water

When the water was boiling, the table set, the meal cooked, we then (and only then) went down to pick the corn. For corn on the cob, we only picked the most perfect ears, pale yellow, the tops not yet ripened. Within minutes (in the corn patch) they were stripped and cleaned of silk. Then we sprinted back and plunged them in the boiling water. They were cooked about 5 minutes, then lifted out and served forth, with plenty of butter and salt.

After that we had dinner.

The reason for all this bother is that, as soon as corn is picked, the sugar in it begins to convert to starch. The process is gradual; it doesn't happen all at once. Corn picked a few hours before cooking will still be sweet, although not quite as sweet as by the above method. In a day or two, however, it is pretty boring; and after a week it will be as tough as old leather.

Corn is one of the very few vegetables I ever cook in large amounts of water; that is because there are very few vitamins to be lost. However, if you prefer, there is another way to cook corn, though I recommend you do only a few ears at a time this way.

Heat under a steaming rack to a boil:

1 cup water

Steam **fresh ears of corn** 5 to 10 minutes, until tender. Serve at once.

Cattail on the Cob

Cattails on the cob are so good that they just about take the edge off one's desire — and endless wait — for fresh ears of corn. Harvest when the slender heads appear, encased in pale green wrapping, not unlike the inner husks of corn. Just break off as many as you need — 5 per serving is about right — and as soon as possible, boil or steam them for 7 to 10 minutes. Remove wrappers, dip in melted butter, and eat as you would corn on the cob.

Choclos

In Peru, where corn on the cob is plentiful, it is cooked in the husk over charcoal braziers (a familiar street sight) and they spread it with things such as:

garlic butter
corn oil mixed with a bit of tomato sauce
butter with grated lemon rind

And I haven't tried it yet, but I bet it would be good with a mild Pesto *(see p. 83)* or good hot Barbecue Sauce *(see p. 77)*.

PURSLANE

Purslane is a spreading, ground-cover plant with tiny, thick-fleshed, darkish-green leaves, which are very good to eat. In India they are domestically grown as a vegetable (the leaves being somewhat larger); here they are classed as a weed. If you are so fortunate as to have your garden overrun with them, leave them there; they don't choke anything out, they look rather nice, and they make good eating, both raw (in salads) and cooked.

Steamed Purslane

Pick off the small sprigs and wash very well:

about 1 lb purslane

Steam over ½ **cup boiling water** for about 5 minutes.

Serve with:
melted butter and lemon juice

WILD MUSHROOMS

If you are fond of foraging for wild edibles, you will sooner or later cast your eye upon wild mushrooms, which spring up from time to time in such abundance. There are two approaches to learning about them. One is to go mushroom hunting with somebody who knows what they're talking about. The other is to get a good, thorough mushroom book with lots of photographs (try the library), collect some specimens, and try to identify them. I favor both methods, used simultaneously, until you're sure you're sure.

Stay away from mushrooms that are similar in appearance to anything poisonous, and mushrooms that are close relatives to anything poisonous, and you'll be safe. There are many more edible mushrooms than poisonous ones; but learn to identify both, for safety's sake. Avoid white mushrooms, because they could be the deadly white Death Angel — there is no known antidote, and it's not an easy death.

Many mushrooms grow in clusters, and all are fruiting bodies of a fungus that actually lives year-round under the ground. It's better to cut them than to pull them up, so carry a jackknife. And if you want to find them again next year in the same handy place, don't take more than 80 percent of the crop.

Chanterelles: Chanterelles are a well-known delicacy in Europe, and they also appear in North America. They form part of the ecosystem growing between mature spruce and fir trees, where you will find them. Chanterelle hunting in the northern woods is pure delight in the heat of the summer, a chance to head off into the cool and bosky woods. The mushrooms are bright orange-yellow, gills running down the stems in an undefined way. Chanterelles are described as funnel-shaped, but actually tend to be flat or wavy on top.

Chanterelles may be lightly poached in soup or sauce *(see Chicken with Chanterelles, p. 138).* I find them best that way, but they may also be sautéed. Chop chanterelles roughly and use very little butter in the pan. If they are fresh, juice will soon bubble in the pan and then dry up. At this point you may add more butter, perhaps a little chopped parsley, and cook a few minutes longer.

Chanterelles may be quite successfully dried *(see p. 261).* I also freeze them raw, whole, or chopped. To thaw, put them in a dry skillet over low heat for 5 minutes, then add butter to finish.

Meadow Mushrooms: These look rather like mushrooms in the store, and in fact are close relatives. However, they are sometimes bigger and are light tan on top, with pink gills that turn to tan and brown as they mature. They occur in dry, sunny sheep pastures with thin soil. Delicious.

SUMMER SQUASH AND ZUCCHINI

Ah, zucchini! Most abundant and versatile of summer vegetables, filling the garden with broad leaves and the larder with heavy fruits. Zucchini plants always seem to provide twice as many squash as any other type of plant, but there are many other squashes to choose from: summer, yellow, crookneck, cocozelle, and vegetable marrow. All have about the same texture and flavor and may be cooked in the same ways.

Summer squash is a short-lived delight; we have tried various methods of canning and freezing them with little success. It is my belief that anything that is mostly composed of water, with very light and tender fibers holding it in place, is at best a tenuous affair and will not keep well by any method. Even under refrigeration, the smallest and best will shrivel in a few weeks. Larger ones will keep a little longer — but they won't taste any better for it.

Generally, the best squash is about 12 inches long, although we pick them all sizes, for various purposes. Some people steam or boil them; I sauté, serve in a casserole, or stir-fry them. They are very absorbent and will pick up almost any flavor or spice you cook them with.

Sautéed Summer Squash

This is a very easy, simple dish. It may be made with any summer squash (such as crookneck, yellow, or zucchini) so long as it is under a foot long.

First, chop the squash. You can slice it into ½-inch-thick rounds, or diagonals, or cut it lengthwise into finger-sized slivers, or just chop it into small bits.

Figure on:
1½ cups per person (it shrinks in the pan)
While you're at it, chop up:
1 onion
Heat in a large, heavy frying pan:
3 Tbsp vegetable or **olive oil**
Arrange as many slices of squash as you can fit in the pan, and sauté them until browned on one side, about 5 minutes. Turn and cook 1 minute or so on the other side; remove them to a warm dish and continue with the rest until they are all cooked. Finally, sauté the onions and scatter them over the squash.

Variation
Return the squash and onions to the pan and toss with:
1 to 2 Tbsp tamari soy sauce per squash
Put a lid on and simmer 5 minutes.

Stuffed Zucchini
à la Restino

Stuffed zucchini is one of those culinary projects that sounds exciting the first time you try it, but all too often turns out to be something your family won't eat. Careful attention to detail — such as how long the squash is parboiled and how long it is baked — makes all the difference. This version has a whole wheat bread-crumb stuffing flavored with sage and bound with beaten egg.

Parboiling: For 2 servings, choose a 10-inch zucchini. Put it in a big pot of boiling water for 10 minutes; remove with tongs and cool in cold water for 10 minutes.

Cut the squash lengthwise. Using a small knife with a narrow blade, make a cut around the squash about ½ inch in from the skin and about ½ inch deep. Using a soup spoon, carefully gouge out a channel the length of the zucchini, in which to put the stuffing.

Stuffing:
In a mixing bowl, beat until foamy
1 egg
Chop fine into separate piles on a breadboard:
insides of zucchini
1 small onion
1 stalk celery
1 thick slice whole wheat bread
3 Tbsp fresh parsley
2 leaves fresh sage or **¼ tsp dried sage**
Mince or crush:
1 clove garlic
Heat in a frying pan:
2 Tbsp vegetable oil
Sauté onion, celery, and bread crumbs for 2 or 3 minutes; toss, add garlic, and cook for another minute or two. Add chopped squash and remove from heat. Add herbs. Allow this to cool a little, then add it to the egg and mix well. Lightly oil zucchini shells and stuff each.

Sprinkle tops with:
1 to 2 Tbsp Parmesan cheese
Cover pan bottom with a film of water, and place stuffed squash in the pan. Bake at 350°F for 30 minutes.

SERVES 2

Summer Stir-Fry

Whether you garden or gather your vegetables at the marketplace, there's so much available in the summer that it's hard to limit yourself. But limit you must to create a stir-fry with character. The important thing is that all the vegetables be fresh, and therefore crisp and tender. Chop and arrange them in bowls or piles just before cooking. Fry them only long enough for heat to penetrate; then add liquid, slap on the lid, and steam them for a few minutes.

It's traditional, and certainly easier, to cook stir-fries in a wok. However, I've been doing it in a cast-iron frying pan for 20 years, and nobody has complained yet. Stir-fries are usually served with rice (*see p. 163*).

Wash, trim, chop, and prepare:
½ **cup baby carrots**
1 **cup chopped summer squash** or **zucchini**
1 **chopped green pepper**
1 **small onion** or **4 scallions**
½ **cup celery** or **Chinese cabbage**
½ **cup sliced mushrooms**
In a wok or heavy frying pan, heat:
3 **Tbsp safflower oil**
Add carrots first; stir and fry them a couple minutes before adding the onion and celery. Stir and sauté these carefully, then add the rest of the vegetables. As you add fresh things to the pan, push those already there back to the edge, where they will cook more slowly. After about 7 minutes, when it all looks good and hot, add ¼ **cup liquid** and cover tightly. Keep heat at medium-high through the whole cooking process.

As liquid you may use plain water or a mixture of water, wine, and tamari soy sauce.

SERVES 4 TO 6

TOMATOES

I put more time than I like to admit into growing tomatoes. In warmer places it must be easier. The most demanding among them are the fat red "beefsteak" tomatoes, very mild and juicy; we grow them in a greenhouse. More prolific and hardy are the smaller fruited varieties. We prune our plants and stake three main stems, then trim blossoms at summer's end to encourage the fruit to ripen. At first warning of a frost (whether by radio or sixth sense) we instantly gather every last tomato. Green tomatoes that have been "burned" by frost, and have brownish spots, will rot instead of ripen.

The next step is to sort. Those that have some red in them may be placed on the windowsill for instant ripening. Those that are still hard and dark green are probably not going to ripen; better to use them in relish or some sort of mixed vegetable dish. The rest of them, if unblemished and unbruised, may be ripened if they are kept warm and dry.

To Ripen Green Tomatoes
1. Pull the tomato plants, roots and all. Inspect fruit carefully and remove those that are discolored or almost ripe or too small and green to ripen. Hang the plant upside down in a warm place and check it every few days for ripe fruit. The advantage of this method is that it is easy to do. The disadvantage is that ripe fruit may fall off onto the cellar floor.

2. Wrap the "ripeners" separately in newspaper; set them in a cozy, dry spot in shallow cardboard boxes, 1 or 2 layers deep. Try to put tomatoes of approximately equal size and color in each box so they will all ripen at the same time. This method requires no special equipment, but wrapping and unwrapping so many tomatoes can be

tedious, and some may go ripe
and rot before you find them.
A variation on this method is
to get your boxes from the
liquor store, with dividers left
in them. Put tomatoes in each
section, separated by crumples
of newspaper. Or see if you can
get a grocer at a nearby store
to save you some fruit dividers,
shaped to hold each fruit
separately, for your tomatoes.
Lay slabs of cardboard between
layers to support them. This
method is best — no sorting
or wrapping.

3. Set tomatoes on the windowsill
    to ripen, unwrapped. They will
    ripen more quickly but will
    taste a little more acidic in the
    middle.

Weekly, go through your boxes and
make up batches of tomato sauce
(see p. 287) with the excess. This
sauce freezes well.

Tomato Salad

Chop, slice, or cut in wedges:
3 ripe tomatoes
Cut in similar style:
1 ripe cucumber
Soak them overnight in a mixture of:
3 Tbsp olive oil
1 Tbsp wine vinegar
1 tsp tarragon or **chervil** (fresh or dried)
1 Tbsp chopped fresh chives
1 tsp salt
½ tsp pepper
Just before serving, add:
2 Tbsp chopped parsley

SERVES 2 TO 3

PEPPERS

Peppers are beautiful and various. Not only do they come in different shapes and colors; they can also be sweet or hot, uncooked, barely cooked, or charred and skinned—offering endless variety in flavor and texture.

In Cape Breton we grow them in a greenhouse, where they are amazingly prolific for plants that never see the unfiltered light of day. Sweet peppers can be green, ripening to red, yellow, or purple; they can be large or small, round or long. They all taste pretty much the same, but offer wonderful visual variety on the crudités platter. Strips of sweet pepper are almost never refused in box lunches, and have legendary amounts of vitamin C. Chopped or in strips, they're a welcome sight in any salad.

Cooked sweet or hot peppers in stir-fries have so much flavor and tender texture that it's worthwhile cutting the pieces large so you can tell what you're eating. They should be finely chopped in a quiche, however, where they make so much difference I can hardly bear to make one without pepper in it.

Char-Broiled Peppers

To char-broil sweet or hot peppers, a Mexican technique that creates a smoky-sweet tang, broil thick-skinned ripe peppers on a grill 4 inches from the heat for 2 to 3 minutes on each side. When they're well charred and somewhat soft, put them all in a covered dish or paper bag for 15 minutes to loosen the skins. Cut them in thirds (over a bowl, to catch the liquid), peel off the skins, and cut away the seeds and inside flesh. If you're working with hot peppers, be careful to scrub your hands thoroughly with soap after this procedure; hot pepper juice, like dried hot pepper, stings eyes or delicate skin. The special flavor of char-broiled, peeled peppers will keep for 2 to 3 days, if the peppers are refrigerated, submerged in olive oil and with a dash of salt. Use them in:

Hors d'Oeuvres: Cut pepper strips and serve with fresh radishes, black olives, green onions, and French Bread (see p. 185).

Stir-Fry: Add strips to summer stir-fries or rice dishes such as Rice Mirepoix (see p. 165) or Chili Chicken Stir-Fry (see p. 137).

FRESH GREEN SALAD

We like to finish meals with a fresh green salad, nicely dressed, with, as my husband puts it, "things to hunt for in it." One of the delights of summer is combining textures, flavors, and colors of different lettuce and other greens — raddichio, arugula, cabbage, and spinach, to name a few. The huntable goodies can be fresh, such as sliced cucumber, tomatoes, or green peppers; or they can be marinated, such as olives or feta cheese. You may also add chopped fresh herbs. Basil, tarragon, dill, chives and parsley are favorites, but you can try finely chopped marjoram, mint and coriander: whatever suits your taste.

Charley's Salad

My husband really enjoys putting together a good salad. For just the two of us, he uses:

about 3 cups lettuce leaves, torn into bite-sized pieces
4 sliced mushrooms
8 Greek olives
½ thinly sliced, ripe, red tomato
1 to 2 Tbsp crumbled feta cheese (optional)
3 Tbsp Suzy's Vinaigrette (next page)
Toss 32 times with a large fork and spoon.

Cucumber Salad

First peel, then score the surface of cucumbers with a fork so that when you slice them, each piece looks like a delicate flower.

Make a dressing of:
3 Tbsp olive oil
1 Tbsp red wine vinegar
½ tsp salt
¼ cup yogurt or **sour cream**
Mix well, then toss with:
3 sliced cucumbers
2 Tbsp chopped chervil or **parsley**
1 tsp chopped dill or **chives**
1 sliced Bermuda onion (optional)
Cover and chill if you are not serving this at once; it will keep for 2 or 3 days.

SERVES 4

Suzy's Vinaigrette

Mix together in a bowl with a fork:
3 Tbsp olive oil
1 Tbsp vinegar
dash of tamari soy sauce (optional)
¼ tsp Dijon mustard
dash of salt
6 grindings fresh pepper

1 SALAD

Mix together in a small jar:
1 cup olive oil
⅓ cup vinegar
1 Tbsp tamari soy sauce (optional)
2 tsp Dijon mustard
1 tsp salt
½ tsp freshly ground pepper
Keep refrigerated. Shake well before using.
Measure 1 Tbsp per serving for salads.

VINAIGRETTE IN QUANTITY

Variation
Add **1 Tbsp Pesto** *(see p. 83)*

Roquefort Cheese Dressing

Use dressing for fairly mature and crisp lettuce, such as celtuce or Romaine. It will keep for a week, refrigerated.

In a small bowl, crumble:
2 Tbsp Roquefort cheese
Add and mix with:
½ cup homemade mayonnaise *(next column)*
¼ cup Suzy's Vinaigrette *(see above)*
3 Tbsp fresh, chopped parsley
Keep tightly covered and refrigerated for several hours before tossing with salad.

Homemade Mayonnaise

Many people make their own mayonnaise. They claim it tastes better, and prefer not to eat preservatives. On the other hand, homemade mayonnaise is more perishable. It must be kept cool, both in the making and in lunch bags. Mayonnaise is traditionally made with 100 percent olive oil. I use half safflower oil because it's less expensive and has a lighter taste.

Making mayonnaise in a beating bowl with a wire whisk is a vigorous occupation. In a blender it's easy: buzz buzz.

Chill:
½ cup olive oil
1½ cups safflower oil
Separate 3 eggs. In a beating bowl or a blender, put:
3 egg yolks
1 whole egg
Buzz or beat them until lemon yellow. Add oil very gradually, starting with a drop or two and working up to a thin stream. The yolks should expand gradually and take up the oil. After it becomes stiff, add:
1 Tbsp lemon juice
½ to 1 tsp salt
¼ to 1 tsp Dijon mustard
If, by chance, the mixture separates, you can rescue it by starting over with fresh egg yolks and oil, and add the separated mixture gradually when it's about half made.

Keep homemade mayonnaise no longer than 7 days, in a labeled jar. Do not allow it to sit around in a warm room.

1 PINT

FALL VEGETABLES

Bonanza . . . the larders overflow. The kitchen is cluttered with box after box of harvest coming in — crates of tomatoes, piles of peppers, sacks of potatoes, every kind of apple, great bundles of herbs drying over the stove, and, surrounding everything, the steady rattle of the canning kettle. A yeasty scent of brewing wine hovers behind the stove; the windows cloud with steam as vegetables are blanched for freezing.

In the midst of all this, almost every kind of vegetable is available to cook with. The few I've listed are really only those you have in such profusion that you hardly know where to put them all — especially those that have to come in before the frost.

And it's a kind of justice, and certainly helpful, that just when you have the least time for preparing meals, the most food is available. You certainly don't have to think too hard to figure out what to eat; it's all around you. In general, use up what you can't keep and save the rest for winter. There's so much.

Gradually, you make some headway through it all, and eventually get it all packed away, in one form or another — just about Thanksgiving time. We gather with our neighbors, bringing pots of this and dishes of that, and pies and stories to share. We push benches along the table until there's hardly room to walk in the kitchen, and all hold hands for a moment in grateful silence, amid the din. Grateful for what? God, the earth, the summer sun? Or just glad to be alive, and done with harvest for another year?

BROCCOLI

A broccoli head is actually a bunch of tightly curled flower buds on very thick stems. If you grow your own, cut it high on the stalk so that you'll get a better crop of small side-florets after the main head is gone. Broccoli should be eaten within a week of cutting. If you buy it in a store, you can pretty well figure the week is up, so use it right away. It is very good with Holiday Sauce *(see p. 80)*, Cream Sauce *(see p. 78)*, grated Parmesan cheese or Gomasio *(see p. 175)*.

Purchased broccoli usually comes with quite a long stem. The stem is delicious, but takes 3 to 5 minutes longer to cook than the florets. If you want all the broccoli to cook the same length of time, peel the stems and cut them into chunks roughly the size of the florets.

The only good way I know to cook broccoli is to blanch it fast in steam or in hot boiling water. After that, add whatever sauce, melted butter, or other ingredients you want. The question of whether you use steam or water is up to you. Steamed broccoli has more vitamins, but the hot water is easier if you have a lot to do.

Steam-Blanched Broccoli

You will need a cooking container with a rack several inches off the bottom and a good tight lid. Bring the water to a full rolling boil for 1 minute before adding the broccoli. Add stems first, unless peeled. Steam florets 5 to 7 minutes (test with a fork). Do not overcook.

Water-Blanched Broccoli

Boil 3 to 4 quarts water in a large pot with 1 tsp salt. Add stems first, unless peeled. Cook florets 3 to 5 minutes (test with a fork). Do not overcook.

If you plan to use the broccoli in a dish that will be further cooked, undercook it by 1 minute and run cold water over it to stop the cooking.

SUMMER CABBAGES

These cabbages, such as Chinese and Savoy, ripen in the fall and don't have firm enough heads to be suitable for winter storage. They are high in vitamin C and more tender than winter cabbages. They do not need as much cooking, and, when made into coleslaw, they may be chopped rather than grated. They will keep for a month or two, becoming gradually less tender and nutritious.

For cabbage recipe; *see p. 50.*

BRUSSELS SPROUTS

Brussels sprouts take a long time to mature but will grow well after the frost, so they make good late vegetables. In places where the frost doesn't strike hard, they will send out more new buds in the spring as well. The plants have a sort of gargantuan beauty.

Brussels sprouts will keep for about 2 weeks, but after storage you may have to pull off the tough outer, yellowed leaves.

To make sure they cook in the middle at the same rate as the outside, cut a cross in the bottom of each sprout.

Steamed Brussels Sprouts

Cook over, not in, rapidly boiling water for 10 to 15 minutes:
¾ cup Brussels sprouts per person
Serve with *one* of these:
butter
Parmesan cheese
lemon juice
Holiday Sauce *(see p. 80)*
Cream Sauce *(see p. 78)*

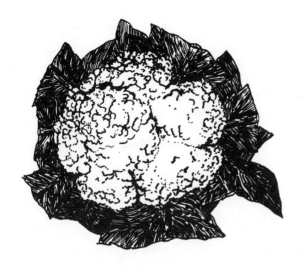

CAULIFLOWER

Cauliflower, a member of the brassica family (which includes cabbage, broccoli, kale, and the like) grows well in cool climates. Fresh cauliflower is tender and sweet, but it doesn't age well; if kept too long, it develops an unpleasant smell and flavor. It can, however, be rescued (if not too old) by adding a couple tablespoons of lemon juice and parboiling instead of steaming it. Cauliflower can be cooked whole: trim off leaves and cut out the middle of the core so that it cooks evenly.

Blanch (boil) whole cauliflower 10 to 15 minutes, florets 3 to 5 minutes

Steam whole cauliflower 20 minutes, florets 5 to 10 minutes

Other Cauliflower Recipes
Cauliflower Cheese *(see p. 102)*

Steamed Cauliflower

Steamed cauliflower works well in sauces or mixed with other vegetables. Be careful; like cabbage, it becomes mushy and smelly when overcooked.

Steam over ½ inch boiling water in a tightly lidded pot:
moderate-sized cauliflower pieces
Check stems with a fork after 8 minutes, and every 2 minutes until done. Serve with one of these:
Fresh Tomato Sauce *(see p. 75)*
Cream Sauce *(see p. 78)*
Holiday Sauce *(see p. 80)*

Cauliflower Curry

In India the spices come into the kitchen whole and are mixed and pounded together before cooking. Garam masala is a preground spice mixture, saving time and producing an equally exotic dish.

Cut into bite-sized pieces:
1 cauliflower
In a heavy skillet, sauté the cauliflower in:
2 Tbsp safflower oil
2 Tbsp butter
Cook over moderate heat 5 minutes, turning once, to lightly brown the florets. Remove them from the pan. Chop and sauté:
1 large onion
1 green pepper (optional)
2 tsp garam masala
¼ tsp chili powder (optional)
When the vegetables are limp, add and sauté for 1 minute more:
1 clove crushed garlic
Then purée, blend, or mash and add:
1 28-oz can tomatoes
2 Tbsp chopped parsley
Simmer, uncovered, until the sauce thickens — about 5 minutes. Add the cauliflower, cover, and simmer over low heat for 15 to 20 minutes, until the cauliflower is just tender. Sprinkle with fresh parsley and serve hot.

SERVES 4

WINTER VEGETABLES

When the world is frost-bound and green things are in retreat, we eat what vegetables can be stored. By far the majority of what we eat in the winter is out of the root cellar. This should be a cool, underground, damp (but well-ventilated) storage place, where you can keep roots and tubers and things like cabbage and apples through the worst of the winter. *(See Root-Cellar Storage, p. 254.)*

We have had various root cellars, but the one that gave me the most pleasure was three barrels set in a hillside. I used to go out there in the middle of January and dig down a couple feet into the snow, pull away hay and spruce branches, open the lids, and pull out, as if by miracle, beets, carrots and potatoes as fresh as the day they'd been stored away. They looked like baskets of Easter eggs, brown, purple, orange and green on the clean white snow, and had the waxy newness of fresh vegetables when we cooked and ate them.

BEETS

Beets are very hardy, and will keep well, right up to warm weather. The larger ones will keep best, so eat up the small ones in the early winter months. Beets aren't particularly strong in any one nutrient, but they have traces of almost every vitamin.

Since beets take a long time to cook, you should either cut them up very small or start them cooking well ahead of dinner. Beets should be cooked separately from other vegetables for this reason, and also because the red juices color everything else pink. (Hash with beets in it is called Red Flannel Hash; if you've ever thrown a red flannel shirt in a white wash you'll know why!)

Unlike most roots, beets can be cooked ahead of time, cooled, and reheated without getting mushy. But they should be cooked as fast as possible, with their skins on, to retain the most vitamins.

Harvard Beets

A fancy name for an old favorite in many an old farmhouse. Wash, dice, and steam for about 1 hour:
½ cup beets per person (plus ½ cup beets for the pot)
Meanwhile, mix together in a small pan:
½ cup vinegar (cider vinegar is best)
¼ cup brown sugar
½ tsp salt
2 whole cloves or **a pinch of dried cloves**
1 Tbsp cornstarch, arrowroot, or **kuzu**
Heat slowly, stirring, as sauce thickens; if you have used cornstarch, set it on low heat to simmer for 10 minutes. When the beets are tender, transfer them to a serving dish and add the sauce. Mix and serve.

Sautéed Beets and Carrots

A colorful dish. Wash, slice, and steam for 15 minutes:

1½ cups beets

Heat in a heavy frying pan:

2 Tbsp light oil

Add:

1½ cups carrots, cut in finger-sized pieces

Sauté for 5 to 10 minutes; then add the beets and:

½ cup water

Cover the pot and steam for 15 minutes.

SERVES 3 TO 4

Beet Salad

Steam for ¾ to 1 hour:

4 to 8 beets

When they are tender through, take them out and chop them up fine. Mix and add to the beets:

3 Tbsp oil
1 Tbsp vinegar
pinch of salt

Let the beets sit in the refrigerator for a few hours before serving. You may add at the last minute, for color and flavor:

2 Tbsp chopped parsley

SERVES 4

CABBAGE

Cabbage is a traditional fall and winter green the world around. It's a glorious sight in the garden; as the season gets colder, the cabbages explode with growth, like late-blossoming flowers.

Cabbage is one of the vegetables that has benefited the most from the broadening of available varieties; in addition to the old-fashioned Ballhead, there are also Red, Savoy, and various Chinese cabbages, and they are all quite different and delicious.

Cabbages are high in vitamin C, iron, and the vegetable fibre we all need to keep our digestive systems working well. They make wonderful salads, stir-fries, and specialty dishes. Cabbage goes well with sausages and potatoes — or rice and spicy tomato sauce.

Ballhead cabbage, the traditional cabbage of Europe, has been bred for tenderness and flavor. Ballhead cabbage keeps better than all other varieties, and is therefore the crispest in late winter for soups, stews, cole slaw, stir-fry, stuffed cabbage rolls, sauerkraut, and other cabbage dishes.

Chinese cabbage is tall and tender, compared to other cabbages, making excellent salad or stir-fry material. The base of each leaf is thick and crisp, the top thin and leafy — so they should be chopped into separate piles and cooked accordingly.

Savoy cabbage is crinkly-headed, much more tender than red or ballhead, and should be used within a week of picking for coleslaw, stir-fry, or soup.

Red cabbage is actually a glowing magenta with white ribs, a very beautiful vegetable to work with. It's sweeter and tougher than ballhead cabbage, lasting well into the winter. Finely chopped, it makes a colorful addition to coleslaw. It also goes well with pork and apples.

Tart Red Cabbage

A very good accompaniment to a big pot of stewed meat and root vegetables, and cornbread or corn pudding; a meal as colorful as fall.

Cut in half:
1 red cabbage
Slice off pie-shaped wedges, 1 or 2 per person, with a bit of the core in the center of each slice to hold it together. Steam them in, not over, an inch or so of water for about 15 minutes, until almost soft.

Meanwhile, heat in a large, heavy skillet:
2 Tbsp oil
Sauté:
1 sliced onion
When the cabbage is soft, fork in the pieces, being careful not to break them up. Sauté them for a minute or so on each side over low heat.

Stir into the remaining cabbage water in the pot enough liquid to bring it to about:
1 cup (water, cider, fruit juice)
2 Tbsp cider or **wine vinegar**
3 Tbsp brown sugar
½ tsp salt
2 Tbsp cornstarch
Heat this, stirring with a whisk, until it is clear and thick. Pour it over the cabbage, cover, and simmer 5 minutes.

Cabbage Tamari

This is a very sophisticated and flavorful version of cabbage; if you weren't the cook, you probably wouldn't believe it was cabbage.

Shred:
1½ cups cabbage per serving (it cooks down a lot)
Heat in a heavy skillet:
2 Tbsp vegetable oil (the best is dark sesame oil)
Sauté the cabbage over high heat, stirring once or twice, for 5 minutes, or until it begins to go limp. Add:
a generous shot of tamari soy sauce
This varies; I never measure it, but I figure about 1 tablespoon for 2 servings. You can make a milder version by adding half tamari and half water. Cover tightly; steam over medium heat for 5 minutes. Serve while cabbage is still somewhat crisp.

Other Cabbage Recipes
Cabbage Rolls *(p. 154)*, Winter Stir-Fry *(p. 51)*

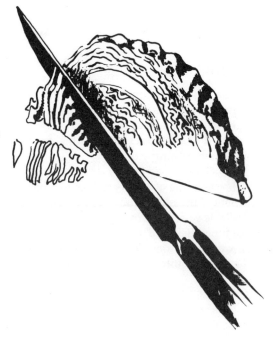

CARROTS

Carrots keep quite well most of the winter, in a cool, damp root cellar. As with beets, the larger ones keep longer, so use up the small ones first.

Carrots have a phenomenal amount of vitamin A. Half a cup of cooked carrots supplies the normal daily need of A (though not much of anything else).

I find plain steamed carrots boring, so before or after steaming them I usually sauté or bake them with a little oil and maybe a pinch of herbs, seeds, or brown sugar and vinegar. Carrots are very good combined with other vegetables, as in stews, Tzimmes *(see p. 53)*, stir-fried vegetables, etc. Grated carrots also combine well with grains in muffins, cakes, and puddings.

Marinated Carrots

Cooked and marinated carrots are a good dish to take along to a potluck party or community supper. You make them up a day ahead, refrigerate overnight, and pop them in the car just before you leave.

Scrub, slice, and steam for 7 to 10 minutes:
2 lb carrots
Meanwhile, mix together in a storage container with a tight lid:
¼ cup vinegar
¼ cup safflower oil
½ can tomato soup
½ cup sugar
½ cup finely chopped onion
¼ cup finely chopped green pepper
salt and pepper to taste
Add the hot carrots and toss them thoroughly. Allow the carrots to cool and toss them again before covering and putting them in a fridge or cool pantry overnight.

SERVES 6

Carrot Salad

Use only very tender carrots for carrot salad. Grate:
2 carrots per serving
Add:
lemon juice and peanut oil to taste
You may also add:
¼ cup nuts or **peanuts per serving, ground into small chunks**
¼ cup raisins per serving, whole or **chopped**
¼ cup mayonnaise
You may season the salad with:
½ tsp dill
or experiment with:
rosemary, chives, tarragon, cardamom, nutmeg, cumin, or **coriander**

Winter Stir-Fry

My winter stir-fries tend to be more rich and delicious than the "fried salads" of spring and summer. This one can be made with or without a little Sweet-and-Sour Sauce *(see p. 82)*.

Slice, chop, or shred *(see p. 25 for directions):*
1 onion
2 carrots
1 to 2 cups red cabbage
1 apple
In a wok or heavy frying pan, heat:
3 Tbsp safflower oil
Add carrots and onion; sauté for 3 minutes.

Move onions and carrots to the outside and add cabbage and apple. Cook a couple of minutes, continue to stir, and cook another 5 to 7 minutes, until things begin to look slightly cooked. Add:
½ cup water
Cover tightly and steam for 7 to 10 minutes, or until carrots taste tender-crisp.

SERVES 4

WINTER SQUASH

There are many types of winter squash, with various qualities, and I count pumpkin as one of them. Squash can be kept in a cool room of the house; it is much more important to keep them dry than it is to keep them cool. The ones with tougher skins keep longer. However, you should check all of them every week or two and use the ones with soft spots right away. You may also freeze squash (cooked and mashed) in plastic containers, for spring and summer use.

Half a cup of squash has enough vitamin A to meet the average daily requirement; pumpkin, being more watery, has about half enough. The other nutrients are minimal.

Squash is an incredibly versatile food. You can bake or steam it in whole pieces, mix it with other vegetables, or flavor it in different ways, since the taste is very bland to begin with. (For this reason, squash makes fine baby food.) You can make a mellow soup with winter squash, or a variety of cakes, pies, and muffins; there is even one old Vermont recipe for Pumpkin Beer!

Steamed Squash

Plain steamed squash doesn't have a very interesting texture or flavor, but steaming is a first step in other cooking processes.

Halve and clean your **squash.** You will need a large and very sharp knife to cut raw winter squash; I sometimes butcher them with an axe, especially the large Hubbards. If you want it to cook very quickly, chop it up into 2-inch chunks or ½-inch slices.

Add the squash to **½ cup boiling water,** lid the pot tightly, and steam until done (20 minutes for pumpkin, 30 minutes for acorn and butternut, 45 minutes for Hubbard and buttercup). When a fork will pierce the squash easily, it is done.

Tzimmes

I often make a tzimmes as a potluck dish, to accompany a roast. It's originally an Eastern European Jewish dish; the carrots symbolize coins (*tzimmes*), a sign of prosperity, while the honey stands for the sweetness of life.

Slice into flat pieces and steam:
1 decent-sized squash
Slice into thin rounds and steam in another pan:
4 carrots (about 1 cup)
Core, peel, and slice when needed:
2 to 4 cups apples
Oil a 2-quart casserole or frying pan and make layers of cooked squash, sliced tart apples, and cooked carrots, in that order, ending with carrots.

Mix together in one of the steaming pans (so as not to have to wash extra pans):
¼ cup oil
½ cup honey
grated rind of 1 lemon
¼ tsp salt
¼ tsp coriander or **a grating of nutmeg**
a squeeze of lemon juice
Pour this over the casserole and cover tightly. Bake at 300° to 350°F for about 30 minutes. You may remove the lid for the last 10 minutes; it makes the dish prettier.

SERVES 6 TO 8

"Baked" Squash

Unless your oven is very hot — around 400° — you do better to steam squash first and then finish it as "baked" squash in the oven. Squash dries out at low temperatures; the vitamins are less damaged with faster cooking.

Halve, clean, and steam until almost done:
about 1 cup squash per person
Remove from the pot carefully and put them skin-side down on an oiled pan.
Paint on top:
oil or **melted butter**
And sprinkle on, if you like:
a little brown sugar or **honey**
a squeeze of orange or **lemon juice**
a pinch of cinnamon, ginger, nutmeg, or **allspice**
Place in a moderately hot oven (350°F).
Bake 10 minutes.

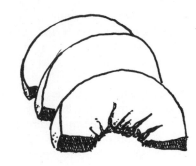

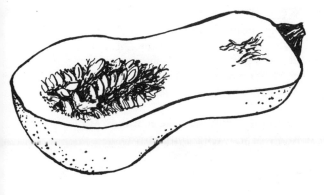

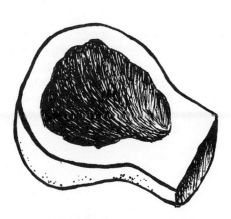

POTATOES

Potatoes are commonly grown on many farms, especially in Maine, the Canadian Maritimes, and points west, wherever the soil is acidic enough to allow them a good growing medium. They are planted not as seeds, but as pieces of potato tuber, each containing an "eye" or growing point.

The food value in potatoes, mostly vitamin C and iron, is concentrated in a waxy layer just beneath the skin; hence the saying, "Eat your potato skins, they're good for you." Unfortunately, today's commercial potato skins also harbor a broad range of pesticide and herbicide residues. Potatoes are one of the most frequently sprayed foods on the market, so unless you grow your own or buy exclusively unsprayed potatoes, you should always peel them.

Potatoes keep quite well, provided they are stored in a cool, dark place, but you should keep in mind that the quality of the tuber changes considerably during storage. Early potatoes have a waxy texture and thin skins, best for steaming, boiling, or dishes in which potato pieces hold their shape. Older potatoes are more "mealy" or crumbly, and make better french fries or baked potatoes. And, even if you're not worried about the skins, you may prefer to peel them off old potatoes. You should also remove any green spots, which result from exposure to light; these are bitter and somewhat toxic (they will give you a stomach ache).

We grow our own potatoes and particularly love the waxy little undersized tubers; since they have more skin, they have more food value. To retain maximum vitamin C and iron (both water-soluble) we steam them (rather than boiling them and throwing away the goodness).

Baked Stuffed Potatoes

These are incredibly good, well worth the extra effort. Start them well before dinner: about an hour before serving, or make them ahead and refrigerate until the final baking. You need not use real baking potatoes, but choose perfect potatoes, evenly shaped and all the same size: about 2½ inches in diameter and 3 to 4 inches long.

Poke with a fork and bake at 425°F for 45 minutes:
1 potato per person
When they can be easily pierced with a fork, take them out and cut each one in half crosswise. Scoop out the middles, turning each shell upside down on the counter. Mash the potatoes with a ricer, food mill, or masher (or a fork).

Add for every 3 potatoes:
½ cup milk mixed with ¼ cup dried milk
    or 1 beaten egg
1½ Tbsp butter
½ tsp salt
1 Tbsp chopped parsley and/or **chives**
a little onion juice (*see Onion Dip, p. 10*)
Refill the potato skins, heaping the mashed potatoes up on top, and put the stuffed potatoes in the wells of a cupcake tin.

To reheat and finish, bake at around 350°F for 15 to 20 minutes until browned.

Scalloped Potatoes

This is a terrific dish to make using a food processor; you can slice the vegetables in seconds. Traditionally baked for 1½ hours, scalloped potatoes can instead be simmered on top of the stove for 20 minutes, then baked only 15 minutes. It's important to use a pot with a good thick bottom for this so the milk doesn't burn. The amount of milk you add will vary; rather than measure, just fill to the top of the sliced potatoes.

Wash, peel (if necessary) and slice ⅛-inch thick:

3 to 4 cups potatoes
1 to 2 onions
Arrange in layers in an oiled, ovenproof pot. On each layer, scatter:
1 to 2 Tbsp whole wheat flour
pinch of salt
1 Tbsp butter, cut in bits
pinch of paprika
Pour over this:
1½ cups whole milk, canned milk, or
double-strength reconstituted dried milk
Cover and simmer over low heat until potatoes can be easily pierced with a fork, about 20 minutes. Remove lid and grate on top:
½ cup cheese (any kind)
½ cup whole wheat bread crumbs
Place in a 350°F oven and bake 15 minutes or until you are ready to serve.

NOTE: If you want to double or triple this recipe, use a broader, rather than a deeper pan; otherwise it will take longer to cook.

SERVES 4 TO 6

Curried Home Fries

4 medium-sized potatoes
1 onion
2 cloves garlic
2 tsp curry mixture
1 tsp curry powder
pinch or more of hot chili powder
1 tsp salt
3 to 5 Tbsp safflower oil
Halve and dice the potatoes into cubes. In a 1 or 2-quart saucepan, bring an inch or so of salted water to a boil. Add and cook the potatoes, covered, for 10 minutes. Remove the lid, drain, and allow to cool slightly as you heat 3 Tbsp of the oil in a large, cast-iron skillet. When the oil is crackling hot, add potatoes and stir well. Cook over lively heat for about 10 to 15 minutes, adding more oil if needed. Chop and add onion; cook 3 minutes. Sprinkle over spices and crushed or minced garlic. Cook 1 minute. Remove from heat. This dish may be served at once or cooled and later reheated; people have even been known to eat it cold, out of the pan.

SERVES 2 TO 3

Other Potato Recipes
Potato Bisque *(p. 18)*, Potato Pancakes *(p. 105)*

Alfalfa Sprouts

From a few tablespoons of tiny seeds comes a veritable jungle of sprouts. It's easy to grow your own. Use ordinary canning jars with two-piece lids. Remove the flat part of the lid and replace it with a 6-inch square of plastic window screening.

For 1 pint jar use: 2 Tbsp alfalfa seeds
For 1 quart jar use: 4 Tbsp alfalfa seeds

Put the seeds in the jar and fill with cold water. Screw on screen top. Soak seeds for 5 to 12 hours. Drain off water. Rinse seeds with cool water and drain again. Place the jar at a slight angle, so it drains continually. It should be at room temperature, but not in full light, for best results. They will grow little green leaves if placed in full sunshine. However, the only thing that can really go wrong with sprouts is that you can forget to water them for more than 24 hours. Try to rinse them more often: every 6 hours is best. Depending on how well you remember, they will be fully sprouted in 4 or 5 days. They keep up to a week if refrigerated, but should be rinsed daily.

Himmel und Erde

"Heaven and Earth," as the old German title proclaims, is this marriage of applesauce and turnips. Fresh turnips need not be peeled, but by spring the skins will be woody and should be removed.

Wash and chop into chunks the size of walnuts:
1 turnip
Put turnip in a pot with an inch or so of water, cover, and boil 15 minutes or until soft. Roughly mash with a fork or potato masher. Don't get out all the lumps. Add to taste:
1 to 1½ cups applesauce
2 Tbsp butter
2 Tbsp brown sugar
½ tsp cinnamon
pinch of nutmeg or **ginger**
Stir well; serve hot.

SERVES 3 TO 4

Herbs & Condiments

THE HERB GARDEN

When we first took up farming I staked out a formal herb garden, close to the house, where I planned to grow everything from thyme to dill, along with decorative little clumps of flowers and a row or two of salad greens. To keep out the chickens and escaping goats and little children who like to pick flowers and big children chasing fly balls and even my husband turning his tractor around, I wove a basketlike fence out of alders and such things, and planted my herbs. Some of them yet survive. There is a big weedy patch of marjoram being taken over by a bigger patch of mint. There are a dozen very decorative clumps of chives, and two enormous Florence fennel plants that get to be about 6 feet tall, with wonderful fronds and flowers.

However, my herb garden is not very well organized, and it certainly isn't the best place to grow herbs, which are all different and have specific needs and special roles to play. Thyme, for example, is a tiny little tangle, easily swamped by grass growing in from the fence. I now grow it in a rock garden behind the house, where it spreads out gloriously on the stones in great mats,

easy to cut for drying, easy to keep weeded. And, after 10 years of losing my basil and early lettuces to the mice who lived near the house, I've learned to plant it up in the hot sunny tomato patch, on black plastic, which heats the soil and discourages mice. Dill and coriander and caraway are tall and weedy; I could grow them in the herb garden, but prefer to interplant them with cabbages and cauliflowers and broccoli, to discourage the cabbage moth. And the sage and camomile and parsley are so pretty that I plant them in the flower gardens.

The herb garden, so called, is still there, although the fence is long gone. It is now home to a lot of tall perennial flowers, a big rhubarb patch the chickens like to root around in, and a pussy willow tree that my kids planted by sticking the branches they'd brought home for me into the wet spring ground. I still go out with notions of order in my head, and dig around in the spring, getting myself in shape for the Big Garden. It's not exactly what I had in mind, but then again, what ever is?

HERBS

Herbs and spices add a whole new dimension to cookery. All herbs are better fresh, and dried herbs and spices have a great deal more ambience if they have been picked and dried within the year. Many aren't hard to grow, if you have space; some are available seasonally at ethnic markets or health food stores.

To dry your own herbs, cut the plants just before they flower, in the early morning of what promises to be a sunny day. Hang herbs to dry upside-down in a warm, dry place, out of the sun. Unless the air is very dry, enclose the herbs in a brown paper bag. Depending on leaf thickness and the humidity, they will take from 3 to 6 days to dry completely. If they are not drying well by the fourth day, take them down and bake them in a slow oven, 120°F, with the door partly open to allow moisture out, or put together a homemade drier (see p. 258).

Crumble the leaves, discarding stems, and put them in a large covered jar in a warm place for 2 days. If no moisture appears on the sides of the jar, consider the contents sufficiently dried. Store herbs in covered glass jars in a cool, dry, dark place. I know this rules out all those nice little spice shelves, but herbs deteriorate in sunlight almost as fast as when exposed to heat.

Another way to store herbs is in the freezer. Delicate flavors such as dill, basil, tarragon and parsley don't carry much of their essence into the dried state, no matter how carefully the process is done. Instead, chop them fine, and pack them by half-cupfuls into little plastic bags. Place the bags in a larger plastic container, label, and freeze.

Anise: Anise is a tall, branchy annual like dill or caraway; it grows best in patches, where the seed is collected and dried late in the summer. Italians like to put it in their sausages, to contrast with fiery peppers and the heavy flavor of meat. You can try it in meatballs, cabbage rolls, and stuffings. In German and Austrian cookery, anise seeds are frequently pressed into cookies. It is said to sweeten the breath after too much cheese and garlic, thus, anise-flavored wines and liqueurs are a favorite.

Basil: Basil is a compact annual with glossy green leaves that are endlessly useful in the kitchen. You can chop fresh basil into salads, fish, tomato sauce, sandwiches, cheese and egg dishes, meats, or chicken. To provide it in plentiful amounts, start the plants early and set them out late into full sun. Clip off growing tips periodically and it will branch instead of flower, giving you more leaves. Basil may be frozen plain or in Pesto (see p. 83). Pesto frozen in an ice cube tray for midwinter noodles or rice will definitely knock your dull old January palate right back into the middle of glorious summer.

Bay: These are the leaves of the edible bay, useful to mildly sweeten stews, soups, and meats, as well as pickles and baked beans. Bay leaves will not disintegrate either in cooking or in your stomach, so remember to remove them from the pot before you serve.

Borage: Borage is a great big leafy plant with tiny blue flowers all over it, grown mainly to make the garden pretty. The flowers taste a bit like cucumbers, and can be used in salads or cold summer drinks.

BOUQUET GARNI

This is a mixture of dried herbs, tied in a bunch or sewn into a little tea-bag-like sack, to be cooked with a stew, soup, or sauce. If you grow your own herbs, these make a very special Christmas present.

Stew Bouquet Garni

3 parts thyme
2 parts savory
3 parts marjoram
1 part rosemary or sage

Vegetable Bouquet Garni

3 parts tarragon
1 part thyme
2 parts savory
1 part rosemary

Caraway: These strong-flavored seeds are used in rye bread, Polish sausage, meatballs, and even, according to Gaelic tradition, on top of cakes and cookies. Caraway's pungent smell is also a marvelous way to mask the smell of cooking cabbage or cauliflower: add a pinch to the cooking liquid.

Celery: Celery has a fresh, crisp flavor and texture and is used with chicken, fish, and in vegetable salads of all kinds. It's also one of the many flavors in tomato sauce, pickles, and stir-fries. Use dried seeds or the fresh plant.

Chervil: This is a delicate cousin of parsley, an annual with lacy leaves and a mild anise flavor. Chopped fine, it adds a nice touch to fish, chicken, salads, eggs, and as a garnish for rice or potatoes. Chervil loses much of its flavor when dried, but may be kept over winter, live on a windowsill or in a greenhouse.

Chili Peppers: Around the equator, foods spiced with hot peppers are served at every meal, along with gallons of thirst-quenching liquids. They are definitely an acquired taste, but once acquired, a meal without a little zip is somehow lacking.

Peppers (hot or sweet) aren't hard to grow, but require a lot of sun for their fruit to ripen.

You may buy chilies fresh, dried, as dried seeds, powder, or *mole,* which, in South American kitchens, is pounded every day because it has more flavor when fresh.

Mild Chili: Dark and flavorful, mild chili powder is often used in combination with hotter chili powders in Mexican cooking, because it has so much more flavor. It's good spread directly on chicken or fish to barbecue or bake.

Chives: Chives are a remarkably resilient little member of the onion family; they grow in hardy clumps, surviving any amount of ice and snow, springing anew each year. They may also easily be transplanted into pots and kept live on the kitchen windowsill for use in winter. They add a wonderful freshness to omelets, potato salad, or broiled fresh fish.

Coriander: Coriander is an annual but, like dill and anise, it grows best in weedy patches that tend to be self-perpetuating. Leaves and seeds of coriander are used a great deal in many kinds of Asian cookery and also in Mexico, where it is known as *cilantro.* Coriander leaves are sometimes used in salads and stir-fries, but the chief use is of the ground seeds, which help to flavor soups, stews, and sauces.

Dill: Dill is a very tall plant (often 5 feet), with feathery fronds and delicate clumps of flowers that become dill seeds. If not all gathered, dill will continue to appear in your garden for years on end. It has a delicate fresh flavor, often used in fish cookery and in salads; it goes well with sour cream or yogurt sauce. It is also commonly used with cucumbers in dill pickles. Dill may be dried or frozen for winter use.

Fennel: Fennel is like celery in that the fresh plant, dried leaves, and seeds are all used in cooking. The raw plant can be sliced or chopped and served fresh as an hors d'oeuvre, or cooked in soup, stew, or stir-fry. Dried, fennel is used both in meat or bean cookery, and can be added to salads or used to lighten the flavor of vegetable dishes such as green beans or cabbage. Dried fennel seeds are also used in cookies *(see Springerele, p. 214).* Fennel has the fresh flavor of anise and may be served to lighten the breath after too much garlic and red wine.

Fines Herbes: This is a mixture of very finely crumbled herb leaves, to be served as a garnish for an omelet, soup, or in a sauce.

Mix any or all of basil, chervil, celery, chopped chives, marjoram, savory, parsley, sage (not too much), tarragon, and thyme.

Garlic: Garlic is an essential ingredient in cookery the world over, alone or in combination with other flavors. To grow your own, separate cloves and plant them, pointed end up, in October. In spring they leaf out like onions, then form a bulb with cloves of its own. When harvested, the stalks may be braided together to hang in the kitchen or pantry as you use them up.

Garlic may be used both raw and cooked, in salads, sauces, dressings, stews, soups, and casseroles. Insert slivers of garlic into fish, chicken, or red meat before roasting or broiling, or crush cloves and smear on the surface of meats or vegetables. To sweeten the breath after eating garlic, serve parsley.

Horseradish: In Victorian England, no roast beef-and-Yorkshire pudding dinner was complete without a dish of freshly grated horseradish with a little vinegar or lemon juice squeezed over it. Horseradish may also be mixed with sour cream, or even (if you're adventurous) added to salad.

Marjoram: Once established, marjoram is a hardy perennial growing in a solid patch, about 2 feet high, with pink flowers. Fresh or dried, it is a mild, sweet herb which is good in soups and stews, especially those made with chicken, veal, or mild fish. Fresh, it may be used in salads. It's also a nice herb to stick in a vinegar bottle. *(See Tarragon Vinegar, p. 63.)*

Mint: A tenacious perennial, mint can take over your whole garden, so be careful where you plant it. It loves wet areas but grows equally well in dry areas, in sun or shade, and in sweet or sour soil. The flavor of mint is common in toothpaste and candy, but it can also be used to pick up the flavor of vegetables such as peas or beans, fruits such as apples or pears, and meats such as lamb or pork. Mint is also a component in many herbal tea mixtures. Fresh or dried, it is a strong flavor; be careful not to use too much.

Mint Sauce

Wash and strip leaves from:
a handful of fresh mint sprigs
Sprinkle with:
½ tsp sugar
Chop coarsely and add:
½ cup vinegar
Leave fresh mint leaves in sauce and serve with lamb or other roast.

Mustard: Mustard is so common in North America that you probably know it as a weed. I always let a few plants go to seed to ensure early spring mustard greens, available long before spinach, kale, or chard come up. As to collecting and grinding the seed, however, I leave it to the experts. There are black, yellow, and white seeds available as whole seeds, ground powder, and the pastes we know as bottled mustard. These range from the almost tasteless yellow hot-dog mustard to the elegant condiments of Dijon; or you may try your hand at making your own.

Simple Mustard

In a blender, mix together:

½ cup mustard powder
¼ cup whole mustard seed
⅓ cup white wine vinegar
⅓ cup white wine
pinch of salt (optional)

Cover and buzz blender on and off, scraping down sides as needed, to make a thick paste or mash with a wooden spoon. Add more liquid as needed to thin it to the consistency you like. Store in a clean bottle in the fridge forever. If it's too hot, remove lid, cover with paper secured with elastic, and age it 1 month in the fridge.

1 CUP

Onions: Onions are basic to cookery throughout the world; it is difficult to imagine stews, soups, curries, or stir-fries without them. When cooking with them, first chop and sauté in a little hot oil or butter, for best flavor.

There are several varieties of onions. The French swear by shallots, which are more tender than our big yellows. Dry purple Bermuda onions are thinly sliced for garnish, sandwiches, and salads.

Onions can be difficult to digest, especially for small children or older people. Try using smaller amounts and chopping them finer. Onions are not bad for you — they just take a lot of energy to process.

Oregano: Oregano is a perennial, a hot little member of the marjoram family from the Mediterranean that adds spice and flavor to tomato dishes like Pizza *(p. 104)* and Spaghetti Sauce *(p. 75)*. It can be used fresh but keeps its strong spicy flavor when dried. To get the most out of it, add some when you start the sauce and some more just before serving.

Parsley: Everybody loves parsley. It's easy to grow, has a lovely, fresh, mild flavor, and does marvelous things for the body. It not only has vitamins A, B, and C — also it has E, which restores health and vigor to jaded tissues. Parsley is also the only sure cure for garlic breath.

Parsley is a biennial, so if you sow it in the same bed 2 years running, and mulch well during the winter, you might get a permanent parsley patch. Or grow it in the winter, in flowerpots or a windowbox. In other seasons, beds of parsley look great among the petunias or marigolds. Dried parsley has very little flavor, so if you can't grow it, buy it fresh and keep it refrigerated in a plastic bag. Use as much as you can to flavor soups, stews, and vegetables. Mountains of chopped parsley can go into sandwiches, stuffings, hamburgers, egg dishes, and salads of all varieties. If you're going to be good to yourself, start with parsley; it's the best.

Peppercorns: Unrelated to chilies, peppercorns are also hot, but much less so. Peppercorns lose their fragrance within hours of grinding, which is why many people keep pepper grinders on the table instead of pepper shakers. The savory aroma of pepper is used in almost all sauces, on meats, eggs, fish, chicken, and on vegetables of all kinds, including pickles.

Rosemary: An aromatic herb with a smell faintly coniferous, rosemary is so difficult to start that the only plants I've had were started in a nursery. Rosemary longs for Greece and will not tolerate frost, but you can set it out and bring it in for years on end. A little bit is all you need to cook with: a sprig in with the beans, a crumbled half-dozen twiggy little leaves in a quiche, a squash soup, a marinade, salad dressing, or fish sauce.

To use fresh rosemary, tear off a dozen leaves, chop them a bit and then smash them with a pestle or the bottom of a cup.

Sage: Sage is marvelously easy to grow and pretty to look at, with gray-green leaves and little blue flowers. It can be started each year as an annual or wintered over; eventually it will become a small, hardy bush. Sage is that special flavor that we're all familiar with in turkey stuffing. One reason I dislike commercial stuffings is that the sage is always stale, giving it an "off" flavor. Stuffing should be made with sage as fresh as possible.

Summer Savory: Savory grows annually in our gardens without difficulty, and is easy to dry fresh each year. Like sage, it's much better used within a year of picking. Savory adds a spicy touch to sausages, stuffed cabbage rolls, tomato sauce, soups, stews, and casseroles.

Tarragon: French tarragon isn't easy to start, but once established will survive winter and become perennial. It's a tall tangle of floppy branches, leaves of which are chopped to add a light, pleasant flavor to fish, chicken, and salad dressings. The elegant, unmistakable flavor of French tarragon is almost lost in drying, but fresh tarragon may be chopped and frozen for winter use. There is also a tall variety called Russian tarragon, which has almost no flavor and is hardly worth bothering with.

Tarragon Vinegar

4 sprigs tarragon
2 to 3 sprigs parsley
1 bay leaf
3 cups white vinegar
4 sprigs tarragon leaves
1 cup dry white wine

Cut and hang tarragon sprigs in a dark, dry place for 2 days or until well wilted. Place them in a plastic container and add parsley, bay leaf, and boiling vinegar. Mark date on the container, cover, and let set in a cool place for 2 weeks.

Sterilize 2 pint-sized canning jars and lids. Place 1 or 2 fresh sprigs of tarragon in each. Strain the vinegar into an enameled or stainless-steel pan and bring to a boil. Divide equally between the 2 jars; add white wine and fill to within ½ inch of the top. Adjust lids.

2 PINTS

Variation
Basil Vinegar: Follow directions for Tarragon Vinegar, substituting basil for tarragon, and red wine for white. You may also add a clove or two of fresh garlic for extra flavor when steeping the basil for 2 weeks.

Thyme: Thyme is a tiny, tangly plant that belongs in a dollhouse rock garden. It does

best, in fact, in a dry, rocky place, becoming a perennial bed that you annually clip and dry. The problem is the stems, which I have never quite figured out how to deal with. Thyme is worth it, however, for the lovely flavor it lends to soups and meat stews; I often tie it in a bunch or bag it as Bouquet Garni *(p. 59.)*

Salt Stretcher

A mixture of dried ground herbs and spices, many people find this helps you get past the need for salt, especially with bland foods like eggs, rice, and potatoes. It's really great in last-minute scrambled eggs. I still use a little salt, but not as much.

Mix:
5 tsp onion powder
1 Tbsp garlic powder
1 Tbsp paprika
1 Tbsp dry mustard
1 tsp thyme
½ tsp white pepper
½ tsp celery seed
Label and store in a closed container.

TISANES & HERBAL TEAS

A great variety of leaves and flowers may be steeped in boiling water to make a wonderfully heartening drink that you may enjoy better than the bitterness of caffeine or the stale smell of commercial herb teas. Some grow wild and some may be grown in your garden. Here is just a small sampling — the ones I gather and grow myself.

Camomile: An annual flowering herb, camomile grows to about a foot in height, in a great tangle of feathery leaves and miniature daisylike flowers. Its flowers alone are picked and dried for tea in the winter.

Clover: I like to gather purple heads of clover, dry them, and fragment them into a tea mixture, which is sweetened by the addition of clover blossoms.

Horsetail: An ancient wild plant that grows along the roads in sandy places, horsetail can be gathered, dried, and used for tea. I drink it for its flavor; it is also said to be good for the lungs.

Lemon Balm: A perennial herb, related to mint, lemon balm gets to be 2 feet tall and bushy with tiny pink flowers. It is picked for the leaves, which have a pleasant lemony scent in tea.

Mint: A perennial herb that spreads by growing runners underground: be forewarned! Any place you put mint it will stay forever, and likely choke everything else out. Mint is grown for its leaves, and best harvested just before it flowers.

Raspberry Leaves: These add iron as well as a fine astringency to herb tea.

Stinging Nettle Leaves: Gather and handle with gloved hands. An ancient Gaelic spring tonic, stinging nettle leaves give body and strength to herbal teas.

SPICES & CONDIMENTS

Allspice: Allspice derives its name from the fact that it smells like a mixture of other spices — cinnamon, nutmeg, and cloves. However, it is actually a whole round seed, often used in this form to pickle vegetables or meats. Ground allspice is a wonderful flavoring combined with molasses in cakes, cookies, and pumpkin recipes. It can also be added to fruit dishes. A pinch can be used to brighten the flavor of a sweet-and-sour sauce, baked beans, or a meat dish.

Almond Flavoring: Almond extract is strong and bitter, so use it with care. Its very special flavor has an affinity for egg whites, nuts, or coconut. Use it in oatmeal cookies. It can also complement chocolate, and is marvelous in fruit sauce.

Cardamom: Cardamom tastes like nutmeg with maybe a little white pepper thrown in. The large seed pods come in three colors: white, green, and black. The white and green pods contain the milder seeds; they are ground for use in Holiday Bread *(see p. 187)* and cookies. The seeds from the smaller black pods are stronger, used to flavor such things as exotic coffee or barbecue sauce. Preground cardamom has little flavor and is not worth buying. To grind by hand, use a mortar and pestle.

Cinnamon: There are two entirely different "cinnamon" plants. Cinnamon sticks are the rolled bark from the cinnamon tree, which grows in Sri Lanka. Ground cinnamon, which is much stronger and more bitter, comes from the bark of the cassia tree in Vietnam. Cinnamon sticks are used in hot drinks such as apple cider, mulled wine, rum toddy, lemonade, or coffee; they are sometimes cooked in pickle juices. Ground cinnamon is the most commonly used spice in North America, probably because it does such wonderful things to apple pie. It's also used in a wide variety of baked goods such as molasses cakes and cookies, in fresh and dried fruit dishes, and in puddings.

Cloves: Whole or powdered, cloves are very strong. A pinch will often do where a teaspoon of cinnamon or half a teaspoon of nutmeg would be appropriate. Cloves have a wonderful aroma and can be used for many things besides gingerbread and pumpkin pie. Buy whole cloves and stick two in an onion to marry with the juices of stew stockpot or baked beans in a marvelous and not-quite-identifiable flavor. A tiny pinch of ground cloves in a stir-fry or casserole will have much the same mysterious effect. Whole cloves, along with other spices, are bagged and cooked with pickle juice. Just make sure that nobody sinks their teeth into a whole clove — they'll know what it is at once! Cloves numb the mouth, and used to be used for toothaches.

Cumin: The strong, nutty flavor of cumin does wonderful things to chicken, meats, and vegetables — even eggs or dried beans. In Eastern cooking it's often used in combination with other spices such as turmeric, coriander, mustard, and chilies. The whole seeds are added to marinades and pickles.

Curry Powder: Western curry powder is not a spice but a mixture of spices. By "curry," Eastern cooks mean a mixture of spiced foods; they add the spices individually to suit the dish and those who are to eat it. Westerners, however, refer to "curry" as a premixed combination of mustard, curry leaf, coriander, cumin, allspice, turmeric, cardamom, and various sorts of hot chilies. Often it is sold as "hot" or "mild" with reference to the chilies. The powder may be used to flavor casseroles, meat or vegetable dishes, or in tiny amounts to pick up the flavor of a cream sauce or gravy.

Ginger: Being a root, ginger will keep for months in a humid refrigerator — you do not have to make use of the greatly inferior dried powder. Freshly grated ginger gives a marvelous tang to molasses cookies and cakes, pumpkin or squash, stir-fry dishes, and sweet-and-sour sauces. When substituting fresh for powdered ginger, use 5 times as much.

Lemon and Orange Peel: The peel of either lemons or oranges may be finely grated into cakes, cookies, and other desserts. It can even be used in sauces for meats or vegetables. The drawback is that who-knows-what is sprayed or soaked into the skins these days, unless you are able to buy organic fruit. Always use whole fruit to grate; remove peel from grater with a stiff brush.

Nutmeg: The kernel of a tall evergreen from the East Indies, nutmeg is famous for its magical flavor. Be careful not to use too much of it. Keep both fresh and ground nutmeg on hand for use in puddings, cakes, and cookies. Nutmeg was also used traditionally for ground meats, sausage, stuffing, and pickling mixtures. Whole nutmeg has more flavor, but must be finely grated as you need it. Ground nutmeg, while having less piquancy, is still good in a pinch.

Turmeric: Turmeric comes from an Asian root (now cultivated in the West). We buy it as a bright yellow powder. In southern Asia, it is very popular in all kinds of meats and vegetable curries, and used to color breads and cakes. Because of its mildly unpleasant smell, it is often combined with strong-smelling spices such as cumin and coriander.

Vanilla: In the good old days when vanilla was cheap, thousands of recipes had vanilla added to the ingredients. Lately, it has become too dear to use so freely. I often use almond extract, orange or lemon peel, or spices such as nutmeg and cinnamon instead of vanilla in my cakes and cookies.

Real vanilla flavoring comes from the bean of a tropical orchid that originated in South America and is now cultivated in Florida, the Caribbean islands, Sri Lanka, Tahiti, and other tropical places. The vines climb shade trees, living to 30 or 40 years of age and producing the aromatic vanilla beans. The beans, 6 to 8 inches long, are annually gathered, dried, fermented for 6 months, and then soaked in fluid (traditionally partly alcohol) which becomes the "vanilla flavoring" we are familiar with. All of this is prodigiously labor intensive, so in the past 20 years, the price of natural vanilla has risen with wages.

Artificial vanilla is much less expensive, but the ingredients that go into it are less widely known. The flavor, moreover, is not as delicious as that of pure natural vanilla.

Vanilla has a warm, friendly taste, and is especially good in puddings, ice creams, cheesecake, and yogurt popsicles. It's also good in combination with other flavorings, such as chocolate, orange, and lemon.

THE PANTRY

Chocolate

Chocolate! There's nothing like it. Almost everybody loves it, even though it's not the best thing for you. Chocolate has hardly any nutrition, and many people are unable to eat it without skin problems, weight gain, or a nervous reaction to the high amounts of sugar needed to make it palatable. However . . .

The chocolate used in cooking is available in several forms. You may buy it as unsweetened or sweetened cocoa, and as bitter or semisweet solid chocolate. Semisweet has some sugar, hence less chocolate. The sugar has been cooked at high temperatures with the chocolate to bond them together, a process difficult to duplicate. When cooking with chocolate, it is best to stick to the type recommended in the recipe.

Carob

Carob is a dark sweet powder made from ground carob beans. It looks like chocolate, but there the resemblance ends; it has a butterscotchlike flavor, and doesn't need the vast quantities of sugar that chocolate requires. Carob goes well with nuts, raisins, and vanilla. I have found that, while my family enjoys it in cookies, cakes, and brownies, they don't like it in uncooked mixtures such as frostings or blender specials.

Yeasts

Two separate products known as "yeast" appear in North American cookery, which the novice cook must take care not to confuse: baker's yeast and brewer's yeast. Baker's yeast, used in breadmaking and brewing, is composed of tiny pale balls, or comes in a solid cake; brewer's yeast, a nutritional food additive, is a pale powder.

Dried Baker's Yeast: Used primarily for baking bread, dried baker's yeast is available in airtight packets, each containing 1 tablespoon; in cans with plastic lids containing larger amounts; or in bulk form from health food stores. There is no difference in these types of yeast. It is important that yeast be kept dry, cool, and dark, and used within 6 months. Some yeasts are sold with expiration dates printed on them.

Cake Baker's Yeast: Baker's yeast used to be sold more often in cake form — little squares of cheesy-looking yeast, wrapped in foil, to be kept in the refrigerator and used before the expiration date.

Using Baker's Yeast: Because it is a living organism, you must take some care in the storage and handling of baker's yeast. Yeast is a simple form of plant, purchased in a dormant stage. It remains dormant until exposed to warmth, water, and oxygen. The extremes of temperature which it can survive are 70° to 105°F, which means that it grows well in water at about skin temperature or a little cooler: tepid water. Hot water will kill yeast, so mix water to the right temperature before adding the yeast.

Yeast growth is controlled by temperature. Low temperatures make for slower growth and a finer-textured bread; high temperatures can cause bread dough to rise more quickly, trapping large air bubbles in this rapid growth. If a dough containing yeast is cooled overnight, it can be reactivated by gradual warming over many hours.

Beer and Wine Yeast: These varieties available at brewing stores and some large supermarkets, are similar to baker's yeast but have a less "yeasty" flavor. They are used in brewing wine and beer because the yeast sinks to the bottom and can be more easily removed.

Brewer's Yeast: A byproduct of the brewing process, brewer's yeast is dead on arrival; it cannot be used to bake bread or brew anything. It has large amounts of B vitamins, and so can be added to milk or baked goods to increase daily intake of these vitamins. Some people like it on popcorn. Brewer's yeast comes in various forms: ordinary, debittered, and a debittered form called Engivita. In England, brewer's yeast is sold as Marmite, a brown spread used on bread.

Baking Soda
Bicarbonate of soda is an alkaline chemical used in baking. It gives off carbon dioxide when combined with an acid ingredient such as buttermilk, yogurt, tea, coffee, molasses, honey, or cream of tartar. The carbon dioxide, released into the batter as it solidifies, causes the batter to "rise," or fill with air holes. Baking soda also neutralizes the acidity of the acid ingredient; for this reason, it is sometimes used in combination with baking powder. If there is no acid ingredient in the batter, it will rise a good deal less and give the product an unpleasant flat taste. Thus, if you have a recipe for cookies that calls for buttermilk and soda, and you are out of buttermilk, either sour the fresh milk first with 1 teaspoon of vinegar or lemon juice, or substitute baking powder for the soda. Baking powder is not as powerful as soda:
2 tsp baking powder = ½ tsp baking soda (plus acid ingredient)
Some people (notably, Adele Davis) object to the use of baking soda because it counteracts vitamin C and the B vitamins. Substitution of baking powder is not a solution, because baking powder contains baking soda. If you feel strongly that you need every vitamin you can get, make your cakes with baker's yeast.

Baking Powder
Baking powder is a combination of bicarbonate of soda and an acid ingredient. You can make your own baking powder by combining:
2 tsp cream of tartar
1 tsp baking soda
However, this doesn't keep well and must be used up right away. Commercial baking powders include a little cornstarch and, rather than cream of tartar, contain mono-calcium phosphate or sodium acid phosphate.

Double-acting baking powder also includes sodium aluminum sulphate, which is a very successful ingredient in that it doesn't act until heat is applied to the batter. However, many people prefer not to ingest aluminum or alum as part of their diet and therefore stick to baking powders that do not contain this ingredient. Aluminum is a substance that is foreign to the body, and has been linked to Alzheimer's disease. Nonaluminum baking powder can be bought in health food stores.

Fats

In cooking, you will find two general kinds of fats: solid (butter and shortening) and liquid (vegetable oils). There are many sources of fat.

Solid Fats: Fats like butter and lard are saturated with hydrogen, making them stable but not easily digestible. Shortenings and margarines are made out of vegetble oils, true, but they are artificially hydrogenated to make them solid at room temperature, so they are actually saturated.

Solid fats are an essential ingredient in crisp light piecrusts, cookies, biscuits, scones and pastries. Many cakes have saturated fats, too, although not in quite such high amounts. Doctors advise many people to avoid or limit their use of saturated fat, and use vegetable oils instead.

Liquid Fats: These are oils pressed from nuts and seeds, such as canola, safflower, corn, peanut, soybean, and sunflower. Such oils are great for frying, braising, pancakes, bread making, salad dressing, and certain kinds of cakes. They have small amounts of saturated fats, and healthy proportions of polyunsaturated or monounsaturated fat.

(The exceptions are tropical oils such as coconut oil, which is liquid but is 92 percent saturated fat.)

Both refined and unrefined seed oils are available. Refined oils are extracted by a series of chemical processes involving caustic sodas, bleaches, and extremes of hot and cold. This renders them clear, flavorless and odorless. Unrefined oils are pressed from seeds or nuts without heat. Because less oil is extracted this way, unrefined oils cost more. They are cloudy in appearance, and carry the distinctive flavors of their origins, and also essential fatty acids, lecithin, and vitamins A and B. Like all fresh produce, they should be stored in a cool dark place and used within six weeks.

Canola Oil: This seed oil has such high ratings that is deserves special mention as having the least saturated fat of them all (6 percent).

Olive Oil: Olive oil is distinctive in that it is pressed from a fruit, rather than a nut or seed. It is traditionally used in Mediterranean and Hispanic cooking. It has a special flavor, especially if cold-pressed, which many people enjoy in cooking and salad dressings.

Butter: Butter is made by churning cream, after the cream is separated from the milk. It is a wonderful spread, marvelously light and flavorful to cook and bake with. However, low temperatures must be used when you fry things in butter, or the milk solids will cause it to burn. Butter is often colored with the yellow annatto seed, and is usually lightly salted, which helps make it possible for it to be kept refrigerated for up to 2 weeks. Unsalted butter will only keep about a week. If you wish to keep it longer, it freezes quite well provided it is carefully wrapped.

Margarine: Dozens of varieties of margarine exist. The best ones have long lists of ingredients with very unfamiliar names. Contrary to what margarine companies would like you to believe, they are not better for you than butter. They're based on unsaturated fats, true, but in order to solidify and stabilize them, margarines are saturated and hydrogenated, like lard or shortening. They have the same number of calories as butter and none of the flavor. However, they are much less expensive than butter.

Shortenings: These are, chiefly, vegetable oils, chemically refined and saturated for stability. They are less expensive than margarines (which are made the same way) because they aren't flavored or colored to resemble butter. Shortening is used in cooking in the same way as butter or lard, in pies, cookies, and cakes. It may also be used in deep-fat frying. It is hydrogenated and saturated, like margarine.

Lard: Lard is a fat made from of the fats of a pig. Home-rendered lard is not stable and should be kept frozen or quite cold. Commercial lard is hydrogenated. Lard is excellent in producing flaky piecrust, cookies, and pastries, provided it is used and kept cold until it goes into the oven. It can also be used for deep-fat frying.

Eggs

The egg, the most common ingredient in cooking, is also one of the trickiest. When cooking them, always use low heat. Too hot a pan causes the delicate protein to shrink and toughen rapidly; too hot an oven will deflate a soufflé, or cause a quiche to separate. Eggs should be heated gradually. When adding eggs to hot sauces or soups, first beat the eggs in a bowl, then add a little of the hot mixture to the eggs, stirring as you do. Continue to stir as you pour the egg mixture into the pot. Be careful not to overcook these mixtures; remove them from the heat when thick. And, until you're familiar with the process, use a double boiler.

Eggs are nutritionally wonderful, but keep in mind that each egg yolk contains 5½ grams of fat. However, eggs contain vitamin A, not available in many other foods, and also lecithin, which helps break down cholesterol.

Homegrown Eggs: Anybody who has ever broken into a homegrown egg can see that they are quite different from the commercial product. The yolk is dark, not light yellow. The white is thick and gelatinous and doesn't run all over the pan when fried or poached. Part of the difference is

that commercial hens, under artificial lighting, lay eggs more often; each egg contains more water. Free-range chickens have a more varied diet, too, which has to account for something. If you feed crab or lobster shells to chickens, the yolks become dark orange.

If you grow your own eggs, you will have noticed these and other differences. Absolutely fresh eggs are wonderful for breakfast, but when making hard-boiled eggs or beating egg whites, choose eggs which are at least 3 days old. Fresh egg whites stick to the shell, making hard-boiled eggs hard to shell. And fresh egg whites absolutely will not expand fully, no matter how long you beat them.

Raw Eggs: Many children and some adults are allergic to raw egg whites. There are many recipes for foods with raw eggs, but I hesitate to use them for this and for nutritional reasons. Avidin, a component of raw egg whites, combines with a B vitamin, biotin, and prevents it from reaching your system.

Sweeteners

Nutritionists often state that there is nothing wrong with sugar as long as you don't eat too much of it, too often, or in place of foods with broader values. The trouble is that people do. Sweet foods are attractive, especially to people on the run. They give you a quick lift and don't require a lot of slow digesting. Sometimes, though, it's more than a lift: it's a rocket launch and crashdown. A snack or short meal made up of sugary foods puts a terrific strain on the pancreas, which is supposed to produce exactly the right amount of insulin, to balance all the sugar. A blood-sugar high is often followed by a dramatic sense of depression. Children are particularly susceptible. After the birthday

ice cream and cake (with candies and icing and pop) it's about half an hour to the first howling casualty.

When you feel the urge for sweets, try to imagine what you'd eat if you were unable to have sugary foods. A piece of fruit? Some freshly cracked nuts? How about some whole grain crackers, cheese, and a cup of hot apple juice? When browsing through dessert recipes, look at the quantity of sugar. Is that what you want to eat? Don't buy cookies or desserts for your kids without tasting them and having a look at the ingredients. I think the answer to the sugar problem isn't whether you use it, but how much, when, and how to go about using less of it.

Various kinds of sugars are available. The most common are:

Molasses: Refined or unrefined, this syrup contains a lot of sugar, and, cup for cup, is as sweet as brown, raw, or white sugar. It also has a lot of minerals, some vitamins, and a very distinctive flavor when used in quantity. You cannot really taste the small amounts used in breads, but it is very noticeable in cakes and cookies. They're browner, chewier, and molasses flavored. It is best to use spices that complement this taste, such as cinnamon, ginger, nutmeg, allspice, and cloves.

Blackstrap Molasses: This kind of molasses has very little sweetness and a very strong taste; some like it, some don't. You'll notice the flavor in anything you add it to. You should consider it not a sweetener but a food additive, like brewer's yeast. It is very high in minerals. You can add a few spoonfuls to bread, cornbread, or grain dishes.

White Sugar: This is a purified form of raw sugar. If kept dry, it doesn't become lumpy in long storage. Its only food value is calories, which enter the bloodstream almost at once and are soon used up. White sugar is very light and easy to work with, and has no flavor of its own.

Brown Sugar: Light brown sugar is popular for cooking; several darker grades are available as well. All are made by adding a little molasses to white sugar. Brown sugars don't have much nutrition but have a slightly richer flavor.

Maple Syrup: Maple syrup is a special treasure in any kitchen. One year we made gallons of our own, and I tried it in everything: cakes, cookies, pies, even our tea. After it was all gone I wished I'd saved some for pancakes and ice cream.

Honey: Nutritionally speaking, honey is not really much better for you than sugar. It is classified as a glucose (rather than a sucrose), which means that it's slightly easier to digest; to some people, that's important. However, sugar is not very difficult to digest either. Honey is certainly not easier on the teeth or the pancreas, and it's not cheap, whether you buy it or produce it yourself. Nevertheless, used in moderation, it has a pleasing taste, and is quite versatile. Honey can be used in baking, but you must alter the recipe: honey is sweeter than sugar and is, of course, liquid. Best stick to honey recipes, available in honey cookbooks.

Chemicals in Food
Food Additives: Many people today are becoming alarmed about the chemicals used in food production and processing. The more processed a product is, the more likely it is to contain chemical substances that may or may not have been fully tested. By comparing labels, you can avoid jelly with food coloring, bread with preservatives, and soup with monosodium glutamate. But you cannot always be so sure about chemical residues in refined oils, or just exactly what has been used to make the "artificial flavoring" in so many products. Until better laws are passed concerning the need for long-term testing of these minute amounts of chemicals — alone or in combination with other minute amounts of chemicals — it's healthiest to eat foods in as whole a form as possible. Buy nuts, raisins, and fruits instead of cookies and snack foods. Stick to juice instead of soda pop, yogurt instead of ice cream.

Fruits and Vegetables: Unless you buy chemical-free organic produce, assume they're all sprayed with pesticides and herbicides. Wash all fruits and vegetables thoroughly as soon as they are brought into the house. Don't wait until later — you might forget. In making the washing a part of the buying process, rather than the cooking process, you can also help other members of the household become aware of the fact that unwashed fruits and vegetables are almost certain to have pesticide residues on them. Most pesticides are water-soluble, so to get rid of them let them soak for 5 minutes in a sink full of cold water, then rinse and wipe off each piece. Dry thoroughly before storing.

Meats: Avoid organ meats such as kidneys and livers from commercial animals. Heavy metals and toxic substances are more likely to be found in these, the "cleaning parts" of the body. Fats are also a storage spot for chemicals, and sometimes there are high concentrations in the neck of an animal, where injections are most often given. Muscle is still the cleanest meat.

Organic Foods: Buy from organic producers whenever possible. Certainly these foods cost a little more. But it's good to support organic growers, because they are the pioneers of the future. The tide is turning against the chemicals in our foods. Organic foods are increasingly available today, and it's worth the extra cost to be sure that your food is all food. As demand increases, cost go down. Consider the difference in price as your contribution to the development of clean food.

fines herbes: celery, parsley, thyme, shallots & tarragon.

Sauces & Marinades

A good sauce is a worthy thing, and is often the touch that turns an ordinary meal into something special. Let's face it — some foods are kind of boring. Others are on the dry side. A good sauce can save the day, if you know how to make it.

It's easy to be intimidated by sauces — there are so many of them, they have such fancy names, and it is not immediately evident what went into them. Actually, there are usually three basic ingredients in a sauce — something liquid, something tasty, and a thickener of some sort to keep the tasty liquid from running all over the plate. The reason there are so many sauces is that there are so many possible combinations of these

three things. The reason they have such fancy names is that they taste so good. Most of them are really uncomplicated, once you understand the thickening process.

If you feel uncertain about trying out a new sauce, save it until you have a quiet, boring dinner to cook and nothing to distract you. You don't need a lot of tools — a heavy iron skillet, a small deep pan and lid (I like a cast-iron enameled pot with a wooden handle), a rotary beater or small whisk, and a spring-type stirring device.

TOMATO SAUCES

Many people are on familiar ground when it comes to tomato sauces — fresh salsa, spaghetti sauce, thick spicy ketchup, and barbecue sauce. Different thicknesses and flavors of tomato sauces are used with different dishes. With plain noodles, for example, you will want a somewhat thinner sauce than with lasagne or pizza. Barbecue and antipasto sauces are very strong and meant to be used in small quantities.

Tomato sauce is basically made with tomatoes, fresh or canned. Tomato paste adds thickness, when needed, but it, too, is simply made of tomatoes. If you have time and the tomatoes, you may make your own paste. *(see p. 76).*

It is traditional to make tomato sauce in a frying pan. This is so that, by taking the lid off the pan for a few minutes, the liquid can easily be reduced.

It is also traditional to cook most tomato sauces for hours upon hours. A crockpot is perfect for this. I have found, however, that it is very successful to cook the vegetables with the tomatoes for a half hour, then allow them to sit at room temperature for 3 to 6 hours before warming and serving. Both these methods allow time for the flavors to "marry."

One final word about tomato sauces: forget about commercially prepared, elaborately presented "spaghetti sauce." I don't know what it is that makes them so utterly tasteless and boring, but I suspect it's the use of a lot of sugar and mono-sodium glutamate. Whatever it is, the addition of one small jar of that stuff to a whole pan full of good tomato sauce will overpower it all with the unmistakable flavor of cafeterias, institutions, and suburban sameness. If you are in a hurry, there's nothing wrong with a nice light sauce of canned tomatoes, onions, and oregano, cooked for 10 minutes.

Fresh Tomato Sauce

Tomato sauce made with fresh tomatoes tastes quite different from sauce made of canned or stewed tomatoes. It's sort of light and tart. It's good on noodles, rice, mashed potatoes, meat, fish, poultry — or just by itself.

Heat in a heavy frying pan:
2 Tbsp olive or **other light oil**
Chop or slice and add:
1 large onion
When limp, crush in:
1 clove garlic
Sauté 1 minute longer. Chop (or buzz in a machine) and add:
4 cups tomatoes
2 Tbsp fresh or dried basil
2 Tbsp parsley
Cover and cook over medium heat for 10 minutes.

SERVES 4

Variations
You may add along with the vegetables:
½ lb ground meat (optional)
Cook the meat gently until it turns gray.

True Spaghetti Sauce

This is the basic sauce for spaghetti, ravioli, gnocchi — anything that doesn't fall apart. It has a wonderful fragrant flavor unlike any canned sauce. It can be made and frozen by the gallon.

Chop small:
1 large onion
1 rib celery
1 green pepper (optional)
Sauté the vegetables in:
3 Tbsp olive oil
After a few minutes, crush and add:
2 cloves garlic
After a minute, add:
28 oz tomatoes
5½ oz tomato paste
1 Tbsp oregano

1 Tbsp basil
⅓ cup red wine (optional)
Refill tomato paste can with water and add to the mixture. Stir, bring to a boil, then cover and reduce heat to a bare simmer for 30 minutes. Turn off heat, leaving sauce covered, and allow to sit at room temperature for 2 to 6 hours. To serve, reheat, adding water if necessary and ½ tsp oregano. You may also add sliced fresh or canned mushrooms.

SERVES 4

Lasagne or Pizza Sauce

Sauce for elaborate dishes such as lasagne, eggplant parmigiana, and so forth must be made thicker than spaghetti sauce, so that it does not disturb the layers of curds tucked in between the noodles. You may make and refrigerate this sauce for one of these dishes up to a week ahead of time, if you can keep it safely hidden from snack fiends.

Follow the recipe for True Spaghetti Sauce *(see previous page)*, but instead of a 5½ ounce can of tomato paste, use:

1 11-oz can tomato paste or **4 patties of homemade tomato paste** *(following)*
Add water as needed, but you should finish with a thick sauce, watching it closely in the last stages of cooking.

SERVES 4 TO 6

Tomato Paste

Chop into quarters:
30 to 40 ripe, red tomatoes
Heat in a heavy, deep pot:
¼ cup olive oil
Add and sauté for 10 minutes:
5 large chopped onions
1 chopped celery plant
Add tomatoes and:
1 Tbsp dried or **1 stalk fresh oregano**
1 Tbsp dried or **10 leaves fresh basil**
1 tsp dried marjoram
10 whole peppercorns
10 whole cloves
2 sticks cinnamon
Simmer all this very slowly for about 4 hours, stirring from time to time to make sure nothing sticks to the bottom. If the bottom should burn, don't scrape it; instead, transfer the paste into another pan and discard the burned part. After 4 hours you may put it through a sieve or food mill, discarding the whole spices. Put it back on the stove and keep simmering it until the pulp becomes too thick to cook safely on top of the stove. Spread it out about ½-inch thick on pyrex, enamel, or china plates or trays, and cut grooves through it with a knife to help it dry through. Set it in the sun (covered with cheesecloth to keep off flies) or cook 2 to 3 hours in a 200°F oven. When the paste is dry enough, rub your hands in:
olive or **other light oil**
Shape into 3-inch patties and submerge them in oil, to keep them from becoming moldy. They will keep up to 3 months in a cool place, in a covered container.

6 CUPS

Mexican Tomato Sauce

This is used in making Enchiladas (see p. 105) and Tamale Casserole (see p. 167). This recipe calls for tomato juice, but you may, if you prefer, use fresh or canned tomatoes; simply process them by blending or putting them through a strainer or food mill for the smooth texture. Although this sauce has dark chili powder in it, there is no hot cayenne and it will not burn your mouth.

Chop fine:
1 onion
1 green pepper
2 cloves garlic
Sauté these in:
2 Tbsp corn or **olive oil**
Stir in:
2 Tbsp dark, mild chili powder
1 tsp ground cumin
1 Tbsp oregano
½ tsp salt
2 cups tomato juice
Cover and simmer 30 minutes over low heat. Allow to sit at room temperature for 2 to 6 hours. To serve, heat and add:
a pinch of oregano

SERVES 4

Sara's Pepper Sauce

This is the perfect thing if you are tired of tomatoes. It looks like, and acts like, but does not taste like, tomatoes.

Chop fine:
4 large red bell peppers (not hot ones)
1 onion
1 clove garlic or **1 inch grated ginger**
Sauté over medium flame for 7 minutes with:
¼ cup olive oil
1½ tsp chopped basil
Add and simmer 10 minutes:
1 cup chicken broth
Purée in food processor 3 minutes, until fully ground but not totally mushy. Return to frying pan for another 5 to 10 minutes to heat and reduce to a nice sauce consistency. Serve on pasta with lots of grated cheese, or on top of flaky whitefish such as cod or haddock that has been delicately poached, broiled, or baked.

SERVES 3

Barbecue Sauce

Barbecues are lovely, outdoors and in, but this sauce is also useful to coat on baked meats, such as chicken, pork, spareribs, and chops.

In a heavy frying pan, heat:
3 Tbsp meat drippings, lard, or **vegetable oil**
Add:
1 finely chopped onion
Sauté until limp; add:
2 cloves crushed garlic
Cook 1 minute longer. Add and simmer for 30 minutes:
1 5½-oz can tomato paste or **2 patties homemade tomato paste**
1 cup water
3 Tbsp cider vinegar or **2 Tbsp wine vinegar**
2 Tbsp tamari soy sauce
3 Tbsp brown sugar
½ tsp salt
1 tsp freshly ground black pepper
1 tsp mustard
¼ cup lemon juice (juice of ½ lemon)
Brush the meats with oil or lard before cooking them. Ten minutes before they are done, coat on the barbecue sauce; 5 minutes before they are done, turn them and coat again.

SERVES 4 TO 6

CREAM SAUCES

This is a catch-all name for a group of white sauces that look and taste creamy, but do not necessarily contain cream. They are thickened with a paste of flour cooked with butter, called *roux* by the French. Roux can be used to thicken milk or cream, in which case the sauce is known as a white sauce, cream sauce, or béchamel. It may be used to thicken fish, meat, or vegetable stock; this is called gravy or velouté. It also pops up in soups, stews, and casseroles. The trick is to add liquid to it gradually, and stir often. Fortunately, making it is a short process.

The best tool for sauce making is a small heavy pan that does not heat up too rapidly: cast iron, seasoned or enameled, or heavy stainless steel. A wire whip, spring-stirrer, or even a plain fork are appropriate tools. Cream sauce may also be made in the top of a double boiler, over boiling water. This takes longer but is a useful when making sauce in quantity, as, say, at Christmas, or when making Lasagne Blanco *(see p. 96)*

Ingredients are variable. You can make a quite nice white sauce using oil instead of butter (this decreases the amount of fat slightly). You may use whole wheat flour instead of white, if it is very finely ground, but do not substitute other kinds of flour. Only wheat has gluten, which binds the sauce.

The liquid in classic béchamel is whole milk, but you can substitute reconstituted dried milk, watered-down canned milk, wine, or a variety of broths and bits of leftover vegetable-boiling water.

A good cream sauce needs no flavoring, but you can make it taste quite different and exotic with a tablespoon of sherry, a bare pinch of mace or nutmeg, or something unusual like tarragon. Curry is popular, and soy sauce is good, although if you start putting soy sauce in everything, you'll soon find that everything tastes alike.

Cream sauce can be made ahead and refrigerated, covered, for several days. To reheat it, whisk in 2 tablespoons warm water and heat in a double boiler, or, constantly stirring, in a heavy-bottomed pan over very low heat.

Basic Cream Sauce

Also known as white sauce, this creamy sauce is actually made with milk. Use a small heavy pan over low heat to melt:
3 Tbsp butter
When just bubbling, sprinkle in:
3 Tbsp flour
Stir until the butter takes up the flour, and cook very gently over low heat for 3 minutes, stirring now and then. It will look strange, but don't worry about it. Now you have roux. Measure into a cup:
1 cup milk
Add ¼ cup of the milk to the roux and stir as the mixture thickens. Add another ¼ cup milk and stir again. When this thickens, add the rest of the milk and stir until it becomes thick. Season to taste.

1 CUP

Variation

Onion Sauce

Read recipe for Basic Cream Sauce. Start with:
4 Tbsp butter
Sauté in butter for 3 minutes:
2 Tbsp finely minced onion
½ clove crushed garlic (optional)
Sprinkle in flour and continue as above.

1 CUP

Mushroom Gravy

This is a great low-cholesterol sauce with no meat or milk products; it takes minutes to make, goes with anything, and tastes delicious.

Chop fine:
1 small onion or **3 to 4 shallots**
½ stalk celery
1 clove garlic (optional)
Sauté these in:
3 Tbsp safflower or **olive oil**
Adjust heat to medium. When the vegetables are translucent, add:
3 Tbsp whole wheat flour
Stir and cook over low heat for 2 to 3 minutes, then add:
1 tsp tamari soy sauce
3 Tbsp white wine
Stir as the sauce thickens, then add:
¾ cup water
4 sliced mushrooms
Cook over low heat until the sauce thickens slightly. Adjust seasonings to taste.

1 CUP

Macrobiotic White Sauce

This has no milk products, but is a surprisingly good substitute for cream sauce or gravy.

Heat in a small, heavy pan:
3 Tbsp safflower oil
Sprinkle in and stir with a whisk or fork:
3 Tbsp unbleached flour
Cook over moderate heat, stirring, for 3 minutes. Then add gradually, stirring as it thickens:
1 cup water
Season with:
2 tsp tamari soy sauce
1 tsp lemon juice
pinch of salt

1 CUP

Cheese Sauce

To Basic Cream Sauce, add:
½ cup milk
Grate into the sauce:
½ to 1 cup sharp Cheddar cheese

1½ CUPS

Velouté Sauce

The success of this sauce depends largely on the quality of the stock you add to the roux. It can be chicken broth, water in which fish or shellfish have been cooked, or a vegetable broth made with carrots, celery, onions, and herbs simmered together for an hour or more.

In a small heavy pan over low heat, melt:
2 Tbsp butter
When the butter is barely bubbling, add:
3 Tbsp flour
Stir until the butter takes up the flour, and cook very gently over low heat for 3 minutes. Measure:
2 cups broth
Add ¼ cup of the broth to the roux and stir as the mixture thickens. Add another ¼ cup of broth and stir again. When this thickens, add broth by half-cupfuls, stirring after each addition until the sauce thickens. Season to taste with salt and pepper.

2 CUPS

EGG SAUCES

A sauce thickened with eggs is one of the most delicious, nutritious, and perishable things in the kitchen. Egg-based sauces have the reputation of being "difficult." This is unfortunate, and untrue. Once you understand what's going on in an egg sauce, everything follows.

Egg yolks thicken when cooked. (For this reason, many egg sauces call for yolks only.) Think of the yolk of a perfectly soft-boiled egg: that's the thickness you want in your sauce. Now consider what happens to an egg yolk when the egg is boiled too long. That's what you don't want to happen. If overcooked, the tiny particles of yolk will harden and the sauce will turn thin and grainy, no matter how well you try to mix it. The great secret is therefore very simple. Take the sauce off the heat as soon as it thickens — never let it sit on the stove more than 15 minutes. Nor can you reheat it. Chefs in restaurants, with six pots of sauces brewing, add a spoonful of béchamel or velouté to make it more keepable, but I seldom have any around at that moment. Fortunately, egg-thickened sauces are perfectly good at room temperature or even cold the next day, if you should have to hold them for any length of time.

I have a personal prejudice against using yolks only, and in many cases have found it unnecessary. Using the whole egg makes egg-thickened sauces so simple that you tend to have them more often.

Holiday Sauce

This is a simple, elegant version of an old favorite, using olive oil instead of butter and a whole egg instead of just the yolks. The result is a thick, rich-tasting lemon sauce that is wonderful on asparagus, broccoli, or fish. Like hollandaise, it must be made over very low heat: a double boiler, woodstove, or the top of a broiler have all worked for me. My father used to make it in a ladle balanced on top of the vegetables as they steamed. The important thing is that the sauce container be just a little bigger than the rotary egg beater, which is a necessary tool.

You may use butter instead of olive oil to make this sauce. It has the more traditional flavor, but is a little more tricky because butter will burn if it is heated too fast.

In a small pan, gently heat:
5 Tbsp olive oil
3 Tbsp fresh lemon juice
In a small bowl, beat:
1 egg
At the last possible moment, pour the egg into the lemon-oil mixture and beat at once with the rotary beater until the sauce thickens. As soon as it thickens, remove from heat.

SERVES 3 TO 4

Variation
Instead of olive oil, use:
6 Tbsp butter
Continue as above.

Sauce Béarnaise

Olive oil instead of butter lends this traditional sauce a distinctive flavor; I like it better. Béarnaise is served on fish or steak, but it's good on vegetables, too.

Cook in a small pan over low heat until reduced by half, about 5 minutes:
½ cup red or **white dry wine**
2 Tbsp tarragon vinegar
1 Tbsp finely sliced green onions
freshly ground pepper
½ tsp dried tarragon
Add:
⅓ cup olive oil
Simmer until it is time to serve. In a small bowl, beat briefly:
1 egg
Pour a little of the hot wine mixture into the beaten egg, stir, then pour the egg into the sauce. Beat at once with a rotary beater until the sauce thickens. Immediately remove it from heat.

SERVES 3 TO 4

Brown Sauce

This is a thick, rich, brown gravy made well ahead of time to serve with slices of roast or something that has no natural gravy-making powers of its own, such as liver. The wise cook has a pot of brown sauce tucked away well before feeding the masses at Thanksgiving or any such gathering. The dark rich color is caused by browning the flour (a delicate operation); the smooth flavor comes from bones and vegetables simmering for hours. This is a good one for the crockpot.

Spread on a large, clean cookie tin:
½ cup whole wheat flour
Bake at 325°F for 20 minutes.
Meanwhile, roughly chop:
1 medium onion
2 carrots
1 stalk celery
1 clove garlic
Sauté these lightly in:
3 Tbsp safflower oil
Remove with a slotted spoon and add to the oil in the pot:
5 Tbsp safflower oil
Over medium heat, add the browned flour. Stir and cook 3 minutes. Add the chopped, sautéed vegetables to the roux, along with:
4 cups water
¼ cup wine (I use vermouth)
2 cups chopped tomatoes (fresh or canned)
1 bay leaf
½ tsp each: thyme, basil, marjoram, salt
4 peppercorns
Cover and simmer 3 hours, or pressure-cook 30 minutes at 15 pounds. Remove bones, strain, and put the limp vegetables through a food mill or food processor into a saucepan. Cook down over low heat until the mixture has the consistency you want, about 1 hour. Season to taste.

3 CUPS

THICKENED SAUCES

Cornstarch, arrowroot and kuzu-thickened sauces become translucent as they thicken. They are also almost tasteless, and are most often used to make sauces that contrast with the foods they accompany. They include sweet-and-sour sauces, soy-flavored vegetable sauce, and piquant sauces flavored with wine, mint, ginger, and so forth.

As a general rule of thumb, it takes:
1 Tbsp cornstarch or **2 Tbsp arrowroot** or **kuzu** to thicken 1 cup liquid
but this varies considerably from sauce to sauce as different thicknesses are desired.

These thickeners are in the form of very fine powders, and will lump if added directly to hot liquid. They must be mixed first with an equal amount of cold liquid and carefully mashed into a paste. Then more liquid may be added and the sauce heated and stirred as it thickens. Or a little liquid may be added to the paste, and the mixture stirred into the hot sauce.

Sauces made with arrowroot and kuzu (which is a Japanese version of arrowroot) are ready to serve as soon as they thicken, and should not be kept hot any longer than 10 minutes. Cornstarch is stronger, and should be simmered gently on low (or over hot water) for 10 minutes to cook out the starchy flavor.

Sweet-and-Sour Sauce

This sauce can add flavor to cooked beets, carrots, onions, parsnips, turnips, or fried apples.

Mix in a small, heavy saucepan:
½ cup brown sugar
1 Tbsp cornstarch
½ tsp salt
pinch of dried cloves
Add slowly, stirring:
½ cup cider vinegar, white wine, or **tart cider**
Make sure the cornstarch is well mixed in before setting it over the heat. Stir and cook on medium heat until very thick (you may thin it further with water if you prefer). Simmer on low heat for 10 minutes, or mix with cooked vegetables and allow to cook 10 minutes.

½ CUP

Stir-Fried Vegetable Sauce

A soy sauce–flavored condiment for stir-fried vegetables, this is also very nice with meatballs, particularly if they're on the dry side.

Heat in a small saucepan:
2 Tbsp oil
Add and sauté for 5 minutes over lively heat:
3 chopped scallions
Add:
¾ cup vegetable or **chicken stock**
a grating of dried or **fresh ginger**
Reduce to medium heat, and let simmer. Meanwhile, mix in a small container:
1 Tbsp cornstarch
2 Tbsp tamari soy sauce
¼ cup cold vegetable or **chicken stock**
Pour this mixture into the simmering stock in the saucepan and stir gently with a whisk or spring stirrer as it thickens. Serve separately or mix it with cooked vegetables.

1 CUP

PESTO

Pesto is a marvelous mixture of mostly garlic and fresh basil, and is good to keep in a jar during the tomato season, when you seem to spend half your life looking for the garlic press. With pesto, you just open the jar, and presto!

Pesto marries well with tomatoes, eggs, and vegetables, and can be used to jazz up a dish of ho-hum rice or potatoes. It transforms a plate of noodles into an elegantly flavored taste of summer. It is often added to salad dressings. It can be coated on meat, chicken, or fish, either as a glaze during baking or during charcoal broiling.

Homemade Pesto

Traditionally, pesto is created by smashing together fresh basil and garlic cloves with a mortar and pestle, then adding olive oil to make it fluid and a handful of cheese to make it even more tasty. It can also be made, more quickly, in a blender or food processor; the whirling blades are just what's needed to pulverize and combine the ingredients. In northern places we are lucky to get enough basil together to make it once a year, but in many modern supermarkets you can buy fresh basil any time and whip up a batch of smooth, green, cheesey sauce to serve on your pasta.

Combine and pulverize:
a bunch or two of fresh basil leaves
a bunch of fresh parsley leaves
4 cloves crushed garlic
1 cup olive oil
¼ cup pine nuts or **walnuts**
½ cup grated Romano or **Parmesan cheese**
This has more flavor the day you make it, but keeps well if refrigerated. Many people make the mixture without cheese or nuts and add them at the last minute.

SERVES 10

Salsa Verde

This is rather like a pesto sauce, but tastes tartly of vinegar and was traditionally served with boiled meat or fish in medieval Italy. I like to mix it with salad dressing or spread it on fish or chicken as it is being broiled.

Chop fine, blend, or process:
2 cups packed parsley
Add and combine:
1 small can of anchovies
1 small clove crushed garlic
1 slice crushed onion (cut onion in small pieces; squeeze through the garlic press)
1 slice whole wheat bread soaked in ¼ cup wine vinegar
1 Tbsp capers
½ cup olive oil
¼ cup chopped sour pickles
2 Tbsp chopped basil
Blend and scrape down until the parsley becomes green flecks in a thick beige sauce. Bottle and label with the date; store in the refrigerator and use within a month.

SERVES 10

MARINADES

Marinades were probably invented to help preserve food, but they also change the flavor and even tenderize it a little. Vegetables used to add flavor to the longer marinades should first be sautéed. Marinades are acidic. Use only Pyrex, ceramic, enameled porcelain, stainless steel, or food-grade plastic containers. Never use aluminum.

Meat Marinades: Stew meats and cuts 2 inches thick can be marinated for 3 to 5 hours. A small roast of 2 to 3 pounds can be marinated for 1 to 3 days, a large roast 3 to 5 days.

Store marinating meats in the refrigerator and turn them over periodically so all parts are evenly exposed to the marinade.

Vegetable Marinades: Among the vegetables commonly marinated are cooked potatoes, green beans, cauliflower, Brussels sprouts, artichoke hearts, cooked or raw mushrooms and all manner of things that are pickled, from peppers to pumpkins.

Marinating vegetables can be as simple as soaking a few tomatoes and sliced cucumbers in a vinaigrette salad dressing or as complicated as brewing a batch of kosher dill pickles.

Marinated vegetables are served as hors d'oeuvres, snacks, and as interesting little additions to salads.

Yogurt Marinade

Good for marinating meats and vegetables to be served in a Middle Eastern concoction. Mix together this amount for every pound of food to be marinated:
1 cup yogurt
1 tsp dill
1 clove crushed garlic
2 Tbsp lemon or **lime juice**

Lemon Tarragon Marinade

I use this on broiled chicken breasts and with fish.

Mix in a ceramic or plastic container:
¼ cup olive oil
1 Tbsp lemon juice
1 tsp crumbled dried tarragon (or chopped fresh)
pinch of crumbled rosemary
Marinate meat for 1 hour at room temperature.

Wine Marinade

Excellent for red meat, this is also good with chicken and fish. This makes a small amount, so increase proportions if needed.

Mix together and let stand for 1 hour:
½ cup red wine
2 Tbsp vinegar
1 Tbsp safflower oil
1 clove crushed garlic
1 slice onion
1 chopped carrot
1 celery top
¼ tsp salt
1 bay leaf
2 whole cloves
½ tsp thyme
1 sprig parsley

Tamari Marinade

This is one of those recipes you should get along with a ring when you get married.
3 Tbsp tamari soy sauce
3 Tbsp safflower oil
1 clove crushed garlic
2 Tbsp lemon juice
Beat well. Anything you soak in this mixture will taste astoundingly good. Try it on steak, pork chops, slabs of tofu, sweet-and-sour pork, fish fillets, chicken breast — anything without much flavor of its own.

Vegetarian Dishes

PROTEIN

The first thing to think about when you fix a meal is protein. Lack of it is what made you hungry in the first place. Protein is what your body converts into energy every day, to work and think, to digest food, to grow, or heal and mend any part of you that may be hurt or sick.

Different people need different amounts of protein at various times. Generally, you can tell how much you need by your appetite; if you're still hungry after eating, plan meals with more protein. You can begin learning how much of it you (and the people you cook for) need by consulting the following chart:

Daily Protein Needs

Infants, age 0 to 1	1 gram per lb
Children, age 1 to 5	30 grams
age 5 to 10	40 grams
age 10 to 12	50 grams
Boys, age 12 to 18	50 to 60 grams
Girls, age 12 to 18	50 to 55 grams
Average woman	55 grams
Average man	65 grams
Pregnant or	
nursing woman	75 grams

Which foods have protein?
In general, the highest protein foods are animal products, such as eggs, milk, milk products, meats, fish, and poultry. Protein is also stored by plants in their seeds. Beans, peas, seeds, nuts, and grains have varying degrees of protein. In most cases, the amount of protein in vegetable foods is lower than the amount in animal foods. Partly, this is because the protein in all vegetable sources is lacking in one or more of the nutrients necessary to make all of its protein available. But if you complement the food with other foods that contain these nutrients, the level of complete protein will be increased. For example, 1 cup of cooked rice has around 3 grams of protein; 1/3 cup cooked kidney beans has 2 grams. But together they provide almost 10 grams of usable protein, the equivalent of an average-sized hamburger. Another example: a bowl of oatmeal has about 3 grams of protein. A glass of milk has about 7. But if you have both at the same time, you will be getting about 12 grams of complete protein, instead of 10, because milk contains amino acids that oatmeal lacks.

Why not stick to high-protein foods?
Traditionally, Americans have depended
mostly on animal-product foods, which do
not have to be complemented to yield high
amounts of protein. It's hard to change
these habits, but it looks as though we're
going to have to.

In the first place, these foods are becoming
much more expensive. If you grow your
own, you have a much more clear idea of
the expense, and it isn't only money. A
quart of milk, an egg, a pound of cheese, a
roast — these are crowning achievements,
not to be taken lightly. Vegetable protein is
cheaper, both in terms of money and in
terms of your own work.

In the second place, high-protein foods are
an extravagant use of the resources of the
earth. As Frances Moore Lappé pointed out
so eloquently in her 1971 book *Diet for a
Small Planet,* livestock must be fed enormous amounts of vegetable protein in order
to produce, for our pampered palates, 1
pound of meat protein. Beef is the worst —
21 pounds of usable protein (not just
measuring grain, or feed, but protein itself)
for our single pound of usable protein on
the chuck wagon. Pork, sheep, venison, and
goat are somewhat better, using 7 to 10
pounds vegetable protein for 1 pound of
meat protein. Chickens and fish use about 5.
A pint of milk protein represents about 4
pounds of vegetable protein, and so do 9
large eggs.

In the third place (and after this, I'll stop, I
promise), it is healthier not to eat so much
meat or the other high-protein foods that
most Americans are used to eating. In
parts of the world where people eat less
meat and more grains, legumes, and
vegetables, they live longer, more physically
rewarding lives. There are other factors, of
course, which contribute to their good
health: lack of psychological stress, regular
physical work, and various things that they
do eat, such as yogurt and whole grains. All

these things work together, in a way. The
earth that produced us supports us best
when we keep an ear tuned to its rhythm.

What is protein? How does it work? The
proteins that people can use are made up
of 22 amino acids, in a particular proportion to one another. Think of it as a sort of
irregularly shaped, 22-pointed star. The
more usable protein a food has, the bigger
the star would be.

However, if you were to measure the exact
amounts of amino acids in each kind of
protein food you eat, you would quickly
find that the stars you drew would all be
different shapes. The only food that is
proportioned absolutely correctly (for us)
is human milk. The next closest is an egg.
Others have varying shapes, and many are
even lacking in a few amino acids. In
some cases that doesn't matter, because
the human body can manufacture some
of the amino acids it needs for itself. But
there are 8 amino acids that the body can't
manufacture. They have to be present in
order for your body to get any protein at
all out of a meal. What's more, they have
to be there in a particular proportion.
Think of the star again, paying particular
attention now to the 8 essential points on
it. If one of them is smaller than it should
be, it doesn't matter how much bigger the
others are. The 8 essential amino acids
have to be present simultaneously (in the
same meal), in the right proportion, in
order for you to absorb all of the available
protein in the food.

COMPLEMENTARY PROTEIN

This sort of chemical attitude toward food can get to be rather a bore, and most people would rather not think about amino acid charts at every meal. But you can form habits, as people have all over the world, of serving certain foods together with other foods to get the most out of both. In most cultures, traditional dishes will incorporate two or three foods that complement each other, or supply the missing amino acids to make the level of protein in the whole meal greater than the sum of its parts. Such dishes are legume-grain combinations, such as beans and corn in Mexico; rice and soybeans or azuki beans in the East; bread or noodles and white beans in western Europe; kasha and lentils in eastern Europe; barley and split peas in Scotland; millet and chickpeas in Africa; rice and black beans in South America; bulgur and chickpeas in the Middle East. Another common combination translated into many cultures is milk products and grains and eggs, which make a good pudding, served hot and cold, sweet and nonsweet. And there are lots of ways to make high-protein snacks out of nuts, seeds, grains and dairy products. All these dishes are the result of thousands of generations of cooking by trial and error, and they are a tribute to the people who invented them, not knowing how or why such foods fed them better together than apart.

We are, by comparison, in a somewhat privileged position, in that we have some idea why such foods combine well to make whole protein out of half proteins. Protein can be measured in grams; amino acids can be counted.

ESTIMATING PROTEIN IN NON-MEAT FOODS

		Usable protein (in grams)	Tryptophan	Isoleucine	Lysine	Sulfureous amino acids
Seafood	tuna, mackerel	18 to 19	B	B	A+	B
½ cup	halibut	17	B	B	A+	C
	salmon	16	B	B	A+	B
	bass, shad, sardines, cod, crab haddock, herring, lobster	14 to 15	B	A-B	A+	A-B
	flounder, sole	12	B	B	A+	C
	scallops, 2 or 3	12	A	B	A+	B
	oysters, 2 to 4	9	A	B	A+	B
Dairy	curds, plain, ½ cup	13	B	A	A+	B
	cottage cheese, ½ cup	11	B	A	A+	B
	ricotta cheese, ½ cup	10	B	A	A+	B
	skim milk, instant, 5½ Tbsp	8	A	B	A+	B
	milk, yogurt, 1 cup	7	A	A	A+	B
	Cheddar cheese, 1 oz	5	B	A	A+	B
	mold-ripened cheese, 1 oz	4	B	A	A+	B
	egg, 1 medium-sized	6	A	A	A+	A
Legumes	soybeans, soy grits	10	A	B	A	C
⅓ cup raw;	mung beans	7	C	C	A+	D
1 cup cooked	broad beans, dried peas	6	C	B	A	D
	black beans	5	B	A+	A	C
	black-eyed beans	5	B	C	A+	C
	kidney beans	5	C	B	A+	D
	dried lima beans, chickpeas	5	C	B	A+	C
	lentils; navy, pea & white beans	4	C	B	A+	D
	tofu, 2 x 2 x 2½ inches	5	A	B	A	C
	soy flour; soy milk, 1 cup	3	A	B	A	C
Grains	whole wheat, bulgar	4 to 5	B	C	C	B
⅓ cup raw;	rye	4	C	C	C	B
1 cup cooked	barley	4	A	C	C	B
	noodles (cooked)	4	B	B	C	C
	oatmeal	3	B	C	C	B
	millet	3	A+	B	C	A
	brown rice	3	B	C	C	B
	whole wheat flour	2	B	C	D	B
	dark rye flour	2	C	C	C	B
	dark buckwheat flour	2	B	C	C	B
	cornmeal	2	C	C	C	B
	wheat germ, 2 Tbsp	2	C	B	A+	B
Seeds and Nuts	sunflower seeds, 3 Tbsp	4	A	B	C	B
	sesame seeds, 3 Tbsp	3	A	C	C	A
	peanuts, peanut butter, 2 Tbsp	3	B	C	C	C
	walnuts, 4 Tbsp	3	B	C	D	B
	Brazil nuts, 8 medium	2	A+	C	C	A+
Vegetables	Lima beans, 4 Tbsp	4	A	A	A	D
	green peas, ¾ cup	3	B	B	A+	D
	Brussels sprouts, 9 medium	3	B	B	A	D
	corn, 1 medium ear	3	D	C	C	B

A = High   B = Adequate   C = Moderate   D = Low

Photocopy this chart and tape it to the refrigerator door for future reference.

Compiled from *Diet For a Small Planet* © 1991
By Francis Moore Lappé. Ballantine Books, NY

KEY TO ESTIMATING PROTEIN

Of the 8 amino acids essential to the human body, 4 are found in most foods in sufficient quantity to make them adequate in the human diet. But 4 other amino acids vary in foods, as indicated in the chart on page 88 by grade letters: A = high, B = adequate, C = moderate, D = low.

Tryptophan and sulphur-containing amino acids are pretty low in most legumes, but high in nuts, and fairly well supplied by most grains.

Isoleucine and lysine are low in grains and nuts, but are very high in legumes.

Usable protein is the amount of protein available if you eat the food alone, without any accompanying dishes. If complemented with a food high in those amino acids that the first food lacks, the amount of usable protein will increase from ⅓ to ½. For more about this, read *Diet for a Small Planet* by Frances Moore Lappé, 20th edition (Ballantine Books, New York, 1991).

DRIED BEANS

Dried beans more than double their size when cooked, and add great richness to casseroles, stews, soups, and salads. Mashed, they can become fillings or fried patties. Combined with grains, dried beans have quite a lot of protein, and are good for you in a great variety of ways.

Always make sure you have cooked dried beans long enough. Soaking them overnight in water to soften them is a good start. In the morning, drain off the water; it may be nutritious, but it causes gas. Add more water and bring beans to a full boil for 10 minutes before simmering them with your favorite flavorings. Boiling the beans is particularly important with large beans like kidney beans, which can cause digestive problems if they aren't cooked at high enough temperatures.

One way to make sure you aren't caught with half-cooked beans is to cook them one day and serve them the next. I find they taste better the second day anyway.

COOKING TIMES FOR DRIED BEANS

Type of Beans	Unsoaked	Soaked	In Pressure Cooker
soybeans	8 hours	6 hours	45 minutes
chickpeas	6 hours	5 hours	40 minutes
kidney beans	5 hours	3½ hours	30 minutes
black beans	3 hours	2 hours	20 minutes
black-eyed peas	3 hours	2 hours	20 minutes
lima beans	3 hours	2 hours	20 minutes
navy beans	3 hours	2 hours	20 minutes
lentils	2 hours	1 hour	10 minutes
split peas	2 hours	1 hour	10 minutes
azuki beans	2 hours	1 hour	10 minutes

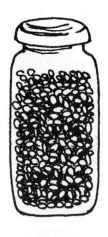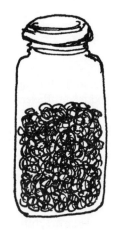

Pasta e Fagioli

This favorite Italian midwinter dish fills the air with such marvelous fragrance that people are attracted from miles around. That is why this recipe makes a large amount.

Pick over, and soak overnight in water to cover:
1 lb kidney beans
In the morning, drain and wash the beans. In a large, deep pot, heat:
2 Tbsp safflower oil
Sauté:
1 large chopped onion
2 ribs chopped celery
2 cloves minced or **crushed garlic**
Add the beans, and:
2 cups chopped tomatoes (fresh or canned)
4 cups cold water
1 bay leaf
¼ freshly ground papper
Bring to a rapid boil for 15 minutes, then reduce the heat, cover, and simmer for 3 hours. Remove bay leaf 30 minutes before serving.

Add to the pot:
1 chopped green pepper
2 Tbsp chopped parsley
Bring a second large pot of water to a boil, and add:
1 tsp salt
2 lbs macaroni or **small shells**

Boil 6 minutes or until barely tender. Drain and add the pasta to the fagioli. Serve hot.

SERVES 8

Variation
Add to beans before cooking them:
1 ham bone
Remove this 30 minutes before serving and add:
1 cup chopped cooked ham
1 cup thinly sliced Italian sausage

New England Baked Beans

White pea beans are traditional, but any bean will do — my favorites are great big kidney beans or speckled trout beans.

Pick over, then soak overnight in 1 quart water:
2 ½ cups beans
Next day drain, rinse, and add:
2 to 3 cups fresh water
1 tsp salt
2 celery tops
1 onion stuck with 2 cloves
Cover and simmer until beans are soft, 2 to 6 hours (*see chart on p. 89*).

Remove onion and celery, and let the beans sit overnight again. Next day heat in a deep pan:
3 Tbsp safflower oil

Sauté:

1 chopped onion

Cool the pan and add the cooked beans, along with:

3 Tbsp molasses

1 Tbsp tamari soy sauce
  or **blackstrap molasses**

2 Tbsp tomato paste

2 tsp mustard

1 tsp cider vinegar

Cover and set in 300°F oven for 1 hour, adding a little water as needed. Stir now and then. After ½ hour, uncover beans to brown the crust. Serve with cornbread (*see p. 197*) and a good green salad.

SERVES 6

Variation

Pork or ham fat may be substituted for oil, and it was traditional for New Englanders to cook a piece of fat in with the beans, as well. Remove fat before serving.

French Bean Dish

Soak overnight to soften:

1 cup white or **navy beans** (or **lima beans**)

3 cups cold water

Next day, drain the water and add:

1 onion stuck with 2 cloves

1 clove minced or **crushed garlic**

1 carrot cut in quarters

1 piece ham fat or **bacon** (optional)

½ tsp pepper

1 tsp salt

2 celery tops

3 cups fresh water

Bring all this to a boil and simmer (covered) until the beans are tender, adding water as needed to keep the sauce liquid — about 2 hours.

Chop into 1-inch pieces and add:

3 medium-sized potatoes

2 stalks fresh celery

½ cup ham or **1 to 2 cups cooked sausage** (optional)

¼ tsp thyme

2 tsp basil

½ cup tomato juice

Cook 25 minutes or until potatoes are soft.

Remove ham fat, celery tops, and carrots. Chop carrots small and return to the pot. Serve hot. (These beans can be kept and reheated very well.)

SERVES 4

Brazilian Black Beans

Served with rice and a good green salad, this makes a surprising combination of flavors.

Soak overnight in 4 cups water:

1½ cups black beans

Next day, drain and rinse the beans, then replenish with:

1½ cups water

1½ cups dry white wine

Sauté together:

2 Tbsp safflower oil

1 chopped onion

2 cloves minced garlic

In a heavy pot, mix beans, onions, and:

3 chopped tomatoes (fresh or canned)

1 peeled, chopped orange

½ tsp salt

2 bay leaves

½ tsp freshly ground pepper

Bring to a boil, uncovered, for about 10 minutes. Then cover, reduce heat, and simmer for 2 hours.

SERVES 6

Dragon Beans

A good hot chili makes your eyeballs snap and your ears tingle slightly. If you have an ulcer or a blind date, don't even think about it. Very good with tortillas, salad, and beer.

The best beans for this recipe are the biggest, such as kidney beans. *(See Dried Beans, p. 89.)* But smaller beans cook more quickly and may better serve your purposes.

Pick over:
2 cups kidney beans (or other beans: *see p. 89*)
Set beans in a pot to soak overnight with 4 cups water. Next day, drain off the water, add fresh water as needed, and add:
1 large whole onion
2 celery tops
1 whole clove garlic
1 bay leaf
1 tsp oregano
1 Tbsp mild, dark chili powder
½ tsp salt
⅛ tsp hot, minced jalapeño pepper
2 cups fresh, frozen, or **canned tomatoes**
Bring ingredients to a full rolling boil for about 20 minutes, then reduce heat to very low, cover the pot, and let it cook 3 hours. It need not be cooked all at once.

Before serving, remove the onion, garlic, celery tops and bay leaf. Adjust flavor, using the tip of a knife to add hot chili powder so the chili doesn't get on your fingers.

SERVES 6

Lentil Stew

In the summer, when you want to run the stove as little as possible, lentils are a good choice; they take only an hour to soften, 2 hours to disintegrate entirely. Cook up a pot of them; use for sauces, soups, and stew. They go well with tomatoes and vegetables.

In a heavy frying pan, heat:
2 Tbsp light oil (olive oil, if you have it)
Chop into big pieces and add:
1 onion
1 tsp basil or **oregano**
1 green pepper
3 stalks celery
1 zucchini squash or **eggplant**
1 cup chopped tomatoes
Cover and simmer until soft. Add:
3 cups cooked lentils
Serve with rice or bulgur.

SERVES 6

Falafels

Falafels are small, fried, meatball-like bean cakes. On every street corner in Israel, they are served along with a mess of chopped lettuce, tomatoes, and cucumbers, in half a pita, and topped with a fiery yogurt sauce. There is no question that this is the best way to eat falafels; however, you can also serve them in a light tomato sauce, or with rice or stir-fried vegetables. Israeli falafels are made with garbanzos and sesame seeds.

Mix:
1 cup cooked, puréed garbanzos
½ cup roasted, ground sesame seeds
¾ cup roasted, ground sunflower seeds
1 Tbsp lemon juice
1 egg yolk
1 Tbsp onion juice
Mix well; add more ground seeds as needed to make the mixture thick enough to shape into small balls. Fry in ½ inch of oil. Drain on brown paper; serve as suggested above.

SERVES 4

PASTA

Some of the best cooking, and the most fun, is also the fastest. It's over before you're tired of it. Such dishes include those with pasta, which cooks in 10 to 20 minutes. Pasta (also called noodles) comes in many shapes and sizes; you can even make your own, with a pasta machine or a lot of energetic work *(see next page)*. Pasta expands considerably in cooking: a 1-pound box will feed 4 or 5 people, especially if you mix in goodies such as cheese, tomatoes, fish, ground meat, vegetables, or tofu. The possibilities are limitless. It is in fact possible to serve noodles 3 or 4 times a week and people may scarcely notice, because each dish is so different.

Be careful not to overcook pasta; it should be *al dente*, as the Italians say, offering a slight resistance to the teeth, rather than becoming mush. If you forget to time them, you can tell by taste or (to the delight of children) by throwing spaghetti noodles at the ceiling: done noodles stick!

Once they are done, drain noodles at once in a colander. If you are not going to serve them right away, rinse briefly in cold water to halt the cooking. They can then be returned to the pot, tossed with a little oil or butter, and reheated.

Cooking Pasta

Pasta will double in cooking, so for every adult allow:

1 cup pasta

Boil a large pot of water — about 4 cups water for every 1 cup of noodles. You may add, if you like:

1 tsp salt

1 tsp safflower oil

The oil is to keep noodles from sticking together and is only really needed when cooking lots of long straight noodles like spaghetti, fettuccini, or lasagne. Alternatively, you may stir the pot about 5 minutes after you add the noodles.

Add the noodles and bring to a boil again. Don't cover the pot — it's likely to boil over.

If you buy noodles in a commercial package, follow the recommended cooking time. Be exact! If you buy noodles in bulk, or make them yourself, allow about 5 minutes for rice-like bits, 10 for spaghetti, 12 to 15 for larger shapes, and 20 for lasagne. Whole wheat or spinach noodles take 1½ times longer to cook than white-flour noodles.

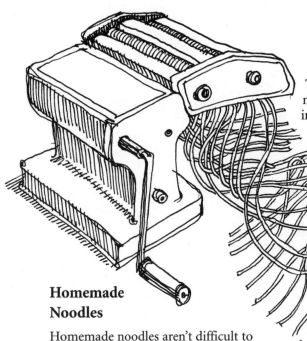

Homemade Noodles

Homemade noodles aren't difficult to make, but they do require time and patience and a flat, smooth surface to roll them out on. For this, marble is the absolute best. You will also find it much easier to use one of those big French rolling pins with no handles.

In a shallow mixing bowl, make a mound of:
2⅓ cups white unbleached flour
Mix together well and add:
2 large eggs
2 Tbsp water
1 tsp salt
2 tsp light oil
Stir these into the flour, lightly, with your fingertips, trying not to get glued in there. Add a little more flour as needed to form the dough into a firm sticky ball.

Clear off the countertop and put a handful of flour in one corner; wipe this across the surface so it is lightly dusted and knead the ball of tough dough until it is no longer too sticky to handle. Push and slap at it with your palms; lift it up and pound it against the edge of the counter. Be loud and un-gentle. In 5 to 10 minutes it will become smooth and glossy. Place it in a covered container in a warm place for 1 hour.

Take out the dough and work it some more. Now divide it with a sharp knife into 4 parts; put 3 of them back in the container and cover. Roll out the first quarter on a flour-dusted counter. It isn't easy to roll out. Try holding one edge with your stomach pressed against the counter edge while you roll away from the edge. Turn the dough often. When it is thin enough to read through, set it aside and start on the next one.

Let the rolled-out dough rest 20 minutes before cutting. To make thin noodles, roll up the sheet of dough in a loose spiral as if it were a jellyroll, and cut the roll into fine slices. Use the scraps for soup noodles.

You may dry the noodles on a rack and store them in a cool, dry place in a paper bag, or cook them immediately for 5 to 7 minutes in lots of rapidly boiling, salted water.

Buckwheat Noodles

Use:
⅓ buckwheat flour
⅔ white flour

Green Noodles

Before mixing up the noodle dough, steam for ½ hour:
½ cup spinach or **fine tender greens**
Put steamed greens in a sieve and press down hard to squeeze out any moisture. Use this water in place of water in the recipe above. Then dump the greens on a board and chop very fine. Add ⅓ cup greens to the noodle dough along with the eggs.

Spaghetti Carbonara

This is an Italian version of macaroni and cheese with tasty bits of ham, bacon, or mushrooms. It's said to be popular in coal mining towns. It's the sort of thing you can make in a terrific hurry out of practically nothing.

Bring to a boil:
1 gallon water
1 tsp salt
1 tsp oil
Add and boil, then stir until separated:
1 lb spaghetti noodles
Cook 10 minutes. Meanwhile, grate:
1 cup sharp Cheddar cheese
In a bowl, beat together:
3 eggs
1 cup sautéed mushrooms
3 Tbsp chopped parsley (optional)
When the spaghetti is al dente, drain and rinse it. In the pot, melt over low heat:
3 Tbsp butter
Return the spaghetti to the pot, still over low heat; then pour in the egg mixture and the grated cheese, and stir as it all melts and cooks. Allow to stand, covered, for a few minutes before serving.

SERVES 4

Variation
Instead of mushrooms your may add:
1 cup chopped cooked ham or **bacon**

Lasagne

Lasagne is a layered casserole of sauce, large flat noodles, cheeses and (sometimes) ground meat. It's a good thing to serve to a lot of people, but is equally good to make one night for dinner and keep the remains around for pickup meals, snacks, and hasty suppers. It is markedly better hot than cold, as the mozzarella cheese in it becomes quite rubbery when it cools down (as at a picnic or barbecue).

There are different ways to approach the making of lasagne. This recipe is for a traditional dish with a tomato sauce, the next uses a white sauce. You may use homemade pasta (the best) or store-bought pasta, or make use of a commercial precooked pasta that need only be layered, uncooked, between a somewhat thin sauce and other goodies. These noodles are a little thinner and not quite so deliciosa as thicker pastas, but they do shorten the cooking time considerably.

First: Make up a big pot of Lasagne Sauce *(see p. 76).* This sauce may contain up to 1 cup ground beef or pork.

Next: Make noodles *(see p. 94).* Cut them into strips which will just fit in your baking pan. Boil until al dente; then place them in a large container of cold water until needed. Alternatively, use precooked lasagne noodles — they're great and not expensive.

Fresh Cheese Filling
Mix:
1 beaten egg or **2 egg yolks**
2 cups dry ricotta or **cottage cheese curds**
2 Tbsp fresh, chopped parsley
Grate:
2 to 3 cups mozzarella cheese
Set aside.

Assembly: In a greased baking pan, spread a very thin layer of tomato sauce. Follow with layers, being careful to keep sauce and curd separated in cooking so they don't get mixed together. I do it this way, starting with the bottom layer:
1. thin layer of tomato sauce
2. noodles going north-south
3. curd mixture
4. noodles going east-west
5. sauce
6. mozzarella cheese
Bake in a 400°F oven for about 30 minutes, until sauce "sets" and cheese browns. Cool 15 minutes and serve at once.

Lasagne is a substantial protein dish in itself and needs no accompaniment other than bread and salad, except perhaps a good bottle of red vino.

SERVES 8

Lasagne Blanco à la Eleanor

This is a truly magnifico dish that can be prepared well before the event of serving. It is actually better if cooked, cooled, and reheated.

The Sauce: In a saucepan with a heavy bottom, gently melt:
4 Tbsp butter
Add and stir in, over low heat:
4 Tbsp flour
Cook and stir the roux for 5 minutes over low heat. Then gradually add, by half-cupfuls, stirring until smooth after each addition:
2 cups milk
Season with:
½ tsp salt
pinch nutmeg
¼ tsp freshly ground white pepper

Noodles and Cheese: You will need 12 lasagne noodles the length of your pan. If they are to be cooked before assembly, submerge them in cold water after cooking to keep them from sticking together.

You will also need:
1 cup finely grated Parmesan or **Romano cheese**
1 cup coarsely grated mozzarella cheese

The Filling: Slice:
2 to 4 cups mushrooms
Chop coarsely:
1 onion
1 green pepper
2 ribs celery
Heat in a skillet:
3 Tbsp olive oil
Add the vegetables and sauté over moderate heat for 5 minutes.

Add and sauté 1 minute longer:
2 cloves minced garlic
1 Tbsp chopped, fresh basil
1 tsp dried oregano
½ tsp dried marjoram
1 cup chopped, cooked spinach
Cover and remove from heat. Allow to cool for 10 minutes. In a bowl, beat together:
2 eggs
Then add and mix in well:
1 cup ricotta or **dry cottage cheese**
Add the vegetables to the egg-cheese mixture to complete the filling.

Assembly: Oil a 9 x 13-inch pan and spread with ⅓ of the sauce. Sprinkle on ⅓ of the

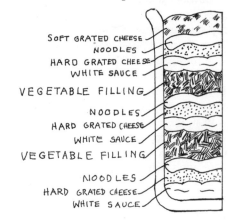

SOFT GRATED CHEESE
NOODLES
HARD GRATED CHEESE
WHITE SAUCE
VEGETABLE FILLING
NOODLES
HARD GRATED CHEESE
WHITE SAUCE
VEGETABLE FILLING
NOODLES
HARD GRATED CHEESE
WHITE SAUCE

Parmesan cheese and cover with 4 noodles. Spread ½ the vegetable filling over this. Follow with ⅓ of the sauce, ⅓ of the Parmesan, 4 more noodles, and the rest of the vegetable filling. Finish with a layer of sauce, the rest of the Parmesan, 4 noodles, and all of the mozzarella cheese.

Bake uncovered at 350°F for 35 to 40 minutes. Cool 20 minutes before serving.

SERVES 8

Eggplant Parmigiana

This dish is an all-day affair with the stove and eggplant. Fortunately you can assemble it on one day and bake it the next.

Sauce: Turn to page 75 and start a batch of spaghetti sauce.

Cheese: You will need two kinds — a hard, aged cheese, such as Parmesan or grating cheese and a soft, melting cheese, such as mozzarella or fresh American cheese.

Eggplant: To prepare the eggplant, slice into ¼-inch slabs:
2 small eggplants
Set them to dry on a rack or paper towels for about 1 hour. Mix:
2 eggs
½ cup milk
Dip the slices in the egg-milk mixture, then in:
flour (maybe a little wheat germ for flavor)
Let them sit again for 1 hour in a cool place, to dry a bit. Then fry them until golden, turning once, in:
½ cup olive or **vegetable oil**
Drain on brown paper.

While you are waiting around for the sauce to get mellow, grate:
1 cup hard cheese
2 cups soft cheese

Assembly: Place in layers in an oiled baking dish: eggplant, sauce, cheese; eggplant, sauce, cheese; eggplant, sauce, cheese.

Set aside until the next day in a cool place, or bake at 350° for ½ to 1 hour until the cheese browns on top.

Omelet for Two

This Italian omelet, served with fresh hot garlic bread and a good salad, makes a wonderful fast dinner. If you have more than two customers, increase the filling but make multiple omelets. Of primary importance is the quality of the ingredients. The butter should not be margarine and the cheese should not be American; the mushrooms and spinach should be fresh. For cheese I've used, variously, Parmesan, feta, and Vermont Cheddar. They were all good.

Vegetable Filling
1 small, finely diced onion
4 or 5 thinly sliced mushrooms
¾ cup washed and roughly chopped fresh spinach
Heat in a skillet:
2 Tbsp olive oil
1 Tbsp butter
Sauté the onion for a minute or two, then add mushrooms and sauté 3 minutes. Add the damp spinach, and pop a lid on the pan. Steam for 2 to 3 minutes, just enough to wilt the spinach. Remove from heat.

Beat together:
3 eggs
1 egg yolk
1 Tbsp fresh chives (optional)
2 Tbsp fresh, chopped parsley (optional)
pinch of salt (optional)
1 tsp salt stretcher (optional; *see p. 64*)
In a shallow omelet pan or a cast-iron skillet, heat until foamy:
3 Tbsp butter
Tip the pan so the butter coats it evenly. Pour in the egg mixture and tilt the pan so the eggs slide around a little as they set over medium heat. When the bottom has set, scatter over the eggs:
2 Tbsp grated or **crumbled cheese**
a grinding of pepper
Vegetable Filling
Arrange the filling so that it covers half the omelet. When the eggs have set almost all the way through but are still moist on top, gently flip the unfilled side over the top of the filling. Cook for 1 minute longer; then divide and serve at once.

QUICHE

Quiche requires a light hand with a piecrust, good ingredients (especially the cheese) and careful attention to temperature and timing. I use half-and-half cream or evaporated milk instead of milk for a creamier filling that doesn't soak into the crust. The crust is also crisper and flakier when baked in a lightweight metal pie dish with holes in it, rather than a heavy ceramic dish. Preheat your oven to 450°F before you put the pie in to bake, and, finally, let your quiche cool before serving.

Quiche Crust

(To read more about piecrusts, see pp. 216–17.)
With 2 knives, cut:
½ cup cold shortening
into:
1⅓ cups unbleached white flour
½ tsp salt
When the pieces are small, switch to a fork or wire pastry cutter. When the mixture resembles coarse meal, gradually add:
3 to 4 Tbsp ice water
Work lightly with a fork into a soft ball. Flatten, cover, and refrigerate for about 1 hour.

Roll out the crust on a lightly floured board to a diameter about 2 inches bigger than the pie dish. Line the dish, then shape the rim into scallops with your fingers. Keep crust cool until you fill.

Asparagus Quiche

Everybody knows at least one cook who comes up with such wonderful things that you always want to ask how it was done. In this case I'm glad I did; I never would have guessed these ingredients.

Make up a Quiche Crust.

Chop and steam in an inch of boiling water for 7 minutes:
½ cup asparagus (3 to 4 stalks)
Chop the asparagus fine. In a small skillet, heat:
2 Tbsp butter
Chop fine and sauté:
1 medium onion
In a mixing bowl, beat together:
3 medium eggs
1¼ cups half-and-half cream or **evaporated milk**
generous pinch of freshly crushed rosemary
½ tsp salt
4 gratings of fresh nutmeg
pinch of cayenne
2 cups (⅓ lb) freshly grated Swiss cheese
Preheat the oven to 450°F. Roll out the crust, line a metal pie pan, and arrange the onions and chopped asparagus in it. Pour in filling and bake at 450°F for 10 minutes. Reduce heat and bake at 350°F for 20 to 25 minutes, until the quiche is firm throughout or "set." Cool at least 10 minutes before serving.

SERVES 5 TO 6

Quiche Charlaine

Make up a Quiche Crust *(see p. 98)*.

Sauté:
3 Tbsp butter
½ cup chopped onion
¼ lb sliced mushrooms
Drain onions and mushrooms. In a mixing bowl, combine:
3 medium eggs
1¼ cups half-and-half cream or
evaporated milk
½ tsp salt
2 cups (⅓ lb) grated sharp Cheddar cheese
3 pinches of cayenne pepper
3 gratings of fresh nutmeg
Preheat oven to 450°F. Line a metal pie dish with crust. Arrange the mushrooms and onion in the pan, then pour in the egg and cheese mixture. Bake for 10 minutes. Reduce heat to 350° and bake for 20 to 25 minutes.

SERVES 5 TO 6

EGG ROLLS

By making egg rolls, you can stretch a small amount of something special into feeding a multitude. One summer, a couple of crab fishermen came visiting and brought more crab than anybody could possibly eat. We boiled it up and went at it valiantly, but by midnight we washed our hands of it and turned to music and ghost stories. In the morning, we stripped the last of the crab out of the remaining carcasses and put it in the fridge for supper. The kids went off swimming. By mid-afternoon I had the kitchen fairly well cleaned of crab and went out to harvest greens for dinner. I was picking snow peas when a large car full of people I had never seen before pulled into the yard. They had just moved to the neighborhood, with their 4 children, and wanted to see our goats, chickens, horses, and garden and meet us. We showed them everything. Our kids came home and the whole bunch of them disappeared down to the creek again. Suddenly I realized that it was dinnertime and all I had in the fridge was a cup and a half of crab. So it was that I happened to make egg rolls the first time we met the Golds. The dinner wasn't hard at all; everything just happened to come together at the right moment. The greens were fresh from the garden, there was crab in the fridge, and there were always eggs in the henhouse. It was a coup of unparalleled luck; Jane Gold turned out to be a fantastic cook and returned the favor many times over, cooking fabulous meals for us and all our friends many times at their famous but short-lived version of the Middle River Inn.

Egg Roll Cases: You can put all kinds of things in egg rolls — cooked cabbage, chopped celery, onions, ground or chopped pork, fish or chicken, sprouts, nuts, seeds, chopped cooked roots — in fact, anything that goes in stir-fried vegetables. This recipe will make 15 to 20 egg rolls, depending on how thin you make them.

In a bowl, mix:
2 eggs
2 cups water
½ tsp salt
1 cup white unbleached flour
Heat up a frying pan. It is easier — but not absolutely necessary — to have a 6-inch frying pan. Grease it with a few drops of oil; you will have to add a few drops every 3 egg rolls or so, when the pan begins to look dry.

Give the batter a stir and pour about 2 tablespoons into the pan. Quickly tilt the pan so the batter spreads around. Fry over medium heat about 2 minutes on one side, 1 minute on the other. Don't let them get hard and crisp.

As you take out each pancake, let it cool; then you can stack it on top of the others without having them stick. Make all the pancakes before you start stuffing.

To stuff them, put about 2 tablespoons of filling in the middle of each egg roll. Fold the sides over and paint them with a glue made of:
2 Tbsp water
1 Tbsp white unbleached flour
Roll them up and seal the flap with more glue. They will seal better if you let them sit for at least 30 minutes before frying.

Fry egg rolls about 5 minutes on each side, until they become golden brown, in:
5 Tbsp oil
Serve hot, with rice *(see p. 163)* and Sweet-and-Sour Sauce *(see p. 82).*

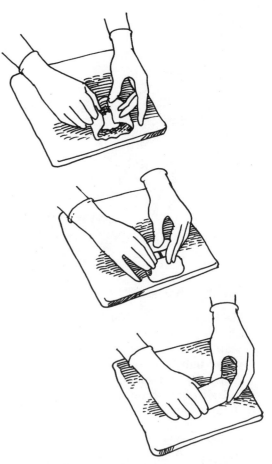

Egg Roll Filling: Egg roll fillings are creative ventures; you can vary the ingredients. If you use mung bean sprouts, they give the meal enough protein so you don't get hungry after dinner. For this you must use fresh sprouts; canned sprouts have had their beans removed and so have little nutrition.

Chop or shred:
1 small onion
½ cup Chinese cabbage or **Savoy cabbage**
¼ cup Jerusalem artichokes or **water chestnuts**
Add:
½ cup drained sprouted mung beans
Sauté these for 5 minutes in:
2 Tbsp vegetable oil
Then add, cover, and steam for 2 minutes:
1 cup crab meat
2 Tbsp sherry or **other sweet wine**
Use 2 tablespoons of filling per egg roll.

Cheese Fondue

A cheese fondue supper is a classic work of art, the ultimate in intimate dinners. The fondue is a hot mixture of cheese and wine (served in a chafing dish at the table) into which each person dips crusty cubes of toasted bread (with a long fork) and is accompanied by wine, salad, and maybe some onion soup, perhaps a good dessert — no more. It requires almost no preparation and very little cleaning up.

A Chafing Dish: You have to have something in which to keep the cheese and wine hot; as soon as they cool, they separate or become gummy. You need a heat source at the table, with a pan to go over it. Usually you acquire along with it some long-handled, two- or three-tined forks with heatproof handles for dipping bread.

Salad and Extra Bread: Make a really good salad, something with things to find in the bottom: cucumbers, or tomatoes, or sprouts, or beans, sliced onion rings, marinated this-and-that, a nice tart oil-and-vinegar dressing. As for the extra bread, slice 2 or 3 pieces per person, and coat each with garlicky butter; wrap in foil and set in the oven.

Fondue: Have everything else ready first; set the table and make sure the heat source at the table is going to work.

Grate:
1 lb Swiss cheese
Toss with:
2 Tbsp cornstarch or **¼ cup unbleached white flour**
Rub the fondue pot with:
1 clove of garlic
Pour into the pot:
2 cups dry white wine
Heat until it bubbles, on the stove, over moderate heat. Throw in the cheese, by handfuls, stirring as it melts. Add:
3 Tbsp Kirsch (or other dry liquor)
As the fondue thickens, taste it; maybe add:
a pinch of salt, a grinding of pepper
Set it on the table and keep it warm. Serve cubes of bread in a basket, with garlic bread on the side. Eat at once.

SERVES 3 TO 4

Cauliflower Cheese

This is such a high-protein dish that it can be served as a main course, along with potatoes, biscuits, and salad.

Break into florets and steam for 5 minutes:
1 cauliflower
In a small saucepan, over low heat, melt:
2 Tbsp butter
Add, stir in, and cook gently for 3 minutes:
3 Tbsp whole wheat flour
Measure out:
2 cups whole milk
Add the milk to the butter-flour mixture ½ cup at a time. After each addition, stir and cook gently until the mixture thickens. Do not allow to boil. When it's all together, add and stir in:
¼ cup grated Cheddar cheese
½ cup grated Parmesan cheese
Remove the sauce from the heat. Lightly oil a casserole dish and mix the sauce and cauliflower in it. Bake at 300°F for 10 to 15 minutes.

SERVES 4

Welsh Rarebit

They've come and they've gone, and what's left in your refrigerator? A bottle of flat beer, half a loaf of stale bread, and a hunk of cheese as dry as a rock. So — grate, grind, pound, or dice:
about 1 lb sharp Cheddar cheese
Heat:
a cup or so of beer
Stir in cheese by handfuls. When it melts, go beat an egg and pour it in, stirring constantly until it thickens; don't let it boil, or heat too fast. Add for seasoning:
½ tsp salt
1 tsp mustard powder or **Dijon mustard**
Some people like to add a pinch of curry. Pour the rarebit at once over:
toast

SERVES 3 TO 4

Blintzes

Traditionally, these are served with applesauce and sour cream; a glorious late Sunday morning brunch, or special supper. You can also serve them with Cream Sauce *(see p. 78)*.

The Pancake Batter
In a shallow ceramic bowl, beat:
3 eggs
2 cups milk
Then beat in:
1 cup flour (white or whole wheat)
dash of salt
Heat a couple of frying pans. It's nice if they're 6-inch pans, but anything will do, as long as they're heavy and don't develop hot spots. When the pans are hot, pour in 2 to 3 tablespoons of batter and tilt the pans so the batter makes a thin, evenly shaped pancake, about 6 inches in diameter. Let them cook about 2 minutes, then turn out on a smooth counter, uncooked side down. Continue cooking pancakes until all the batter is used up.

The Filling
Meanwhile mix up:
1½ cups dry curds or **drained cottage cheese**
1 egg or **1 egg yolk**
1 Tbsp soft butter
1 tsp grated lemon peel
Put 1 heaping tablespoon of the cottage cheese mixture on each pancake, spread out in a line, and roll it up tightly. (You can tuck in the edges as you roll it up.)

Heat a large iron skillet with ¼ cup vegetable oil. When the oil begins to crackle, fill the skillet with blintzes, but don't let them touch one another. Cook until brown on each side. (You may have to move the pan around to keep just the right heat under it.) Drain on brown paper and keep warm until they are all done. Serve at once, with applesauce spooned on top.

SERVES 4

Variation

Instead of milk in the batter, use:

2 cups water
⅔ cup dried milk

TOFU

Tofu could be the food of the future. Derived from soybeans, it has all the protein of eggs, cheese, or meat, but less fat and no salt. A pound contains 4 servings. It comes stored in a container of water; it will keep for a week or longer if the water is changed daily.

The first step to preparing tofu is to drain and lightly press out some of the water. Cut the tofu into 4 slabs about ½ inch thick, and place them on absorbent paper or cloth. Put this inside a folded section of towel or newsprint; cover with a bread board or flat plate, to press the tofu for 1 to 2 hours. You may change the absorbent material to extract more liquid if you like.

After pressing, I like to tear my tofu into irregular fragments. Just because it's easy to chop it into identical cubes doesn't mean that's the most appealing way to serve it.

Mix up a marinade (one of these or your own invention) in a plastic container with a tight lid. Roll the tofu in the marinade, cover, and refrigerate until time to cook — from an hour to a couple days.

PRESSING TOFU

WEIGHT
CLOTH
TOFU
CLOTH
PAN

Lemon Marinade

¼ cup safflower oil
¼ cup white wine
1 Tbsp lemon juice
salt
a grating of lemon peel

Tamari Marinade

¼ cup safflower oil
3 Tbsp tamari soy sauce
1 Tbsp lemon juice
1 clove crushed garlic

Tofu Stir-Fry

A stir-fry is a good way to introduce tofu. Press out the excess moisture and marinate *(see above):*
1 slice tofu per serving
Put on a pot of rice to cook *(see p. 163).*

While it is cooking, assemble and cut up vegetables:
1 medium, coarsely chopped onion
1 to 2 stalks diagonally sliced celery
1 to 2 diagonally sliced carrots
Before you start cooking, tear or chop tofu into bite-sized pieces.

Vegetable Options
1 cup broccoli flowerets
½ sliced green pepper
6 to 12 sliced mushrooms
½ cup mung bean sprouts
Heat in a wok or cast-iron skillet:
2 to 3 Tbsp vegetable oil
Sauté carrots and broccoli over high heat 2 to 3 minutes, then stir them around and add onions, celery, and green pepper. Add mushrooms, tofu, and bean sprouts last. Stir continually, then add:
2 Tbsp water or white wine
Cover the pan and let it steam for a couple minutes. When the carrots are tender, serve at once.

No-Problem Pizza

Nowadays people do anything and call it pizza, but the pizza with pizzazz has a crisp crust of fresh bread under a very thin layer of sauce and a lot of fresh melted mozzarella cheese. It is not hard to make, especially the crust, which is the same dough as *pain ordinaire (French Bread; see p. 185).* Like *pain ordinaire,* it is cooked hot and fast.

Before you heat your oven to extrahigh temperatures, make sure it (and your pizza pan) are entirely clean. Old black cookie tins smoke at 400°F and above. Pressed aluminum pans work well.

Pizza Dough: Start 2½ hours before dinnertime; most of this time is bread-rising time. To start the dough, mix up:
2 cups warm (not hot) water
2 Tbsp baker's yeast
pinch of sugar
Stir well and leave the bowl in a warm place for 10 minutes. Keep an eye on it. When it gets good and foamy, pour it into a mixing bowl and add:
1½ tsp salt (optional)
2 cups unbleached white flour
Beat the dough vigorously for 5 minutes or so. Then add, by half-cupfuls, beating after each addition:
1 to 2 cups white unbleached or whole wheat flour
After the first cupful, the dough will be hard to beat; at some point, it will become physically impossible. Switch to kneading by hand on a floured board, on a suitably low counter or table. You may want to underlay the board with a newspaper to keep flour from making a mess. Place the dough on the floured board, and with floured hands, pat and work it lightly until it takes up enough flour to be kneadable. Fold and press and add flour until it will take no more. *(For more on kneading, see p. 180.)*

Put the dough back in the bowl, cover with a clean cloth, and place it in a warm spot (it should stay at 70°F) to rest and grow for at least 2 hours.

Assembly: Preheat oven to 500°F. Punch down the dough, turn it out, and cut it in half, kneading each piece into a smooth bun. Flatten the buns by hand until they are the size of the pizza pans. Scatter in each pizza pan:
1 tsp cornmeal
Place the dough in the pan. Spread the middle of each pizza thinly with:
¾ cup Pizza Sauce *(see p. 76)*
1 Tbsp dried oregano
1 tsp dried basil

Toppings: You may top the sauce with any (or none) of the following:
green pepper rings
thinly sliced mushrooms
thinly sliced, cooked sausage
chopped, cooked bacon
pitted black olives
chopped, sautéed onions
chili pepper flakes
canned pineapple chunks

Cheese: Cover each pizza with:
1½ cups freshly grated mozzarella cheese
For a bubbly crust, allow the pizza to rest for 5 to 15 minutes before it goes into the oven. To make sure the crust is crisp, pour a cup of boiling water into a pan and place it on the bottom of the oven. This will make the oven steamy, which for some reason makes the bread crust crisp.

Bake the pizza for about 12 minutes, until the cheese bubbles and the crust browns.

Slide the pizza on a wooden board and cut with a rolling pizza cutter.

2 SMALL PIZZAS

Mexican Enchiladas

Enchiladas are thin corn tortillas wrapped around a tasty filling, covered with a little sauce and cheese, and baked in the oven for around 20 minutes. Due to the fragile nature of the tortilla, it is important to cook each one separately first, then keep the filling on the dry side, and, finally, cover them with very little sauce. Enchiladas are usually not "hot" in the chili sense, but are served with both "hot" and "cold" salsa *(see p. 83),* along with yogurt or sour cream.

Sauce: Sauté in a heavy skillet:
1 finely chopped onion
2 cloves minced or **crushed garlic**
1 tsp cumin
1 Tbsp oregano
Then add and cook over low heat 30 minutes:
2 cups puréed tomatoes or **tomato juice**

Fillings: The classic enchilada is filled with sharp, grated cheese (such as cheddar or jack) and chopped, raw onions. Not everybody will eat raw onions, however.

Alternative fillings: chopped or ground, cooked hamburger; sausage, chicken, or sautéed sliced mushrooms; crumbled goat cheese; mashed, dry, cooked beans; grated cheese; diced, sautéed eggplant; garlic with grated cheese

Tortillas: Frozen tortillas are even available in Cape Breton now. Thaw for 1 hour:
8 to 10 tortillas
In a heavy pan, heat:
1 cup safflower oil
Don't let this get too hot; turn it down a little if it crackles. Have ready brown paper for draining, well away from the fire. Using tongs, dip the tortillas in hot fat for 30 seconds, then remove and drain them, one by one. Alternatively, you may dip tortillas in hot tomato sauce to soften before arranging them with stuffing in the pan.

This is less traditional but safer and less fattening.

Stuff each tortilla with a tablespoon or two of filling, and arrange one-layer-deep in a shallow oiled casserole. Pour over a cup or less of the sauce — just enough to moisten it. Grate a little cheese over all as a garnish. Bake at 350°F for 15 to 20 minutes. Remove at once and serve hot or cold.

SERVES 4

Potato Pancakes

Potato pancakes aren't at all like flour-based pancakes; they're crunchy on the outside, mushy in the middle, and very quick and easy to make. Together with a jar of applesauce and some sour cream or yogurt, maybe jam or maple syrup, they're a meal that anybody can whip up in half an hour (and they taste like "city food," say my kids). They are one of the foods made easier with the grater attachment of a food processor. Grate:
about 1 small potato per serving
½ onion per serving
(Do the potatoes first because the onions make your eyes weep.) Add:
2 Tbsp white or **wholewheat flour per serving**
1 beaten egg for every 2 servings
This makes a rather runny, gray mixture. Never mind. Heat until almost crackling:
4 Tbsp corn or **safflower** or **peanut oil**
Spoon about 3 tablespoons of the potato mixture on the hot skillet and spread it out thin to about 4 inches in diameter. Repeat until skillet is full (you can use 2 skillets at a time); cook on each side until the cakes are a rich brown. Stash finished cakes in a 200°F oven until they are all done. Serve good and hot.

CALZONES

When I was little, we used to drive in to the city to visit our grandparents. Sometimes we spent the night and sometimes we didn't, but invariably when it was time to go home we were always starving. My mother and her mother would be running around trying to decide whether there was room in the car for one more box (of sheets, towels, magazines, paints, crockery).

"There's bread in the fridge," they'd say. "Make yourself a sandwich." But the bread always turned out to be a small stale end, at which point my grandfather would grandly say, "Get on your coats."

And, as we went out the door: "We won't be a minute." Released into the cool, crisp air, we would run all the way to the corner, wait for a grownup hand to accompany us crossing the street, and then dash importantly into the crowded Italian bakery where my grandfather bought us calzones: steaming hot, fresh pockets of Italian bread, filled with chopped sausage and enough for all of us.

When we got back, the car would be loaded, my parents in the front seats, waiting, and here we'd be, with dinner. Saved by a grandfather. As we drove through the city, the lights coming on, the bridges thick with evening traffic, we'd savor the wonderful, fragrant taste of the city. And then, content, we'd fall asleep.

Calzone Bread

Mix in a measuring cup:
½ cup warm water (not hot)
1 Tbsp baker's yeast
pinch of sugar
Stir well and leave the cup in a warm place for 10 minutes. Keep an eye on it. When it gets foamy, pour it into a bowl and add:
½ cup warm water
½ cup warm milk
2 cups unbleached white flour
Stir vigorously for 5 minutes. Add flour as needed, turn out on a floured board, and knead it into a fine, smooth dough. *(For more on kneading, see p. 180)*. Oil the ball lightly, return it to the bowl, cover with a clean cloth and set in a warm place to rise for 2 hours.

Sausage Stuffing
This stuffing is a combination of greens, sauce, and sausage. We have found kale to be the best greens because they are both delicate and pack loosely; our favorite sausages are the hot, fresh Italian ones, crumbled and cooked right before filling the calzones.

Tear the leaves off the stalks of:
10 kale or cabbage leaves
Steam leaves over boiling water in a tightly lidded pot until tender, 5 to 7 minutes. Cool and chop fine.

Dice and crumble:
5 hot, fresh Italian sausages (or 1 cup hamburger meat)
1 large onion
In a lightly oiled skillet, sauté the meat and onions over moderate heat until tender, 5 to 10 minutes. Add greens and:
1 cup Pizza Sauce *(see p. 76)*

Calzone Assembly
Chop the dough into 6 equal portions and make each into a bun, stretching the dough and tucking it in the bottom so that when flattened it will make a smooth,

elastic surface without holes. Flatten or roll each into an 8-inch round. In the center of each, place ½ cup filling.

Beat in a small bowl:
1 egg
1 Tbsp water
Use this mixture to paint around the edges of the dough, so when sealed the calzones won't leak or fall apart. Move them carefully to a cookie sheet lightly sprinkled with:
1 tsp cornmeal
Paint tops with more egg mixture. Sprinkle on top of each:
1 tsp sesame seeds
Allow calzones to rise for 1 hour before baking in a preheated 375°F oven for 20 to 30 minutes, or until golden brown.

7 TO 10 CALZONES

Vegetarian Filling
Make calzones as above but omit sausage or hamburger. Instead, grate on top of filling in each of them:
½ cup mozzarella cheese
Fold, seal, and bake as above.

Special Cooking

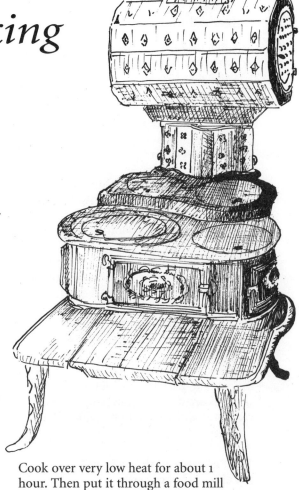

This chapter is a series of short discussions about preparing food for special occasions. They are: baby food, cooking for a mob, breakfast, recovery food, and traveling food.

BABY FOOD

No two babies start eating whole foods at the same time, nor will they eat the same foods. But some general principles may be applied: for example, most babies are started out on grains and fruits, and other foods are added one at a time, gradually. You need not worry too much about a "well-balanced diet," especially at first. It is more important to give healthy foods that the baby likes, so as to work up some enthusiasm about the whole idea of food — which, to a little baby, is kind of weird in the first place. A very good section on introducing foods appears in *Baby and Child Care* by Dr. Benjamin Spock, which you should have anyway because it covers so many aspects of caring for babies (like how to tell measles from scarlet fever, and so forth).

First Cereal

This is what I always fed my kids for the first 2 or 3 months of their eating adventure.

Put:
1 cup rolled oats
into a pot with:
3 cups boiling water

Cook over very low heat for about 1 hour. Then put it through a food mill using the smallest holes. Store in a covered plastic container in the refrigerator; it will keep for 1 week.

To serve, mix a little cereal in a small enamel pot with:
a little pasteurized milk (or reconstituted dry milk)
Heat until it's just your skin temperature. You may add some:
fresh mashed banana or **applesauce**
However, any cereal mixed with banana should not be put back in the refrigerator.

For Other Cereal Ideas, see Grains, *p. 172*

Puréed Fruits

Slice and cook in a little water:
apples, plums, berries, peaches, apricots
 (whatever you have)
When they become soft, put them through
a food mill. Don't use a blender for this,
because berry seeds and fruit skins should
be sieved out.

If you think the fruit needs it, you can
cook into the purée:
a little sugar
If it isn't thick enough, mix into the cold
purée:
a little cornstarch (1 Tbsp per cup)
Heat and stir until thick and clear. Keep 1
week if refrigerated, or you can freeze
baby-sized portions in an ice cube tray,
dumping them out into a communal bag
or container when hard.

Puréed Soups

Though most babies are not thrilled about
vegetables and meat, if you cook together a
whole mess of vitamin-rich vegetables and
a few chicken bones and some rice, and
put it through the mill (discarding the
bones), they'll probably love it. By the time
you get around to introducing such
sophisticated fare, your baby might
appreciate a little texture in the food. So
put it through the coarse plate of the mill,
and maybe throw in a little whole, cooked
rice grains, too.

Instead of (or along with) chicken
flavoring, you may add a little miso or
tamari soy sauce just before serving.
Babies love them.

Puréed Vegetables and Meats

Generally I find little babies aren't over-
enthusiastic about plain puréed vegetables,
with the possible exception of carrots,
winter squash, or pumpkin. I wouldn't
argue about it. As soon as they get teeth,
they'll be only too happy to sink them into
all sorts of raw vegetables, so don't worry.

This is even more true for meats — babies
and even small children very often will not
eat meat at all, no matter how much you
grind it up. So, why bother? There's lots of
other stuff to feed them.

Other Good Baby Foods

Cottage Cheese

For a very little baby, mash with a fork.
Otherwise serve plain. A meal my children
always used to enjoy was cottage cheese,
raw slices of summer squash (to pick up
and chew and throw around) and a small
cup of tomato juice. (Baby lasagne?)

Baby Custard

Mix:
1 egg yolk
¼ cup milk or **fruit juice**
a touch of honey (if needed)
Bake at 300°F for 20 minutes in a heatproof cup. Cool before serving.

NOTE: it is unwise to serve any food with a
high concentration of egg whites to small
children. They may develop an allergy to
egg white if it is eaten too soon.

Egg Yolk

Hardboil:
1 egg
Mash the yolk with a fork. Add.
**a sprinkling of ground toasted sesame
 seeds**
a tiny touch of salt
about 1 tsp milk (to soften it)

Tofu

Plain tofu may be tasteless to us, but babies love it, and it's good for them — all protein, no salt, no fat, nothing to upset the little digestive systems. Mash it up by sieving, blending, or food-milling small amounts.

COOKING FOR A MOB

You were just planning supper, having on hand for the purpose two flounder fillets and a handful of fresh greens, when in walks Jack and Penny and their two kids, over to visit from their farm 30 miles away, bringing to meet you their old buddies, Low and Allie, from West Virginia. Low, it turns out, went to school with your sister, and is interested in goats, so you go down to the barn. After you get through rapping about Toggenburgers vs. Nubians and showing them the weird chickens that lay blue eggs (when they lay), they remember a six-pack of warm beer in the car and you, suddenly, remember that you have a dinner to cook and the stove must be nearly out. What on earth are you going to make?

Having been faced with this situation several hundred times in the last 25 years, I would like to make a few astute observations:

1. Forget about fancy cooking. Make something easy, which you can cook with your eyes closed and one hand tied behind your back, which is, more or less, the general effect of having visitors in the house.

2. Make some discreet inquiries about people's eating habits. Some people have allergies or aversions to certain foods.

3. Don't worry too much about quantity. People will eat less because they're talking so much. Better to provide a continual stream of munchies and 1

basic dish than an entire well-balanced meal of the sort you usually serve.

Munchies

One friend I have always pours a cup or two of sunflower seeds into a frying pan and stir-roasts them as soon as guests show up. That's a pretty good start. And you can always slice up a bowlful of raw vegetables: carrots, Jerusalem artichokes, turnips, celeriac, celery; and, in season, green peppers, tomatoes, peas in the pod, green beans, cauliflower, broccoli florets. Cheese is always good, and, of course (if you have them) bread or crackers. Pickles are terrific.

BREAKFAST

If you're going to do any work during the day, breakfast is your most important meal. That doesn't mean you have to mound your plate with six kinds of food; but it does mean that you need a good stash of complete protein under your belt. It could be oatmeal and milk; or it could be last night's leftover beef stew.

What we eat in the winter, ordinarily, is hot cereal; in the summer, we eat home-made Familia or granola, with fresh berries. Once in a while, though, I get inspired in the morning and make something like:

- hot biscuits, scrambled eggs, home-fried potatoes

- blintzes (they take forever; it'll be brunch, really), applesauce, and sour cream

- french toast

- pancakes with fruit syrup

- toast and cheese (goat cheese in brine is very good for breakfast) and a piece of fruit

Some people hate breakfasts. For them, something special should be provided; whether or not they like it, they still need it. Perhaps they might like:

- yogurt with fruit

- leftover rice or other grain, scrambled with an egg and fried in a frying pan

- a toasted cheese sandwich, or a ham sandwich

- a milkshake of milk, yogurt, honey, and fruit

- a couple of hot muffins or toasted bagels

- leftover pudding

- homemade granola personalized with some special ingredient — almonds, apricots, or slices of dried mango

RECOVERY FOOD

When somebody in the house is sick, they usually can't (or don't want to) eat the same food as when they're well. Particularly, they aren't too interested in foods that are difficult to digest. That's sensible. The energy the body normally puts into working, thinking, and digesting should be all going into getting better. Which is why, as you recover, you feel stupid, lethargic, and not too hungry.

The body still needs some basic things, though. It needs a minimum level of protein. It needs quite a lot of liquid, and it needs vitamins.

For protein, the best thing is clear soup. It could be meat stock soup or miso soup.

Both are easy to digest and both are adequate for the minimum protein needs of average recovery. You might add noodles or brown rice to the soup — it's good to have a little roughage, keep the system working. A piece of toast or crackers, maybe. But go easy on the butter; substitute jam, or honey. Have lots of juice, cold or hot. You can make the juices into gelatins, for a solid version of the same thing.

Extra vitamin needs depend on the nature of the illness. If there's any kind of infection, vitamin C will help. You can't get too much vitamin C; if you do, your system can easily eliminate it (this is a medical fact). Some people like to take it by pills; I like to make up a lemonade or fruit juice, heavily spiked with powdered or granular ascorbic acid, such as they sell in supermarkets for canning. We keep a lot of that around in the early spring, when vegetable supplies run low and cold bugs seem to be on the rampage. A stash of canned blackberry, rhubarb, or other juice helps add variety to the juice pitcher. Or throw in a few canned or frozen berries.

If you wind up having to take antibiotics, make sure to get enough B vitamins, since many will be destroyed by the antibiotics. Have wheat germ in your bread or cereal, or sprinkled on acidophilic yogurt. After antibiotics, take acidophilus (as yogurt or pills) to reestablish intestinal flora.

For other special vitamin needs, consult *Jane Brody's Nutrition Book: A Lifetime Guide for Good Eating & Better Health & Weight Control* by Jane Brody (Bantam Books, NY, 1987). And ask the doctor when you get a chance; even mention that you heard such and such was helpful for your problem. Many doctors simply forget to give dietary advice until you ask.

TRAVELING FOOD

Once you get used to eating real food, it's hard to swallow the stuff they pass off as food in most eateries. Not to mention the incredible cash output they demand for their plastic-packaged morsels of synthetic, stale, tasteless junk. So, whether you're off to town for the day, or en route to visit your sister in New Mexico, it's a good idea to pack up some traveling food.

Grains: Bread was probably invented for traveling purposes. Dense, compact, slightly damp bread keeps longer than light, well-risen breads. If the weather is very dry, store in plastic; otherwise, don't — it'll just mold after a few days. (You can slice mold off, though — it doesn't mean the bread is bad to eat; it just isn't tasty.) Store bread in closed paper bags or in paper-lined tins.

To pack traveling grain, take along plastic containers of sprouts and grains to soak. Crackers keep well, stored in airproof containers. Quickbreads don't keep at all; they become dry and crumble easily. Make up some Familia and granola, and carry dried milk. Make some carrotcake muffins to take along.

Protein: Cheese, of course, is the best traveling source of protein. Take along several kinds if you can: variety helps a lot in limited circumstances. Stop at a super-market for a bit of ham, sausage, or milk products such as yogurt or cottage cheese. They will keep for a couple of days without refrigeration. Sprouts and nuts are also good protein sources. Nuts are available as nut butters in health food stores.

Vegetables: If you're in the woods, equip yourself with a good foraging book, such as *Stalking the Wild Asparagus* by Euell Gibbons. There's no point in backpacking turnips when you're surrounded by good stuff to eat. Even if traveling by super-highway, a true forage fanatic can spot wild edibles alongside the road, or find them near a campsite. It's sort of fun to find out what grows in different places, anyway. If you're in too much of a hurry to stop, take along things that keep: roots mostly, and vegetables that can be sliced and munched raw.

Fruits: Stock up on your favorite dried fruits before you leave. Buy fresh fruits along the way. Fruit is good travelling food.

Other: If you're going camping and cooking, take some oil and a little flour. Oil is about the hardest thing to supply to the foraged diet. Take nuts, which have fresh oils in them or fresh nut butters.

Fish and Shellfish

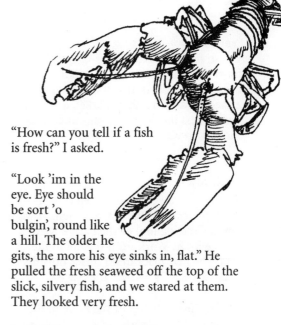

The old man looked up at me, his gray eyes lively as he swung the crates of fresh fish off the rocking deck of his Cape Islander boat, onto the creaking wharf.

"Lobsters," he said. "Y'cin have 'em, for all the trouble they are." He stood up and pushed his cap back on his forehead. With one hand spread wide, he counted his fingers, one by one.

"First, you got to build 'em traps. No easy job, that. Then" — he bent back another finger — "you got to find a place t' put 'em. You wouldn't believe the wars been fought on this very shore over whar you can put a lobster trap. Whole families divided. Terrible." He shook his head. "And, if you git a good northeaster, you can lose the whole business in a single day: traps, buoys, lines and all." He paused. "Lobsters. You git them home, snappin' and crawlin', and boil up some water to git them cooked, and then" — another finger bent back— "you got to spend nearly as long gettin' the good out of them as you did catchin' and haulin' them. No, sir. You c'n have your lobster." He bent down and heaved another crate of slippery silver fish up on the wharf. "Give me fresh mackerel, any day. Sweet, fresh mackerel is. Especially th' fall, when the fish run fat. Lovely stuff, mackerel. You like mackerel?" he asked.

"I do," I smiled.

"Lots o' people think it's mucky, because they've only had it old. If you put fish straight on ice, they'll be wonderful fresh for a day. Next day, they'll be good, but not as sweet. Three, four, five days" — he spread his enormous hand, and gestured with a clean sweep — "No good. You never want to eat a mackerel again."

"How can you tell if a fish is fresh?" I asked.

"Look 'im in the eye. Eye should be sort 'o bulgin', round like a hill. The older he gits, the more his eye sinks in, flat." He pulled the fresh seaweed off the top of the slick, silvery fish, and we stared at them. They looked very fresh.

"How do you cook them?"

"Ah," he leaned back, pleased. "My wife likes to bake 'em in the oven, because it's so easy. I like that. But I like 'em best of all cooked on a rack over a fire on the beach. On a piece of bread, I know, by the light of the silvery moon — that's the very best way to have fresh mackerel."

Well, I am fond of both lobsters and mackerel, so I bought both, and brought them home, and cooked mackerel the first day and lobster the second. They were so good. But I minded what the old man said, so it wasn't long before we tried it his way: we loaded beach gear, towels, bottles of juice and wine, and a batch of biscuits into the back of the car, and took off for a day on the beach. And that night we ate our fish by the light of the silvery moon, sand on our fingers and the smokey smell of the burning driftwood as the only flavoring. He was right. It is the very best way to have fresh fish.

PREPARING FISH

Freshness

A fresh fish has bright bulging eyes, is pink under the gills, and has a slick skin. It flops when you handle it. If you're buying fillets at the fish store or supermarket, don't take them unless they're moist and smell good. There is no way to rescue rancid fish.

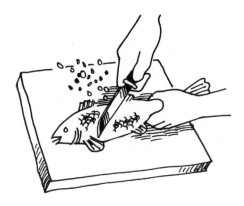

Cleaning

To Remove Scales: The first step is to remove the scales, if the fish has them, using a special scaling tool or the back edge of a filleting knife. Work from the tail to the head. The best place to do this is outside, because scales fly all over the place.

Gutting: Insert the tip of the knife in the vent with the blade edge toward the head. Hold the knife tilted so you cut only the belly flesh and skin, and slit up to the gills. Remove entrails, cutting them free at the gills. Scrape and rinse.

To Remove Fins: Cut slits on either side, at a slight angle, and pull the fins out. This way you also get the bones under the fins.

To Remove Head: Cut in a curved line from the top of the head back around the gills on both sides. Bend the head back sharply to snap the spine. If the fish is large, you may do this on the edge of a table.

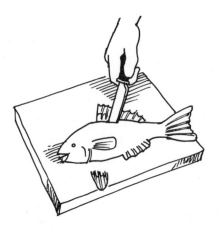

To Remove Tail: Cut through it just above the narrowest point.

Filleting

The fine art of filleting is basic to much of fish cookery. Leave the fish intact as much as possible if you're going to cut off the fillets — don't clean it or take off the head or tail. Use a very sharp knife *(see Knives, p. 293)*.

Make a shallow cut behind the gills, down one side of the backbone, across the tail at the narrowest point, and back up the belly to the vent.

To remove a fillet, hold the knife parallel to the ribs along the backbone, and cut the meat off gently, back to front in one or more cuts, pulling the fillet away from the ribs with your other hand.

After you remove the fillets, you may wish to skin them. Hold the fillet firmly, skin side down, and slide the knife under the fillet, sawing gently to remove skin.

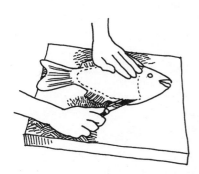 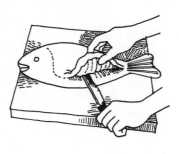 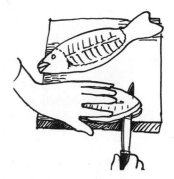

Removing Bones

By taking the backbone out, it is possible to remove most of the bones of a good-sized fish that you may wish to stuff. Clean the fish, making the belly cut extra long, right up to the jaw. Then slide the knife on top of the rib cage up to the backbone on each side, from head to tail. The sharper your knife, the less fish will go with the rib. This does not work on small fish.

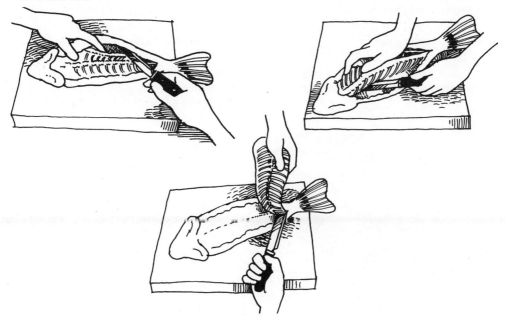

Codfish Cakes

When we first came to Cape Breton and lived beside the Bras d' Or Lake, we had very few resources — but one of them was a boat and jig line. My husband went out whenever it was fine and brought home huge cod. There were only two of us then, and fresh fish doesn't last very long, so I used to bake these monsters in the oven, flake them into plastic containers, and use the fish to make codfish cakes all winter.

Chop fine:
1 onion
In a heavy, deep pot, heat:
¼ cup bacon fat, butter, or **safflower oil**
Sauté onion 3 minutes. Add:
1 cup water
6 peeled, sliced potatoes
½ cup powdered milk
Cover and cook 15 minutes over moderate heat. Take care the pot doesn't cook dry.

Remove from the heat when the potatoes are soft and mash with a fork or potato masher. Add:
1 cup flaked, cooked codfish
1 tsp salt
1 Tbsp chopped parsley
Mix well. Thicken, if need be, with a little flour, or thin with milk, to make a texture that can be shaped nicely into cakes and browned on both sides in:
bacon fat or safflower oil

SERVES 4

Cod Pepper Stew

This is a very Portuguese sort of thing: chunks of fish and potatoes simmered in a light tomato sauce. It should be very lightly flavored with herbs to complement the tenderly cooked fish.

Chop coarsely:
1 medium-sized onion
1 to 2 stalks celery or **½ cup celeriac**
3 carrots
1 green pepper
Sauté these vegetables in:
2 Tbsp olive oil
for 5 minutes, then add:
2 cloves crushed garlic
and cook another minute. Add at once:
½ cup vermouth or **white wine**
6 chopped, canned or **fresh tomatoes**
4 chopped potatoes
Tie in a small cheesecloth bag:
1 bay leaf
3 green peppercorns
4 sprigs thyme or **¼ tsp dried thyme**
1 piece fresh lemon peel
1 frond fennel (optional)
6 peppercorns
Immerse the bag in the pot and simmer, covered, for 15 minutes. Add:
1 lb fresh or **frozen cod, haddock, halibut**
 or **perch, cut in chunks**
Simmer 5 minutes if fresh fish, 10 to 15 minutes if frozen. Remove the herb bag.

Serve hot with:
garlic croutons
freshly chopped parsley, fennel or **dill**

SERVES 4

Large-mouth bass

Oven-Crisp Fish

This is an excellent way to cook small fish or small pieces of fish. It preserves the delicate flavor and texture so often lost in frying — and yet, like frying, is very crisp and quick.

Preheat oven to 400°F. Allow:
½ lb fish per serving

Roll each piece of fish in milk (or butter-milk), then allow them to dry 5 minutes.

In a paper bag, mix:
1 cup whole wheat flour
1 tsp garlic powder (optional)
pinch of thyme
Toss in the fish and shake the sack around. Spread a baking pan lavishly with:
5 Tbsp vegetable oil or **melted butter**
Put the fish in the pan, rolling the pieces around a bit to coat them with fat. Place in the oven and bake at 400°F, 5 to 10 minutes, or until pieces flake apart. Serve with:
lemon slices

Sole Fillets with Mushrooms

Sole fillets are such delicate morsels. They do very well smothered in butter and mushrooms, served with rice or a baked potato, and a fresh green vegetable.

Preheat oven to 350°F. Allow :
½ lb sole per serving

Oil a heatproof baking dish, or line it with lightly oiled aluminum foil.

In a frying pan, heat up:
3 Tbsp butter
Add and sauté until golden:
3 chopped green onions
6 sliced mushrooms
1 clove crushed garlic
Remove from heat and add:
1 Tbsp fresh lemon juice
Pour this over fish, and distribute the

mushrooms on the fillets. Bake for 10 minutes and serve with:
lemon slices

SERVES 4

Stuffed Striped Bass

Striped bass run to vast sizes. The best for cooking are around 6 to 8 pounds, perfect for stuffing and baking. These may be boned *(see p. 115)* or not, as you choose. Before placing the fish in the pan, line it with heavy foil, lightly oiled. This will make it easier to remove the baked fish to a serving platter, where it can be admired at the table.

Assemble Stuffing
2 cups sliced mushrooms
¼ cup sliced green onions
½ tsp finely crumbled or **chopped sage**
2 Tbsp finely chopped parsley
pinch of finely crushed or **chopped rosemary**
Sauté the mixture in oil or butter for 5 minutes, stirring constantly. Remove from heat.

Preheat oven to 400°F.

Wipe the fish with a cloth, and rub it inside and out with lemon juice. Stuff the interior and skewer the sides together. Place in an oiled pan. Sprinkle on the fish:
3 Tbsp sherry
chopped green onions
sliced mushrooms
Put the fish in the oven and turn the heat down to 325°F at once. Bake 10 minutes for each inch of thickness. Baste with sherry again, and serve.

SERVES 4 TO 6

Broiled Bluefish Fillets

Bluefish are very popular with sport fishermen, who catch them in the surf all along the Atlantic coast of North America. The best of them are young and should be cooked within 24 hours of being caught. *(To fillet fish, see p. 115.)* Be careful to remove the dark midline meat along the backbone, which has a strong flavor. Broiling is ideal for bluefish, but other fish fillets may be substituted. The vegetables add a festive touch.

Allow:
1 to 2 fillets per serving
Sprinkle with:
lemon juice and pepper
Allow to sit for 15 minutes. Pat dry and rub each fillet with a mixture of:
1 tsp olive oil
pinch of thyme
pinch of basil
1 clove crushed garlic
To cook them, cover a cookie sheet or broiler rack with aluminum foil, and lightly oil it before arranging the fish on it. Arrange on top of the fillets:
thin slices of Bermuda onion, tomatoes, and strips of green pepper
Preheat broiler for 10 minutes before cooking the fish. Allow 10 minutes per inch of thickness. If the fillets are young and small, 5 minutes is probably enough.

Hake à l'Orange

Hake is like cod, but a little firmer, and more solid, unsuited to long immersions in milk in the oven. This is a nice little fish sauté with a tart lemon sauce for a hot summer day.

Allow:
1½ lb fresh hake
Cut the fish into serving pieces and dip each in:
cornstarch
Wash, then grate:

1 orange rind
1 lemon rind
Cut the fruits in half and squeeze out all the **orange juice** and about **1 Tbsp lemon juice.** Mix this in a bowl with the grated rind and:
½ cup white wine (optional)
In a heavy skillet, heat:
2 Tbsp sesame or **safflower oil**
Sauté the fish 2 minutes on each side, then add the juice mixture. Cover and cook 2 minutes over moderate heat. Serve at once, garnished with:
finely chopped chervil or **parsley**

SERVES 4

Baked Bass Fillets

Basted with juices and wrapped in foil, these fillets can be baked in the oven or grilled on a barbecue. If wrapped individually, they have the added advantage of staying warm while the rest of the meal is served.

Simmer together:
2 Tbsp lemon juice
2 Tbsp tamari soy sauce
1 tsp celery salt
2 cloves crushed garlic
3 Tbsp finely minced parsley
Arrange 4 to 6 fillets on 6 x 12-inch rectangles of aluminum foil. Top each with a few spoonfuls of the lemon-garlic mixture and:
1 tsp sesame seeds
chopped green onions
1 thin slice lemon
Fold up the foil and seal each along the top, so the steam does not escape. Barbecue or bake at 350°F for 5 to 7 minutes. Do not turn.

SERVES 4 TO 6

Broiled Halibut Steaks

A halibut is a large, flat fish, related to sole and flounder. Because it is so large, it can be cut into steaks about ½-inch thick, which have a firmer texture than that of fillets. Fresh fish steaks can be baked, broiled, or barbecued, but whatever you decide, don't cook them very long. They need not be turned during cooking, but you should coat them with oil or marinade sauce before cooking.

To cut fish steaks: Leave the skin on. Cut vertical slices 1½ to 2 inches thick from behind the gills to just above the tail. Make the last piece somewhat larger, 3 inches or so.

Allow:
⅓ lb halibut per serving

Marinade
3 Tbsp tamari soy sauce
3 Tbsp white wine
1 clove crushed garlic
½ tsp dried oregano
3 Tbsp vegetable oil
Shape a piece of aluminum foil into a crude dish for the fish, so no juice can escape. Combine marinade ingredients, pour over the fish, and let sit 5 minutes. Turn fish and let it sit another 5 minutes. Preheat broiler for 10 minutes. Lay the steaks, foil and all, under the broiler; cook 5 minutes. Do not turn. As you serve the steaks, pour the juice over them.

Solomon Gundy

(Pickled Herring)

Small, dense-fleshed herring, called *milter* or *matje,* are used in Europe for pickled herring. North American herring are bigger and fatter, so they are usually salted before cooking, to draw out some of the moisture. After cleaning them, sprinkle liberally with coarse salt and let sit overnight. Meanwhile, bring to a boil in a stainless steel or enamel pan:
¾ cup vinegar
1¼ cups water
1 Tbsp fresh pickling spices (bay leaf, whole mustard, pepper, coriander)
⅔ cup white sugar
Boil 10 minutes, then cool overnight. Do not refrigerate.

Next day, cut off the herrings' heads, and cut a slit down each back. Then cut a shallow slash across each side at the narrowest part of the tail, and, using the tail as a handle, peel the skin off each side, tail to front. Fillet them in the same direction, using your fingers to separate the meat from the long bones. The smaller bones will dissolve in the pickle mix. Rinse the pieces and dry them.

Peel and slice thinly:
1 onion
Grind or chop fine:
milt from herring (optional)
Tear the herring into small pieces as you layer it with onions and milt in a suitable container. I use wide-mouthed canning jars, but crocks or food-grade plastic can be used as well. Strain the spices out of the pickle mix and pour it over the fish and onions. Cover and refrigerate 1 week to 1 month.

Rolled Sole

Fillets such as sole and flounder have so little flavor of their own, you do well to lend them a lot — say, roll them up with basil pesto, chill, then lightly sauté them in olive oil. Serve each with a spoonful of salsa and a squeeze of lemon juice.

Allow:
1 to 2 sole fillets per serving, 1½ to 2 lb in all
Have Pesto *(see p. 83)*, and sliced whole wheat bread ready.

In a small frying pan, heat until bubbling:
2 Tbsp butter or **olive oil**
4 level Tbsp basil pesto
crumbled slice of whole wheat bread
Allow this to cool slightly as you lay out:
4 to 8 fillets (sole or **flounder)**
Spread each with some of the mixture. Roll them up. Don't worry if they split. Place them end-down on a tray or plate and chill up to 30 minutes, or until stiff.

In a small bowl, beat:
1 egg
2 Tbsp cold water
In another, place:
1 cup flour
Heat 2 Tbsp safflower oil in a frying pan. Dip rolls in egg, then flour, then into the hot oil. Sauté each side 2 to 3 minutes over medium heat. Remove from pan with a slotted spoon on to brown paper, then roll them around and on to the plate. Cover each with:
1 Tbsp Salsa *(see p. 83)*
a squeeze of lemon juice

SERVES 4

Shark Kebabs

Shark is a very dense, white meat, tender and tasty if treated properly — soaked before cooking in salt water, milk, or an acidic marinade, any of which will remove the very slight ammonia smell found in some kinds of shark.

One hour before serving, mix together:
¼ cup white wine (optional)
3 Tbsp lemon juice
2 Tbsp tamari soy sauce
½ cup safflower oil
1 tsp freshly grated ginger
2 cloves crushed garlic
For 8 kebabs, cut into bite-sized chunks:
2 lb shark steaks
Put the meat into the marinade, cover, and let soak for 30 minutes at room temperature, or 1 hour refrigerated. Soak bamboo skewers in cold water 1 hour. Alternate fish on skewers with:
1 pepper cut in 1½-inch squares
large mushroom caps
cherry tomatoes
small onions, parboiled 5 to 7 minutes
sliced, small zucchini squash
scallops
shelled and deveined shrimp
partly cooked squares of bacon (optional)
Coat with:
marinade or safflower oil
Place kebabs on the grill 6 inches from coals or fire. Barbecue 4 to 5 minutes on each side, basting with marinade.

8 KEBABS, SERVES 4 TO 6

Poached Salmon

Dense and heavy, the salmon is a fish like no other in the kitchen or in nature. The best method for cooking it is to poach it tenderly in a fresh, homemade bouillon.

Bouillon
4 cups water
½ cup vermouth or **white wine** (optional)
1 large, chopped onion
1 stalk chopped celery
5 peppercorns
1 bay leaf
1 bunch of parsley
Bring to a boil, cover, and simmer 30 minutes. Meanwhile, rinse fish and measure its thickness.

To Poach: Poach fish in bouillon 10 minutes to the inch *(see The Canadian Rule, following).* Keep bouillon just under the boiling point. Remove from bouillon with slotted spoon or spatula; or you may wrap, poach and remove it using a clean cloth, as pictured.

To Skin and Serve: Remove skin by peeling it back from tail to head; use a knife to free it where necessary. Scrape the flesh carefully, following the grain, to remove the

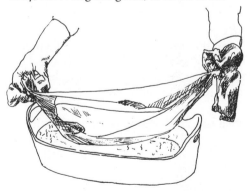

"underskin." You may also make a long V-shaped cut down the spine to remove the strip of dark meat. Salmon may be served hot with Holiday Sauce *(see p. 80).* Or you may cool it and serve with mayonnaise.

Cold poached salmon, laid out on a serving dish and surrounded by lettuce, parsley, slices of lemon, tomatoes, cucumber, and stuffed hard-boiled eggs, is quite an impressive dish.

SERVES 6 TO 8 (OR MORE)

THE CANADIAN RULE
Cook fish for 10 minutes per inch.

This means inch of thickness, not length, and it applies to all kinds of fish cookery: boiling, broiling, baking, frying, and all types of fish: cod, haddock, salmon, trout, shark, whatever.

Modern amendments to the Canadian Rule are to double this if the fish is solidly frozen, and to put it somewhere in between if it is partially thawed. Also, add a few minutes if you're baking it on a heavy ceramic platter.

The internal temperature of a fish, when done, is about 140°F.

Fish Facts
Fish, once frozen, does not have the same firm texture and moistness as fresh fish. It isn't bad, or unpalatable, but it isn't the same. It does better chopped into a stew, sauce, or soup, or it can be fried.

Never overcook fish. When it's done, remove it from the heat. You may cover it to keep it barely warm, reheat it slightly, or serve it with a hot sauce. Whatever you do, don't apologize. It'll be fine.

Pan-Fried Small Fish

This method is excellent for trout, mackerel, small salmon, smelt, and snappers. Many people who fish carry a small pan and a bit of butter with them, and cook their catch by the waterside. They are very good this way. Snappers should be scaled and their spiny fins and bony bottom section trimmed.

Allow:
½ lb fish per serving
Clean and wash fish, but leave on the heads and tails. Dust the fish with:
white flour or **corn flour**
You may add:
a dash of paprika, pepper, tarragon or **chervil** (but not salt, which would dry the fish)
In a cast-iron skillet, heat:
3 Tbsp butter
When the butter bubbles, add the fish and sauté until it is just golden on each side. If the fish is quite round (as with mackerel), reduce heat and cook very slowly for 5 to 7 minutes, turning as needed.

To make an excellent quick sauce, remove the fish from the pan as soon as it is done and pour in:
¼ to ½ cup white wine
Tilt the skillet and let the liquid bubble for a minute or two as it cooks down. Pour the sauce over the fish. Serve garnished with:
lemon slices

SHELLFISH

Common along the New England and Maritime coast are a dozen or so species of clams, oysters, mussels and scallops that make wonderful eating, especially after you have spent all afternoon gathering and cooking them. Our family is especially fond of mussels, which are also available in a fatter and more tender (if possible), cultivated variety.

When you bring your mollusks home, put them loosely in a container, uncovered, in a cool, dark place. If they contain sand, you may remove it by soaking them in clean salt water (or sea water) for 12 to 24 hours with some cornmeal sprinkled on top. (Fresh water kills shellfish.)

Shellfish Safety Measures: Consult local advice as to whether the shellfish are safe to eat before setting out to gather some. Shellfish can pick up pollutants and sometimes carry hepatitis and other serious diseases. However, shellfish beds are monitored by government agencies, and the information is available from the Department of Health as well as from the Department of Fisheries.

Shucking Shellfish
Scrub the shells with a stiff brush before opening them, and trim off the beards, seaweed, and anything that might harbor sand. Rinse in cold salt water.

Shellfish can be opened raw by carefully inserting an oyster knife or a thin, rounded piece of hard metal between the shells and twisting them open.

Quahogs are stubborn, but as children we learned that if you leave them in a bucket of cold (salt) water, in a quiet place, for an hour or so, and then return alone, stealthily slipping them out and quickly inserting the knife, it's a lot easier to work

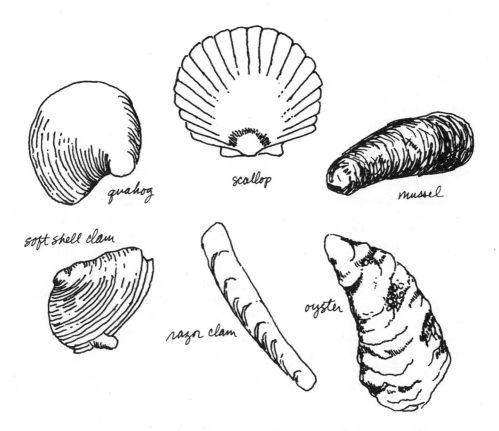

quahog

scallop

mussel

soft shell clam

razor clam

oyster

your way through a bucketful. Another trick is to get them very cold by putting them in the freezer for a half-hour (no more). As you open them, use three bowls: one for juice, one for clams, and one for tough neck trimmings or muscles.

Opening raw oysters is an art. It sounds simple: break the "bill" or thin edge with pliers, insert knife, open oyster. But only experience can tell you where the best place to break it is, and how to strike it so that bits of shell don't get inside. Work slowly, and watch your hands: oyster shells are very sharp. Once you get it open, inspect under good light for shards of shell. Rinse (alas) if you suspect. Drain juice into one container, set oysters in another.

After shucking raw shellfish, strain the juice through a sieve lined with a clean dishtowel or a Handywipe. It can be used for making sauce or chowder.

Shellfish and Seafood Sauce

The best shellfish for serving raw are, of course, oysters, but cherrystone clams are a close second, and I've eaten lots of mussels and soft-shell clams raw and enjoyed them. Larger clams can be a little tough.

Strain the juice and cut shellfish free of their shells; return the meat to the shell and pour juice over it. You may mix the juice with lemon juice or a little vermouth.

Put through a food mill or buzz in blender:
1 cup chopped fresh tomatoes
2 Tbsp wine vinegar
1 Tbsp grated horseradish
1 Tbsp grated onion
1 clove crushed garlic
1 tsp tamari soy sauce
½ tsp white pepper
Chill, covered, 3 to 24 hours.

ABOUT 1 CUP

Shellfish Spaghetti

When fresh mussels are available we often assemble this favorite meal. It can also be made with fresh or canned clams. If using fresh clams, you should plan to steam, cool, and shuck the clams ahead of time, discarding the tough necks and chopping the clams fine. You will need about 1 lb fresh mussels, in their shells, or ½ can of clams per serving. If there are not enough, the dish may be stretched with mushrooms, sliced and sautéed.

To begin, put a large covered pot of (salted) water on to boil for the pasta.

Steaming the Fresh Shellfish: Dump noisily into the sink, pick through, rinse and throw the live ones into a pot. Any shellfish that will not stay closed when pressed should be discarded. Add to the shellfish:
½ cup white wine or **water**
Bring to a boil, turn down heat, and cook 5 to 7 minutes, covered, until the shells open. Remove from heat and allow shellfish to cool uncovered.

Sauce
Chop fine:
1 onion
1 cup parsley or **spinach**
1 tsp dried oregano
2 heads fresh basil or **1 tsp dried basil**

Mince or put in a garlic press:
1 large clove fresh garlic
In a heavy-bottomed skillet, heat:
3 Tbsp butter or **olive oil**
Sauté the onion gently until limp, then add garlic, sauté 1 minute longer, and add greens, herbs, and shellfish liquid. Cover and simmer over low heat.

By now the spaghetti water will have come to a boil. Remove lid and add to the water:
1 tsp safflower oil
1 tsp salt
1 lb spaghetti noodles
After a minute, stir vigorously so they won't stick together. Boil, uncovered, 5 to 7 minutes.

Meanwhile, shuck shellfish. Pour cooking liquid into the sauce. Reserve shellfish meats until the last possible moment, then add them to the sauce and cook over moderate heat for 1 or 2 minutes.

When spaghetti is al dente (cooked but not mushy), pour at once through a colander and run cool water to halt the cooking. Toss with shellfish and serve at once with:
freshly grated Parmesan cheese
toasted garlic bread
white wine
tossed green salad

SERVES 3 TO 4

Mussels

Mussels in France and Belgium are called *les huîtres des pauvres,* suggesting they're much cheaper than oysters, which they are in most seacoast places. But in their different way they're at least as delicious as oysters. In Antwerp, the delis have cold, steamed mussels in mustard sauce, tomato sauce, and mayonnaise, and they sell them by the ton for hors d'oeuvres. As long as their beards have not been scrubbed off, mussels can be kept in the refrigerator for several days. (Beards are dark threads, also called byssus threads, that attach the mussels to rocks.) If mussels are tightly closed they're usually still alive and fit to eat, although the occasional closed mussel shell may be full of sand and tightly closed. You can spot a sand-filled mussel because it's heavier than a live mussel of the same size.

Mussels Jambalaya

This dish is not authentic anything, but is a good spicy way to go with rice and mussels.

Pick over, rinse, and steam open over an inch of boiling water:
3 to 4 lb fresh mussels
Chop, slice, and dice:
1 large onion
2 stalks celery
1 large clove garlic
1 large green pepper
1 cup mushrooms
4 Tbsp parsley
Sauté the vegetables gently in:
3 Tbsp olive oil
Then add:
3 Tbsp bottled chilies or **salsa**
4 Tbsp tomato sauce
liquid from cooking mussels
Simmer, uncovered, for 5 or 10 minutes while you set the table and pour out something thirst-quenching. A few minutes before serving, add the mussels and:
1 Tbsp lemon juice
Serve with rice and freshly steamed greens or salad.

SERVES 4

Mussels Steamed in their Own Broth

Heat in a skillet:
2 Tbsp olive oil
2 cloves sliced garlic
When the oil is very hot, add:
2 to 3 dozen fresh mussels with their
  beards scraped off
Cover tightly and cook full tilt for about 10
minutes or until the mussels are open. For
variety you can throw in:
1 tsp chopped basil or **oregano** or **a pinch
  of red pepper**
Then ladle the broth and mussels over a
mound of pasta on each plate (linguini is
best, but almost any pasta will do if it's a
little undercooked).

Except for the oil, the broth in this recipe
comes entirely from inside the mussels and
is very salty, so when you cook the pasta,
put in only half as much salt as usual.

Adding ½ **cup grated Gruyère cheese** and
2 Tbsp cream to the broth at the end of
the cooking will make the broth into a
sauce. **A cup of diced zucchini** thrown in
the skillet at the beginning of cooking
makes this dish a complete meal, and, if
you gather your own mussels and pick
your own zucchini, a remarkably
inexpensive one.

SERVES 2

Crab Feed

In Pleasant Bay, Nova Scotia, they go out
for the big, spiderlike snow crabs in July
and August. Unlike lobster, the crabs don't
live long once they're pulled up from the
briny deep, so they have to be cooked right
away. After that you can either freeze them
or sit right down and have a fine mess of
crab. What you serve with crab is:
nutcrackers or **kitchen shears**
beer

I once had snow crab at a three-star
restaurant, surrounded by soft music,
twinkling lights, excellent company, and a
small army of waiters bowing and zipping
around. There were all kinds of vegetables
and side dishes, none of which would fit on
my plate. Worst of all, I realized, as I tackled
the beast, I was wearing my best clothes.

The best way to serve snow crab is on the
beach, cooked over a driftwood fire. You
can throw the shells anywhere; seagulls will
clean up at dawn.

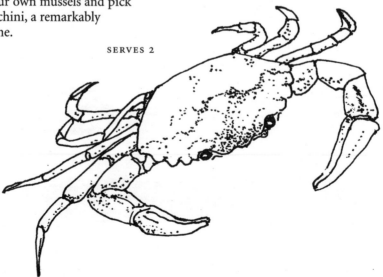

Lobster

The sweetest and tenderest lobsters are small and lively. Keep them cool until you are ready to cook them. If one dies, discard it.

Allow:
1 to 2 lobsters per serving
If there are too many, cook all and use them for sandwiches or salad the next day.

Bring to a boil:
2 to 4 gallons water
Grasp lobsters firmly behind the head and plunge them into boiling water, head first, one at a time. Cover and boil 10 to 15 minutes. Remove at once with tongs, and cool under running water for 1 minute. Turn each lobster on its back and split it down the middle, using a sharp knife.

Lobsters are an expensive treat unless you happen to live near a lobster port, but even then remember that five pounds of lobster on the hoof yields only one pound of meat. The largest chunk of meat is in the tail; the next largest in the claws; the next in the joints of the large legs. The meat in the small legs and tail flippers are only tiny morsels, and it takes lots of patience and skill to squeeze them out of the shell, but they are particularly sweet and tender. For the brave and bold, there is the green liver known as the tomalley, or the bright red egg mass known as coral, both edible.

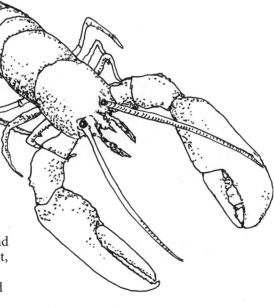

Inedible parts are the small sack of sand at the head; the gut, which is a dark vein running the length of the lobster, and the feathery white mass on each side of the back, near the head.

Serve lobster with:
melted butter or **garlic butter**
hot toasted French bread or **garlic bread**
a good crisp salad
white wine or
Canadian beer

Poultry

CHICKEN

Whenever I think of becoming a vegetarian I remember chicken. Chicken is much loved the world over, easy to digest, and there are about a million ways to cook it. If you're worried about calories, you can remove the skin (containing almost all of the fat) and cook it in a liquid sauce with lots of flavors. If you're pressed for time, you can roast it; if you're low on supplies and cash, you can chop it into small pieces and add it to rice or noodles. Recipes for all these methods are in the following pages.

There is quite a difference between the quality of store-bought chicken and homegrown chicken, despite the fact that most chicken raised for meat is of the same variety. The difference has to do with the way the chickens live and the age at which they are butchered. Homegrown chickens tend to run around more and get fed less consistently than commercial chickens. They eat more different kinds of things. They also tend to be butchered later. The result is that the meat is a little tougher, especially in the legs, than that of commercial chickens. They're better suited to long, slow cooking, roasting or braising,

than to fast, hot cooking. On the other hand, homegrown chickens definitely have more flavor.

Young chickens, whether homegrown or store-bought, have hardly any flavor. You won't notice this when eating, say, hot barbecued chicken wings, but it makes a tremendous difference in something like chicken soup. It is hardly worth throwing the bones of a young chicken into a soup pot. You get more out of a carrot.

Homegrown roasted chickens are a four-day affair. The first day it is roasted. The second day there are leftover cold cuts. The

third day there is a casserole of some sort with bits of chicken in it, and the fourth day, there is this marvelous soup. This sort of economy makes them well worth whatever hassle it is to raise and butcher them.

Raising Meat Birds

For as long as anybody around here can remember, we've raised meat birds every summer and popped them into the freezer every fall. Newly hatched chicks can be shipped by bus or mail for 24 hours, because for the first day they don't need to eat or drink. Every year I go down to the post office or bus depot and pick them up. For the first couple of days we keep them in the house in the box they came in, while we hunt around the farm for the various pieces of chick-raising equipment. We have, somewhere, a wooden lobster crate with a hinged lid, a tiny feed rack, chick-watering devices and a heat lamp. New chickens have to be kept warm. They are endlessly amusing. Even the collie, content to live outside most of her life, insists on coming in to watch them run around the pen, her nose in the box and her tail moving gently from side to side in a slow collie grin.

After a couple of days, weary of incessant peeping (which starts up at first light), we move them out into a chick brooder in a little varmint-proof A-frame in the yard. The collie takes to barking and patrolling with great vigor, especially at night. The chicks grow rapidly, going through stages of being housebound, then allowed into a little pen on the lawn, and, finally, in about 3 weeks, moved out next to the brook, where they become true free-range chickens. We feed them twice a day and lock them up tight at night.

We feed our meat birds traditional chick starter, and, later, chick grower, which are very high in protein foods such as soybeans and fish meal, to duplicate the chick food of life in the wilds (mostly bugs). In late summer we fatten them on sunflowers and squash.

We buy males and females mixed, and butcher them at different times. The males grow faster, develop longer, tougher legs, and are butchered at 7 to 8 weeks for frying, barbecue, and braising (things like Coq au Vin). The females sit around eating instead of running around fighting, and can be kept until they reach 6 or 7 pounds, making very high quality roasting birds.

Regardless of gender, it's essential to finish them off before the onset of very cold weather, or you will have a lot more feathers to pluck.

People always ask, "How can you bear to butcher them, after you raise them yourselves?" The answer is that meat birds are bred for fast growth but not long-term survival. If you keep them into the winter, they fight, get injuries, and succumb to diseases that never seem to bother laying hens.

Butchering

Butchering is a lot easier once you develop a system. Ours is very low tech; we start by building a campfire to heat water outside the shed where we pluck them. We used to pluck feathers outside, but were discouraged by wasps. On butchering day we don't feed them, but let them have water while we round up tools and clear the decks. We sharpen knives. My husband, who does the actual dispatching, props a ladder against the barn to hang chickens from. The dog follows us around with great interest.

The Art of Dispatching Chickens: There are more ways of doing in chickens than there are mousetraps. What you should do is ask around your neck of the woods as to the socially acceptable way of dispatching chickens. Find somebody who knows. If possible, get them to demonstrate.

Dipping to Loosen Feathers: After we're sure the chicken is dead, we dip it in almost-boiling water, at 180°F for 20 to 30 seconds. It's important not to leave them in too long, or the skin becomes yellowish and fragile. The test I use is tugging on a big wing or tailfeather; when they come out without a big struggle, the bird's ready to be plucked.

Plucking: We've learned to lay out a big old piece of plastic under the plucking operation, and to provide chairs for the pluckers. Hang chickens from both legs so that when they stiffen, they'll be symmetrical, at least — if you can do this fast enough, they'll still be flexible and you can set them on a rack, legs bent.

Start by pulling the large feathers, then roll great clumps of feathers off the legs and torso, getting all the large areas clean. Rub vigorously; you'll be surprised how fast it goes.

We dispatch and pluck chickens two by two. At a dozen we stop for a break and use a propane torch to remove hairs and pin feathers. To remove head and feet, we cut the skin in a circle, then twist them off.

Cleaning Birds: We clean birds on an outdoor porch on a big table covered with five or six layers of newspaper, keeping various plastic containers around, including a garbage container. I also bring out a couple of plastic cutting boards and my sharpest knives. Before and after butchering, wash all knives and boards in hot soapy water to discourage stray bacteria. Wash your hands, too, or use surgical gloves.

To clean a bird I lay it on its back and take up a generous pinch of flesh above the bird's vent. This enables me to get a knife blade under the skin without poking holes in anything but the skin. Once you have made the initial cut, it's not difficult to extend the cut in any direction, keeping the blade turned upward so as to cut only through the skin. Cut in this way all the way around the vent hole, then up to the breastbone.

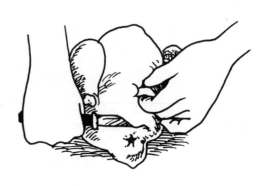

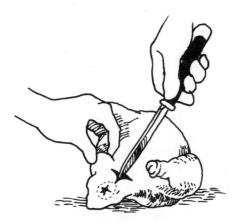

in a big old washtub full of chickens and let it run overnight in the shed. (The shed is tight enough to keep out varmints and, of course, there is the dog, who is keeping a close eye on the whole procedure.)

Packaging

Whole Birds: Tuck wing tips behind the upper joints.

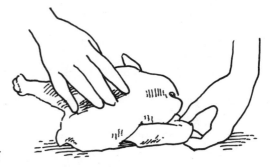

Make a second cut at a right angle to the first. This T-shaped cut will allow you to snake in your hand and clean out the inside of the chicken. The vent and intestines go into the garbage, of course. Better things include the gizzards (cut free and set aside to deal with later), heart, and liver. The liver has a dark green bile sack; if it breaks, the bile will spoil the liver, so I cut into the liver to free it. I throw hearts and livers into a container of cold water as I butcher. Beyond the heart are lungs, wedged in between ribs; I scrape them out with my fingers and throw them away. I also cut and twist off the neck and trim back all dangly things. Necks go in with hearts and livers.

To tuck the legs in close to the body, make a second horizontal cut parallel to the first, just below the tip of the breastbone.

I leave gizzards until last because of the danger of dulling my knife if I cut in too far; the inner sac is full of small stones. Cut the outer gizzard as if cutting open a clam, without cutting into the thick inner skin, and discard the inner sack.

Tuck both legs into this band, if you can. If not, the bag enclosing the bird will hold the legs close to the body.

Chilling: Freshly butchered meat has a slimy quality; it should be chilled at least 12 hours. This may be done in a cooler or in cold water. Because we have an endless supply of gravity-fed water, we set a hose

In each whole bird, I like to put a small plastic bag containing: 1 heart, 1 neck, 1 gizzard, and a small bunch of fresh parsley. These can be used to start broth for the gravy when roasting the bird.

Parts of the Chicken

Thighs: These are nice chunks of dark meat, very good for braising, barbecue, or roasting.

Lower Legs: Very popular with the younger set, drumsticks are the darkest and toughest meat. When cooking older birds, relegate them to the soup pot.

Wings: Wings have the lightest and tenderest meat, but not much of it. They are wonderful barbecue fare. The uppermost wing joint (closest to the bird) is the best one to give a small child, having only one bone and no cartilage or gristle.

Back: This hardly has any meat except two morsels tucked tenderly in bone enclaves. Backs make good soups and stocks *(see p. 14).*

Breast: The white meat or *suprême,* as the French call it, has two sides, each with a layer of tender outer meat and even more tender inner meat. A chicken breast may be cooked in a little butter or oil for 6 to 8 minutes; it may be marinated and broiled or rolled as in Chicken Kiev *(see p. 137).*

Subdividing Poultry

Many recipes call for uncooked chicken cut into serving pieces. If yours came whole, you can easily cut it up. You will need a sharp knife *(see Knives, p. 292).*

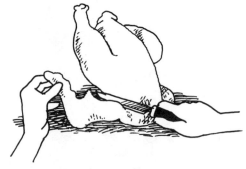

To Remove Wing: Pull wing tip away from the bird, and make a shallow cut just where the wing joins the body. Then turn the bird over and make a second, deeper cut at a right angle to the first, slipping the knife blade under the bone as you pull the wing outward.

To Remove Leg and Thigh: Grasp bird firmly by the leg, and starting from the center of the bird, make a gradually deepening cut toward the tail, along the side where the thigh connects to the back. Bend the leg outward to disconnect the socket, and then make a second cut, front to back, to remove the entire leg and thigh.

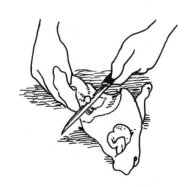

To Separate Leg and Thigh: Bend leg and thigh back and forth as you feel for the place where the two bones hinge. Lay the piece on your cutting board, skin-side down, and cut through the hinge first. Then, with a straight, clean cut, separate the rest of the meat.

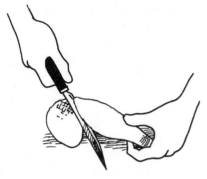

Separating Breast and Back: Insert the knife, blade facing toward you, through the side of the bird just where the upper and lower ribs meet. Cut toward the back. Repeat on the other side. Then grasp breast and back firmly and pull them apart as if hinged at the neck. Cut through remaining meat and skin.

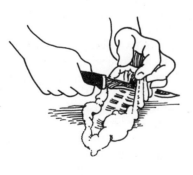

Boning the Breast

To remove breast meat entirely from the bone, leave bone whole, but remove skin. Cut a line through the breast meat slightly to one side of the breastbone ridge, as deep as it will go.

Peel the flesh from the bone, using the knife to pry and cut free the bottom half of the meat.

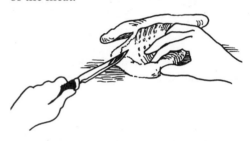

Breast meat separates easily into two pieces; the inner, smaller one is more tender.

Cutting the Breastbone in Half: This can be done with one well-placed blow of a Japanese cleaver, but it can also be done, less professionally, by simply cutting toward the front and back from the middle, along a line slightly to one side of the central ridge, with the breast turned upside down. This sort of cutting dulls knives.

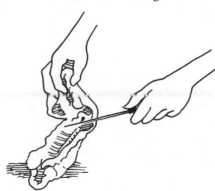

Part of growing and butchering your own chickens is freezing and defrosting them. (*To freeze chicken, see p. 280.*) Chicken defrosted slowly in the refrigerator may take longer and use up space, but it will be more tender, an important consideration when the bird is large and mature. Defrost whole birds fully wrapped.

Defrosting Chicken
For whole chickens allow:
36 hours for a 6-lb bird
48 hours for a 12-lb bird
3 days for anything larger

For cut-up chicken, allow:
6 hours in the refrigerator
3 hours at room temperature

Add 2 hours to crockpot cooking time if using frozen, cut up chicken.

Roasting Tips
To Roast a Bird: A roasted bird looks wonderful, tastes delicious, and is very little work for the cook. You may stuff or not stuff the inner cavity. The skin should be intact, as it has a thin layer of fat beneath it, which automatically keeps the meat basted. This fat is thinnest at wing tips and on the drumsticks. If the bird is large and is to be cooked for a long time, it may need extra basting in those areas. When roasting ducks and geese, there is often a great deal of fat around the tail. To drain this, you should poke holes in the skin around the tail area, to release some of the fat as it roasts.

Always roast your bird on a rack in a roasting pan. This is so that it will not fry in the fat that accumulates in the pan during the latter part of roasting. Tuck the wing tips behind the upper wing joint, and tie or tuck the legs down so they are close to the body of the bird. If you have a meat thermometer, insert it between the thigh and body. **Done is 185°F for all birds.** If you don't have a thermometer, estimate the approximate amount of time from the Poultry Roasting Chart at right and test by twisting a leg. It should feel a little loose when the bird is cooked through.

A large bird should be basted and covered loosely with foil once it browns, or the meat may dry out under the crisp skin. Smaller birds may be roasted for the last half hour or so at a slightly higher temperature (350°– 375°F) to make sure they brown.

Carving Tips
A roasted bird will retain heat for quite some time, so you can remove it from the oven up to an hour before serving. Cover with foil and a towel to keep in the warmth, and don't carve it or serve the stuffing until you are ready to eat.

If you plan to save the bird for future eating, carve one side only, leaving the skin intact on the other side. Cover and refrigerate. Use within 4 days. Cooked leftover meat may be used in a variety of ways (*see pp. 137–38*) or frozen for use within 4 weeks.

To Carve a Bird: Always use a sharp, well-honed knife. Remove wing, thigh, and drumstick, and set them on a serving plate before attempting to cut thin slices of white meat from the breast. Cut small slices at first, at the top, then larger slices parallel to the bone underneath. Lift each slice onto the serving plate as you go. Cut up some pieces of skin as well and put them on the plate for people who like crisp, brown skin.

ROASTING POULTRY

Bird	Minutes (per lb)	Oven Temp.	Temp. on Meat Thermometer When Done
Chicken, under 3 lb	35	300°F	185°F
Chicken, over 3 lb	60	225°–250°	185°
Duck	35	300°	190°
Goose	30	300°	185°
Turkey, 10 to 12 lb	25	300°	185°
Turkey, 12 lb or more	15	300°	185°

Gravy Broth

Broth for gravy may be started when you put the bird in the oven to roast.

Assemble:
2 cups water
½ tsp salt
¼ tsp pepper
poultry neck, liver, heart, and giblets
3 celery tops
1 small onion stuck with 2 cloves
Simmer ingredients gently in a small, covered pan. When the bird is done, place it on a serving platter and cover lightly with foil to keep it warm. Scrape and pour drippings from the roasting pan into a measuring cup and let sit a few minutes. When the fat rises to the top, measure out 4 Tbsp of chicken fat. You may use this to make gravy (see below).

1½ CUPS

Chicken Gravy

After you have made gravy a few times, you won't have to measure things anymore; you simply heat the drippings, add flour to "take up the fat" and then add liquid, stirring until it looks right. Many cooks do this right in the roasting pan, to save time and dishes. If there isn't enough fat to work with, add some butter or vegetable oil. If there's too much, pour some off.

4 Tbsp rendered chicken fat
4 Tbsp flour
1½ cups chicken broth
Heat the fat in a small, heavy pan, and when it begins to bubble, add the flour, stir with a fork, and reduce heat. Cook, stirring occasionally, over low heat for 3 minutes. Then add the broth and drippings, gradually, in 3 parts, stirring after each addition until the gravy thickens. Cook gravy gently for about 3 minutes. If it gets too thick, add more liquid.

Additions of all kinds can be made to a good gravy. For seasoning, try light herbs such as chopped parsley, chervil, or tarragon. You may want to add a dash of salt, a grinding of fresh pepper. To some it isn't gravy unless the liver, heart, and giblets are added — all chopped fine, of course. Others prefer a few sliced, sautéed mushrooms. You may also substitute a little white wine or sour cream for part of the liquid. Gravy is a terrific leftover. To reheat, add a little liquid (water or milk) and stir until smooth. Then heat gently, stirring from time to time. Add more liquid as needed. Add to chopped, cooked, leftover poultry; serve on toast.

1½ CUPS

Fresh Bread Stuffing

Store-bought stuffing is a poor imitation of what stuffing can be. There are 2 essential ingredients. One is whole wheat bread; white bread simply doesn't have enough body to make good stuffing. In our house, we crumble "heels" or ends of loaves into a basket on the warming oven of the woodstove. The other important ingredient in stuffing is good sage. To be sweet and pungent, sage should be grown and dried within the year. Sage, more than most herbs, becomes musty after a year or two — especially when prepackaged with a lot of breadcrumbs. Fortunately sage is a lovely herb to grow, even on a balcony, and you don't need a lot to make a good stuffing.

Chop moderately well:

1 onion

1 stalk celery

1 clove garlic (optional)

3 Tbsp parsley

½ cup mushrooms (optional)

In a heavy frying pan, heat:

1 Tbsp safflower oil

Tilt to coat pan evenly, then throw in vegetables and cook over rapid heat, tossing and turning until they begin to brown. Remove pan from heat. Add to it:

2 cups crumbled whole grain bread

1 tsp chopped, fresh sage or **½ tsp dried, rubbed sage**

1 tsp chopped, fresh savory or **½ tsp dried, rubbed savory**

Stir thoroughly. No further cooking is needed. Stuff the bird with it. I have never found any need to rub salt into the bird before stuffing, and have also never bothered to sew the bird up; if the cavity isn't covered, it doesn't matter.

1½ CUPS

Sesame Chicken

This is a good recipe to make use of in a hectic moment — infinitely expandable and easy to prepare, cook, and serve.

Mix together a marinade of:

4 Tbsp sesame oil (or **vegetable oil**)

2 Tbsp tamari soy sauce

1 Tbsp lemon juice

2 Tbsp white wine (optional)

Pour the mixture over:

4 chicken legs and thighs, separated

Cover and let sit for 30 minutes, or refrigerate and allow to sit up to 3 hours. Turn the pieces if you have time. Remove chicken from marinade and sprinkle with:

paprika

sesame seeds

Place in an oiled pan and bake at 325° to 350°F for 30 minutes. From time to time, baste with leftover marinade or juice from the pan. This chicken may be served hot, warmed-over, or cold.

SERVES 4

Chicken Suprême aux Herbes

Suprême is the breast, or white meat, of the chicken. Allow 1 breast per serving. Marinated in lemon and olive oil, a delicate morsel indeed.

For every serving, mix:

2 Tbsp olive oil

2 tsp lemon juice

½ tsp tarragon

pinch of rosemary

Crumble the herbs into the mixture and marinate the chicken breasts for ½ to 1 hour. These may be broiled, 4 minutes per side, but I find it easier to simply pan-fry them over moderate heat, 3 to 4 minutes to a side. There is no need for any more fat or oil than in the marinade.

Serve with Roasted Brown Rice *(p. 163)* and "Baked" Squash *(p. 53)*.

Chicken Kiev

Golden *roulades* of chicken breast, saturated with garlic butter and parsley, batter-fried. Very choice. Serve with rice and good green vegetables. No sauce is necessary, but you may accompany with a slice of lemon.

Depending on the size of the chicken, you can make 2 or 3 rolls per side of breast. Each side has an outer and an inner, more tender, fillet. Both may be pounded thinner, but be careful pounding the inner fillet so it doesn't fragment. The outer fillet may, if large enough, be sliced laterally into 2 pieces. Both are then pounded. A rolling pin or heavy bottle are good for pounding.

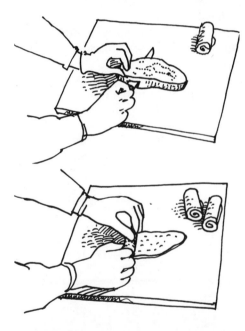

Mix together:
¼ cup softened butter
¼ cup chopped parsley
2 cloves crushed garlic
Pound and flatten:
4 to 6 chicken breast pieces
Roll the butter mixture into little sausages and place one on each piece of meat. Roll the meat up, put on a small plate, and chill 1 hour, refrigerated, or 15 minutes in the freezer.

Beat in a small bowl:
1 egg
Put in another bowl:
1 cup unbleached white flour
Dip each meat roll in egg, then in flour. Heat in a heavy pan:
½ cup safflower oil
When hot, but not smoking, place the roulades in, seam-side down, and gently fry until golden. Be careful not to cook them too fast or too long; they will become dry and tough if overcooked. In the original recipe they are sautéed in butter, a very delicate fat. Turn as necessary to brown all sides, a total of 10 to 15 minutes. Drain on paper before serving.

SERVES 4

Chili Chicken Stir-Fry

Chop into ½-inch cubes:
1 cup cooked chicken
Roll pieces in:
dark chili powder (not the super hot kind)
Sauté in:
2 Tbsp safflower oil
Add to stir-fried onions, carrots, peppers, celery, sprouts and fresh chopped herbs (*see p. 40*).

SERVES 4 TO 6

Variations
Use pork instead of chicken. Use uncooked chicken. Select white meat only. Cook as above.

Chicken Pilaf

This dish is full of rich, delicious spicy aromas, but is actually quite easily prepared, low in cholesterol, and inexpensive — 1 cup of chicken feeds 4.

Chop fine:
1 onion
Crush or mince:
1 clove garlic
Choose a heavy pan suitable for making rice. Heat in it:
2 Tbsp safflower oil
Add the onion, garlic, and:
2 cups uncooked brown rice
1 to 2 tsp curry powder
Cook and stir over lively heat until the rice turns light brown and smells nutty. Turn off heat, stir as it cools a little, then add:
4 cups water or **chicken stock**
2 cups chopped, fresh, canned, or **frozen tomatoes**
1 tsp thyme
1 tsp salt
Cover and cook 30 minutes over low heat until all liquid is absorbed.
Toss in:
1 cup well-chopped, cooked chicken

Variations
You may also add:
½ cup roasted almonds
1 sliced, sautéed green pepper
½ cup sliced, sautéed mushrooms
½ cup raisins or **dried currants**

SERVES 4

Chicken with Chanterelles

Chanterelle mushrooms *(see p. 37)* abound in Cape Breton. Easy to identify because of their lurid orange color, they are found under spruce trees in late summer. They have a smokey, woodsy flavor that goes well with chicken. I find it best not to sauté them; just throw them in the pot, whole or sliced.

Divide into serving pieces:
1 whole chicken
Dust lightly with flour and sauté pieces in:
3 Tbsp safflower or **olive oil**
Remove chicken from the pan and sauté:
1 chopped onion
2 stalks chopped celery
2 cloves minced garlic
1 tsp basil or **tarragon**
Return chicken to the pot and add:
1 cup chopped, canned tomatoes
1 cup water
½ cup vermouth, white wine, or **water**
Cover closely and simmer over very low heat for 2 hours. Fifteen minutes before serving, stir into the gravy:
1 cup whole or **sliced chanterelle mushrooms** (or ordinary mushrooms)
Serve with rice or pasta, and green beans or salad.

SERVES 4 TO 6

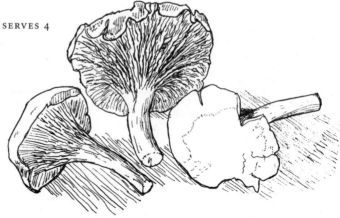

Coq au Vin

You can make this with just about any kind of wine, sweet or dry, even a little sour. I often make it with Amontillado, which is terrific, if a little rich.

Divide into serving-sized pieces:
4 to 6 pieces chicken
Dry and dredge in flour.

Heat:
3 Tbsp light oil
Sauté for 5 minutes:
1 sliced carrot
1 sliced onion or **4 sliced green onions**
1 clove crushed garlic (optional)
Remove vegetables; sauté chicken until golden, about 20 minutes. Add vegetables and:
1 cup chicken broth
½ cup sherry or **1 cup wine**
bay leaf
½ cup mushrooms (optional)
½ tsp ground pepper
pinch of thyme
Heat until liquid just bubbles; cover and simmer on low heat for 1 hour.

To finish with a wonderful glaze, put it in a 350°F oven for the last 10 minutes. Serve with rice and cooked vegetables. Remove bay leaf before serving.

SERVES 4 TO 6

Thai Chicken Curry

This recipe comes from a young couple who work in Emergency Medicine. They like to come home from a wearying day and cook each other fabulous meals. (This recipe reflects their concern with health; it has little fat, even though it tastes juicy and delicious.) The chicken is first poached with vegetables in wine, and then a mixture of coconut and tahini (sesame butter) is added to give the dish its distinctive flavor. If you make it with breasts, it cooks in about 15 minutes. If you use thighs, allow 30 minutes cooking time.

Mix together in a heavy-bottom pan:
2 cups coconut milk (see below)
2 Tbsp curry powder
2 Tbsp tahini or **¼ cup almond butter**
Set this aside. Remove skin from:
4 to 6 pieces chicken
Dust the pieces lightly with:
curry powder
in a heavy pan, mix together:
½ cup white wine
1 Tbsp tamari soy sauce
4 cloves crushed garlic
½ to 1 inch fresh, sliced ginger root
Set the chicken in this mixture, cover tightly, and cook over low to medium heat 15 minutes or longer until the chicken is almost done. Meanwhile, prepare:
1 cup julienned or **sliced carrots**
1 cup thinly sliced green peppers
1 head broccoli flowerets
1 to 2 stalks chopped celery
Place these on top of the chicken, cover, and steam 5 to 7 minutes. Remove from heat. Add the coconut mixture and cook, covered, over low heat for 3 to 5 minutes. Serve at once with rice (see p. 163).

SERVES 4

Coconut Milk: If you have no fresh or canned coconut milk, soak together:
2 cups unsweetened coconut
2½ cups warm water
Let stand 10 to 20 minutes, then wring out coconut in a cloth, or press in a sieve, to get:
2 cups coconut milk

Duck à l'Orange

My mother, in Connecticut, has raised ducks with some success. They are so endearing that it is hard to actually butcher them. On the other hand, eating duck is a great thing, a dark, dense, delicious meat. It has, however, a great deal of fat, and less meat than chicken. To drain fat, poke holes in the skin before roasting, especially around the tail and back, and set the bird on a rack at least ½-inch high. Poke holes before and during cooking.

Roast duck 35 minutes per pound at 300°F to an internal temperature of 190°F. When the duck is almost done, drain pan drippings into a tall glass container and allow fat to rise to the top (5 to 10 minutes). Remove all fat from drippings; save or freeze for other cooking (such as sauce for leftover duck the next day).

In a small pan, mix:
1 Tbsp unsweetened cocoa
1 Tbsp cornstarch or **2 Tbsp arrowroot**
3 Tbsp sherry or **port**
Mash this into a paste, then add:
½ cup skimmed duck drippings
juice of 3 or **4 fresh oranges** (**⅔ cup orange juice**)
Put the pan over low heat, stirring occasionally, for 15 minutes. It should thicken. If it's too thick, add more drippings or orange juice. For piquancy, add:
1 to 2 Tbsp red wine vinegar
2 Tbsp currant jelly or **brown sugar**
grated orange and lemon rind to taste

2 tsp tamari soy sauce
salt to taste
Cook sauce, covered, over low heat for another 15 minutes. Meanwhile, remove duck from the oven, carve it, and arrange on a heated platter. This is better done in the kitchen than at the table, as it is messy. Serve sauce in a gravy dish at the table.

SERVES 4 TO 6

Maccheroni con Tacchino
This recipe, created to disguise leftover roast turkey as something new, may be used for any sort of leftover roast meat.

Set on high heat:
1 large pot salted water (covered)
Meanwhile, coarsely chop:
1 medium onion
2 stalks celery
½ green pepper
½ cup mushrooms (optional)
Sauté these until tender in:
2 Tbsp olive oil
Then add:
2 cups chopped roast turkey
1 28-oz can tomatoes, mashed with a fork or potato masher
1 tsp basil
1 tsp oregano
Cover tightly and simmer gently. When the hot water comes to a boil, add:
1 lb large shell pasta
Boil, uncovered, 20 minutes. When al dente, drain, rinse with cold water, and mix with sauce. Serve with Parmesan or other grated cheese.

SERVES 4 TO 6

Meat

American meat is famous the world over; we're fortunate to live on a continent able to support so many meat animals. In most parts of the world, roasts and steaks such as we commonly serve are unheard of. People who eat meat in Asia and Africa usually chop it fine and use it for flavoring and added protein in vegetable and grain dishes.

Meat is very high in protein — and protein, as you may have discovered, becomes tough when it's cooked at high temperatures. You may want to lightly sear the meat over high heat on the outside to seal in the juices. But if you want it to be tender and juicy in the middle, better turn down the heat.

There are three ways to approach meat cookery:

Pan-Frying, Broiling, or Cooking over the Coals: For tender meats, cut 1 to 1½ inches thick. Sear first, then cook slowly for 5 or 6 minutes, keeping a close eye on it.

Roasting: Roasting is good for large solid chunks of fairly tender meat, especially hind legs and pieces from the back. The heat should be low and the pieces covered in fat, one way or another, to prevent the meat from drying out.

Stewing or Braising: This means cooking in liquid. The pieces may be large (as in pot roasts) or small (as in stews). They may be tough or tender; they will, in any case, be tenderized by long, slow cooking in liquid. Often these meats are browned or seared first, to firm the shape of the meat and improve the flavor, but the main part of the cooking is gentle simmering in liquid. A crockpot or woodstove is ideal for this.

ROASTING MEAT

A good roast is a wonderfully easy thing for the cook to prepare, and sure to please. If your meat is frozen, allow time for it to defrost in the fridge *(see p. 280)*; it will be more tender.

I like to roast meat at low temperatures. The slower meat cooks, the more tender it remains when cooked. When roasting very fat meats, such as pork, you can sometimes get away with higher temperatures and shorter cooking times. However, the leaner the meat, the slower the oven should be.

Meat should be set on a rack before roasting; this is to keep the bottom of the roast from getting fried in the escaping fat. If there is no fat on the roast, some should be applied, in some way. Brush meat with oil before and during roasting, rub it with lard, or attach thin slabs of pork or other tasty fat with toothpicks over the top before you put it in the oven.

The best way to be sure about what has happened inside your meat is to use a meat thermometer and cook until the thermometer registers the right temperature. Insert the thermometer into the thickest part of the meat (not next to bone or into fat) and keep an eye on it. If you plan to take it out early and keep it warm for a while, until your guests arrive, take it out when it registers 5 degrees below the desired temperature.

Roast Pork

Pork is a fat, juicy meat, and may be cooked at somewhat higher temperatures than other meats. Put it in an oven pre-heated to 500°F, but immediately reduce heat to 350°F for roasting. Bake until done to at least 170°F, or until the juice from the center runs out clear and gray.

Pork should never be rare. The heat destroys a parasitic larva called *trichinae*, sometimes found in pork muscle. Trichinae are actually killed at 131°F, which is a lot more rare than you would ever want to eat it, but the custom of cooking pork until it is thoroughly gray has served us well, and continues to be popular.

Roast Venison

Venison is a lot like beef, but leaner and a little tougher (depending on the age of the deer). If cooked slowly, however, it makes a good roast. To avoid a gamey taste, remove all venison fat, replacing it with bacon or thin slabs of pork fat attached to the top with toothpicks.

ROASTING MEAT

	Oven Temp.	Minutes (per lb)	Internal Temp. When Done
Beef	325°F	25	140° rare
		30	160° med.
		40	170° well
Veal	325°	35	170°
Venison	275°	50	135° rare
Mutton or		60	150° med.
Chèvre		70	160° well
Lamb, leg	325°	35	180°
shoulder		45	180°
Fresh Pork	350°	35	170°
Spareribs	325°	30	170°
Cured Pork	325°	35	160°

Using a Roast

Nowadays, with the rising cost of meat and the recognition that it isn't healthy to eat a lot of it every day, people don't cook big roasts as often. However, they can still have a place in your cookery, if you use them economically. Just because you cooked a great whack of meat doesn't mean you have to eat it all at one sitting. Serve a variety of foods along with your roast the first night, and keep it chilled for use in other dishes, cold cuts, or sandwiches. I'm reminded of an old ditty called "Vicarage Mutton."

Hot on Sunday, cold on Monday, hashed on Tuesday, minced on Wednesday, curried on Thursday, broth on Friday, cottage pie on Saturday.

How to Tell if Meat Is Tender

There is no easy way to tell if meat is tough or tender just by looking at it, but there are clues.

All meat is tender when it is young, and gets tougher as it gets older. The meat of animals that are fat and sedentary, such as pigs and sheep and cows, is more tender than the meat of animals that bound around, like deer and rabbits. Fat cools the meat and bastes it as it cooks, making it less likely to shrink and become tough.

You can also do some guessing if you know what part of the animal the meat came from. The most tender cuts come from the back; the rump is a little tougher, the shoulder tougher than the rump, and the lower legs and neck toughest of all. The more tender it is, the more expensive the cut.

Tough meats should be cooked long and slowly in liquid that, if you are lucky, will tenderize it; in any case you can make a good gravy out of it. Tender meats may also be cooked long and slowly, but will not require quite so much time. With tender meats, however, you also have the option of cooking them rapidly, as in a steak, chop, Chinese stir-fry, or dry roasting.

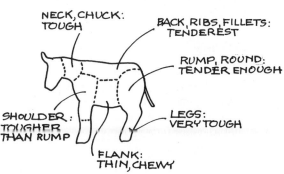

NECK, CHUCK: TOUGH

BACK, RIBS, FILLETS: TENDEREST

RUMP, ROUND: TENDER ENOUGH

SHOULDER: TOUGHER THAN RUMP

LEGS: VERY TOUGH

FLANK: THIN, CHEWY

GRAVY

Gravy, like cream sauce, is a mixture of fat, flour and liquid. Pork, lamb and well-marbled beef give off enough fat during roasting to make the gravy base. If there isn't enough fat, as is often the case with veal or venison, you may add butter to make up the difference. For the liquid, you can use canned beef or chicken stock or a bouillon cube with water, but the best stock is made by cooking together a little meat sliced from the roast before cooking, together with an onion, carrot, celery, parsley, salt, and water to cover. Bring to a boil, cover, and lower heat to simmer 30 minutes or more. Strain before using in gravy.

To pick up the flavor of a good meat gravy, add any juices released in cooking and carving the roast. If your gravy tastes a little flat, try adding a dash of wine or beer. Or a pinch of thyme or summer savory.

If your gravy has no flavor at all and you really want something delicious, add a few dollops of sour cream and a handful of sliced mushrooms, sautéed in butter.

To darken gravy, see Brown Sauce, *(p. 81)*, or try adding one of these:
1 tsp tamari soy sauce or
½ tsp instant coffee or
1 tsp unsweetened cocoa
(The flavor of coffee or cocoa isn't noticeable in a strong meat-flavored gravy such as lamb, pork, or beef.)

Pan Gravy

As you put the roast on to cook, start a meat stock *(see above)*. When the roast is nearly done, move it to another pan. Measure out of the roasting pan into a small heavy-bottomed pan:
3 Tbsp drippings

Heat the drippings, then add and stir in:
3 Tbsp flour
Cook and stir over moderate heat for 3 minutes. Then add gradually:
1 to 1½ cups meat stock
Cook and stir and add liquid until gravy is at the thickness you want. You may serve at once, keep warm, or cool and reheat — but be careful not to burn it.

SMOKE ROASTING

If you have a smokehouse or can easily devise one, you can cook and smoke meats at the same time by smoking them at temperatures around 200° to 250°. Beef, venison, and pork are particularly good this way, and birds are terrific. Smoked meat makes wonderful cold cuts and will keep a little longer than ordinary roast meat.

The meat can be cured in ordinary brine mixture (6 Tbsp salt to 1 qt water) for two days to the pound, if desired. That will change the flavor, but because it will be cooked meat after hot-smoking, it won't keep for months on end — a few weeks, refrigerated, at the most.

Birds, generally, are split and placed on racks; or they can be disjointed. Care must be taken to coat young broilers and turkey with plenty of fat or oil, otherwise they will dry out. With a very large bird, use a meat thermometer to gauge when it is done; if it's smoked all day and you're tired of waiting around, you can always pull it out and finish roasting at 300° in the kitchen oven.

If a very strong smoke flavor is what you want, smoke the meats first at low temperatures (75° to 85°F) for 2 hours or more. Then raise the temperature and roast them, as in roasting meat *(see p. 142)*.

Hang meat by a strong cord, threading under skin or tying securely around it with half-hitches; or place it on racks, covered with perforated aluminum foil. Set dripping trays under meat. Coat with herbs and spices if desired. Preheat smoke oven 200° to 225°, and follow information in Meat Roasting Chart *(see p. 143)*.

HAM

Having a baked ham in the kitchen is a great richness: useful in times of need, although a bit much to have on a daily basis. Most of the time I zip right by the processed meat counter without giving it a second thought. Bacon, sausage, ham, salami, baloney and hot dogs all have less nutritional value and more fat than most other foods, and also contain nitrosamines, which many people prefer not to add to their diets. Not to mention all that salt.

However, there is a time of year when ham is tempting. When the frost is on the pumpkin, and the scent of baking beans and breads and apples fill the kitchen; when there are suddenly a lot of people hanging around the stove, and they're hungrier than usual — that's when a ham goes with everything. And I'm not just speaking about sliced roast ham for dinner, or ham sandwiches. There is a whole cycle of dishes, starting with eggs and cheese, potatoes, vegetables, casseroles, baked beans, and spicy tomato-sauce treats, all of which can be improved by bits and scraps, bones and even chopped fat from a roasted leg of ham. Ham also has the advantage (due to its salt content) of keeping longer than other meats, so you can buy large and spread it out over a week or 10 days.

Remember, when you bring home a ham, that it may not be cooked at all and, like all fresh pork, should be heated to at least 140°F through and through before it is declared safe to eat *(see Roast Pork, p. 146)*.

Baked Ham

Ham may be simply baked, but it's tastier by far if first simmered in a pot of water for an hour or two, to get at least some of the salt out of it. It can then be trimmed, decorated with brown sugar and cloves (not necessary, but attractive) and baked, usually for about the same amount of time as the simmering. The water in which ham has been simmered is great stuff to soak and cook beans in, or can be used to boil vegetables such as turnips, carrots, and potatoes. Precooked ham need not be simmered; simply bake it *(see Meat Roasting Chart, p. 143)*

Ham may be added to:
    Omelets *(p. 97)*
    Quiches *(p. 98)*
    Scalloped Potatoes *(p. 55)*
    Cabbage *(p. 50)*
    New England Baked Beans *(p. 90)*
    Spaghetti *(p. 95)*
    Lasagne *(p. 95)*
    Calzones *(p. 107)*
    Pasta e Fagioli *(p. 90)*
    Spanish Rice *(p. 164)*
    French Bean Dish *(p. 91)*
    Stuffed Squash *(p. 39)*
    or any kind of stuffing *(p. 136)*

BRAISED MEAT

I have always thought of braising as cooking the juice out of meat and then cooking it back in again. Since meat is mostly protein, it should be cooked gently, to stay tender and juicy. If you doubt me, try a crockpot, which cooks at 200°F (Low) or 300°F (High). It makes things very tender to cook them long and slowly.

The flavor of the dish depends largely on what else you put in the pot — onions make it sweeter, carrots give it strength, turnips give it a turnip taste, and acids, such as tomatoes, lemon juice, wine, or even beer or a small amount of vinegar, help balance the strong meat flavor. Acids also help tenderize the meat.

Cocido

There are many recipes combining stewing meat and pork sausage. This is a Spanish version, which also includes garbanzos (chickpeas) and tomatoes.

Cut into 1-inch chunks and roll in flour:
1 lb stewing beef
Brown the meat lightly in:
3 Tbsp olive oil
Remove meat from the pan and sauté in the oil:
1 chopped onion
2 stalks chopped celery
3 cloves minced garlic
Return the meat to the pan and add:
½ lb chopped sausage
1 cup cooked garbanzos *(see p. 89)*

3 cups chopped, canned or **fresh tomatoes**
1 cup tomato juice or **water**
3 Tbsp chopped parsley
1 Tbsp chopped, fresh basil or **1 tsp dried basil**
freshly ground pepper
Cover tightly and cook over very low heat for 1½ hours, or use a crockpot at Low for 6 to 8 hours or High for 3 to 4 hours. Serve with millet, corn mush, or rice.

SERVES 4

Pork Roast Carbonnade

Pork pot roast cooked in beer fills the house with a wonderful fragrance as it simmers slowly on a woodstove or in a crockpot half the livelong day. Served with rice and salad, it makes an excellent gala dinner for friends or family.

Place in a heavy pot over very low heat:
6 lb pork roast
2 cups Canadian dark ale
2 cloves garlic
1 tsp tarragon
1 tsp salt
¼ cup sliced scallions
1 cup sliced mushrooms
Simmer, covered, 4 to 5 hours at very low heat. If you are using a crockpot, cook on High for 4 to 5 hours or on Low, for 6 to 8 hours. Remove the roast, slice, and arrange on a platter; serve the sauce separately, in a warm gravy bowl with a ladle, to pour over rice.

SERVES 6 TO 8

Variation
Turkey Carbonnade: Use 6 turkey legs instead of pork roast. Substitute light for dark ale and cook only 3 hours. Cool slightly and remove meat from bones, cutting into bite-sized chunks with a sharp knife. At the last moment, add:
½ cup finely chopped parsley

Boeuf Bourguignon

This is one of those mixtures that is transformed by long slow cooking into something magical and marvelous; you can't exactly tell what the great taste is, but it's there.

Cut into 1-inch chunks:
1½ lb stewing beef
Spread on a dish:
3 to 5 Tbsp white flour
1 tsp garlic powder
Toss beef in flour, then sauté pieces in:
3 Tbsp pork fat or **olive oil**
Brown meat lightly on all sides, then remove and sauté:
1 chopped onion
2 cloves minced garlic
Turn off heat; return meat to a deep stewing pot, along with:
½ cup red wine (Burgundy is recommended)
1 cup water
3 Tbsp tomato paste
1 Tbsp chopped parsley
¼ tsp thyme
freshly ground pepper
Cover pot closely and simmer for 1½ hours at very low heat. Alternatively this can be done in a crockpot, at Low for 6 to 8 hours, or at High for 4 to 5 hours.

The next part of this recipe involves:
12 little white onions
Cut tiny crosses in their bases, to keep them from falling apart, and steam or boil them for 3 to 5 minutes to loosen their jackets. Cool and peel them. Heat in a skillet:
3 Tbsp butter
Brown the onions on all sides, carefully controlling heat and stirring as you do. For extra browning, you can sprinkle them with a pinch of sugar and sauté them for an extra minute or two. Add them to the pot of meat. Finally, sauté:
3 Tbsp butter
1 cup sliced mushrooms
Add browned mushrooms and onions to the meat. Simmer 10 to 15 minutes or until onions are tender. Garnish with:
freshly chopped parsley
Serve with French bread and rice or pasta, a good green salad, and a good red wine.

SERVES 4

Osso Buco

My mother makes this exquisitely flavored Milanese veal stew with shin bones and their tasty marrow. After cooking, before serving, she discards the hollow bones.

Dip in olive oil, then in seasoned flour:
2 lb veal shin bones, cut in 6 pieces
Prop them together upright, so as to keep the marrow intact, and brown the veal slowly in olive oil for 10 to 15 minutes. They should be pale brown. Remove the bones, and in the same pot, lightly sauté:
1 cup finely chopped onion
½ cup finely chopped carrots
½ cup finely chopped parsley
Sauté these for 5 minutes, then add:
1 clove crushed garlic
Sauté 1 minute longer. Then add:
1 cup dry white wine or **vermouth**
and the veal bones. Cover the pot or arrange in a deep casserole and bake at 325°F for 1½ hours. Baste every ½ hour if you have time.

Gremolata Garnish
Prepare and mix:
grated rind of 1 organic lemon
¼ cup minced parsley
1 large clove crushed or **minced garlic**
Remove the bones and transfer the meat to a heated platter. Sprinkle the gremolata garnish over the meat. Serve with rice and the gravy in a bowl.

SERVES 4

TENDER CUTS

The tenderest muscles are those that get used the least. Being tender, they can be cooked in a hurry when time is short. Tender cuts are usually those along the back of the animal, so they include the loin cuts (tenderloin, sirloin) and T-bone, not to mention rib chops of all kinds. Also tender are the organ meats such as calf's liver.

To Pan-Fry Tender Meat: Oil the pan lightly and heat until nearly smoking. Throw in the meat and sear it rapidly on both sides, less than 30 seconds each. Then turn the heat down to medium and cook more slowly for 4 to 5 minutes on one side and 2 to 3 minutes on the other. The only way to be sure is to cut into it — you will notice that red juice runs from rare meat, pink from medium, yellow from done, and none at all from overdone.

To Broil Tender Meat: First of all, make sure the broiler (and the oven, if connected) is very clean. Second, preheat the broiler for 10 minutes. Coat meat lightly with fat or oil and place it 4 to 6 inches from the heat. Cook 4 to 5 minutes on one side and 2 or 3 minutes on the second.

Steaks and Chops
For steaks and chops, you want the tenderest meat, the loin cut, which is along the back just inside the ribs. This is cut about 1 inch thick and sold as sirloin, porterhouse, T-bone, and lamb or pork chops.

These cuts may be broiled or pan-fried. In this recipe the meat is served under a heap of lightly sautéed peppers and onions.

Sara's Chinese Pork Chops

My sister Sara, on the fly between home and job, relies on recipes like this one to keep body and soul together.

Per chop:
¼ tsp rosemary
½ clove crushed garlic
⅛ tsp freshly grated ginger
lots and lots of tamari soy sauce
Cook under the broiler, 8 to 10 minutes per side. Of course, she concludes, it is best to marinate this for 2 hours, but it works at the last minute, too.

Pepper Steak

Mix together:
2 Tbsp olive oil
½ tsp oregano
1 or 2 cloves crushed garlic
freshly ground pepper
Rub this mixture on both sides of:
steaks or **chops**
Let sit at room temperature for 1 hour.
Slice into strips about 2 inches long:
green pepper
onion
mushrooms
Preheat the pan or broiler before putting the meat on to cook. Lightly oil the pan or grill. If you are using a pan, sear the meat lightly on each side, then turn down the heat and cook it slowly for 5 or 6 minutes, or until done to your taste. Under a broiler, cook it for 4 to 5 minutes on the first side, 2 to 3 minutes on the other side. Meanwhile, heat in a frying pan:
2 Tbsp olive oil
Sauté the vegetables, stirring often, for 5 minutes. Remove from heat when done and serve them heaped on the meat.

Wiener Schnitzel

A friend used to work in a restaurant specializing in German food. I'll never forget the German waitresses hollering to the kitchen, as they came in: "Vun SCHNIT-zel!" Schnitzel was popular because of its speed of delivery: the gourmet version of a hamburger.

Pound flat, using a rolling pin or a bottle, and douse in flour:
4 veal scallops
Heat in a heavy iron skillet:
¼ cup butter and 2 Tbsp oil
Over fairly high heat, brown on both sides. How long you cook it varies from 2 to 5 minutes per side, depending on how thin you pounded it. Prick with a paring knife; when yellow juice runs out, it's done.

Braised Veal Scallops: To braise scallops, pound, flour, and sauté them first, as above, but use only:
1 Tbsp butter and 1 Tbsp oil

Braised in White Wine: Remove scallops and sauté in the butter:
3 sliced green onions
1 cup sliced mushrooms (optional)
Sprinkle lightly with:
1 Tbsp flour
and cook for a couple of minutes to take up the fat. Then add:
1 cup chicken or **veal broth**
½ cup dry white wine or **¼ cup vermouth**
2 tsp tarragon or **chervil** (optional)
Boil this sauce down to about ⅔ cup liquid, which should be thick. You may add, if you like:
½ cup sour cream
Return veal scallops to sauce and just heat them, over mild heat, about 2 minutes.

Braised in Tomato Sauce: Remove sautéed veal scallops from the pan and, using the fat there, make a Fresh Tomato Sauce *(see p. 75)*. Lay the pieces of meat in it, ladling some sauce over them; cover and set the pan on the side of the stove to stay just-warm for 30 minutes.

If the scallops are thick, or if other cuts of veal are used instead, bake at 250°F for 30 minutes or until the meat is tender.

SERVES 4

Spareribs

Spareribs are most often pork, but any meat may be used. We found venison spareribs delicious. You don't have to serve a lot of them; the sauce is very rich.

Dust meat lightly with flour (it can be in large or single-rib pieces). Rub a heavy iron skillet with a little suet, and brown meat on both sides, 2 or 3 minutes. Remove meat and make up:
Barbecue Sauce *(see p. 77)*
Along with the onion in the sauce, you may sauté other vegetables, such as:
½ cup chopped carrot, eggplant, or **summer squash**
Cover and simmer meat in sauce or bake at 300°F for about 2 to 3 hours, until meat is tender. If pork is used and the sauce tastes and looks too fat, remove it and skim off fat; return to pan and reheat. Serve spareribs with noodles or rice.

Pan-Fried Liver

Dredge calf, baby beef, or chicken liver in flour and shake off excess. Cut into serving-sized portions; separate joined chicken livers.

Heat in a heavy iron skillet:
4 Tbsp bacon fat or **sesame oil**
When the fat crackles, add the liver. Cook until brown on one side; turn and brown. To see if livers are done, slice into them with fork and paring knife. Thin cuts cook faster; remove as done and serve dinner at once.

STRETCHING MEAT

We eat meat for two basic reasons: it tastes good and it provides lots of protein. Other foods also contain protein, however, and cost less than meat. It is also better for our health to include a variety of foods in our diet than to eat a large portion of meat daily. *(To find out more about protein, see pp. 85–88.)*

Recipes in this short section combine meats with other foods to "stretch" the meat. Other recipes which can include smaller amounts of meat are:
    Pasta e Fagioli *(p. 90)*
    Dragon Beans *(p. 92)*
    Lasagne *(p. 95)*
    Calzones *(p. 107)*
    Pizza *(p. 104)*
    Enchiladas *(p. 105)*

Noodles Nonnioff

Back in the days when I was going to college in Vermont, my friend Nonny used to cook this stuff up by the gallon, to feed to the starving thousands. It was sublime.

Boil a large pot of:
noodles (1 lb or so)
Heat a heavy skillet and sauté until soft:
1 large, chopped onion
Crumble in and stir until gray:
1 lb ground hamburger
Add:
2 cups or more sour cream
Keep just warm but don't let it boil, for about 10 minutes, or until noodles are done. Add:
¼ cup wine or **sherry** (any kind — the better it is, the better it will taste)
Drain noodles. Serve meat over noodles, immediately.

SERVES 4

Pat Nixon's Hot Tamale Pie

This recipe was contributed to a cookbook published by The Daughters of Job (Iyob Filiae) of Grand Junction, Colorado, in 1957, by Pat Nixon, wife of then–Vice President, Richard Nixon. My friend's mother, who bought the cookbook, my friend, and I have based countless variations on it ever since. It is great stuff.

Just for posterity, I have put all the variations in **bold italics,** so that Pat's original recipe is recognizable. I make it with hot Italian sausages, removing the casings and crumbling the meat with chopped onions and garlic before cooking.

We have found it best to make and cool the cornmeal hours in advance; otherwise the crust tends to run into the filling.

Cornmeal Crust: Measure out and have ready:
3 cups cold water
In a medium-sized saucepan, mix and heat, stirring constantly:
1 cup cold water
1 cup cornmeal
1 tsp salt
As the cornmeal thickens, turn down the heat and add the 3 cups of water gradually as you stir. The idea is to keep it from lumping. When the water is all in and the mixture is smooth and creamy, allow it to cook with the lid off for at least ½ hour.

Meat Filling: Sauté in a cast-iron skillet:
2 Tbsp fat or *oil*
1 chopped onion
2 pimientos or *green peppers*
2 cups chopped beef, pork, or *turkey*
2 cloves crushed garlic
1 Tbsp mild, dark chili powder
1 tsp ground cumin
1 tsp oregano
Stir and cook over moderate heat for 5 minutes. Then add:
2 cups chopped, fresh, or **canned tomatoes**

salt and pepper to taste
Let this simmer, covered, for at least 10 minutes.

Now line an oiled casserole with thick, cool, corn mush, reserving ⅓ of the corn mush for the topping. Fill the center with meat filling. Cover top with flattened patties of mush. Garnish with:
6 ripe olives
Bake at 350°F for 45 minutes.

Variation
Corn-bean filling: Sauté in a heavy skillet:
2 Tbsp safflower oil
2 chopped onions
1 large, sliced green pepper
1 tsp ground cumin
1 tsp oregano
1 Tbsp mild chili powder
When the onions are limp, but not yet brown, add:
2 cups chopped, fresh, or **canned tomatoes**
2 cups whole, cooked kidney beans
  (see p. 89)
1 cup fresh, canned, or **frozen corn**
Let this simmer, covered, for at least 10 minutes. Assemble as above.

SERVES 4 TO 6

Moussaka

An ancient Balkan recipe, thought to be divine in origin, in which layers of eggplant and stuffing are topped by a thick layer of cheese pudding. A moussaka is baked, chilled, and then reheated: the original party food. Janey Stone, when she sent me this recipe, said to credit James d'Entremont.

Meat-onion filling: Sauté:
2 Tbsp olive oil
1 cup ground meat (lamb is traditional)
1 large, chopped onion
Remove from heat and add:
1 cup red wine
1 Tbsp tomato paste
¼ cup finely chopped parsley
bare pinch of cinnamon
grated pepper
Place over low heat and simmer until the wine is taken up (about 10 minutes).

Eggplant: Slice thinly:
1 medium-sized eggplant
Dry pieces, if necessary, with a towel and sauté them in olive oil.

Cheese sauce: Melt in a separate pan:
2 Tbsp butter
Blend in:
1½ Tbsp white flour
Add and stir until the mixture thickens:
1 cup warm milk
Cool somewhat before adding:
1 beaten egg
½ cup ricotta, cottage cheese or **crumbled feta**
a grating of nutmeg (if all you have is pre-ground nutmeg, use about ¼ of a pinch)
You will also need:
½ cup whole wheat bread crumbs
4 Tbsp Parmesan cheese
Grease a loaf pan. Lay in an overlapping layer of eggplant, then a layer of meat-onion filling, then a sprinkling of bread crumbs and Parmesan. Repeat until these ingredients are all in the pan. Then top with cheese sauce. You may decorate the top with:
black olives
Bake 1 hour at 350°F. Cool, then cover top before refrigerating. To reheat, bake 1 hour at 350°F. Moussaka is also delicious cold.

SERVES 4 TO 6

Meatball Mix

This is a mixture of bread crumbs, eggs, and flavorful ingredients that transforms ho-hum hamburger into delicious stuff. It can be used to make meatballs, meat loaf, stuffing for cabbage rolls — whatever use you have for hamburger. The mixture may also be added to crumbled tofu *(see p. 103)*, cottage cheese curds, or mashed cooked beans, to make meatlike balls or patties.

Whole wheat bread crumbs are an essential ingredient in this mixture.

Beat in a mixing bowl:
2 eggs
Add and crush in:
1 cup whole wheat bread crumbs
When the bread is moistened, add and mix in thoroughly:
3 Tbsp ketchup
1 tsp tamari soy sauce
½ tsp salt
3 Tbsp finely chopped parsley
freshly grated pepper
3 Tbsp minced onion
2 cups ground meat
Mix and shape firmly into balls, burgers, or a loaf. A shaped loaf can be decorated with lines of ketchup, bits of green pepper, or sliced mushrooms.

Bake meatloaf at 350°F for 45 to 60 minutes.

SERVES 4 TO 6

To make hamburgers: Shape the ground meat mixture into firm patties, about 3 inches in diameter and 1 inch thick. Sauté them over medium heat 5 minutes on one side and 3 minutes on the other. Serve hot.

To make meatballs: Shape the ground meat mixture into balls about 1 inch in diameter. Sauté them over medium heat 3 minutes; then turn them or shake the pan to roll them around and evenly sauté the other sides. Reduce heat and cook 3 to 5

minutes before serving or adding to a sauce. Meatballs may be kept warm in a low 200°F oven or in a covered warm pan, up to 1 hour.

Sweet-and-Sour Stir-Fry

One year I planted a crab apple tree and now, every fall, I have these little round red crab apples hanging around my kitchen. Eventually I make them into jelly, but from time to time they wind up in mixtures like this, providing a tart counterpoint in a pork stir-fry.

Dice:
½ lb pork
Marinate in Tamari Marinade *(see p. 84)* for 30 minutes.

Half an hour before dinner, cut into discs:
2 carrots
1 kohlrabi or **½ turnip**
1 onion or **5 green onions**
2 stalks celery
Quarter and cut out the cores of:
5 crab apples
Heat in a heavy wok or frying pan:
3 Tbsp sesame oil
Stir-fry the vegetables, starting with the carrots and kohlrabi and ending with the crab apples. Then add and brown meat on all sides, along with:
2 Tbsp sesame seeds
Pour in the leftover marinade liquid, and clap a lid on the pan to steam the contents for 5 minutes.

Meanwhile, mix:
2 Tbsp cornstarch
3 Tbsp water
2 Tbsp brown sugar
1 Tbsp cider vinegar
Mix just before pouring into the pan. Stir as mixture thickens; add water as needed to make the sauce smooth. Serve with rice.

SERVES 4

Cabbage Rolls

One afternoon I walked into the Ryans' kitchen, next door to our home on Boulardarie Island in Cape Breton, and found myself in a cabbage roll factory. Peggy and her two youngest daughters were boiling, stuffing, and freezing cabbage rolls by the dozen. It was a practical idea; the cabbages, freshly harvested, were flexible and tasty; the stuffing and sauce was made en masse, and the pans of finished rolls were available in the freezer for special meals and potluck suppers all winter.

You can be flexible about the stuffing; it might contain ground meat, crumbled sausage, grain, tofu, or bread crumbs. It can be flavored with curry, hot chili, oregano, sage, rosemary, or thyme. The sauce, too, can be varied; you might use White Sauce *(see p. 79)* or Spaghetti Sauce *(see p. 75)*.

Break off and steam in a covered pan over boiling water for 5 minutes:
10 to 12 well-shaped cabbage leaves
Set these aside to cool while you mix up:
1 cup cooked rice
1 cup ground beef
½ cup minced onion
4 Tbsp minced parsley
1 tsp dried savory
1 beaten egg

To assemble the rolls, lay a cabbage leaf on the counter, rib-side out, and put 2 or 3 tablespoons of filling into it. Fold in the sides of the leaf, then roll it up as pictured. If the central ribs are too stiff to roll, trim them so they aren't so thick. Place cabbage rolls in a 9 x 9-inch pan, seam-side down.

When the pan is full, pour over the rolls:
2 cups fresh Tomato Sauce *(see p. 75)*
Top with:
¼ cup grated Parmesan cheese
  (or other cheese)
Bake at 350°F for 40 minutes. If you are going to freeze them, as Peggy does, don't bake them until you take them out of the freezer.

SERVES 4 TO 6

Old-Fashioned Sausage Dinner

This is a very satisfying, down-home dinner. There are now turkey meat sausages available for those who don't want to eat pork. If you sauté sausage for 20 minutes in a frying pan, you will fill up the house with smoke in spite of watching them. Instead, boil them with potatoes, then brown them briefly.

Peel, if necessary, and chop so they are roughly the same size:
4 large potatoes
Put them in a good-sized saucepan, along with:
1 cup water
6 to 8 sausages
Cover tightly and boil for 20 minutes. Remove sausage, drain, and put into a lightly oiled frying pan. Sauté 3 minutes on each side.
Meanwhile, remove potatoes from the water and keep warm. Add:
4 wedges of cabbage
and boil for 10 minutes. Drain and serve with sausages and potatoes.

SERVES 4

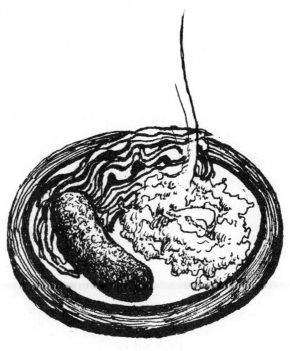

Grains, Nuts & Seeds

GRAINS

A field of ripe grain is very impressive to the eye; it almost sings as the wind moves across it. It holds the seeds of promise, of fulfillment and harvest, of survival and rebirth. An Austrian friend described, one night, the process of mowing and harvesting and threshing the grain by hand at times in his youth when the machines (like all machines) broke down, and they all pitched in to get it done.

"It was awful hard work," he said. "At the end of the day, you had chaff in your hair and dust in every pore of your body; our faces were black with it, our arms ached, we longed only for bed. But I tell you, when you look at a big pile of grain on the threshing floor, you really feel rich; and there is nothing like it — no money or anything money can buy compares with it."

I can see how that is. Grain is at the very base of our food chain, the broad bottom of the pyramid. Most of what you eat in a day comes from grain. Well, cereal, you say. That's grain. Sure, and so is bread, and muffins, pie, and cake; so are noodles, and so is beer and even crackers. No dairy, poultry, or meat products would be possible without grain. In fact, grain is at the source of almost everything you eat, except fruits and vegetables.

Food Value in Grains

Grains provide three general categories of important food value: protein, vitamins, and roughage. These values are not highly concentrated, as they are in some special foods such as liver or brewer's yeast. On the other hand, most people don't want to eat liver every day, or make up special concoctions of brewer's yeast and wheat germ. Most people don't even need to do that anyway, unless they have a particular vitamin deficiency. It is easy enough to keep a steady flow of the nutrients you normally need by cooking and eating with whole grains every day.

The protein in grains: All grains have a certain amount of protein; it varies a little with the type of grain and the richness of the soil it grew in, but in general it is about 9 to 15 grams per cup of cooked grain. (Or, about 5 to 10 grams to a cup of whole grain flour; that is because there is more air in flour than in unground grain, not because it has less protein.)

The vitamins in grains: All whole grains provide well-rounded amounts of vitamins A, E, and the dozen or so substances spoken of as the B-vitamin complex. They also contain the oils and minerals needed by your body for various purposes, including that of absorbing the vitamins they have. These vitamins, minerals, and so forth are subtle things. You would not notice the lack of them overnight; rather, you would "wonder where some people get all the energy" or feel tired and stiff after an ordinary day's work; you'd take naps, not think too hard, wouldn't be much interested in sex, and feel in general as though you were getting old. Many people do lack these nutrients because they are mostly concentrated in the germ of the grain, which is sifted out of refined grain products. "Enriched" cereals and flours replace only tiny amounts of some of the vitamins, which is of little use; the reason they are called the B complex is that they operate together. If you lack one, you lack all the others; if you're low in one, you're low in all.

Other than grains, there are very few sources of this B-vitamin complex in the average human diet. You can get them from pills, or shots, but you might not be able to absorb them unless you balance them with other B vitamins, and have some oil at the same time, and so forth; body chemistry is a complicated business, and I think it is better not to spend your time worrying about levels of this and that, as if your body were a test tube. If you stick with whole grains, you won't have to.

Roughage in grains: In every kernel of whole grain, there are there parts: the germ, the starch, and the bran. The germ, the innermost part, we know to be full of vitamins and oils; the starch around it contains much protein. The outer bran has little nutrition. It is mostly used as "roughage"; it goes right through the system and, together with other solids, passes out.

For a long time, nobody thought this was very important. Now, however, it appears that people who lack roughage because of eating refined-grain products instead of whole-grain products have a much higher incidence of bowel troubles. The solids from other foods, such as meat, or milk products, or even vegetables and fruits, don't form as substantial a bulk in the intestines. Sometimes they linger there, too hard or too pasty a substance to be passed. After a day or two this becomes very uncomfortable. The repeated strain of trying to eliminate, however, will eventually lead to hemorrhoids. Sometimes infections can occur from these problems; and continual intestinal difficulties often lead to more serious illness, even cancer of the bowel, which is virtually unknown in parts of the world where grains are eaten whole, and where roughage from the bran is a part of the daily diet.

So bran, and other grain roughage, is not unimportant at all. They have always been a part of the human diet, and should be still.

WHEAT

Long ago, most people harvested their own wheat, and took it, every fall, to the miller, who ground it up for them with two huge millstones driven by water or other power. Time went by, technology proliferated, and people gravitated to the cities. Flour was grown and ground on a more massive scale. Roller mills, which were developed during the first part of the nineteenth century, came into wide use. When wheat is ground by this process, the germ and bran are flattened rather than chopped into particles, making it easy to sift them out. Because wheat germ spoils rapidly due to its oil content, it was to the advantage of the milling companies to sift it out along with the bran, and market only the fine white starch, which, having all the gluten necessary for making breads or thickening sauces, was acceptable to most people. Moreover, it resembled the fine white flours that had heretofore been available only to the very wealthy. White flour became a status symbol and, finally, a common commodity. Wheat germ and bran were fed to pigs and other animals.

Eventually, however, it began to be evident that people who ate white-flour products exclusively lacked the elements in their diets once supplied by the germ of the wheat. During World War II, widespread vitamin deficiencies caused the British government to enforce "enrichment" of flours by adding synthetic vitamins. The development of enriched bread, with wheat germ put back in, was due to this recognition of the need for vitamins in the daily diet. Eventually American flour producers followed suit and started to advertise "enriched flour." They also put on the market "bran" or "graham" flour, with the bran put back in; but no commercial American flour is sold with wheat germ put back in, because it will spoil easily unless kept refrigerated or frozen.

Food Value in Wheat

What, exactly, are the beneficial results of wheat germ? And is there anything for you in the bran? These questions are easy to evade because the results of vitamin deficiencies aren't rapidly evident or uniform; that is, you don't feel them overnight, or in a week, and not everybody feels them in the same way. It has been shown over the years, however, that people who eat whole grains and whole-grain products do not contract the same illnesses in their later years as do people who eat white-flour products. Heart disease, for one, is almost unknown in cultures where vitamins B and E (such as whole grains have) are present in large quantities in the daily diet. The oil that spoils so rapidly in wheat germ also contains some lecithin, thought to be the element needed to break down cholesterol in the bloodstream. And good old bran has now come into the forefront as supplying the crude fiber needed to keep the bowels healthy and functioning regularly.

So, while it is true that white flour isn't, really, in itself "bad for you," it's missing some essential elements. You need what it has, so why bother with the other stuff? It is true that white flour does make some foods (to which we have become accustomed) easier to make and to store. Bread made with white flour and chemical preservatives keeps practically forever. Bread made with whole wheat keeps only for a week; therefore you must make it yourself, freeze it, or pay a high price for it. Piecrust and some breads and cakes are hard to make with hard whole wheat flour. They can be made with soft flours, but it is not as easy to find soft whole wheat flour, and it has to be kept refrigerated.

Of course, in the end whole wheat costs less, when you consider the cost of hospital bills, vitamin pills, and so forth. Besides, the more people demand whole-grain flours and products, the more facilities will be built to handle them. Whole wheat flour will never be as cheap as white flour is but it's a far more valuable product.

Steamed Cracked Wheat

To Steam: In a deep, heavy pot, bring to a boil:

2 cups water

Add slowly, stirring:

1 cup cracked wheat

½ tsp salt

Cover closely, lower heat, and simmer 20 minutes. Remove from heat. You may stir cracked wheat during cooking to be sure the bottom does not scorch.

Variations

To Sauté and Steam: In a deep, heavy pot, heat:

2 Tbsp light oil

Add and cook over moderate heat, stirring, for about 5 minutes:

1 cup cracked wheat

Let the pan cool for a minute, then add:

2 cups boiling water

½ tsp salt

Cover closely, lower heat, and simmer 15 to 20 minutes.

Roasted Whole Wheat: Freshly roasted grain has a flavor like no other. Very popular with the highchair set.

Roast over medium heat in a cast-iron frying pan:

1 cup whole wheat berries

Stir the wheat as it roasts for 5 to 7 minutes. When a rich, nutty smell fills the kitchen, remove from heat. Grind at a loose setting twice in a Corona mill or buzz in the blender until the pieces are about the size of ground cornmeal.

Place in a small saucepan and add:

2 cups boiling water

½ tsp salt (optional)

Bring to a boil, cover, and simmer for 20 to 30 minutes. Allow to cool slightly before serving.

Steamed Whole Wheat

Cooked whole wheat berries are very chewy; that can get to be a bore if you serve too big a plateful at once. Stick to small quantities and serve with a good sauce — say, cheese or miso, or as a nutritious breakfast treat, with honey and milk.

Combine:

1 cup whole wheat berries

2 cups water

½ tsp salt

Cover tightly and cook 30 minutes.

Variations

Add along with the salt:

1 Tbsp tamari soy sauce

Use leftover whole wheat berries in bread (¼ to ½ cup per loaf) — especially a dense loaf with rye flour in it.

Add whole wheat berries to meatloaf. Some people like them in egg dishes.

My kids like them for breakfast, with milk, blueberries, and honey.

BULGUR

The great advantage of bulgur (as compared to whole wheat) is that it can be cooked more rapidly. A little of it goes a long way. It is very loose and dry, so it combines well with rice.

To Make Bulgur

Put in a colander, and submerge in a large bowl of water:

2 to 4 cups whole wheat berries

Rub the wheat between your hands until the water is cloudy. Discard the water and fill the bowl again; wash 3 or 4 times. Then put the wheat in a pot with water to cover. Bring to a boil; simmer for about 30 minutes, or until the water is absorbed and the wheat is soft.

Spread the wheat by handfuls on a cookie sheet, one kernel deep, and roast it in a very slow oven (150° to 200°F) for about an hour. Sometimes it takes an hour and a half. I test it by taste; when it's no longer the slightest bit squishy, it's done.

Put it through a grain grinder, adjusting so it comes out in chunks too small to be recognizable as wheat berries and too large to be flour.

Store bulgur in a closed jar, in a cool, dark place.

Steamed Bulgur

To Steam: In a deep, heavy pot, bring to a boil:

2 cups water

Add:

1 cup bulgur
½ tsp salt

Cover closely, move to lower heat, and simmer 20 minutes. Remove from heat.

To Sauté and Steam: In a deep, heavy pot, heat:

2 Tbsp light oil

Add and cook over high heat, stirring, for about 5 minutes:

1 cup bulgur

Let the pan cool for a minute, then add:

2 cups boiling water
½ tsp salt

Cover closely, lower heat, and simmer 15 to 20 minutes. Remove from heat.

Other Uses for Wheat

See Simmered Grains *(p. 172)*, wheat in bread *(p. 183)* and quickbreads. Wheat is also the chief ingredient in pasta *(p. 94)*.

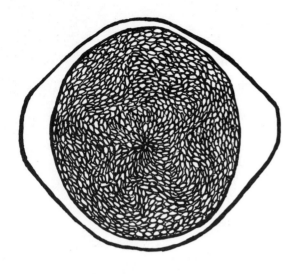

RICE

Rice is the staple food for nearly seventy-five percent of the world. It grows well in so many places, and is easy to prepare for people who have limited tools and fuel supply. Rice is delicious, easy to digest, and in its natural form (brown rice) has an abundance of B vitamins.

In the nineteenth century, it became the vogue to "polish" the outer bran off rice kernels. Whether it was done in order to make the rice less sticky, or to cut down the cooking time from 45 to 12 minutes, one result was massive, grim epidemics of beri-beri, all over the Far East.

Nothing then was known about vitamins, and it was not until 1911 that a Polish scientist named Kasimir Funk discovered that there are, after all, substances that the human body cannot do without; he named them *vitamines,* and advised against polishing rice. The beri-beri subsided. Not all the effects of B-vitamin deficiency are as dramatic as beri-beri, however, and today many Americans suffer from ailments directly traceable to their B vitamin shortage: difficulty in digesting food, short tempers, and general fatigue.

TYPES OF BROWN RICE

Short-Grain Brown Rice: A good deal of this is grown in California. This rice is full and fat and noticeably browner than other types of rice. When steamed, it has the most flavor and nutrition of any type of rice, and is also slightly sticky.

Medium and Long-Grain Brown Rice: These are grown in California, Louisiana, and Texas. Long-grain rice is lighter colored, ranging from pale tan to off-white; the grains are thinner and, when cooked, less sticky than short-grain rice.

Sweet Rice: This is grown in California or imported from Japan, where it is popular. It is a tan or greenish, round grain, and when cooked, is very sticky and glutinous. It is used for sushi, breakfast cereal, and desserts such as rice pudding, or pounded to make rice cakes.

Steaming Brown Rice

One of the most important things to have in the kitchen is a good rice-cooking pot. To cook rice well it is necessary to surround each grain of rice in the pot with water or steam for at least 45 minutes. In order to do this, you must use a pot that holds steam. That means a tight lid as, for example, a pressure cooker (you don't have to use the pressure). My Dutch oven isn't tight enough; steam leaks out, and the top grains stay dry. Your pot must also be heavy, so the rice doesn't scorch on the bottom. The outer layers of rice grains are very starchy. If you stir the rice while it is cooking, you will loosen the starch and make the rice gummy. Some cooking methods call for washing the rice first; you can do this, but it will cost you a few vitamins in the outer layers. In any case, it should not be stirred after water is added. If you want to peek at the bottom and see whether all the water has been absorbed, a quick poke with a small spoon will suffice.

Another way to see if the rice is done is to taste a few grains on top.

Brown rice takes about 45 minutes to steam. However, if you roast or fry the grains first, they will take slightly less time to cook.

After the rice is cooked, it is best to let it rest for 15 minutes, in the pot with the lid on, but off the heat. This will help finish the rice and let each grain "set" before you serve it.

Salting the Rice: Some people cook rice without salt, but they serve it with soy sauce, which is very salty. Others use as little as possible: about ¼ teaspoon per 1 cup of dry uncooked rice. Americans, accustomed to much salt in their cooking, tend more toward 1 teaspoon per cup. I like it in the middle: ½ teaspoon per cup. You should not take salt for granted; find your own level.

Proportions of Water to Rice: Each crop of rice is a little different. Some batches of brown rice take 2 cups of water per 1 cup of rice; others, 2½ cups water.

Brown Rice

This method of cooking brings out the most natural flavor of the rice. It is a very good way to cook short-grain brown rice, or sweet rice; very chewy and delicious.

Bring to a boil, in a deep, heavy, 1-quart pot:

2 cups water
½ tsp salt (optional)
Add gradually:
1 cup brown rice
Boil for 1 minute. Cover the pan closely and turn down to simmer. In 5 minutes, check to make sure it's not boiling furiously. Cover again; cook 40 minutes. To see whether it is done, taste a top grain,

then poke lightly at the bottom with a spoon. When the water is absorbed, remove rice from heat; let it sit 15 minutes, with the lid on.

SERVES 2 OR 3

Variations
Flavoring Rice: If you wish to add herbs, fresh or dried, chop or crumble them into the water before cooking the rice. Use parsley, thyme, chives, saffron, or a tablespoon of Pesto *(see p. 83).*

On the other hand, if you are adding spices such as curry, cumin, coriander, or turmeric, they will generate more flavor if you toss them in after cooking and let the pot sit for 15 minutes.

Roasted Brown Rice

If the kernels of rice are roasted or fried before steaming, the texture and flavor is completely changed. The grains will be both fluffier and firmer; the taste will be nutty.

Put in a deep, heavy pot:
1 cup brown rice
Place over medium heat, shaking the pan lightly now and then to keep the rice from burning. A pleasant nutty smell floats up, full of promises; the rice turns yellowish brown. Let the pan cool, so there won't be a volcano, and add:
2 cups water
½ tsp salt
Cover closely and simmer gently 35 to 40 minutes.

Almond Pilaf

This is a good fresh vegetarian meal. Rice and fresh peas are often served as a main dish in India. Almonds add flavor and texture, and also increase the protein by complementing the rice and peas *(see pp. 85–89)*. If you've never tried freshly fried almonds, you're in for a treat. Be careful not to overcook or burn them.

Roast and set to boil *(see p. 163)*:
2 cups brown rice
While the rice is cooking, chop up:
1 onion
1 green pepper (optional)
1 stalk celery
Allow about:
1 Tbsp almonds per serving
Leave them whole or crush them (we leave some whole, crush some) with a pestle, rolling pin, blender or food processor. Whatever you do, don't grind them too fine. When the rice is done, steam:
1 cup peas *(see p. 32)*
In a heavy skillet, heat:
1 Tbsp cooking oil
Add the onion, pepper, and celery and sauté 3 minutes. When they are almost done, add the almonds.

Sauté 1 minute, then remove from heat. Mix rice and peas; top each serving with the almond-vegetable sauté.

SERVES 4

Variations
Add any or all of the following:
2 tsp curry
⅓ cup dried currants
½ cup sautéed mushrooms

Spanish Rice

Spanish rice is made by flavoring steamed rice with tomatoes and bacon or ham fat.

Bring to a boil in a deep, heavy, 2-quart pot:
4 cups water
1 tsp salt (optional)
Add gradually:
2 cups brown rice
Boil for 1 minute. Cover pan and turn down to simmer. Cook 45 minutes without removing lid or stirring the rice. Remove from heat. While rice is cooking, sauté over medium heat or broil:
6 to 8 strips bacon or **4 pieces fatty ham**
Drain the fat as it heats, reserving it to sauté:
1 chopped onion
1 chopped green pepper
1 chopped stalk celery
After 5 minutes, add:
1 cup tomato sauce or **½ cup stewed tomatoes and ½ cup tomato paste**
1 tsp basil
Simmer until the rice is done; you may add to it bits of seafood or ham. Mix rice and sauce lightly. Some people think you should crumble bacon in (in memory of days when bacon was thicker), but thinly sliced bacon just gets lost; serve it separately, crisp.

SERVES 4

Wild Rice

Wild rice, a staple for Native Americans who live near the shallow northern lakes, was traditionally gathered by shaking the full heads of grain into canoes. It's actually a grass, not a rice, and should be washed and soaked before cooking to soften the kernels. Wild rice is fairly expensive, but can be combined with brown rice to make a festive dish for a special occasion.

Pour into a bowl or pan:
1 cup wild rice
Cover with cold water. Remove any bits that float to the surface; drain the rice, then cover with boiling water and allow to sit for 30 minutes. Drain and rinse in cold water again. Then put the rice in a 1-quart saucepan with a good tight lid, and add:
1 cup brown rice
1 tsp salt
4 cups boiling water
Bring to a boil, cover, reduce heat, and simmer for 45 minutes, or until all the liquid is absorbed. Meanwhile, sauté:
3 Tbsp butter
½ cup chopped onion or **scallions**
½ cup sliced mushrooms
Serve the rice with the vegetable garnish on top.

Other Uses for Rice
Minestrone Soup *(p. 20)*, Cabbage Rolls *(p. 154)*, Stuffed Zucchini *(p. 39)*, Chicken Pilaf *(p. 138)*

Rice Mirepoix

Heat in a deep, heavy pot:
2 Tbsp vegetable oil
Add and stir:
1 cup brown rice
After 5 or 10 minutes of cooking and stirring, let the pot cool, then add:
2 cups boiling water
½ tsp salt
You may also add:
1 Tbsp tamari soy sauce
1 cup chopped, sautéed vegetables
  (onions and celery)
Cover tightly and simmer gently for 35 to 40 minutes.

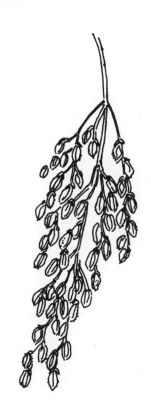

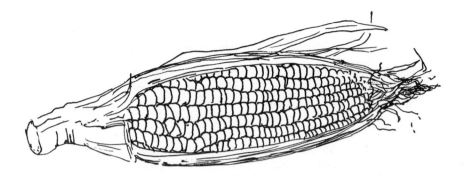

CORN

Corn, the staple grain of the Native Americans, was shared with the first European settlers. It was a long time before these settlers branched out and began growing other kinds of grains, so it's small wonder they had so many recipes for corn, or that many of them are so simple, involving little more than grain, salt, and water.

Fresh corn was then (as it is now) eagerly awaited each year; it was called "green corn" while it was still sweet and tender. But piled in open slatted corncribs, it soon became as hard as nails. It was easy enough to get off the cob, but pretty tough eating. Once it dried, it could be ground up between two rocks but, as any hard-working Native American woman could have testified, it was a slow process, so other means were found to make it palatable.

Milling

Once mills appeared, corn could be ground into coarse meal, or twice ground into a fine powder. Cornmeal can be boiled with water, to make "grits" or "mush." The mush firms as it cools; it can be refried for another meal. Uncooked ground corn can be mixed with salt and water and a little fat, and fried or baked as corn dodgers. If you add milk and eggs you can make cornpone, batter cakes, hush puppies, and Indian pudding. A Southern favorite was spoonbread, an egg-rich corn pudding, served hot and puffy; in the

North they liked to make what they called johnny bread, or journey cake, crisp and thin, for carrying on a day's march.

Corn is still an important staple in Mexican, Central American and South American cooking (*see Masa Harina, p. 167*).

Varieties such as blue-black corn are specially grown for their flavor and color.

Despite the evidence of the hardy folk who have made so much use of it, corn is the least nutritious of all grains, having only slightly more than half the amount of protein in wheat, rye, oats, or rice. It also has fewer minerals and B vitamins, although it does have a substantial amount of vitamin A. Natives and settlers alike depended much more on meat and fish for their protein.

Corn Mush, Polenta, or Grits

Combine in a deep, heavy pot:
4 cups water
1 tsp salt
1 cup coarse cornmeal
Bring to a boil, stirring as it thickens.

When it is completely thick, cover and move to low heat. Simmer 20 minutes.

If you forget to stir, the cornmeal will become lumpy. If this happens, put it through a food mill or a sieve to make it smooth again. Or start over, and this time, stir!

Variations
After cooking polenta, before serving, add:
1 cup grated hard cheese (Parmesan or Cheddar)
Cool and then refrigerate the mush in a greased loaf pan. Slice into thick slabs and fry in olive oil, butter, or bacon fat.
Serve corn mush with poached eggs on top, and ham or sausages on the side.

Cool the cooked corn to a temperature your hand is comfortable in; mix it with 2 or 3 beaten eggs. Bake at 400°F for 30 minutes, until crisp. Serve, if you like, with thick tomato sauce *(see p. 75)*.

Masa Harina

Masa is a fine corn flour, treated with lime-impregnated water to duplicate the traditional corn flour with which much Mexican cooking is done. Masa is what makes cornmeal tortillas hang together, and what gives that distinctive flavor to tamales. To cook with it, mix (as below) with cornmeal and cook as any cornmeal. It will make a finer, smoother, more tasty dish.

If masa is not available in your usual stores, try health food stores.

Masa Tamale Casserole

Mexican dishes tend to build on one another. In this cornmeal casserole, there's an optional cup of Mexican Tomato Sauce *(see p. 77)*. Leftover casserole can be fried, steamed, or made into tamales for days to come. It's also heart-smart and vegetarian.

In a heavy, ovenproof pot, sauté:
2 Tbsp olive oil
1 finely chopped onion
2 cloves crushed garlic
½ cup chopped green pepper
Remove from heat and add:
⅔ cup yellow cornmeal
⅔ cup masa harina
3 cups water
1 cup Mexican Tomato Sauce *(see p. 77)*, **tomato juice,** or **water**
½ tsp salt
1 tsp cumin
1 Tbsp mild chili powder
½ tsp hotter chili (not cayenne)
1 Tbsp oregano
½ tsp cinnamon
½ cup fat black olives (optional)
1 cup fresh, frozen, or **canned corn**
Heat, stirring constantly, until this mixture boils and thickens. Then lower heat or move into the oven and cook at low heat (325°F) for 1 hour.

Garnish with:
grated cheese
additional Mexican Tomato Sauce *(see p. 77)*

Other Uses for Corn
Hoecakes *(p. 194)*, Cornmeal Pancakes *(p. 195)*, Whole Cornbread *(p. 197)*, Enchiladas *(p. 105)*, Indian Pudding *(p. 222)*

OATS

Oats are a plump, pale, delicious, high-protein grain, and they are easy to grow in any northern climate. The only real practical drawback to homegrown oats is that whole oats have a tough husk that doesn't grind up very well, either in the hand-operated mills or in one's mouth. It sort of flattens, like wheat chaff, and then sticks in the throat.

This husk softens easily in water, however, and by a simple method of steaming and flattening we have rolled oats, which are not only palatable and nutritious, but also partly precooked, so that they can be eaten without cooking. Rolled oats can be bought in 50- or 100-pound sacks from bulk health food distributors for very little, and are a good deal no matter how you look at it. You can add milk and a handful of raisins and have very good instant food; or cook them briefly for a quick hot bowl of oatmeal. You can mix rolled oats with a little oil and honey, and toast them in the oven to make your own granola. Or you can bake them into all sorts of oatcakes, bars, cookies, cakes, and breads. The Scots traditionally mixed oats and water with ground or diced meats for a kind of cereal-based sausage; they stuff all sorts of things with this mixture, including a sheep's stomach, their famous haggis. Rolled oats are very easy to grind into a fine, heavy flour, which has many uses. It is much better for dredging meats or vegetables than is whole wheat flour (which tends to be on the gritty side). This flour is good to bake with, too. Being very high in fat, it is terrific for cookies and piecrusts, especially mixed with wheat germ or bran.

Roasted Oat Cereal

Spread on cookie sheets and roast at 150° to 200°F for 30 minutes:
1 cup wheat germ
1 cup chopped walnuts
1 cup coconut
2 cups rolled oats
Mix everything together in a big wide bowl and add:
1 cup chopped, dried apples
1 cup chopped, dried dates
2 Tbsp nutritional brewer's yeast
  (optional)
Mix by hand; store in a glass jar. Serve with milk as instant food.

Familia

If you don't have a grinder, you can leave the rolled oats whole and bash up the nuts with a mortar and pestle, or buzz them in a blender.

Set a grain grinder very loose and put through it:
3 cups rolled oats
1 cup whole unroasted almonds
Put these in a big wide bowl and add:
1 cup rolled oats, unground
½ cup sugar
1 cup currants
1 cup chopped, dried apples
1 cup roasted wheat germ
Mix well with your hands and store in a glass jar. Use as breakfast cereal, uncooked.

Sam Brooks's Granola

Homemade granola is superior to store-bought in the same way as homemade bread. It can reflect your personal tastes or income — and, best of all, it's fresh. I also use it to make granola bars *(see p. 207)*, which everybody loves as a snack.

In a large bowl, pot, or bucket, combine:
8 cups rolled oats
(Sam favors large flakes; I like a combination of large and small, with a cup of rye flakes thrown in)
1 cup sunflower seeds
1 cup chopped nuts (walnuts, almonds, and filberts)
½ to 1 cup coconut
In a small pan, over gentle heat, mix and heat:
¼ cup safflower oil
¾ to 1 cup honey
Pour this mixture in a thin stream over the dry ingredients, and mix everything together with clean hands. Strew the mixture evenly on cookie sheets, about 2 cups per sheet. Bake at 350°F for 10 minutes or until it begins to brown. Remove and cool before adding:
1 to 2 cups dried fruit: raisins, currants, or chopped apricots
Store in an airtight container in a cool place. Serve as cereal, in a bowl with milk, or eat as a snack out of your hand.

Oatmeal

Oatmeal should be firm, not soupy. If you are cooking it quickly, for less than ½ hour, use less water than if cooking for a long time. For breakfast, always have something else with oatmeal; milk is easy, but it could be eggs, or cheese, or meat, or even tamari soy sauce and roasted sunflower seeds; any of those will bring the level of protein in 1 cup of oatmeal up from 9 grams to 12 grams, as well as adding flavor to it.

Quick Oatmeal

Bring to a boil:
3 cups water
¼ tsp salt
Add:
1½ cups small-flake, rolled oats
Reduce to low heat, cover, and cook 10 minutes.

SERVES 2

Roasted Oatmeal

In a heavy iron skillet over good steady heat, put:
2 cups rolled oats
Roast, stirring constantly, for about 5 minutes, until oats begin to smell nutty. Then add:
3½ cups water
Steam 10 minutes. Serve with tamari soy sauce, gomasio *(see p. 175)*, roasted sunflower seeds, and/or butter.

SERVES 2

Other Uses for Oats
Simmered Grains *(p. 172)*, in bread *(p. 178)*, Porridge Bread *(p. 188)*, Oat Raisin Treats *(p. 211)*, Oatmeal Spice Cake *(p. 201)*, Coconut Oatcakes *(p. 209)*, Oaten Cakes *(p. 195)*, Granola Bars *(p. 205)*, Date Bars *(p. 206)*

MILLET

Steamed whole, millet makes a dense, bland grain with a curious crunch. It has more flavor if it is first roasted, dry or in oil. Like buckwheat, it is best when combined with other grains or vegetables. It cooks quickly, in 10 to 15 minutes.

Ground millet is almost exactly like cornmeal and may be used in recipes instead of cornmeal; unlike corn, it is very easy to grind.

Millet is widely grown in Africa and in other areas where the climate is too warm for wheat or rye and too dry for rice. A lot of people depend on it for their daily grain; but among those who have the choice, rice is more popular. Nevertheless, millet is more nutritious than rice, having more amino acids; it's closer to being perfect protein for human consumption than any other grain.

Steamed Millet

Heat a deep, heavy pot and put in:
1 cup millet
Shake the pan a little to roast it evenly for 5 to 10 minutes. Let the pan cool and add:
2 cups water
½ to 1 tsp salt
Cover closely, bring to boil, and simmer for 10 to 15 minutes, until the water is taken up. Shake the pan and let it sit, covered, for 10 minutes.

Variation
Use half buckwheat, half millet; roast and cook as above.

BARLEY

Barley was once a staple in the English, Scottish, and Northern European diet; those old cookbooks are full of recipes for barley stews and puddings and breads. It was easier for the small farmer to grow than wheat. Nowadays, with wheat readily available, few people realize how versatile and useful barley can be in the kitchen.

Barley bought in stores is "pearled," the inedible outer husk being partly or wholly removed. As with most grains, many vitamins are on the outside, so barley that is less rigorously pearled is more nutritious. (You can tell; good barley is brownish, best found in health food stores). Barley is almost as high in protein as wheat, especially if it is grown in rich soil (the best comes from Minnesota and South Dakota).

The two best uses of barley I have found are in breads (ground) and in soups (whole). It makes the bread chewier, denser. In soups, it should be cooked for 3 hours; it is edible in 2, but not nearly so good as after hours and hours of simmering.

RYE

My relationship with rye is ambivalent. Sometimes I use it in cooking binges (usually in the winter) having to do with pickles and herring, sour cream and borscht, black bean soup, slabs of funky cheese, and great crusty loaves of solid, chewy, sour rye bread. Rye speaks to me of troikas, and potato moonshine, and endless snow, the vast steppes shining under the fierce cold stars. Rye tells of a sustenance that goes beyond the moment.

Rye is the wheat of the north, and is in fact very much like wheat, both in the way it's used and the nourishment it gives. As a flour, it grinds up finer than wheat, and thus makes a much denser bread. Rye is harder than wheat: difficult to grind, heavy to knead, and slow to chew. Rye breads are often made with some sourness in them, such as whey, or sourdough yeast, to liven the mouth, and set juices flowing. But rye itself has a special flavor, a tasty tang that curls around the tongue and stays with you. And a loaf of rye bread, being less airy than a loaf of wheat, doesn't dry out as fast. It's better bread for traveling, for keeping.

Rye has other uses: it can be used whole, as cereal; steamed and rolled rye may be eaten like rolled oats, or added to them; rye crackers are terrific. But bread remains the most common use of rye grain, at least around my house.

Soaked Grains

Grains soaked in water until they soften are delicious and very high in vitamins. They become slightly sweet and chewy. You can eat them out of your hand (instant food, good on trips) or add them to potato salad.

Soaking grains is a lot like sprouting them, except it doesn't take as long. Put 1 cup of grain in a wide-mouthed quart jar and fill with water. Different types of grain take different amounts of time to soften:

wheat	2 days
oats	6 hours
barley	4 hours
buckwheat	3 hours

If you decide, after all, to cook them, soaked grains cook up very much faster than raw grains. For example, soaked barley cooks soft in 30 minutes, compared to the 3 hours needed for dry barley.

Overnight Cereals

Whole oats, cracked wheat, cracked rye, ground corn, and samp (a traditional New England mixture of cracked wheat and ground corn) are at their best if simmered, at very low heat, for 6 to 8 hours or overnight. You can do this on a woodstove or in a crockpot. If you are not sure the heat will be slow the whole time, you should do it in the top of a double boiler, over simmering water. It can even be done in a wide-mouthed thermos; good for camping. The hot cereal will be ready for eating just as you stumble down the stairs or ladder buttoning your shirt and on your way out to milk the goats. It's much better than a dry hunk of cold bread for breakfast after milking.

Simmered Grains

Bring to a boil in a deep, heavy pot:

3 cups water
1 tsp salt

Stir in:

1 cup whole oats, ground corn, cracked wheat, or **samp**

Cook rapidly for 15 minutes; then move to a slow spot and let simmer 6 to 8 hours or overnight.

Creamed Cereals

Creamed cereals make good breakfast cereals or baby food; have them with tamari soy sauce and butter instead of milk and sugar. Little kids love soy sauce. You can make up cereal creams every 3 days and store them, refrigerated, for easy instant infant food. For grownups, however, too much rice cream can be constipating.

Rice Cream

Roast light in a dry skillet:

1 cup brown rice or **sweet brown rice** *(see p. 162)*

When golden brown, take off the heat and grind or buzz in the blender to a sort of gritty flour. Put the ground rice in a deep, heavy pot with:

1 cup hot water

stirring as it thickens. Then add:

3 cups hot water
½ tsp salt (optional)

Bring to a boil, stirring from time to time; then cover tightly and simmer on low heat 45 to 60 minutes.

Oat Cream

Bring to a boil:

3 cups water
1 tsp salt

Add and boil 5 minutes:

1 cup rolled oats

Cover tightly and simmer 30 minutes. Put through a food mill.

BUCKWHEAT

Buckwheat, also called kasha or groats, is not a grain nor, as some suppose, a legume. It's a member of the smartweed family, which includes, of all things, burdock and rhubarb. It is high in protein, minerals, and B vitamins like the true whole grains, and it is cooked (more or less) as they are, so we usually think of it as grain. Buckwheat seeds are oddly shaped — little tetrahedrons, like tiny pyramids.

As a plain, steamed grain dish, buckwheat is seldom a popular item. It is better roasted first, either dry or in oil, and better yet combined with yogurt, which somehow changes the dry texture into something quite a lot tastier.

Buckwheat is easy to grind, and makes a very delicious nutty-flavored flour. This flour is a little heavy to use alone but it is good combined with wheat in breads, muffins, and especially pancakes, or good combined with ground or minced meat, in meatballs, meatloaf, and in stuffings for poultry or game. Soaked, uncooked buckwheat is delicious in green salads.

Steamed Buckwheat (Kasha)

Roasting firms the texture, which is otherwise mushy and dry, and brings out the strong, nutty, buckwheat flavor.

In a deep, heavy pot, heat:
3 Tbsp oil
and add:
1 diced onion
1 cup buckwheat
Cook rapidly 5 to 10 minutes, stirring. Cool the pan a bit and add:
2 cups water
½ to 1 tsp salt
Simmer 15 minutes, until dry. Toss in:
½ to 1 cup yogurt
The yogurt disappears; the grain becomes tender and delicious. Serve at once for breakfast, lunch, or dinner with fresh steamed vegetables and omelets.

Variations
Use clear broth (any kind except fish) instead of water.

Mix with cooked millet, or cook millet and buckwheat together.

Mix with cooked rice.

Sauté green pepper, celery, or ground meat along with the onions. After cooking, substitute tomato juice for yogurt.

Other Uses for Buckwheat
Soaked Grains *(p. 171)*, and buckwheat in bread *(p. 178)*

SEEDS AND NUTS

Seeds and nuts are similar to grains in their nutritional value, but their goodness is more concentrated. They're richer food, and we eat them in smaller amounts.

You can buy nuts and seeds shelled or unshelled. Unshelled, they will keep 6 months to a year. With the shells off, however, the high oil content soon causes them to go rancid, unless you keep them (along with your wheat germ) in the freezer.

Different kinds of nuts and seeds have different uses (and prices). Buy a variety and learn to use them in your cooking. They are more fresh and flavorful whole; chop or slice them yourself rather than buying them that way.

Sesame Seeds: Especially good when toasted. Sprinkle them on bread and rolls, or mix in toppings for casseroles. Roasted and coarsely ground with a little salt, they make gomasio, a delicious garnish for rice, fish, and any grain dish *(see p. 175)*.

Sunflower Seeds: These are very high in protein and very inexpensive compared to other seeds and nuts. Dry-roasted or sautéed in oil, they make good nibbling in the afternoon or evening. Add them to granola, or roast them and add to meusli. Or roast and mix them with dried fruits and other nuts for a hiking mix or traveling food; they supply the oil that any survival expert will tell you is hard to forage in the wilds. *(To roast sunflower seeds, see p. 12.)* Raw or roasted, they may also be ground, added to breads, cookies, and cakes, or used as part of the "flour" for whole-grain piecrust. Roasted and coarsely ground, they may be used as a variation on gomasio.

Almonds: Almonds are hard nuts, with a very special flavor that fades soon after shelling. You may slice or grind almonds and use them on cookies, or in meusli; or you can chop and sauté them in a little butter and mix them with green beans or on top of fish.

Brazil Nuts: Large, soft nuts, Brazils are very good in cookies or as topping for yeasted rolls and pastry.

Cashew Nuts: Cashews are a soft, sweet nut, very good raw in a hiker's mix, or roasted as a snack. Sometimes used on yeast rolls.

Filberts or Hazelnuts: Fresh filberts have a wonderful flavor, brought out even more by roasting. Use like almonds: in meusli, granola, or baking.

Pecans: Pecans are ridiculously expensive. Softer than walnuts, with a gentle flavor, they are good raw or baked. Very good in custards, pies, or ice cream.

Walnuts: Walnuts are an old standby in baking, but they aren't as good raw; they have a funny bite unless they are very freshly shelled. Use them in cookies, nut breads, nut loaves, in cakes or on breads. Deep-fried in hot oil for a minute or so, they are terrific.

Peanuts: Peanuts are a great buy, raw or shelled. Roast them for snacks or "pocket food"; make tamari peanuts or even fancy beer nuts. To make peanut butter, roast them 1 hour at 150°F, then grind them and add a little oil. Or you can roast and grind them coarsely, for dessert toppings or as a condiment traditionally served with an Indian curry. Many people cannot easily digest peanuts, some people are severely allergic to them. Always serve them separately, as a snack or optional garnish.

Gomasio

Gomasio, goma shio, or sesame salt, is a garnish of ground sesame seeds and salt, commonly found on the Japanese table; it is served with rice or other bland foods. It tastes a little like peanut butter. Kids love it.

Sesame seeds must be imported, so to us they are expensive — but it's well worth it for gomasio. Since only a few tablespoons are used in a meal, a pound or two of sesame seeds will do my family for a year.

The main trick to gomasio is roasting the seeds without burning them. You can do this in the oven, for 20 to 30 minutes at 275°F. In 45 minutes they will burn, so if you don't use a timer, it's better done in a frying pan, stirring constantly for 10 to 15 minutes over low heat.

In any case, roast:
1½ cups black, brown, or **white sesame seeds**
Add:
1 tsp salt (macrobiotic cooks favor sea salt)
Grind loosely in a blender, grain mill, or with a *suribachi* (a Japanese mortar with a scored surface) and pestle until the seeds are mostly pulverized — leave about ¼ of them whole, so the gomasio is crunchy rather than pasty.

Gomasio loses much of its flavor within a few days, so you shouldn't try to make too much at one time. Store in a tightly lidded jar in a cool place.

Breadmaking

Some of my earliest memories are of my father or mother making bread. Home-made bread leans more to ritual than recipe: first of all, there is the moment when you realize you're almost out of bread, and plan a day to make the next batch. Then there's the mixing, deciding which goodies go in this time: Shall we make raisin bread? Is there a little wheat germ around? How about one loaf mixed with thyme and garlic? Then the kneading; my mother used to put the big enamel baby bathtub with dough in it on the kitchen floor and let us pound and fold it as long as we liked (with clean hands). Even when I don't have children around all the time, I still find kneading a relaxing, therapeutic activity; a combination of meditation and exercise. Finally, the whole house is transformed by the smell of baking bread, and anyone in it suddenly finds some good excuse to hang around the kitchen, waiting for a "test" slice. The big loaves cooling on clean cloths, a lovely sight, and when a neighbor stops by, you give one loaf away because — how can you not? It's such a luxury to have fresh bread — you feel so rich, and yet have spent so little.

EQUIPMENT

Equipment for making bread varies from house to house. You need a very large container. I recommend:

A Heavy Ceramic Bowl: It should be large enough for the dough to double in, and thick enough so that in rising the heat is distributed evenly. The sides should not slope out too much. Metal bowls don't keep the dough as warm. Wooden bowls, alas, eventually crack. For years I used a plastic bucket, but I have to admit that ceramic bowls are infinitely superior.

Cloth: A clean cloth wrung out with warm water covers the bowl during rising so that the dough doesn't get cold and crusty on top from evaporation. Better not use terrycloth; if the dough rises up to touch it and sticks, you will have a tough time washing it off. Use woven cotton instead.

Kneading Surface: Knead your bread on a good, flat board, about 15 x 15 inches square. Open a newspaper under it. Scatter flour on it.

A kneading surface should be low enough to work on without getting tired shoulders. The more you enjoy your work, the more you will knead, and well-kneaded bread is the best, no matter what the recipe.

My counter is too high to knead on comfortably, so I usually do it on the kitchen table. However, using a mat for my knees, I have also been known to do it on the floor, on a board, over a newspaper.

Wooden Spoon: Some people like a rubber spatula for stirring up the first mixture of liquid and special ingredients, because it's very good for scraping down the sides. I prefer a wooden spoon, because I can measure some ingredients with it (yeast, salt) and because it's nicer to look at.

Baking Pans: As long as they're smooth inside and aren't smaller on top than at the bottom, you can use about anything. Bread pans, cookie sheets, casseroles, frying pans, muffin tins, cake pans, pie plates, flower pots — to name a few.

INGREDIENTS

Most of what you do or don't do, and how long it takes, depends on the ingredients of the bread you're making. It is good to understand how they work. The two most essential ingredients are:

Flour and Water: One loaf takes about 1½ cups of water and about 4 cups of flour, give or take a cup. One reason this varies so much is the weather: on damp days, flour will absorb water from the air. Another reason is that the same amount of flour will measure out to more cupfuls if it is freshly ground or sifted than if it is scooped out of a sack, where it has gotten packed down. So you add flour until the texture is right, rather than depending on measurements.

Gluten in Flour: Mature wheat contains a great deal of a substance called gluten. If you put an equal amount of wheat flour and water together and stir, it will look and feel like cereal: grainy and easy to stir. But if you let it soak some hours at 70°F, it begins to soften and turn gluey. You can easily feel the difference. Lift up the spoon in the mixture; great strings of it will trail behind. This is what you want when you make yeast bread. If you leave it to soak overnight at 70°F, even more gluten will be softened, and you will find it hard to lift the spoon at all without bringing the whole mixture along.

Hard winter wheats, such as those grown in southern France and in Deaf Smith County, Texas, are exceptionally high in gluten, and make bread that is tougher and bouncier than bread made with ordinary wheats. Other flours, such as rye, oat flour, or cornmeal, have very little or no gluten at all. However, when combined with a high-gluten flour, you can make marvelously strong but tender breads. Spring wheat is soft, has less gluten than hard wheat, and makes good pastry but poor quality yeasted bread.

Yeast: Yeast is a living organism, and when you buy it, either in dry or block form, it is dormant. It stays alive but asleep until given warm (not hot) liquid, a little something to eat, air to breathe, and a nice temperature in which to grow: 70° to 100°F, or, roughly, skin temperature. It will continue to divide and multiply, turning sugar into alcohol and oxygen into carbon dioxide, until it runs out of food or air, gets too cold, or is killed by a trip to the oven. The alcohol is what smells so divine; the carbon dioxide is what makes the bread rise.

When this carbon dioxide is released into a dough of nonglutinous flour, it doesn't rise much and it makes a dense, crumbly sort of bread — very tasty, but heavy. When it is released into glutinous dough, however, the gluten stretches around the bubbles of gas like little balloons. A lighter, higher bread, not so likely to fall apart, results. This sort of bread is best for making sandwiches.

However, there are many other uses for bread besides sandwiches, and many other sorts of good bread besides yeasted or glutinous bread. You can also make breads by combining different flours with wheat. The wheat will provide the gluten, and the other flours will give your breads texture, variety, and flavor.

Rye Flour: Rye makes a very fine, dense flour. It's hard to grind, and makes the dough harder to knead. I therefore use a

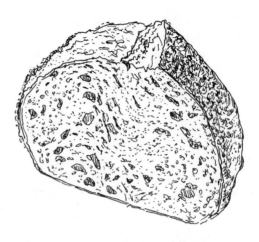

little more yeast in a dough with rye in it, and let it rise longer. The flavor is finer and a little sour or dry compared to wheat flour. Rye goes well with sourdough starter yeast, molasses, and sour milk products such as yogurt or whey. Or you may head in a different direction — with honey, eggs, cardamom, and lemon or orange rind. Rye makes a firmer, denser-textured bread; ¼ to ½ cup per loaf, added to whole wheat bread, makes better sandwich bread than wheat or rye flour alone.

Buckwheat Flour: Buckwheat is a heavy, dense flour, although it's easy to grind. It has a strong nutty flavor, which is even more pronounced when the buckwheat is roasted. A little of it will go a long way; ½ cup per loaf makes fine "buckwheat" bread.

Oats: Oats make a delicious addition to wheat bread. I have not found there to be any difference between using raw rolled oats, cooked oatmeal, and oat flour. Bread with oats in it is tastier, and has a chewier texture than all-wheat bread.

Cornmeal: The addition of cornmeal makes bread crunchier on the outside, crumbly on the inside. It's excellent for rolls or gravy-sopping bread.

Soy Flour: One cup of soy flour to every 8 cups wheat is enough to increase the protein level of your bread by about a third. Soy flour won't add any noticeable taste to your bread, but it does make it somewhat heavier; I usually add an egg and increase the yeast to balance this. Soy flour should be stored frozen or refrigerated; use within a month.

Beans: In the absence of soybeans, you can add almost any kind of ground beans to bread. They will also bring up the protein level, although not as much as soybeans do.

Ground Seeds: Ground seeds, such as pumpkin, sunflower, and sesame, add delicious flavor to bread. They are even tastier if roasted. You need not add much; a few tablespoons per loaf are sufficient. They contain a lot of natural oil, so you should decrease the oil a little in the recipe.

Wheat Germ: Wheat germ, like soy flour, supplies the amino acids missing in wheat flour. Half a cup for every 10 cups of flour will bring up the protein level tremendously. Wheat germ is sweet and light, and does not "weigh down" a loaf. The only thing to watch out for is that it goes rancid easily — so keep it refrigerated or, over longer periods, frozen.

Dried Milk: Dried milk adds crunch to the crust and makes the inner bread lighter and tenderer. It's also good for you, cheap, and easy to keep. Half a cup per loaf, added to the water in the beginning, is a good addition to bread. If you are using non-instant dried milk, though, mix it with an equal amount of flour for easier mixing.

Eggs: Eggs do amazing things to bread; they make the loaves both lighter and stronger. They are very good to add to sandwich breads for this reason. You can use up to 3 eggs per loaf, if you have a surplus. Eggs are traditional in holiday loaves — that sweet, luxurious touch to the otherwise ordinary.

Sweetening: All sweeteners make the yeasts grow faster, since yeast feeds on sugar. Bread can be made without them, however, since grains have natural sugars in them.

My preference in all breads is for molasses, because it has so many minerals and B vitamins, both of which are lacking in white sugar and are much less concentrated in honey and maple syrup. Besides, we like molasses — it tastes good.

Shortening: You can make bread with no fats at all (such as French bread). It will taste great for a day, good for two days, but it gets pretty dry by the end of the week. You may use solid shortening or vegetable oil. The difference is not noticeable. I like to use unrefined cold-pressed safflower oil, because it assures me of getting some of it in our diets every day.

Lecithin: A very thick, golden, viscous substance derived from soybean oil, good for the body because it helps break down hydrogenated fats. Lecithin also helps bind bread together, even in very small amounts. Used particularly in dark rye.

How Long Does It Take?

In general, plan to bake bread 4 to 6 hours after you start it. Much of that is rising time, but plan to spend ½ hour or so vigorously kneading, and to keep an eye on it throughout the process.

Proofing Yeast: The first step is to mix yeast with tepid water (not cold, not hot) and a bit of sweetening for the yeast to eat. Yeast doesn't wake up immediately, but in about 10 minutes it should be noticeably foamy. If not, your yeast may be dead, due to old age or too much heat. Throw it out and get new yeast, which "proofs" successfully. *(See pp. 67 and 178 for more about yeast.)*

Mixing Other Ingredients: Mix all the other ingredients before adding the proofed yeast. If the shortening is solid, melt to liquefy it. You should end up with a mixture that is between 70° and 100°F, so that when you add the yeast, it goes on growing.

Making a Sponge: The flour you use in whole-grain breads will become stretchier if it's softened. To do this, combine all ingredients except ⅓ of the flour. Mix well, cover, and let sit in a designated "warm spot" for an hour or two. The dough will foam up. When you stir it down, you will notice the activated gluten following the spoon in long wet strands.

Adding Flour: As you add the last of the flour, the bread dough becomes stiffer. At first you add it by cupfuls, then half-cupfuls, and then by handfuls. I like to work out of an open can of flour, set by the board on the newspaper. After each addition, mix flour in thoroughly, at first by stirring with a wooden spoon, then by folding and kneading the dough on the board.

KNEADING

The purpose of kneading bread is twofold: (1) to mix in more flour than is humanly possible with a spoon; (2) to stretch the gluten in the flour so that, when the yeast releases carbon dioxide into the dough, tiny bubbles will form, with the softened gluten around them like little balloons.

At least 15 minutes of kneading the finished dough will always give you a better bread. You may find it easier to knead bread dough in divided batches. I find 4 loaves at once to be hard work, and any more seems impossible.

You should knead on a smooth, lightly floured surface. From time to time wipe the surface with more flour. Keep a pile of it handy in one corner to keep your hands dry too.

When you first turn the dough out, it will be very sticky. Keep the surface lightly floured; pat and fold, rather than digging in. Gradually, it will become more workable, and you will become more vigorous. The idea is to keep stretching it, so work it out into a flattened round, using the heels of your hands. As you do so, you may find the middle is still a little sticky, so powder it evenly with a little flour, spread it around, and then fold the dough.

Give it a half-turn on the board and begin again. Continue around and around for about 15 minutes. Take your time, and when the dough doesn't seem sticky, don't add any more flour, but keep kneading for a while. You can't knead bread too much, or too vigorously. (Kids love kneading — they can punch it, slap it, pound it.)

White-bread recipes say to stop when the dough is smooth and glossy. But whole wheat bread, or other whole-grain breads, will not have a glossy dough, especially if the flour is home-ground in a small mill. Well-kneaded whole-grain dough will hold its shape in a rounded mound, and should be evenly textured throughout. Dough with a large proportion of rye should still be slightly sticky when done; too much rye flour will make the bread heavy.

Letting the Dough Rise

A steep-sided ceramic bowl is best for rising dough. It distributes heat evenly and keeps warmth in, too. Whole-grain dough needs the sides of the bowl to "climb" on, so don't grease the bowl. Sometimes people grease the top of the dough lightly, to keep it from drying out and forming a crust, but I find that if you cover the bowl with a damp tea towel, large enough to fold the edges under the bowl, it isn't necessary to do anything else. The tea towel helps keep warmth in, too.

The temperature in a woodstove warming oven is too hot for rising whole-grain bread dough. It is better to raise it more slowly and evenly. Use a thermometer to find a spot that will stay at 80° to 100°F, out of drafts and away from hot spots. Usually these places are high up in the room — on a shelf or fridge. Also, it'll be out of the way of marauding pets and kiddies.

Let the dough rise until it just doubles in size — an hour, usually, unless otherwise indicated in the recipe.

"Knocking Down" Rising Dough

Dough can rise to triple its original size, but it's best to knock it down before that, when it's about doubled. You can just punch it down, if you're in a terrific hurry, but it's better to do it with a little care. Take it out, scraping down the sides of the bowl. Knead it for a minute, carefully flattening all air bubbles, and finally tucking the sides in to the center. Put the dough into the bowl again, tucked-side down. Wet the towel and replace it tightly.

Letting Dough Rest

Bread dough is easier to shape after it has rested. If you knead it, knock it down or cut it into pieces, and you want to roll it out in a long tube or shape it, first let it rest 10 minutes. You'll find it more relaxed.

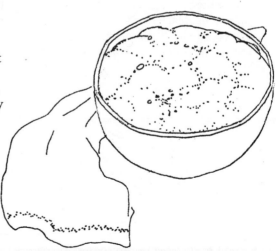

SHAPING LOAVES

To shape any kind of loaf — whether it is to be baked in a pan with high sides or on a flat sheet — don't roll it into a shape. Flatten it slightly, and bring the edges together. Pinch them firmly, without leaving any air holes underneath *(see below)*. Place it on the pan tucked-side down. This stretches the gluten on top of the loaf to form an even crust.

Generally, I weigh out dough, to divide it evenly among pans. I find 2 pounds of dough is the right amount. Unevenly divided, some loaves will be smaller, rise faster, bake quicker — no end of bother.

To form buns and rolls, you may use the same method with smaller pieces. To make bread sticks or fancy rolls, chop pieces of dough the size of your fist and roll them out, slowly, into ropes. These can be baked straight, or wrapped into fancy shapes for supper rolls.

Greasing the Pans

Grease the pans lightly with lard or shortening. Make sure you get every corner. People tell me you can use oil instead, but I never have had any success with it.

BAKING BREAD

It is important to preheat the oven. Bread baked in a rising oven will burn, either on the bottom (in a gas or electric stove) or on top (in a woodstove).

Opening the oven and putting bread in will automatically cool a modern oven. To get around this, preheat the oven to 50° or 100°F higher than the temperature called for, then turn the thermostat down after you put in the bread.

If you continue to have burned bread, try using bricks or tinfoil on the bottom of the oven to deflect the direct heat.

When Bread Is Done

Take a loaf out of the oven and shake it out of the pan. Tap it lightly on the bottom. It should be crisp, light brown, and sound hollow. It shouldn't be soft or shrink slightly.

If it's done, lay it on one side on a rack or tea towel to cool for about 2 hours. Hot bread is hard to slice — except, of course, the heel, which is best hot and stolen.

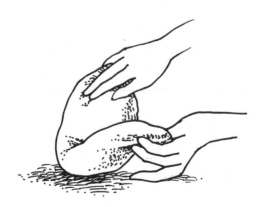

Whole Wheat Bread

This is my basic bread recipe — the one I don't need a recipe to know how to make. It makes 3 loaves of good, firm sandwich-and-toast bread.

In a small bowl, mix:
1 cup water at room temperature
2 Tbsp dried baker's yeast
1 tsp molasses
Allow this to sit for 10 minutes, until foamy (*see Yeast, pp. 67 and 178*). Then pour it into a large ceramic bowl, along with:

3½ cups tepid water
2 cups milk (or **reconstituted dried milk**)
½ cup sweet molasses
½ cup safflower, sunflower, or **corn oil**
1 Tbsp salt
Beat in:
10 cups whole wheat flour
Cover and set to rise or double in 1 hour. Beat down and add, one at a time, beating after each addition:
7 to 8 cups whole wheat flour
Knead and add flour as needed until the dough becomes smooth and workable. Knead an extra 10 minutes. Cover and let rise again, for 1 hour.

Divide dough into 3 equal pieces. Grease 3 loaf pans. Shape loaves (*see p. 182*) and let them rise 30 minutes or until doubled in size. Preheat oven to 400°F, but turn down to 350° as soon as you put the loaves in to bake. Bake 40 minutes. Remove from pans to cool 2 hours before storing.

The White Flour Finish: if you desire a lighter loaf (both in texture and in color), substitute unbleached white flour for whole wheat flour in the last stage of mixing, when you knead flour in. The amount needed will vary

3 LOAVES

Big Baddeck Brown

I made up this recipe for my father who likes rye bread without any sweet flavor.

Mix in a small bowl:
½ cup warm water
1 Tbsp dried baker's yeast
pinch of sugar
Let this sit and proof (*see p. 180*) for 10 minutes. Meanwhile, mix up:
4½ cups warm water
½ cup blackstrap molasses
¼ cup safflower oil
1 Tbsp salt
1 egg
2 Tbsp caraway seeds
6 cups unbleached white flour
1 Tbsp lecithin (optional)
Beat this vigorously, cover, and let it sit in a warm place for 1 hour or until doubled. Add by cupfuls, beating after each addition:
8 to 9 cups dark rye flour
Knead in flour until dough becomes workable, although still slightly sticky unless dusted with flour. Return to the bowl, cover, and let rise for another hour. Cut into 3 equal pieces. Grease 3 pans and shape loaves; let them rise until doubled (about 45 minutes). Preheat oven to 400°F. Turn down the oven to 350°F and bake bread 45 minutes or until browned and crisp on top and bottom. Cool 2 hours before storing.

3 LOAVES

SOURDOUGH BREADS

Sourdough is really the same yeast we buy, dried or in cake form, to make bread with. The difference is that when sourdough is made, the yeast is allowed to remain in the flour and water mixture at the right temperature for growth for a much longer time. It eats up not just some, but all, of the sugar in the flour. It creates a great deal of carbon dioxide, and, finally, running out of air and food, it dies — not, however, without leaving some seeds behind, dormant, just in case conditions should ever happen to improve.

The reason it is called sourdough is that in eating up every last iota of sweetness, it makes the flour sour-tasting.

Sourdough is, according to most cookbooks, supposed to be kept in a sealed, sterile container in a cool, dark place, and renewed once a week or so. However, I have heard stories of trappers who came upon deserted cabins and scraped the crud off the inside of the old sourdough crock back of the rusty stove and used it to get bread going. So I think maybe sourdough is a little more durable than they say in the books.

The sourdough I have is purported to be 22 years old (going on 23). I keep it in a jar in the pantry. Sometimes it gets warm; sometimes it freezes. I use it around once a month. It always works.

Sourdough Starter

Soak together in a clean jar:
½ Tbsp dried yeast
½ cup water
When the yeast dissolves, add:
1 cup water
⅔ cup flour (rye or wholewheat)
Set in a 1-quart plastic container, covered, in a cozy draft-free spot, around 75°F, to

rise and fall for a day or more. When it stops working, store it in a cool place.

2 CUPS

Sourdough Bread

Sourdough bread is very simple compared to yeasted bread; however, you do have to start it the night before. This recipe makes 2 loaves, and it takes 3 or 4 hours (not counting the overnight).

The night before you make sourdough bread, the culture must be renewed — that is, warmed up and fed something to wake up the yeast.

Mix in a ceramic bowl:
1 cup sourdough starter
3¾ cups warm water
4½ cups whole wheat flour
This mixture must fill only half a bowl. Cover with a damp towel and leave in a draft-free place to rise overnight.

In the morning, take out 1 cupful of the batter and refrigerate it in a clean jar — this is starter for another batch if you've used up all the other. To the remainder, add:
½ cup oil
1 Tbsp salt
2 cups unbleached white flour
3 cups dark rye flour
Add flour gradually, by half cups, beating after each addition. When the dough comes easily away from the bowl, but is still sticky, knead for 5 minutes, adding flour as necessary. Sourdough should not be mixed as dry as ordinary yeasted bread — it should remain on the sticky side.

Shape into 2 loaves and place in very well oiled and floured pans. Do not fill pans above half full; sourdough will not support itself much above the level of the pan. Slit the tops, and sprinkle with seeds if you like (caraway is nice).

Sourdoughs take a long time to rise and are unpredictable; I've had some rise in 2 hours; others went all night and were just right by morning. Usually it just sits doing nothing for a long time and then within 30 minutes rises all it's going to. Keep an eye on it; when you see it increasing its girth, see to the fire. Bring the oven to 375°F.

Bake from 1 to 1½ hours at 375°F. For a crisp crust, remove loaves in the last 15 minutes of baking and brush on water — with a duck's tailfeather, says Bobby Dann, who gave us the culture.

2 LOAVES

French Bread

Making French bread is a great thing. It is a very simple mixture of water, flour, yeast and salt. It has no capacity for storage at all; it should be eaten (or frozen) within 24 hours of baking. It is not any kind of replacement for real whole-grain breads, with all their deep ecological satisfaction. On the other hand, everybody agrees about French bread. It's great.

This dough can also be used to make pita bread (Arabic pocket bread), pizza, calzones, or instant crackers.

In a small bowl, mix:
1½ cups tepid water
1½ Tbsp dried baker's yeast
While that brews, measure into a large warm ceramic bowl:
3 cups unbleached white flour
2 tsp salt
When the yeast dissolves and bubbles, make a well in the flour and stir in the yeast with a wooden spoon. Stir vigorously. Cover and let rise 2 hours, or until fully expanded and almost falling down. Stir down.

Scatter flour on a kneading surface and scrape the dough out on it. Fold and pat in:
½ to 1 cup unbleached white flour

Knead bread thoroughly (see p. 180). Keep dough warm at all times. Return to bowl, cover, and let rise 1 to 2 hours, until doubled.

To Make French Loaves
Cut the dough in half and tuck the cut part in as you shape the bun. Cover and let dough rest 10 minutes. Gluten needs to relax after stretching, before it will stretch again. Work each bun into a loaf shape by flattening it out and then folding it in half and pinching the edges together. This should be done twice. Then roll each loaf out into a baton by starting with both hands in the middle and gradually moving them out to the ends of the loaf.

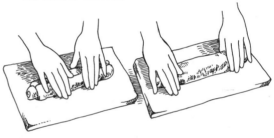

Sprinkle a clean baking sheet lightly with fine cornmeal, rather than greasing the pan. (Grease will burn at high temperatures.) Place loaves on pan. Some French breads are baked in curved pans known as gutters, but if you shape the bread properly you will not need them.

Allow bread to rise 1 to 1½ hours at 70°F until the loaves are about 4 inches in diameter.

Preheat oven to 450°F. Bring to a boil:
3 cups water
Pour the water in a loaf pan and stick it in the bottom of the oven; humidity will make the loaves crisp. If you wish to paint on egg white, scatter sesame or poppy seeds, or lightly slash the top with the sharpest of razors, now is the time. Bake 15 minutes at 450°F.

2 LOAVES

Variation
Instead of white flour, you can use all whole wheat, which makes a rather dense loaf, or half white and half whole wheat, which is a nice compromise.

Pita Bread

Cut 1 recipe French Bread dough *(see p. 185)* into 6 pieces, and shape into individual buns. Cover with a cloth and let them rest for 10 minutes. Preheat oven to 450°F. Scatter finely ground cornmeal on clean baking sheets. Roll out pitas to 6- to 8-inch diameters, rolling and stretching from the center out. Place pitas in fully preheated oven and bake 5 to 7 minutes. Remove and place them in a paper bag to cool.

6 POCKETS

Sesame Crackers

Our friend Claire made these so easily, one night, that I just had to ask. What she does is set aside some of the dough from a batch of plain brown bread (yeast, water, salt, and whole wheat flour). In a bag it goes, and into the fridge, where she punches it down if it rises too much. She pulls it out when the notion strikes her and makes instant pizza, breadsticks, and these terrific little crackers.

Spread liberally on the breadboard:
¼ cup sesame seeds
Put a cup or so of French bread dough *(see p. 185)* on these and roll it out, turning often and re-distributing sesame seeds until the bread is thick with them. Roll the dough out to about ⅛-inch thickness. Preheat oven to 375°F. Place the dough on a cookie tin and scatter over it:
¼ tsp salt
Cut the dough into diamonds, triangles — whatever strikes your fancy. Bake 20 minutes or until browned.

See also:
Pizza *(p. 104)*, Calzones *(p. 107)*, Fruit Pizza *(p. 219)*

Maple Syrup Bread

Samantha Smith made this bread for the West Brattleboro farmer's market for years. It always sold out.

Heat together over low heat:
⅓ cup vegetable shortening
1 cup milk
When the shortening dissolves, pour the mixture into a large mixing bowl. Add:
3 cups cold milk
This will cool the mixture enough so that you can add:
4 Tbsp baker's yeast
½ cup grade C Vermont maple syrup
Allow the yeast to dissolve for 10 minutes. Then mix in:
2 tsp salt
4 eggs
2 cups rolled oats
9 cups whole wheat flour
Samantha does not actually measure the flour so much as stop adding it when it becomes unmixable. She then turns it out on a board thinly coated with:
1 to 1½ cups white flour
and kneads white flour until it holds together like a good batch of dough should. Allow it to rise in a draft-free place, for 1 hour or until doubled. Punch down, cut into 4 and work each piece into a loaf. Allow to rise 15 to 20 minutes; then bake at 375°F for 30 minutes.

4 LOAVES

Holiday Bread

Traditionally, I make this rich, light, braided bread on Christmas Eve and the day before Easter. It is a glorious lovely thing with which to decorate the holiday breakfast table, and people can snatch chunks of it all day, to eat with the goodies from their stockings or the jelly beans and chocolate rabbits.

In a warm ceramic bowl, mix together:
⅔ cup tepid milk (not hot)
2 cups tepid water
2 Tbsp dried baker's yeast
2 Tbsp sugar
Allow to sit, covered, until the yeast dissolves. Then add and beat in:
2 cups unbleached white flour
Beat this well and allow it to sit and rise for about 1 hour. Then add and mix in:
1 cup sugar or **½ cup honey**
2 beaten eggs
1 tsp almond flavoring
½ tsp mace (optional)
1 tsp cardamom or **cinnamon**
¼ cup melted butter
1 tsp salt
Gradually add, mixing after each cupful:
3 cups unbleached white flour
3 cups whole wheat flour
Add more flour as needed to make a smooth, workable dough. Turn out and knead for 10 minutes. Knead in:
1½ cups raisins or **dried currants**
Return to bowl and let rise 1 hour or until doubled. Turn out on board and knead into a smooth bun. Cut into 3 portions and shape each into a bun. Let them rest 10 minutes. Then roll each gradually into a long thin rope.

You may find this easier to do in 3 stages. Roll each out to about 12 inches, then 18, and finally 24 inches, letting each one rest between each stage. To roll them longer, start with your hands together, and,

rolling back and forth, move your hands out gradually to the ends of the roll. Repeat as needed.

Braid the ropes together and arrange on a lightly oiled cookie sheet, either as a straight braid or in a circle. Let rise 45 to 60 minutes or until doubled. Preheat oven to 450°F, but reduce heat to 400°F when you put bread in the oven, and bake 30 to 40 minutes or until gloriously golden brown and crisp. Cool 2 hours before icing (*see p. 214*).

(*see p. 214*)

1 LARGE LOAF

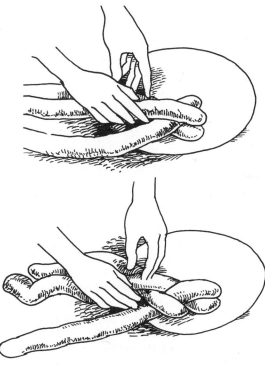

Raisin Bread

A sweet, tender bread with a crisp crust and a hint of cinnamon about it.

Mix in a small bowl:

1 cup warm water
pinch of sugar
2 Tbsp baker's yeast

Allow to sit for 10 minutes in a warm place until it foams. Meanwhile, mix in a small pan:

1 cup raisins
½ cup water
½ tsp cinnamon

Bring to a boil, then let the raisins sit, covered, at room temperature until needed. In a large ceramic bowl, mix:

1 cup warm water
½ cup dried milk
½ cup honey
2 tsp salt
3 Tbsp safflower oil

Add yeast mixture, stir, and then add:

3 cups whole wheat flour

Beat well. Then add and beat in:

2 cups unbleached white flour

Cover the dough with a clean dishtowel and set in a draft-free place for 2½ hours, until doubled in size. Punch down the dough. Spread out some newspaper, then spread on a breadboard:

½ cup unbleached white flour

Scrape the dough on to the breadboard and knead *(see p. 180)* until smooth and pliable. Cut the dough in 2 pieces and flatten each; then spread half the raisins on each and knead them into the dough. Grease 2 bread pans and set the loaves in them to rise for 1 hour or until they double in size. Preheat the oven to 400°F. Put loaves in oven and turn it down to 350°. Bake 40 minutes or until browned to top and bottom. Turn out of pans to cool.

2 LOAVES

Porridge Bread

Bread with oatmeal in it is traditional in Cape Breton. It makes a slightly moister, better-lasting bread than does all wheat flour. Excellent for sandwiches.

Measure into a large ceramic bowl:

1 cup rolled oats
½ cup molasses
2 cups boiling water

In a smaller bowl, mix and set to proof:

½ cup warm water
2 Tbsp dried baker's yeast
pinch of sugar

Allow oats to cool to skin temperature before mixing it with the yeast. Mix in:

2 tsp salt
¼ cup safflower oil
2 cups whole wheat flour

Beat vigorously for 5 minutes. Cover with a clean dishtowel and leave in a draft-free place for a couple hours. Then beat and add:

2 to 3 cups unbleached white flour

The finished dough is slightly sticky to touch. Return it to the bowl and allow to rise for 2 hours, until doubled in size. Turn it out on a floured surface and knead for 2 to 3 minutes, using a scant handful of flour to work the dough with. Cut the dough into 4 equal pieces, and shape each into a smooth bun. Grease 2 bread pans and fill each with 2 buns. Break into a small bowl:

1 egg

Beat it well and brush the tops of each bun lightly with the beaten egg. Allow the loaves to rise in a warm, draft-free place for 30 minutes.

Preheat oven to 400°F. Bake for 10 minutes, then reduce heat to 350° and bake for 35 minutes. Remove loaves from their pans and cool them on a wire rack or clean dishcloth for several hours before storing.

2 LOAVES

Beer Bread

Bread is risen with a yeast very much like the yeast that ferments beer and wine. It occurs naturally in grape juice, explaining how people learned to use it to brew wine. It is less obvious, however, how yeasted bread came to be invented, unless you stop to consider that most things in earlier times were made with what was at hand: water, beer, whatever. Those first risen loaves, baked on hot stones by the open fire pit, must have tasted a little like this.

Mix:
2 Tbsp dried baker's yeast
½ cup water
Allow this to sit 10 minutes until foamy. Meanwhile, heat together in a small pan until dissolved:
¾ cup beer or **ale**
2 Tbsp honey
1 Tbsp butter
Allow this to cool to room temperature before adding it to the yeast mixture, along with:
1 tsp caraway seeds
1 tsp salt
1 clove crushed garlic
1 cup unbleached white flour
½ cup rye flour
Beat smooth. Add gradually, mixing and kneading in:
1 cup white flour
1 cup rye flour
Use more flour as needed. Knead and shape into a round loaf. If you want to stick sesame seeds to the top, use a little beaten egg. Let it rise 45 minutes or so. Preheat the oven to 375°F and bake for 25 to 30 minutes. Brush or dot with butter, and let it cool on a rack.

Serve with beer, cheese, lots of salad, and something terrific that you make ahead: Chowder (p. 19) or Pasta e Fagioli. (p. 90).

1 LOAF

Focaccia

A flat, round bread, thicker than pita and flavored with olive oil and herbs, focaccia is traditionally served with lentils, hummus and salad. If you freeze it soon after baking, it keeps quite well.

Mix in a small bowl for 10 minutes:
1 Tbsp yeast
1 cup water
1 Tbsp flour
When foamy, add:
½ tsp salt
2 cups whole wheat flour
⅓ cup olive oil
Beat well, cover, and let sit in a warm spot until doubled (1 to 2 hours). Beat down and add gradually, by half-cupfuls:
1 to 1½ cups unbleached white flour
Knead until the dough is smooth and elastic. Cut, then shape into 4 buns (see p. 182). Flatten each and smear on each:
1 Tbsp olive oil
a sprinkling of rosemary leaves
Stud each with:
5 to 6 pieces of black olives (optional)
Let rise 20 minutes. Preheat oven to 450°F and bake 20 minutes or until rich brown. To crisp and warm it before serving, toast at 400°F for 5 minutes.

4 SMALL LOAVES

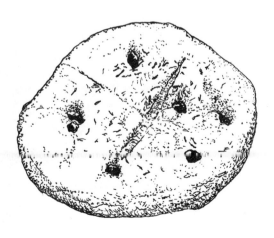

English Muffins

For years I tried to duplicate commercial English muffins, thinking nothing else would do. Then one summer during a heat wave I was mixing up a batch of bread dough, and I thought, why not? So I rolled it out, cut out a few circles, let them rise, and baked them in a pan on top of the stove — which is, no doubt, how English muffins first got their start in the world. Any bread recipe will do, although I find it works best if you double the yeast and keep the flour very light. This is the one we use now:

Break into a 2-cup measure and beat slightly:
2 eggs
Fill the rest of the measure with:
warm water
Place this mixture in a large ceramic mixing bowl and add:
1 cup dried milk
1 Tbsp dried yeast
⅓ cup sugar or **honey**
1½ tsp salt
2 Tbsp oil
2 cups whole wheat flour
Allow this sponge to rise for an hour. Then beat in:
½ cup whole wheat or **soy flour**

Dump **½ cup white unbleached flour** on a smooth work surface. Turn the dough out on it and sprinkle some more white flour on top. Knead in white flour as needed (in all, about a cup) until the dough is smooth and elastic.

Let the dough rise in a warm place, covered, for 1 hour; or, if you're in a hurry, you may make up the muffins at once. To make muffins, roll out the dough ½-inch thick. Cut into circles with a round cookie cutter or tuna fish can.

Sprinkle a cast-iron frying pan lightly with cornmeal and place the muffins in it. (They won't all fit; you will wind up doing it in 2 or 3 batches, or in several pans). Let them rise until doubled (30 minutes to 1 hour, depending on the temperature in the kitchen). When they're ready, put a lid on the frying pan and put it over medium heat. Bake about 10 to 15 minutes on each side, checking the middle muffin now and then to make sure it isn't burning. The main thing is to have medium heat evenly distributed over the entire pan. Cool the pan (in cold water) before placing the second batch of dough in it — or use 2 pans, and have 1 batch baking while the next is rising.

24 MUFFINS

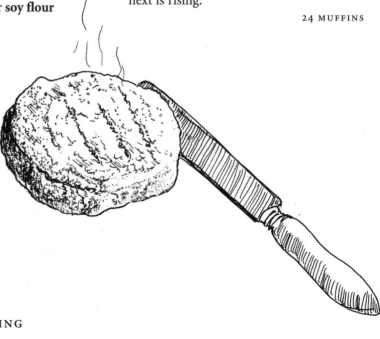

Picnic Rolls

My mother invented these fat delicious rolls to serve with hamburgers at the student picnics that they annually held for my father's classes (and friends, and former students). A week or two before the picnic, she baked them for 3 days running, in batches of 35, and stored them in the freezer.

Starting first thing in the morning, combine and beat for 2 minutes:
3 cups scalded milk
⅔ cup shortening
1 Tbsp salt
⅓ cup sugar
1 Tbsp yeast dissolved in ¼ cup tepid water
4 cups unbleached white flour
Cover and allow to rise for 1 to 2 hours in a warm place. When the dough has doubled in size, punch down and add:
1 beaten egg
½ cup small-flake rolled oats
½ cup wheat germ
Mix thoroughly. Then add gradually, mixing in half cup at a time:
2 to 3 cups unbleached white flour
When the dough becomes too stiff to mix, turn it out and knead until smooth and elastic. Return to bowl and let rise until doubled. Cut into 16 pieces and shape each into a flattened bun *(see p. 182)*. Roll each bun in:
poppy seeds

Arrange rolls six to a cookie sheet, not touching, and let them rise until doubled. Bake 12 to 15 minutes at 350°F.

16 ROLLS

Bagels

Bagels are easy to make, and popular, too, and don't have as many calories as brownies or cookies.

Mix together:
1 Tbsp dried baker's yeast
1 Tbsp white sugar
1½ cups warm water
Let this sit for 10 minutes, or until bubbly. Add:
1½ tsp salt
2 cups whole wheat flour
1 cup white flour
When the dough gets too stiff to stir, turn it out on a board floured with:
½ cup white flour
Knead into a smooth, pliable dough *(see p. 180)*. Let it rise in a warm place covered with a dishtowel for one hour or until doubled in size.

Bring to a boil:
1 gallon water
1 Tbsp salt
Meanwhile, chop the dough into 8 or 10 pieces. Roll each one out about 10 inches long, and link the ends together by mashing them. Drop them, 3 at a time, in the boiling water. They will sink, then rise. Fish them out in 5 seconds and put each on a lightly oiled cookie sheet. Let them rise until doubled, about 20 minutes. Preheat oven to 400°F. Bake them 20 minutes, until golden brown. Cool 1 hour before storing.

8 TO 10 BAGELS

Quickbreads

Quickbread is a convenient name for muffins, biscuits and pancakes, which contain a lot of flour and other good things, but are (for the most part) raised with baking powder or soda instead of yeast. The texture is different; rather than "bringing out" the gluten in the wheat, the aim in quickbread is a "light crumb," meaning as little gluten as possible.

Ingredients

Baking Soda and Powder: Most quickbreads are leavened by baking soda or powder, and here's how they work: when bicarbonate of soda is combined with something acid, it gets fizzy, letting off little bubbles of carbon dioxide. If this happens in the batter, it fills the bread or cake with nice little holes. But for it to work, you have to use it with something acid: buttermilk, sour milk, yogurt, sour cream, whey, molasses or honey; even tea or coffee. Baking powder, on the other hand, doesn't need something acid, because what's in it is baking soda combined with something acid (in dried form): namely, cream of tartar. So all you have to do to activate the baking powder is to dampen it.

As soon as you start the reaction, either with soda or powder, the fizzing starts, and all the bubble making that's going to occur happens within a few minutes. That's why many recipes say to mix up wet and dry ingredients separately, and all recipes say to stir the final batter quickly and pop it in the oven. Baking powder is a little slower acting than baking soda, responding to heat as well as moisture, but you still get a lighter end product if it's lightly mixed and quickly baked.

Many people are beginning to wonder if these leaveners are really good for you. Baking soda, of course, neutralizes acids: not only in foods, but also in your stomach. Without stomach acids, your body cannot digest B vitamins (which you went to such work to get, if you use whole-grain flours). It seems to me that if you use very little soda or powder, only using soda in combination with acid foods, that the alkaline substance will be all used up by the time you eat it; but, of course, it's up to you. Baking powder and soda are not included in the macrobiotic diet, incidentally; they are considered too yang.

If you prefer not to use these leaveners, you can substitute beaten egg whites in many recipes (muffins, pancakes, loaves) and leave them out altogether in thin pancakes or biscuits.

Flour: If you grind your own, do it well, or sift out the rough stuff when making quickbreads. That's because the flour is only dampened for a brief period between mixing and baking; there'll be no soaking to soften the grit. Another version of many of these recipes can be made by substituting half hard whole wheat flour and half soft whole wheat pastry flour.

Milk: You can use whole milk, or skim, or reconstituted powder. If buttermilk, sour milk, or yogurt is called for in a recipe, the sourness is usually important: baking soda needs an acid ingredient to set it fizzing and bubbling. You can sour a glass of milk at room temperature by adding a tablespoon of vinegar or 2 tablespoons of lemon juice and letting it sit for 15 to 30 minutes in a warm (not hot) place.

If you just don't have time, use milk, and substitute baking powder for baking soda. Use about twice as much baking powder as the amount of soda called for.

Eggs: Eggs help make cakes and quickbreads moist, and also help hold them together.

Grains: I like to experiment with the various densities and flavors of different grains. If you have your own grinder, you can mill flours freshly; they taste better and are better for you.

Sweetening: This is one place where you can use honey and molasses in place of sugar. Quickbreads use little sugar in any case. Their strength lies not in their sweetness but in their fresh-cooked flavor.

Fats: In making most quickbreads, it doesn't matter much if you use a liquid fat such as oil, or a solid fat, or even if you melt the solid fat. However, you should only use cold, solid shortening to make biscuits.

Scones

Scones are a traditional form of biscuit all around the British Isles — and, of course, in Cape Breton, where they are served fresh and hot from the oven. The reason they are so popular is, at least partly, that they are not difficult to make; you can throw a batch together in time for tea, or a midnight snack, or before breakfast. They can be served plain, with butter and jam, or covered with sliced fruit and whipped cream. Preheat oven to 350°F.

Sift together:
1 cup whole wheat flour
1 cup unbleached white flour
4 tsp baking powder
½ tsp salt
½ cup sugar
Cut in, using first 2 knives, then a pastry blender:
⅓ cup cold butter or **shortening**
In a separate bowl, beat together with a fork:
½ cup milk or **buttermilk**
1 egg
Stir the liquid lightly into the dry ingredients. Be careful to handle the dough as lightly as possible as you flour a board and pat the dough into a round about 1 inch thick. Scones may be cut into dia-monds or rounds, or you can divide the dough into 10 separate pieces and pat each into a round. Set pieces at least 1 inch apart on an ungreased pan and bake 20 minutes at 350°F.

10 SCONES

Raisin Scones

The night before you make these, you can set to soak:
½ cup raisins or **currants**
in:
½ cup warm water
Add soaked fruit to mixture with milk and egg. Bake as above.

GRIDDLE COOKING

Except for pancakes, griddle cooking is seldom done anymore. For one thing, modern stoves don't turn low enough to bake on top. So the gentle art of English muffinry, of hoecakes and oatcakes, has gone the way of soups and breads: people get them from the store.

There are various ways to get around the limitations of the 20th century, however. If you are able to get hold of a plate from a cast-iron woodstove, use that between the heat and your frying pan to disperse the heat evenly. A cast-iron pan will work by itself if the heat will turn low enough. If you have a woodstove, you will find that top-of-the-stove baking is a welcome relief in the summer. On camping trips, set a flat-topped stone near the fire to heat, and cook on that.

Here are a few basic principles:

• Bake thin and small. Pour pancakes no bigger than your flipper can handle. Stiffer doughs can be cut in individual shapes or in a large circle, then divided into wedges, or "farls" as the Scotch called them.

• Prick the surface of dense doughs to allow steam to escape, so they cook evenly.

• Keep all forms of sugar at a minimum; they heat up too much and burn easily.

• Preheat pan, rather than greasing it, and scatter the surface lightly with cornmeal.

Hoecakes

We call them hoecakes to differentiate them from pancakes — actually, they are pancakes, but they don't taste like them. However, there's no way our primitive ancestors ever had these ingredients, so I don't imagine hoecakes were ever really made on a hoe. At any rate, they are terrific bits of bread to make hastily on top of the stove and serve with soup or beans.

Heat together, stirring as you do:
2 cups water
2 cups cornmeal
When this thickens, remove from heat and add:
1 to 3 Tbsp finely chopped onion
1 tsp salt
½ cup dried milk
When it has cooled, mix in:
1 or 2 eggs
Hoecakes are very good fried in bacon or ham fat, but if the pan is preheated, you may also cook them in a dry pan. The results are different but equally delicious.

10 HOECAKES

BISCUITS

In the making of biscuits it is important that the fat be solid, as in butter, shortening, margarine, and lard. It should never be melted, and, in fact, the colder the better. This is because, as in making piecrust, you want to break or slice the fat into tiny fragments, keeping them intact and separate from the flour, so that when the high oven heat hits them, the fat melts in pockets, flattened by the rolling pin between layers of flour, thus making a "flaky" biscuit.

If you prefer to use oil, try another kind of quickbread.

Whole Wheat Biscuits

These are fine and light, but have a more nutty flavor than white biscuits. Make sure the shortening is cold and the oven is hot. Preheat oven to 425°F.

Sift together:
1½ cups whole wheat flour
1½ cups unbleached white or **whole wheat flour**
2 tsp baking powder
½ tsp salt
Cut in with 2 knives, then use a pastry blender or fork until the mixture resembles coarse meal:
½ cup solid shortening (lard, butter, whatever)
Add gradually and mix in well:
¾ cup sour milk, buttermilk, or **water**
Knead lightly for a minute until the dough sticks together. Refrigerate dough if it has to wait for a hot oven. Roll out ½-inch thick and cut into shapes with a small glass or biscuit cutter. Set on an ungreased sheet; bake 15 minutes at 425°F, until brown.

15 BISCUITS

Oaten Cakes

These are thin and crisp, with a delicious nutlike flavor; everybody around our house eats them up as fast as they get made. Thankfully, they don't take long to make.

Grind up rolled oats coarsely to make:
2 cups oat flour
Add and mix in with your fingers:
½ tsp salt
And then:
2 Tbsp butter or **corn oil**
And:
2 cups rolled oats
Mix in with a fork:
½ cup hot water
Turn the dough onto a board sprinkled with oat flour, and press into 2 tight balls. Flatten and then roll out each ball to around ¼-inch thickness, trimming the edges if you like; cut into 4 wedges, and prick each wedge with a fork.

Preheat a cast-iron frying pan and sprinkle lightly with oat flour. Bake the farls about 5 minutes on each side over medium heat with a lid on the pan (you can tell when the first side is done because the edges will curl up slightly).

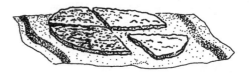

Cornmeal Pancakes

These are always popular with the pancake set. They are tender, crisp, and lighter than whole wheat pancakes.

In a heavy ceramic bowl or a thick pot, put:
1 cup cornmeal
2 Tbsp molasses
1 tsp salt
Stir as you pour in:
1 cup boiling water
Cover the bowl, and let it sit for a few minutes (while you make the coffee, scout up the maple syrup, and feed the cat). Then add:
2 eggs
½ cup dried milk
2 Tbsp safflower oil
½ cup whole wheat or **unbleached white flour**
2 tsp baking powder
½ tsp salt
Lightly rub a heavy frying pan or two with a few drops of safflower oil on a bit of paper, and heat the pans thoroughly before making pancakes. Make the cakes on the small side, no more than 3 to 4 inches wide.

SERVES 3 TO 4

Mother Earth Pancakes

These are the original famous pancakes we always used to make. They are firm and sustaining, while light enough to eat by the pile. We often used to make them as a favorite dinner when the kids were little, serving them with lots of applesauce and cottage cheese, and little dabs of maple syrup or jelly.

Beat together:
2 eggs
¼ cup safflower oil
1½ cups milk (or **reconstituted dried milk**)
Add and beat in:
1¾ cups whole wheat flour
2 tsp baking powder
½ tsp salt
Preheat a cast-iron frying pan, lightly oil it, and cook the pancakes one at a time. Adjust the heat to keep the pan from smoking. When small holes appear on top of the cake, flip it over with a spatula and cook the other side, which will take about half as much time to cook. Remove from the pan and serve at once.

Variation
Fruit Pancakes: Blueberry or raspberry pancakes may be made by adding **½ to 1 cup fresh** or **frozen** (not defrosted) **fruit** to the batter. To make apple or banana pancakes, place the slices of fruit directly on the hot griddle and pour or spoon batter around them. Cook as above.

SERVES 4

Crêpes

French pancakes are very thin and delicate, not at all like our lumberjack behemoths of the Western hemisphere. They are the basis of blintzes *(see p. 102)*. In all pancakes, breads, and quickbreads, you can use reconstituted dried milk.

In a shallow ceramic bowl, beat:
3 eggs
Add:
2 cups milk
½ tsp vanilla or **grated lemon rind**
1 cup whole wheat flour
½ tsp salt
Beat briefly with a whisk. Heat a skillet — any kind will do as long as it is good and hot. Test with a few drops of batter; if it sticks, it's not hot enough. If it separates into hopping spatters, it's too hot.

Put about ¼ cup (or less) batter at a time in the pan and tilt to spread it around. When the top looks dry and the edges have curled up a little, turn them over and cook a minute or so longer.

17 CRÊPES

Oatmeal Pancakes

Thick and hearty, with a nutty flavor, these pancakes are a good way to include roughage on a holiday menu.
2 cups milk or **reconstituted dried milk**
2 cups rolled oats
¼ cup vegetable oil
2 eggs
1 cup whole wheat flour
2 tsp baking powder
½ tsp salt
Combine milk and rolled oats and let them sit for 5 minutes. Add oil and eggs, and beat well. Then add flour, salt and baking powder. Combine with a few swift strokes. Heat a cast-iron griddle and pour pancakes about 4 inches across. Cook until brown, turn, cook again, and serve hot with butter and maple syrup and/or applesauce.

SERVES 3 TO 4

Whole Cornbread

Whole kernels of corn gives the bread a juicy quality, but this recipe is also very good without the whole corn. If you prefer to bake it as corn muffins, preheat the oven to 425°F and bake for 5 minutes less.

For cornbread, preheat the oven to 400°F. Brush a 9-inch square pan with oil or shortening and set it in the oven to heat up for a couple of minutes so the crust will be crisp. Meanwhile, beat together:

1 egg
½ cup buttermilk
2 Tbsp corn oil
Add and mix in swiftly:
½ cup yellow cornmeal
½ cup unbleached white flour
3 tsp baking powder
1 Tbsp brown sugar
pinch of salt
1 cup whole corn
1 Tbsp finely chopped parsley or **chervil**
Stir only to mix, and pour at once into the hot pan. Bake for 20 minutes at 400°F, or until crisp on the sides and light brown on top. This is especially good with beans or stew.

1 SMALL LOAF

Blueberry Muffins

These are big, puffy muffins, sweet and delicious and stuffed with blueberries. Barely mix the wet and dry ingredients.

Preheat the oven to 425°F. Combine and mix together in a large bowl:
**2 cups flour (unbleached white, whole
   wheat pastry,** or **a mixture)**
2 tsp baking powder
½ tsp salt
½ cup white sugar
2 cups fresh or **frozen blueberries** (do not
   defrost)
In another container, beat together:
2 eggs
⅓ cup milk

1 tsp vanilla
¼ cup melted butter
Butter the muffin cups before mixing wet and dry ingredients. Combine them lightly and almost fill the muffin cups. Bake 15 minutes or until the tops spring lightly back when pressed. Allow them to cool before taking the muffins out of the tin.

12 MUFFINS

Janet's Muffins

Janet and Bill live in a magical home in the woods. It started as a school bus that carried them from Connecticut to Cape Breton. The various additions have since taken over; still, the original bus is in there, along with the tower, the parlor, and the summer kitchen; all very quaint and tidy. Janet welcomes you with a cup of her own herbal tea, and, if you're lucky, these homemade muffins fresh from the oven.

Preheat oven to 350°F.

Mix together:
1½ cups water
2 Tbsp safflower oil
¼ cup molasses
1 egg
Dump on top and mix in hastily:
2 cups whole wheat flour
½ tsp salt
1 tsp baking powder
handful of raisins
Lightly oil 2 six-cup muffin tins, fill each ⅔ full, and pop them in the oven. Bake 20 minutes. Cool before unmolding.

12 MUFFINS

Desserts

BAKING

Baking is best done in batches. In the old days, it was traditional to bake on Saturdays. First thing in the morning, the flour barrel was opened, lard brought up from the basement, and whatever else was at hand was peeled, pitted, chopped, and mixed. The old woodstove was fired up, and a continuous stream of cookies, pies, cakes, squares, and goodies came out hot and fresh.

Baking day still makes sense. This is partly because of the mess, which is the same whether you bake one thing or ten. You might as well get the most mileage out of flour on the floor, tools and ingredients out of the cupboards, and chaos in the sink. You'll soon find yourself recycling tools, bowls, and pans with a quick rinse and a wipe as you go. And, of course, it's more efficient to heat the oven once, than to heat and reheat it over and over, whether the fuel is wood, gas, or electric.

Baking is personal. Sometimes you feel like baking and eating more whole-grain foods. The added nutrition tastes good. The crunch and chew of brown breads and biscuits, and the level of sweetness natural to grains and nuts are just exactly what you want to eat.

Other times, you might want some glorious thing to celebrate — or console yourself with. Sometimes it's enough just to read the recipes, and dream about the goodies you're going to make whenever you find the time.

CAKES

The art of baking cakes is not nearly as exacting as many cookbooks would have you believe. Some recipes tell you to sift even the sugar. But generations of perfectly good cooks have slapped together trillions of cakes, and seen them all disappear before they even had a chance to cool.

It's true that not everything can go into a cake; there are some ground rules. But once you get a basic sense of ingredients and proportion, you can vary and invent, put things in or leave them out. The best way to go at it is to pick a recipe you like, and make it often for a couple of months, varying ingredients as you go. Eventually you won't have to look at the recipe, or measure things; you'll know by the consistency and taste of the batter what the cake is going to do.

Suzy's Coffeecake

I've been making this cake for 25 years. I've made it with every conceivable lack, substitution, and variation, and in a chancy oven; I've made it with oil, lard, butter, and no shortening; with sugar, molasses, honey, and no sweetening; with no egg, 1 egg, 3 eggs; with the egg whites beaten and no rising powder; with milk, yogurt, buttermilk, sour milk, sour cream, dried milk, whey, and no milk at all. I've also made it with white flour, whole wheat flour, half whole wheat and half anything from rye to soyflour. I've used it as the basis for upside-down cake, banana bread, raisin cake, muffins, coffeecake; flavored with cinnamon, almond, coriander, nutmeg, berries, apple juice, oranges, lemons, coconut. It stands.

Preheat oven to 350°F. Mix:
⅓ cup oil or **¼ lb softened butter** or **shortening**
½ cup sugar, molasses, honey, or **a mixture**
Add:
1 to 3 eggs, whole or **separated, whites beaten stiff**
¾ cup milk, buttermilk, sour milk, or **½ cup dried milk mixed with water** or **whey**
Beat, then add:
1½ cups whole wheat flour or **half whole wheat and half any other flour**
2 tsp baking powder (omit if egg whites were beaten)
½ tsp salt
Flavor with:
1 tsp almond, vanilla, or **grated lemon rind,** or **¼ cup orange, lemon,** or **apple juice**

Upside-Down Cake
Grease the pan well with butter, and sprinkle with flour before lining it with:
a layer of overlapping sliced fruit (apples, berries, peaches, pineapple or **½ cup of nuts)**
You may sprinkle over the fruit, if tart:
½ cup brown sugar
¼ cup whole wheat flour
Pour on the batter, and bake at 350° for about 30 minutes. If the temperature is lower, it will be a denser cake but still good.

1 SMALL CAKE

Apple Streusel Cake

A wonderful coffeecake with apples in the middle and crunchy stuff on top.

Streusel
Measure into a bowl:
¼ cup whole wheat flour
½ tsp cinnamon
⅓ cup brown sugar
Chop in small pieces, then mash in with a fork:
3 Tbsp cold butter
Add:
½ cup chopped nuts

Cake
Preheat oven to 350°F. Cream together in another bowl:
⅓ cup softened butter
¾ cup brown sugar
Add and beat in:
1 cup buttermilk or **sour milk** *(see p. 68)*
1 egg
Sift in together:
1 cup unbleached white flour
1 cup whole wheat flour
3 tsp baking powder
1 tsp salt
Mix well.
Core and chop fine:
2 cups apples
Pour half the batter in a well-greased cake pan. Distribute the apples and half the streusel; pour in the rest of the batter. Top with streusel and bake at 350°F for 45 minutes.

1 LARGE CAKE

Variation
Instead of apples, use **2 cups fresh** or **frozen blueberries.**

Gingerbread Cake

This continues to be a popular cake with many people because it contains no sugar. It keeps very well, and is especially good on a cold winter afternoon with apple-sauce and a dollop of sour cream. It is best baked in a tube or loaf pan.

Preheat oven to 350°F. Combine in a mixing bowl:
1 egg
½ cup safflower oil
1 cup molasses
1 cup sour cream or **yogurt**
Beat well, then add:
2½ cups whole wheat flour
½ tsp salt
1½ tsp baking powder
1 tsp cinnamon
1 to 2 Tbsp freshly grated ginger
Beat thoroughly. Grease, then flour a tube or loaf pan. Fill pan and bake the cake at 350°F for 45 to 50 minutes, or until a knife slipped in the middle comes out clean. Cool before unmolding.

1 MEDIUM CAKE

Variation
Instead of sour cream or yogurt, use:
1 cup water
Just before pouring into the pan, add:
½ cup raisins or
    currants
Raisins dusted with flour are less likely to sink.

Oatmeal Spice Cake

This is a very popular cake, easy to make, and nicely moist with a hint of spice. It can be dressed up with Coconut Topping *(recipe follows)*, or served as it is.

Preheat oven to 350°F. Break into a mixing bowl:
2 eggs
Beat them with:
⅓ cup safflower oil
2 Tbsp molasses
In a measuring cup, combine:
1 cup warm water
1 tsp baking soda
Add this to the batter. Then sift in together:
1 cup whole wheat flour
1 cup unbleached white flour
1 tsp cinnamon
½ tsp nutmeg
½ tsp salt
Mix well. Then stir in:
1 cup brown sugar
1 cup rolled oats
Grease and flour a tube pan or cake pan, and pour in batter. Bake single cake 40 minutes at 350°F. Cool before removing from pan. Very good with Coconut Topping.

1 MEDIUM CAKE

Aunt Carrie's Carrot Cake

My husband's Aunt Carrie gave me this recipe long ago, and I have doubtless changed it a good bit, but it's still a family favorite. More than once I have made it as muffins, for travelling food; it keeps well.

Preheat oven to 300°F. Grease 2 loaf pans or 1 removable-rim tube pan or 14 muffin-tin cups.

In a large mixing bowl, combine:
4 eggs
1 cup safflower oil
1½ cups sugar
Beat well, then sift in:
1 cup unbleached white flour
1 cup whole wheat flour
1 tsp salt
1 tsp baking soda
2 tsp cinnamon
1 tsp allspice
Beat thoroughly. Wash, then grate in:
3 cups carrots
Fold in:
1 cup walnut pieces
1 cup raisin or **currants** (optional)
Bake cake 1½ hours, loaves 45 minutes, muffins 30 minutes. Traditionally topped with Cream Cheese Frosting.

1 LARGE CAKE

Coconut Topping

Melt in top of a double boiler or over very low heat:
½ cup butter
1 cup brown sugar
Stir in, cooking for 5 minutes:
3 Tbsp milk
1 cup unsweetened shredded coconut
1 cup walnut pieces
Spread at once on cooled cake, and cool before serving.

COVERS ONE LAYER CAKE, TOP AND SIDES

Cream Cheese Frosting

Mash together:
½ cup (8 oz) room-temperature cream cheese
3 Tbsp butter
Sift and work in gradually:
2 cups confectioner's sugar
Flavor with:
½ tsp vanilla
½ tsp almond flavoring

COVERS TOP OF 1 LAYER

The Most Incredible Chocolate Cake

From a nutritional standpoint, there is just no excuse for this cake. It is absolute sheer total sin. And worth every bite.

Preheat the oven to 375°F. In a small pan, mix and melt slowly:

½ cup water
3 oz unsweetened baking chocolate or
7½ Tbsp unsweetened cocoa

Meanwhile, mix together in this order, beating well after each addition:

½ cup room-temperature butter
pinch of salt
1½ cups sugar
2 beaten eggs

Then add and beat in the chocolate and:

1 tsp vanilla

In the chocolate pan, mix together:

¾ cup cultured buttermilk, yogurt or
sour cream
1 tsp baking soda

Add to the batter, by half cups, alternating with the buttermilk and soda mix and beating well after each addition:

1½ cups white unbleached flour

Pour the batter into a well-greased cake or tube cake pan and bake at 375°F for about 30 minutes. Cool before unmolding. This creature has the tenderness of cake, the richness of candy, the slight crunch of brownies, and is very very good with a generous dab of whipped cream, or French Butter Icing.

A ONE-LAYER CAKE

French Butter Icing

This is a rich, sweet icing. If you want to make it less sweet and more nutritional, substitute ½ cup non-instant skim milk powder for ½ cup confectioner's sugar. You can make it pink by substituting cranberry sauce for cream, or yellow with 1 egg yolk.

Allow to sit at room temperature until soft:

¼ cup butter

Mash in:

1 tsp vanilla
3 Tbsp cream or **evaporated milk**

Then add and mix well:

2 cups confectioner's sugar

Spread on top and sides of cake.

COVERS ONE LAYER, TOP AND SIDES

Orange Butter Cake

This is a nice simple little cake with an elegant flavor; very good with Mocha Java Icing (*see p. 203*), or sliced fruit, or ice cream.

Preheat oven to 350°F. Grate rind of:

1 organic orange

Cream the peel into:

½ cup room-temperature butter
½ cup sugar

Add and beat in:

2 eggs
¾ cup buttermilk
juice of 1 orange

Then sift in and beat well:

2 cups unbleached white flour
2 tsp baking powder
½ tsp salt
½ cup dried currants

Turn into a greased loaf or single cake pan and bake at 350°F for 30 minutes. Remove and cool before unmolding. Excellent with Mocha Java Icing (*see p. 203*).

A ONE-LAYER CAKE

Plain Butter Cake

Omit orange juice and add instead:

¼ cup milk
1 tsp vanilla

Mix and bake as above.

Chiffon Cake

Large, light, and moist, chiffon cake must be baked in a separating-type tube pan. The pan is not greased, so the cake can hold on to the sides as it bakes. It is then literally cut out of the pan. Lemon, orange, and chocolate variations follow.

Separate:
7 eggs
Place the yolks in a big mixing bowl and beat them until light and foamy. Then add gradually, in a thin stream, as you beat:
½ cup safflower oil
¾ cup milk or **water**
1 tsp vanilla
Sift in together:
2¼ cups unbleached white flour
1 cup sugar
1 tsp salt
1 Tbsp baking powder
Mix well.

Preheat the oven to 350°F. Beat with a clean eggbeater, until stiff:
7 egg whites
½ tsp cream of tartar
Add egg whites to batter, folding them in with a plastic scraper or your flattened hand. Bake at 350°F for 1 hour, or until a knife inserted in the middle comes out clean. Cool upside down for 30 minutes, before removing from the pan.

1 LARGE CAKE

Chocolate Chiffon Cake

Sift in along with the dry ingredients:
6 Tbsp cocoa
½ extra cup sugar
Use milk for liquid. Use in all:
1 cup milk

Lemon Chiffon Cake

Grate the peel of:
1 organic lemon
Add to egg yolks. Cut the lemon in half and squeeze juice into a measuring cup. Add water to make, in all:
¾ cup liquid
Use this in place of the milk or water. Omit vanilla.

Orange Chiffon Cake

Grate the peel of:
1 organic orange
Add to egg yolks. Cut the orange in half and squeeze the juice into a measuring cup. Add:
1 Tbsp lemon juice
Add water or orange juice to make in all:
¾ cup liquid
Use this in place of the milk or water. Omit vanilla.

Mocha Java Icing

½ cup room-temperature butter or **margarine**
1 tsp freeze-dried instant coffee mixed with 2 tsp hot water
1 Tbsp unsweetened cocoa powder
1 Tbsp buttermilk or **yogurt**
2½ cups sifted confectioner's sugar
Mix together and spread evenly on tops and sides of 2 layers of cake. Chill to set.

Separating tube pan

Rhum Baba

The Cake: Mix together in a large warm ceramic bowl:

1 cup warm water
1 Tbsp dried yeast
½ cup sugar
1 cup whole wheat flour
½ cup dried milk

Let this rest 5 minutes; beat well for 30 minutes. Then beat in:

4 eggs
½ tsp salt
⅔ cup oil or **melted butter**
2½ cups whole wheat flour

You may add, if the spirit moves you:

1 cup raisins

Beat, knead, and work this dough until it is glutenous. Cover with a cloth and set to rise in the warming oven for about 1 hour, until it doubles in size.

Butter and flour well a deep mold or two, or cupcake tins. An 11-inch tube pan will do all of it, but if your pan is smaller, use 2, or put the extra in muffin tins. Fill whatever you are using only half-full, and let it rise 1 hour, until doubled. Preheat oven to 350°F.

When the dough is ready, bake it for about 30 minutes (20 minutes for small cupcake-sized cakes). Cool before unmolding.

The Syrup: As children, we delightedly imagined rum cakes to be soaked in straight rum, and lurched around accordingly. Actually, it's mostly sugar syrup, flavored with a little liquor.

Boil together for 10 minutes:

2 cups water
1 cup sugar (or **¾ cup honey**)
juice of ½ lemon
grated lemon rind

Cool and add:

½ to 1 cup rum or **sweet gingery wine,
    such as dandelion**

Put the cooked cakes in a large pan, upside down, and poke them all over with a skewer as you pour on the syrup. Let them sit 15 minutes; then pour off the excess syrup and dose them again. Continue doing so until all the syrup is used up.

1 LARGE CAKE OR 12 MUFFINS

Sponge Cake

This is a very nice little cake with no oil or shortening of any kind and no keeping power whatsoever. Very good under fresh strawberries or blueberries and sour cream.

Like Chiffon Cake (*see p. 203*), its lightness is supported by the pan, an ungreased separating-type tube pan (*see p. 203*).

Preheat oven to 350°F. Beat until light:

3 egg yolks

Add gradually:

1 cup sugar

Grate in:

rind of 1 organic lemon or **orange**

Beat in:

¼ cup boiling water
2 Tbsp lemon juice

Sift in:

⅞ cup unbleached white flour
2 tsp baking powder
¼ tsp salt

Stir to mix. Using clean beaters, beat until stiff:

3 egg whites

Fold the egg whites lightly into the batter, using a plastic scraper or the flat of your (clean) hand. Pour at once into the ungreased separating tube pan and bake for 40 minutes, or until uniformly browned on top. Keep upside down until completely cooled.

A ONE-LAYER CAKE

Apricot Almond Fruitcake

I always bake our Christmas fruitcake in a pan shaped like Santa coming out of the chimney, and it takes us months to eat it all. I suspect this is its real purpose; no matter how bare the cookie tin, there is always some fruitcake left somewhere. This version of fruitcake is cakelike, and the fruit is tart, without any peel or molasses. The almonds are an important part of it. Use kitchen scissors to chop apricots and dates.

Soak overnight together:
1½ cups chopped apricots
1 cup golden raisins
1 cup currants
½ cup chopped dates
1 cup orange juice
Next morning, preheat oven to 250°F. In a large bowl, beat:
4 eggs
½ cup honey
Cream together:
¾ cup butter
1 cup brown sugar
Add egg mixture and:
¾ cup buttermilk
Sift in together:
2 cups unbleached white flour
1 tsp baking powder
¼ tsp salt
¼ tsp mace
½ tsp allspice
½ tsp cinnamon
Add fruit mixture and:
1½ cups whole or **sliced almonds**
Fill cake pans or muffin tins ¾ full. Bake at 250°F for up to 2 hours, until a knife inserted in the middle comes out clean. Cool before unmolding. You may soak this cake with any amount of rum, brandy, or cognac, or simply wrap it up in foil and keep it cool until you are ready to serve it.

1 LARGE CAKE AND 1 OR 2 LOAVES

BARS & SQUARES

Granola Bars

These are worth making granola for. They remind me of the exotic little cakes my cousin used to send us when she lived in Florence, Italy.

Preheat oven to 350°F. Mix together:
¼ cup softened butter
½ cup whole wheat flour
Press into a lightly oiled 9-inch square pan, and bake at 350°F for 20 minutes. Meanwhile, mix up:
2 beaten eggs
1 cup brown sugar
1 cup granola cereal *(see p. 169)*
½ cup slivered almonds
½ cup candied fruit rind (optional)
1 tsp vanilla
Pour the mixture over the crust, return to the oven, and bake at 350°F for 25 minutes. Cool completely before cutting into squares.

9 SQUARES

Maple Nut Squares

Preheat oven to 350°F. Lightly oil a 9-inch square pan.

Mix together:
1 cup whole wheat flour
¼ cup safflower oil
1 Tbsp sugar
Press these into the pan, and bake for 10 minutes. Meanwhile, combine:
1 cup maple syrup
2 Tbsp melted butter (optional)
2 eggs
2 Tbsp whole wheat flour
pinch of salt
½ cup chopped nuts (I use brazil nuts)
Take the base out of the oven and pour in the topping. Bake 20 to 25 minutes. Cool and cut into squares.

9 SQUARES

Itty's Breakfast Bars

Isabelle Bartlett told me I ought to be writing a novel instead of a cookbook, but she was so kind as to give me this recipe anyway. If you use margarine, it has no milk products.

Preheat the oven to 350°F. Combine in a small bowl and let sit:
⅓ cup frozen orange juice concentrate
¼ cup raisins
½ cup shredded unsweetened coconut
½ cup chopped nuts
In a larger bowl, mash together:
½ cup room-temperature butter or **margarine**
1 cup brown sugar
2 eggs
Add and mix in:
1 cup flour
¼ tsp baking powder
¼ tsp salt
¾ cup All-Bran cereal
½ cup rolled oats
2 Tbsp sesame seeds
grated rind of 1 organic lemon
This makes a *very* stiff dough. Press half of it thinly into a greased 9-inch square pan. Spread the fruit-nut filling on that, and top with the rest of the dough, using wet hands to press it into flat sections before piecing it out over the filling. Bake 35 to 40 minutes or until browned on top. Cut into bars.

9 SQUARES

Date Bars

The sticky date center is so sweet that the cookie layer on each side hardly needs to be sweet at all.

Place in a small pan:
1 cup pitted dates
Add:
½ cup boiling water
Cover tightly and cook over low heat 10 minutes or until dates soften. Meanwhile, mix together:
¼ cup cold butter
1 cup whole wheat pastry flour or **half white, half whole wheat flour**
Cut these together with 2 knives and a pastry cutter until they are a fine crumble. Then add and mix in:
½ cup rolled oats
½ cup unsweetened dried coconut (or **more rolled oats**)
½ cup nuts or **seeds** (optional)
Then combine and mix in:
½ cup honey
¼ cup safflower oil
Lightly oil a 9-inch square pan. Set a bowl of water at your elbow and use it to moisten your hands as you flatten pieces of dough to thinly cover the pan, using half the dough. Then flatten pieces of dates in the same way, and finally cover with a top layer of dough. Bake at 350°F for 30 minutes or until rich and brown. Cool before serving.

9 SQUARES

Coconut Meringue Squares

This is as fancy as a cake with icing, but tastier. The cake goes into the oven in 2 layers, and comes out finished. This cake is a favorite with some of my friends who especially like to beat the egg whites.

Preheat the oven to 350°F. Grease a 9-inch square pan. Separate into 2 bowls:

3 eggs
Beat the yolks and add to them:
½ cup white sugar
2 Tbsp room-temperature butter
Then add and beat in:
½ cup milk
pinch of salt
1 cup unbleached white flour
1 tsp baking powder
1 tsp vanilla
Mix well. In the other bowl, beat the egg whites with a clean eggbeater. Then gently fold in:
½ cup white sugar
1½ cups unsweetened coconut
1 tsp almond flavoring
Pour the yellow batter into the pan. Scoop white on top, and spread it around. Scatter a little coconut on top. Bake for 25 to 30 minutes or until lightly browned.

9 SQUARES

Snowy Day Squares

Squares are often made for a tea or lunch served at a community gathering. They usually have separate layers, baked together, and are made in a 9-inch square pan so that pieces may easily be cut and handled in a social situation.

Preheat the oven to 350°F.

Base: In a small pan, melt:
5 Tbsp butter or **margarine**
Add and mix in:
1 cup graham cracker crumbs
1 tsp cinnamon
2 Tbsp brown sugar
Butter a 9-inch square pan and press this mixture into it. Bake the base for 10 minutes while you mix up the topping.

Topping: Beat with a whisk or fork until foamy:
2 eggs
Add and mix in:
¾ cup brown sugar
½ cup walnut pieces
1 cup unsweetened coconut
1 Tbsp unbleached white flour
1 tsp almond flavoring
½ cup chocolate chips (optional)
Take the base out of the oven and pour the topping directly on it. Return to the oven and bake for another 30 minutes, or until nicely browned on top. Cool, then cut with a cold, wet knife.

9 SQUARES

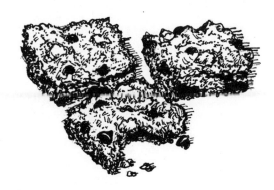

Chocolate Raspberry Brownies

Rich, dense chocolate brownies on the bottom, raspberry filling, and chocolate icing on top: an ode to chocolate. Allow time for the raspberries to set; make this at least 2 hours before you plan to serve it.

Brownies: Melt together over very low heat or in a double boiler:
1 cup sugar
½ cup butter or **margarine**
2 oz unsweetened baking chocolate
In a mixing bowl, beat until foamy:
2 eggs
½ cup unbleached white flour
½ tsp baking powder
Pour in the chocolate in a thin stream, mixing as you do. Beat well. Bake in a 9 x 6 x 2-inch baking pan for 20 minutes or until the middle bounces back when pressed lightly. Remove from oven but leave in the pan until cool.

Raspberry Filling: Combine in a small pan:
1 cup fresh or **frozen raspberries**
¼ cup sugar (omit if the berries are pre-sweetened)
2 level Tbsp cornstarch
Cook until thick, then pour over the cooled brownies.

Chocolate Icing: Melt over very low heat or in the top of a double boiler:
1 cup chocolate chips
¼ cup butter or **margarine**
Pour the icing over the raspberry filling, rolling the pan to coat the berries evenly. Cool until firm. Cut in pan, and lift pieces out with spatula.

8 SQUARES

COOKIES

Cookies can be flat and crunchy, fat and soft, plain and satisfying, or full of surprises. They don't have to be very sweet; they can have interesting flavors or textures instead.

The great virtue of a cookie is its portability. You can always stuff a handful in your pocket, your knapsack, your saddlebag, or your lunchbox.

Ingredients

Fats and Oils: The reason cookies are so crunchy and keepable is that, generally, they have a high measure of oils or fats. Solid fats make cookies lighter; oils make them denser, and, after a day or two, not so crunchy. But oils are better for you.

Flours: If you're used to white-flour cookies, you can probably switch to whole wheat pastry flour for more nutrition; nobody will know the difference. Hard wheat is nutritionally better for you, but it must be very finely ground to be really good in cookies (because they bake so fast and hot). Oat flour is nice — sort of dense, but tasty. A little ground millet or cornmeal adds crunch.

Milk and Milk Products: Milk makes the insides of cookies tender and the outsides crisp. Cultured buttermilk or yogurt does it even better.

Sweeteners: These affect the texture as well as the flavor. Sugar and brown sugar make a light, dry cookie. Molasses or honey makes them chewy; molasses is chewy with a distinct flavor.

Eggs: Watch out for eggs and oats. The high temperatures used in baking cookies often make eggs tough, especially when mixed with oat flour. When I first began inventing cookies I used lots of eggs;

all my cookies were soft and tender for about 1 hour, after which they became so hard that the only way you could eat them was to put them in a tin for a month with a slice of apple. Eggs do hold cookies together; but use other liquids, too.

Ground Nuts, Seeds, and Wheat Germ: These all have a lot of oil, so they're very good cookie materials. You may roast and grind them for more flavor, or leave them raw for more nutrition. Brazil nuts, walnuts, and pecans are the softest; they can be added in big chunks, but hard nuts, such as almonds and filberts, should be sliced or ground.

Baking Soda, Baking Powder, (see p. 68)

Almond Cookies

These are very healthy cookies, compared to most.

Sift together:
1½ cups whole wheat flour
1 cup whole wheat pastry flour or **white flour**
1½ tsp baking powder
½ cup sugar
Mix in by hand, very thoroughly:
½ cup safflower oil
Mix in a measuring cup and add:
⅓ cup cold water
2 tsp almond extract
Mix well and shape into balls the size of large walnuts. Set on a cookie sheet and press to flatten slightly, ½ inch thick.

Mix in the measuring cup:
1 egg yolk
1 Tbsp water
Paint tops of each cookie. Set on each:
1 whole almond
Bake at 350° to 400°F for 10 to 15 minutes.

30 TO 40 COOKIES

Coconut Oatcakes

Light crisp oatcakes are the national dish of Cape Breton Island. This is a large recipe, but they keep very well.
Sift together:
2 cups unbleached white flour
1 cup whole wheat flour
1 cup white sugar
1 tsp salt
2 tsp baking powder
Chop with 2 knives, then cut in with a pastry cutter:
1 cup cold shortening (**butter** or **lard** for flakiness, or **margarine** if you must)
½ cup butter
Mix in:
2 cups small-flake rolled oats
1 cup unsweetened, shredded coconut
Then mix in:
¾ to 1 cup buttermilk (or **1 cup yogurt**)
1 tsp almond flavoring
Shape the mixture into 3 or 4 rough balls. Turn each out on a lightly floured board and roll out ¼-inch thick. Cut into squares with a pizza cutter. Preheat oven to 350°F and bake 15 minutes or until lightly browned.

60 TO 70 COOKIES

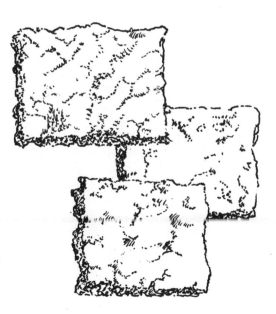

Peanut Butter Cookies

Once upon a time there was a little boy named Captain Peanutbutter, who used to go on amazing adventures over the oceans blue in his boat, which was named the Good Ship Peanutbutter. He sailed all over the world. And if he ever got into trouble, all he had to do was eat some peanut butter and he became so strong he could lick a dozen tigers. This was partly because of the good things in peanut butter, which all kids know. This is why they like Peanut Butter Cookies.

In a large mixing bowl, mash together:
1 cup peanut butter
1 cup brown sugar
¼ cup peanut oil
⅓ cup water
1 cup dried skim milk powder
1 egg
Sift in together:
1 cup whole wheat flour
½ cup unbleached white flour
2 tsp baking powder
½ tsp salt
Mix thoroughly.

Preheat oven to 375°F. Lightly oil a cookie sheet or two. Roll the dough into 30 or 40 balls about the size of walnuts. Flatten them slightly with a fork. Bake at 375°F for 15 to 20 minutes, or until lightly browned.

30 TO 40 COOKIES

Fat Archies

This is a substantial molasses cookie which has brightened many a lunchbox. For special flavor, try grating in an inch of fresh ginger root, instead of using dried ginger powder.

Preheat oven to 350°F. Mash with a fork:
½ cup shortening
Then add and beat in:
1 cup molasses
1 egg
1 tsp baking soda
dissolved in:
½ cup buttermilk
Sift in together:
3 cups unbleached white flour
1 tsp cinnamon
½ tsp cloves or **allspice**
pinch of salt
Grate in:
1 inch peeled fresh ginger root or **1 tsp ground ginger**
Add:
¾ cup raisins
Stir everything together. Drop by spoonfuls on a lightly oiled cookie sheet and bake for 10 to 12 minutes at 350°F. Cool before storing.

40 TO 50 COOKIES

Birdseed Brittle

Thin, crunchy squares of nuts, seeds, and dried fruit, these are always a big hit at picnics and parties.

Scatter on a cookie sheet and roast at 300°F for 10 to 15 minutes:
1 cup sunflower seeds
½ cup sesame seeds
½ cup chopped nuts (cashews, brazils, or **walnuts)**
1 cup large-flake rolled oats
In a mixing bowl, combine:
1 egg
1 cup honey
3 Tbsp safflower oil
¼ cup water
pinch of salt
Add cooled seeds, and:
1 cup dried currants
½ cup finely chopped dates
Oil cookie sheets. Spread the mixture evenly (more or less) on the 2 pans, and bake at 350°F for 20 minutes or until evenly browned. Cut into squares with a pizza cutter, or simply tear into fragments. Allow them to cool before storing in a tin. They keep very well.

Oat Raisin Treats

These are crisp, tasty, tender little oat cookies to slip in a lunch or grab a pocketful of as you scoot out the door.

Preheat oven to 350°F. Mix together:
¼ cup safflower oil
½ cup honey
Add and beat in:
1 egg
2 Tbsp water
Then mix and add:
¾ cup unbleached white flour
1 tsp cinnamon
½ tsp baking powder
¼ tsp salt
Mix and beat smooth, then mix in:

2 cups small-flake rolled oats
½ cup raisins
½ cup walnuts or **sesame seeds**
With wet palms, lightly roll the stiff batter into balls (about 2 Tbsp each), then flatten on cookie sheets. They will not spread much, so you can put them close together. Bake 10 minutes or until golden. Cool on racks or clean cloths before storing in airtight containers.

ABOUT 45 COOKIES

Spice Cookies

A soft cookie with fruit and lots of flavor.

If the ingredients are at room temperature it will be much easier to mash together:
½ cup shortening
1 cup brown sugar
Then add and beat in:
1 egg
¼ cup cider or **water**
Sift in together:
1 cup unbleached white flour
1 cup whole wheat flour
1 tsp baking soda
½ tsp salt
1 tsp cinnamon
1 tsp cloves
Chop well and add:
1 cup apples or **other soft fruit**
½ cup chopped nuts
1 cup currants
Put cookies on lightly oiled cookie sheets and bake in a preheated 400°F oven for 15 minutes.

30 COOKIES

Peppernuts

Peppernuts are funny crisp little cookies about the size of hazelnuts, very nicely flavored with spices that blend to make them tasty. In old-fashioned German households, they were served alongside gingerbread with milk or coffee.

In a large, wide bowl, mix:
3 cups sugar
1 cup shortening
Add and beat in:
4 eggs
1 cup milk
Then sift in together:
3 tsp baking powder
¼ tsp salt
1 tsp each cinnamon, cloves, nutmeg, and white pepper
7 cups unbleached white flour
Shape the dough into 4 flattened balls, and wrap each in waxed paper. Refrigerate at least 2 hours, up to 2 weeks.

Preheat oven to 350°F. Lightly oil a couple cookie tins. Cut dough from 1 packet into 4 pieces, then roll each out by hand on a lightly floured board to the diameter of a thick pencil. Cut the dough in snippets the size of an eraser with a knife or scissors. Scatter them on the cookie sheet and bake at 350°F for 10 minutes, or until lightly browned.

HUNDREDS

Gingerbread Figures

When we first moved to Cape Breton in the early '70s, we landed on Boulardarie Island next door to the Ryan family. It was, for me, a great piece of luck. Peggy Ryan, mother of twelve, was a wonderful cook and took it upon herself to educate me. It was from her that we learned how to make gingerbread "by the ton," as she said. She never measured the flour, and made them fat and soft. I don't measure either, except at Christmas, when we cut out stars and gingerbread people to ice and hang up as decorations. To punch holes for hanging them, use a straw.

Beat together until creamy:
¾ cup shortening
1 cup brown sugar
Beat in:
2 eggs
1 cup molasses
1 tsp salt
1 tsp cloves
1 tsp allspice
2 tsp ginger
Mix together and add:
½ cup milk
2 Tbsp yogurt (any flavor)
1 tsp baking soda
Peggy added flour until she could roll it out; she used:
6 to 7 cups white flour
If you'd rather use whole-grain flours, I'd suggest you use less, and make drop cookies. You could use:
3½ cups whole wheat flour
3 cups white flour or **whole wheat pastry flour**
Beat well and chill 2 hours before baking. To make ordinary cookies, press large spoonfuls onto a cookie sheet. To make ginerbread figures or other shapes, follow the directions on the next page. Bake at 350°F for 10 to 15 minutes.

50 COOKIES

CUTTING OUT COOKIES

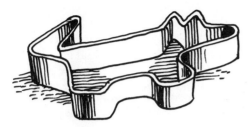

Cookie cutting has always been a Christmas event in our house. We have piles of cookie cutters: traditional trees and Santas and reindeer, men and women, horses, flowers, hearts, and also elephants, palm trees, and crocodiles; my family takes special delight in finding me the most outrageous shapes.

It is traditional to roll them out on the kitchen table. To keep things tidy, spread newspapers first. You will also need:
- a container of flour
- a small pot of water
- a breadboard
- a rolling pin

Chill cookie dough before rolling it out. You may use Gingerbread Figure dough, Sugar Cookie dough (p. 215), or any dough that is firm and does not spread too much as it bakes.

Lightly flour the board and rolling pin before you begin and as you go along, to keep the dough from sticking to the board or rolling pin.

Some cutters are small, some are large. Try to make each trayful the same, because large thick cookies will take much longer to bake than small thin cookies.

If you want to be able to hang these cookies up on the tree or around the house with yarn or ribbon, punch holes in them before you bake them, using a fat drinking straw.

To make stained-glass gingerbread, you will need colored sourballs or Life Savers. Cut out large cookie shapes, such as people or flower or houses. Cut holes in them about ¾-inch square (as for windows) or 1 inch diameter (the size of doughnut holes). Place the cookies on a clean cookie tin and put a hard candy or Life Saver in the middle of each hole. Bake as above. When the cookies are ready and the candy melted, take them out, but don't touch them for 5 minutes. Then quickly slide your spatula under each one. It's not necessary to move them else-where, just get that spatula under each one at the 5-minute mark. (If you do it sooner, they glom up and stick to the spatula; if you do it later, they're stuck to the sheet.) No use greasing the sheet. This is a single-method operation, no alternatives.

Decorating

Use nuts, seeds, bits of candied fruit rind, coconut, or sugar; for children, you may put each kind of decoration in the cups of a muffin tin, so they won't spill. Avoid raisins or currants on top because they just swell up and blacken. Remember you can use dough for decoration, too, if stuck on with water. Patterns can be made with blunt knives, chopsticks, forks, etc.

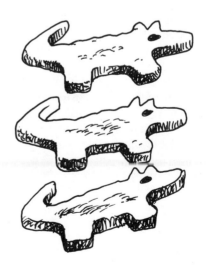

Springerle

When I got married, my brother gave me a springerle rolling pin "with which to dent the head of your husband in an interesting pattern," as he said. It is such a highly specialized piece of equipment that I have felt responsible for producing the springerle every Christmas since then. It is a very sweet, dense anise-flavored cookie, which, because it hardly rises at all, keeps the imprint of the springerle mold, whatever that may be. It is baked very slowly and when done is hard as a rock. When cool, you put them in a tin with a slice of apple for at least 15 days, and they become soft again, in texture rather like marzipan.

Beat together in a mixing bowl:
4 eggs
1 tsp vanilla
Add gradually, beating as you do:
2 cups sugar
Sift together, then add gradually, beating as you do:
3½ cups white flour
½ tsp baking powder
½ tsp salt
Using your hands, work in another:
½ cup flour
Spread a little flour on a flat surface, and roll out the dough with a floured rolling pin to about 1-inch thickness (this is very thick). Sprinkle on the board:
2 to 3 tsp fresh anise seeds
Lay the dough over the seeds and roll it lightly with the rolling pin so the dough will pick up the seeds on one side.

Lightly dust your mold with flour. On the other side of the dough, print the pattern, using either a flat springerle mold or a rolling pin. Cut the cakes apart. Set on lightly oiled cookie sheet, seed-side down, not touching. Allow them to rest 12 to 24 hours.

Preheat oven to 200°F. Bake cookies 45 minutes or until light brown on the bottoms. Cool before storing. Place them in a tightly covered tin with slices of apple (arranged so that the apple slices do not touch the cookies.) They should be softened in about 2 weeks, but have been known to take longer, possibly due to the constant opening of the tin to check them.

50 SQUARE COOKIES

Cookie Icing

Cookie icing takes an extraordinary amount of sugar and very little liquid. It may be flavored with vanilla or almond extract, or a little Christmas spirits such as rum or brandy. To make lines and squiggles, put the mixture in a plastic bag, then cut off the tiniest bit of a corner with sharp scissors. Icing is not a good project for little hands.
1 cup sifted confectioner's sugar
2 Tbsp milk
½ tsp almond flavoring
Combine ingredients. *(To color icing, see French Butter Icing, p. 202.)*

Allow iced cookies to dry for several hours before stacking them together.

MAKES ¼ CUP ICING

Sugar Cookies

These crisp, delicious little morsels are just what you want to serve with a fruit or custard dessert.

Bring to room temperature:
½ cup shortening
½ cup butter (important for flavor)
Mash in:
¾ cup white sugar
¼ cup brown sugar
Beat in:
1 egg
1 tsp vanilla
Mix together and sift in:
2 tsp baking powder
2½ cups unbleached white flour
¼ tsp salt
Mix the batter well, then drop by tablespoonfuls on an oiled cookie sheet. You may decorate cookies with a half cherry, an almond, or a walnut. Bake at 350°F for 8 to 10 minutes.

30 TO 40 COOKIES

Variation
Chill dough, then roll out on a lightly floured board and cut shapes; decorate with bits of candied peel, nuts, or sugar.

Fabulous Chocolate Chip Cookies

You could start a restaurant based on a cookie like this. The main thing is to make sure the oven is up to the right temperature before you put the cookies in the oven.

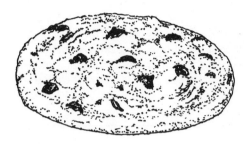

Allow to come to room temperature:
½ cup butter
Add and blend in:
1 cup brown sugar
Then add and mix in:
¼ cup vegetable oil
1 egg
1 tsp vanilla
1 tsp almond flavoring
Sift together and mix in:
2 cups unbleached white flour
2 tsp baking powder
½ tsp salt
Mix well.
Add chips, nuts, whatever, at the last. I like:
½ cup chopped walnuts
½ cup chocolate chips (or **carob chips**)
Refrigerate the dough while you preheat the oven to 375°F. Shape the cookies into 30 walnut-sized balls and flatten them slightly on a lightly oiled cookie sheet. Bake at 375°F for 12 to 15 minutes.

30 COOKIES

PIECRUSTS

Piecrusts serve two purposes. One, they enclose the contents of the pie, so that it can be served in elegant wedges instead of glomps; and, two, the crisp crust provides a contrast to the middle of the pie, which is usually soft and sweet.

The making of a good piecrust is a delicate operation. To make a flaky white piecrust, use white flour and cold solid shortening, either lard or butter. You can also make piecrust with whole wheat flour and oil. It will be crispy, like a cracker, but delicious in its own way.

Ingredients
Flour: To make a flaky white crust use unbleached white flour. To make a whole wheat crust, the best choice is whole wheat pastry flour.

Shortening: For a flaky white crust, the absolute best shortening is homemade lard, which is harder than commercial shortenings. Chilled commercial lard, or its vegetable-derived look-alikes are what most cooks use. Butter has delicious flavor, and is sometimes used in combination with lard. Mild-flavored oils such as safflower, corn, or peanut make good crisp crusts, and are better for you than hydrogenated fats *(for more about fats, see p. 69)*. Oils do not, however, make a flaky piecrust.

Liquid: For the lightest, flakiest, melt-in-your-mouth piecrusts, use only water. If, on the other hand, you desire a durable crust that can be put together by a pair of twelve-year olds and carried, intact, to the county fair, try Elsie's Foolproof Piecrust with egg and lemon juice *(see p. 218)*.

Mixing White Piecrust
To make a flaky white piecrust by hand, measure the flour and salt into a bowl, and add chilled shortening. Cut the shortening in small pieces with 2 knives, then use a pastry blender or fork to chop the shortening into fragments so small they are no longer identifiable. When the mixture resembles hot cereal, measure out cold water and add it gradually. Use just enough to make the mixture stick together. Too much, and the piecrust will be solid and dense, rather than flaky. Too little, and the piecrust will fall apart as you try to roll it out. The amount will vary with flour and daily humidity.

Piecrust is easier to roll out and work with if chilled for at least half an hour before you make your pie. Wrap it in waxed paper or a plastic bag to retain moisture.

Rolling Out the Dough
If you are making a pie with both top and bottom crusts, you will need ⅔ of it for the bottom, ⅓ for the top.

Roll pie dough out on a movable wooden board or on a pastry cloth. Flour will stick to the slight roughness of the wood; therefore the dough won't stick to floured surfaces.

Rolling out the dough makes it thin enough to surround the pie; it also flattens the particles of shortening and flour so the crust will become flaky in baking.

Start with dough in a rough patty, and roll it from the center outward, with a light, firm touch. Turn and move the crust to make sure it isn't getting stuck underneath. Roll to ⅛-inch thickness. If a hole appears, make a patch of rolled dough and stick it in place with a finger dipped in water.

Pie Pans

The best pie pans are thin metal, with gently sloping sides, and have little holes in the bottoms to allow moisture to escape. You will not be able to bake crisp piecrusts in deep ceramic vessels.

Moving the Crust

Getting piecrust from the counter into the pie dish has caused much despair in novice piemaking. It is trickier with whole wheat than with white flour crusts, but any crust can fall apart in transit, so be wary. One good way is to invert the piepan over the crust and board and then turn the whole thing right-side up. The crust will fall into the pan. The top of the pie, being smaller, is easier to handle.

Finishing Touches

To close bottom and top, you may use dabs of water on your finger, or the pressure of a fork, or flute it with your thumb and index finger. Slash the tops of berry pies to keep the edges from steaming open.

Baking

Good piecrust requires a very hot oven, cooling slightly as it bakes: 450°F, going down to 375°F. *(See Using the Stove, p. 298.)*

If baking berry or rhubarb pies, which are likely to boil over, it is wise to have something underneath them to catch the drips.

To Bake an Empty Pie Shell: Line piedish with crust; trim the edge wide to allow for even more shrinkage than usual. Prick sides and center with a fork and line the shell with tinfoil to hold dried kidney beans that will keep it from bubbling up. Bake at 450°F for 10 minutes or until browned. Remove beans and cool piecrust before filling.

Single Whole Wheat Piecrust

For the whole wheat flour in these recipes, you may use either hard whole wheat bread flour or whole wheat pastry flour. Hard wheat makes a tougher, denser crust than pastry flour, but hard wheat has more flavor. Pastry flour is lighter both in color and texture, and the crust is less likely to fall apart as you move it from the rolling surface to the pan.

Sift or mix together:
1¼ cup whole wheat pastry flour
1 tsp salt
In another bowl, mix together:
⅓ cup safflower oil
3 Tbsp water
Make a well in the flour. Beat oil and water together and into the flour with a fork. Work with fork until it is all one solid mass. Roll out with a little white flour or with minimum handling, to 1 inch larger than the pie shell. Invert on pie shell as carefully as possible. Bake an empty piecrust in a preheated oven at 400° for 12 minutes.

1 BOTTOM PIECRUST

Single White Piecrust

This may be baked with the filling in, as with quiche, or baked without a filling, and later filled with pudding.

½ cup cold shortening
1⅓ cups white flour
½ tsp salt (optional)
3 to 4 Tbsp ice water
To mix and bake the piecrust, *see pp. 216–17.*

1 BOTTOM PIECRUST

Crumb Crust

This can be made with any kind of cookie crumbs, really. To smash them up use a blender, food processor, or a plastic bag and a rolling pin.

Melt:
⅓ cup butter
Add and mix in:
1½ cups ground graham cracker crumbs
¼ tsp nutmeg or 1 tsp cinnamon
Lightly butter a spring-form pan and press the crumb mixture in as best you can. You may bake this crust for 5 or 10 minutes at 350°F, or not, as you choose, before pouring in the filling. It will be crunchier if baked. I prefer to refrigerate it for 2 hours. It will not be tidy-looking in any case but will keep the filling from sticking to the pan and will taste divine.

1 BOTTOM PIECRUST

Variation
Instead of butter use ¼ cup safflower oil

Elsie's Foolproof Piecrust

Elsie Kirkham showed me how to make a decent piecrust that will not fall apart.

Mix together:
⅓ cup ice water
1 egg
1 Tbsp lemon juice
In a large mixing bowl, measure out:
4 cups white flour
1 tsp salt
1¼ cups cold shortening
Cut shortening into flour *(see p. 216).* Then add water and lemon mixture. Shape into 2 balls, each of which is enough dough for a two-crust pie. Refrigerate for 1 hour before rolling it out.

2 TWO-CRUST PIECRUSTS

Strawberry Rhubarb Pie

Make and refrigerate:
1 recipe Single White Piecrust *(see above, left)*
Mix together in a 2-quart saucepan:
3 cups fresh or frozen chopped rhubarb
2 cups fresh or frozen sliced strawberries
1 cup sugar
Heat until the rhubarb softens. Remove from heat and allow to cool until there is ½ cup liquid in the pot. If there is not enough, add a little water and mix it in; if there is too much, simmer gently to evaporate the excess. In a small bowl, combine:
3 Tbsp cornstarch
4 Tbsp water
Mix these well, then add:
½ cup liquid from the pot
Stir, then add the mixture to the fruit in the pot. Heat until the cornstarch clarifies and thickens the fruit mixture.

Preheat oven to 450°F. Line pie dish and trim the edge generously. Fill pie and top with piecrust in plain or latticed strips. Bake at 450°F for 25 minutes or until nicely browned. Cool before serving.

ONE 9-INCH PIE

Lemon Meringue Pie

Lemon meringue has always been my favorite pie. It isn't difficult to make, even from scratch, and is very elegant looking as long as you chill it before serving. There are three separate procedures.

1.) Make a **Single White Piecrust** *(p. 218)*, a **Single Whole Wheat Piecrust** *(p. 217)*, or a **Crumb Crust** *(p. 218)*, and bake it in a hot oven, at 450°F, for 15 minutes. Cool the crust before filling.

2.) Meanwhile, separate **3 eggs,** putting the **yolks** into a small saucepan and the **whites** into a mixing bowl. Beat yolks together in the pan, then add to them:
grated rind of ½ organic lemon
3 Tbsp lemon juice
¾ cup sugar
1½ cups water
3 Tbsp cornstarch
Heat very slowly, stirring with a whisk or spring stirrer until it thickens. Stir and heat 1 minute over low heat, then pour into the piecrust.

3.) In the mixing bowl, beat the 3 egg whites with a clean rotary beater until they stand up stiffly. Fold in gently:
3 Tbsp confectioner's sugar
Scoop the egg whites on top of the pie, sculpting them a bit, and bake at 350°F for 15 minutes or until lightly browned at the tips.

Cool for a minimum of 3 hours before serving, or overnight if your life is that organized.

ONE 9-INCH PIE

Blueberry Apple Pie

I have thought about growing blueberries close to home, but truth is I like travelling to pick them, especially on a mountainside with a long view. We always freeze several gallons for year-round use. The blueberries stain the apples reddish purple — very colorful.

Make up and refrigerate:
2 recipes Single Whole Wheat Piecrust *(see p. 217)*
Preheat oven to 450°F. Roll out the piecrust and line a pie dish.

Mix together:
2 cups sliced apples
2 cups fresh or **frozen blueberries**
2 Tbsp cornstarch or **flour**
½ tsp cinnamon
½ cup sugar
Put filling in the pie and cover with top crust. Cut slits in top. Be sure to place something under the pie to catch drips. Bake at 450°F for 10 minutes, then reduce heat to 350° for 35 to 40 minutes.

ONE 9-INCH PIE

Fruit Pizza

Just when you thought you'd heard everything. Fruit Pizza? Yes! It's terrific! Even good for you!

Make and allow to rise:
1 recipe Pizza Dough *(see p. 104)*
Roll out a piece about the size of a small melon to ¼-inch thickness. Arrange on it:
4 to 5 sliced apples, pears, nectarines, peaches, kiwi, or **a mixture of these and other fruits**
Sprinkle over them a mixture of:
2 Tbsp sugar
¼ tsp cinnamon (optional)
Bake at 425°F for 15 to 20 minutes, until browned around the edges. This is as good cold as hot and a popular thing to bring to a potluck.

ONE 14- TO 16-INCH PIZZA

Apple Crisp

Traditionally a favorite for feeding the masses, apple crisp is as delicious as pie, much easier to make, and has no saturated fats.

Toss together:
4 to 5 cups sliced apples
½ tsp cinnamon
½ tsp nutmeg
¼ cup water
½ cup sugar (only if the apples are sour)
Put in an oiled 9-inch square baking pan.

Topping
In a bowl, mix together thoroughly:
½ cup whole wheat flour
½ cup brown sugar
2 tsp cinnamon
½ cup safflower oil
Then add and mix in lightly:
1 cup rolled oats
½ cup wheat germ
Spread the mixture on top of the apples and bake at 375° for 35 minutes. Serve hot or cold.

SERVES 6

Variation

Rhubarb Crisp

Follow directions above, but instead of spices, toss **4 to 5 cups sliced rhubarb** with:

1 cup sugar
3 Tbsp cornstarch
and omit the ¼ cup water. Mix topping and bake as above.

Ultimate Cheesecake

Light, rich, and delicious, with a raspberry glaze topping, this is the sort of cheesecake people dream about. Our innovative daughter supported herself for a while making these for patisseries and coffee shops to sell by the slice. She recommends a spring-form pan, with a separating bottom, but she has also made it in a separating tube pan. It should be made 12 hours before serving, and completely chilled. It keeps quite well refrigerated — up to a week.

Prepare and chill:
1 recipe Crumb Crust (*see p. 218*)

Filling: Allow to sit for ½ hour, or until at room temperature:
2 large packages (2 cups) cream cheese
Beat until creamy, with an electric beater if you have one. Add and beat in:
1 cup white sugar
3 eggs
1 Tbsp lemon juice
rind of ½ well-washed lemon
2 tsp vanilla
1 cup sour cream
Into the batter fold:
2 Tbsp white flour
Pour the batter into a 9-inch spring-form pan, lined with the Crumb Crust. Bake at 350°F until a knife inserted into the batter comes out clean (about 1 hour). Remove cake from oven and allow to cool. Cover with topping. Cool and chill for at least 5 hours in the pan, before taking the pan apart.

Raspberry Topping
Mix together in a small pan:
2 cups fresh or **frozen raspberries**
½ cup sugar (or to taste; if using sweetened raspberries, omit)
1 Tbsp lemon juice
grated rind of ½ organic lemon

4 Tbsp cornstarch

Stir well, then cook gently for 5 to 10 minutes, until thick and clear. Spread on the cheesecake and allow to chill for at least 2 hours.

Yogurt Cheesecake

From the kitchens of Mrs. Restino, we bring you a cheesecake that entered our back door as milk and eggs. Thick, tangy, and rich-tasting, but relatively low in calories (68 calories per 2-inch slice as compared to cream-based cheesecake, which is 250 calories per 2-inch slice). Despite the low calorie count, this is rich stuff.

You will need:

1 qt yogurt

Line a bowl with 4 or 5 layers of cheese-cloth; dump in the yogurt, and tie up the cheesecloth. Hang the bag to drip over the bowl for a couple of hours, but don't squeeze it; the yogurt will come through.

Make:

1 recipe Crumb Crust *(see p. 218)* chilled for 30 minutes.

When the yogurt is thick enough (down to about 2 cups) scrape it out into a bowl and add:

2 egg yolks
1 whole egg, beaten in
1 grated lemon rind
1 cup sugar or **¾ cup honey** (or a mixture)

Since every batch of yogurt is different, I sweeten to taste rather than by recipe. I used some really strong stuff that had been forgotten in back of the warming oven for 24 hours one time; that took 1 cup sugar *and* ½ cup of honey. If you want this to be a Neapolitan Cheesecake, you can add:

½ cup whole pine nuts
¼ cup chopped candied lemon or **orange rind**

Pour the yogurt mixture into your Crumb Crust and bake at 300°F for about 30 minutes, or until the top begins to swell and crack. Cool before serving.

Fruit Topping: A plain cheesecake is very nice covered with:

1 to 2 cups fresh or **frozen fruit: blueberries, apples, peaches, cherries, strawberries,** or **raspberries,** sweetened to taste

Heat the fruit in a saucepan; pour off a few tablespoons of liquid and mix with:

4 Tbsp cornstarch

Return the liquid to the fruit and stir as the sauce becomes thick and clear. Pour over the cheesecake and allow the fruit to "set" on top of the cake for a couple of hours in a cool place before serving.

ONE 9-INCH PIE

CUSTARDS AND PUDDINGS

Desserts such as these are easy to make, and there are so many ways to make them. The commercial-ice-cream generations are getting robbed; strawberry, chocolate, and vanilla all taste the same, and so handy in their plastic containers; nobody knows anything about the astonishing variety of textures and flavors that used to grace our tables. Branch out: learn about egg custards, gelatins, and cream whips. Serve up your precious home-canned or frozen treasures in a dozen different forms. Save sugar; strawberries taste more like strawberries when they're a little tart. Think about your meal: does it need a light ending, or a generous scoop of pudding? Could it use eggs or milk for protein, or some fruit to balance a lack of vegetables? Invest in a few fake cut-glass dessert dishes to make gels and whips in. Or some nice brown custard cups. Remember, too, you don't have to serve desserts for only dessert. They're very good in the afternoon, with a cup of tea. And many a wise parent has discovered that children who normally despise breakfast willingly devour a trim egg custard, or a raisin Indian pudding.

Baked Custard

Delicious in its utter simplicity, a custard is anybody's favorite. Be sure to bake it in a slow oven, though, or it will toughen and separate.

Beat together:
3 eggs
2 cups whole milk
⅓ cup honey
1 tsp vanilla
pinch of salt
Pour into a greased casserole or ovenproof custard cups (teacups work nicely) and set them in a cake tin of hot water (to keep the bottom from toughening). Bake at 300°F to 325°F for about 1 hour. When a knife inserted in the center comes out clean, it's done.

4 SERVINGS

Indian Pudding

Native Americans probably made this with water, corn, and maple, perhaps a little piece of fat thrown in to render as the grain cooked. It was quickly adapted by settlers to include more ingredients; it is the sort of food that takes well to adaptation. You put in what you think is right.

Scald:
1 qt milk
Sprinkle in and stir:
½ cup cornmeal, cracked wheat, or **samp**
   (samp is a mixture of the two)
When thick, remove from heat and add:
⅓ cup molasses
⅓ cup maple sugar or **brown sugar**
½ tsp salt
½ tsp cinnamon, ½ tsp allspice, and
   ½ tsp nutmeg
½ cup raisins and ½ cup chopped nuts
   (optional)
1 Tbsp butter (optional)
Mix well, pour into a buttered baking dish, and bake at 300°F for about 2 hours.

4 SERVINGS

Orange or Lemon Sponge Custard

Custardlike on the bottom, frothy on top, and fruit-flavored, these elegant desserts must, like all egg custards, be baked in a slow oven or they will toughen and shrink. Bake them in 4 custard cups or in a small, deep casserole for best results.

Beat together:
3 egg yolks
5 Tbsp sugar or **3 Tbsp honey**
2 Tbsp melted butter
1 cup whole or **skim milk**
grated rind of 1 lemon or **orange**
3 Tbsp unbleached white flour
juice of 1 lemon or **orange**
Beat until stiff; fold in just before baking:
3 egg whites
Bake in a greased casserole or custard cups and set in a pan of hot water for about 1 hour at 300°F.

4 SERVINGS

Raspberry or Strawberry Sponge Custard

Substitute for the lemon or orange juice and rind:
⅓ cup raspberry or **strawberry juice**
2 Tbsp lemon juice
After folding in the beaten egg whites, fold in:
1 cup fresh or **frozen berries**
Bake as above.

4 SERVINGS

HOMEMADE ICE CREAM

We used to have one ice cream freezer in our neighborhood. Whenever anybody had a birthday it arrived, along with ice, cream, and ice cream mixture and was ritually filled, assembled, and passed around the room. It took one to hold it and one to turn the handle, and periodically it had to be taken out and repacked with salt and ice, but eventually ice cream began to thicken and the churning got heavy. That was the signal to speed up to as-fast-as-you-can-go. The bucket was passed around as people's arms fell off and finally everybody wanted to have a look: Was it ice cream yet? It was never really hard ice cream, unless you let it sit in a freezer for half an hour, but nobody ever waited any longer than it took to light the candles and sing Happy Birthday.

Now we have ice cream freezers, made with some kind of space-age material. You stick them in the freezer, then fill them with syrup and cream, and turn the handle once every minute for 20 minutes. They are very handy devices, making it possible to have home-made ice cream once a week, instead of just on people's birthdays, and without that terrific mess from cracking the ice and packing the bucket. But it is not as much fun.

Ingredients
Unlike store-bought ice cream, which contains an amazing assortment of chemical flavorings, colorings, and preservatives, homemade ice cream is really very simple stuff — basically it's just cream, or milk, beaten as it's frozen. Sugar or honey sweetens it; fruits, vanilla, or chocolate flavor it. In strongly flavored ice creams, you can use canned evaporated milk instead, but you must disguise the taste. For a really smooth texture, mix up the syrup the day before and keep it refrigerated.

Included here are two kinds of ice cream.

Creamy Ice Cream, in which the milk and sugar are bound by cooked eggs, so that the mixture holds together even if it begins to get warmer.

Philadelphia Ice Cream, which begins to melt when it gets warm. The advantage, however, is that you need not cook or chill it. Just mix it up and go for it.

Churn-Freezing
First, fill the churn or inner container with the ice cream mixture *(see recipes on next page).* It should never be more than ⅔ full, as the mixture will expand by ⅓. Adjust churn, dasher and lid before packing ice and salt in the outer compartment. You will either need 3 bags of ice cubes for this purpose, or a couple of gallons of frozen water, crushed in a sack with a hammer or baseball bat. Any salt will do. Layer ice about 6 inches deep, then spread a handful of salt; continue to top.

Second, churn the ice cream steadily, not rapidly, for about 20 minutes. This is a long time for one person. Four or five people taking turns is better. Add more salt and ice as needed.

When the ice cream begins to get thick, churn a little more rapidly. Don't give up until it's impossible.

Third, remove dasher, replace lid, and cover churn with wet towels and ice. Allow to sit and harden for 30 minutes if you like your ice cream frozen hard.

Creamy Vanilla Ice Cream

This is a basic recipe, because most ice cream flavors are a variation of vanilla. And it's a favorite, most frequently asked for by neighborhood children, for each of whom, traditionally, I make a birthday batch. Try it with Chocolate Fudge Sauce or Raspberry Melba Sauce *(see p. 225)*.

Mix in the top of a double boiler and heat over boiling water:
1 cup whole milk
¾ cup white sugar or **⅓ cup honey**
Meanwhile, beat in a mixing bowl:
2 eggs
pinch of salt
When the milk mixture is hot, pour it, a little at a time, as you stir, into the eggs. Return this mixture to the pan, still stirring, and cook about 10 minutes, stirring intermittently, but remove from the heat when it thickens. Cool, then pour into a container and chill for a minimum of 4 hours in the fridge or 1 hour in a freezer.

To make ice cream, put this mixture in the churn, and add:
1½ cups half-and-half cream
½ cup whipping cream
2 tsp vanilla
To pack and churn, see above, or see instructions on your ice cream–making device.

MAKES 1 QUART

Creamy Chocolate Ice Cream

In the top of a double boiler, heat over boiling water:
1½ Tbsp butter
¼ cup unsweetened cocoa powder
¼ cup sugar
Proceed as with Creamy Vanilla Ice Cream, pouring milk and sugar into the melted chocolate. Omit vanilla. You may use evaporated canned milk instead of half-and-half cream when making chocolate ice cream; the chocolate will disguise the flat flavor.

Philadelphia Ice Cream

Please read about ingredients *(see p. 223)*.

Basic Vanilla: Mix in the churn:
4 cups half-and-half cream
1 cup sugar
pinch of salt
2 tsp vanilla

Coffee: Add to Basic Vanilla:
**3 Tbsp freeze-dried espresso mixed with
   3 Tbsp hot milk**

Chocolate: Add to Basic Vanilla:
**2 squares (2 oz) melted semisweet
   chocolate**

Mix some of the cream into the chocolate, then add to the churn.

Butterscotch: Combine in a small saucepan:
1 cup brown sugar
⅓ cup butter
1 cup cream
Stir over very low heat until butter melts and sugar dissolves. Add to the rest of the cream and salt in the churn.

MAKES 1 QUART

Creamy Strawberry Ice Cream

You can use this method for all sorts of fruits: peach, for example, is very elegant and delicious.

Follow directions for Creamy Vanilla Ice Cream, but in addition to vanilla, add:
2 Tbsp lemon juice
Instead of 2 cups of cream, at the end of the recipe, add:
½ to 1 cup fruit purée
1 cup whipping cream

MAKES 1 QUART

DESSERT SAUCES

Since these are very sweet, and a bit of an extra bother, I don't make them often. But supposing it is someone's birthday, and a blizzard is raging outside. . . .

Fruit Sauce

Usually I make these out of a **1 pint jar of canned fruit (blueberries, apples, cherries,** or **peaches).** I drain off the syrup and mash a bit of it with:
2 Tbsp cornstarch
The rest of the syrup is heated, then the cornstarch is stirred in until it thickens. Then I add, by tablespoons, until the flavor is sweet enough:
sugar or **honey**
Sometimes I add:

2 Tbsp butter
Finally I add the fruit, and stir, and serve. If I had some, I'd add:
2 Tbsp brandy or **sweet wine**
Serve with ice cream, yogurt, Sponge Cake *(see p. 204)*, or Butter Cake *(see p. 202)*.

2 CUPS

Raspberry Melba Sauce

The absolute epitome of elegance.

Heat together slowly:
½ cup currant or **apple jelly**
1 cup raspberry juice
Dip out a bit of juice and mix with:
1 Tbsp cornstarch
Return to the mixture and stir until it clarifies and thickens a little. Cool 1 hour, bottle, and store refrigerated. Use on ice cream, cake, or custards.

1 CUP

Chocolate Fudge Sauce

Dreadful stuff! Guaranteed to rot your insides and curl your hair. You keep it in a small pot in the fridge and heat it up to go on ice cream or strawberries.

Melt together over low heat:
3 Tbsp butter
5 Tbsp unsweetened cocoa
Stir this well, and then add:
½ cup boiling water
1 cup sugar
Bring to a full rolling boil and cook for about 5 minutes. The longer you boil it, the thicker it will get; after 10 minutes it will be the kind of stuff that hardens on ice cream.

MAKES ⅔ CUPS

Dairy

Of all the things that I do in the kitchen, the most adventurous, it seems to me, is working with milk. I think that's because you start with such a common, simple thing (milk), and wind up making so many various and marvelous products: butter and yogurt, hard cheeses, soft cheeses, exotica like gervais and crème fraîche, or a little feta crumbled in your salad.

It does take a fair amount of work. One gallon of whole milk goes into 1 pound of hard cheese or 2 pounds of soft cheese (such as ricotta). Two and a half gallons of milk have about 1 quart of cream, which will make 1 pound of butter. Clearly, it only makes sense to work with milk if you have an endless supply.

There are two other considerations. One is equipment. In some places you can pick up things like butter churns, separators, and cheese presses secondhand, but not always. The other consideration is the time spent washing up after cheesemaking. To work with milk, you have to commit yourself to a certain level of cleanliness that goes far beyond the merely visual. It takes gallons and gallons of hot water.

When we first started farming, we had two goats. In a couple of years they turned into a whole herd that still didn't give enough milk, so we got rid of the goats and got a cow. We had enough milk then, all right. It was all I could do to keep up with it. I was making cheese every day, butter twice a week, and washing bottles and separators and churns and presses and bits of cloth every 5 minutes. Eventually we went back to goats. Now I make cheese and other milk products in the early summer, and slack off when the garden gets busy. During winter, production goes down to a quart a day, and that's about what we drink or cook with. In the spring, there I am, trying out a new cheese again.

I haven't listed all the kinds of cheese there are to make, by any stretch of the imagination. It's a collection I've worked with, had success with. There are more comprehensive books on cheesemaking. The one that I know and love is *Cheesemaking Made Easy* by Ricki and Robert Carroll, who also run a mail-order business called New England Cheesemaking in Ashfield, Massachusetts.

MILK

Milking is a habit of rhythm; at first it seems a little weird, and gradually it becomes part of your life. You learn always to keep your nails clipped short, always to wash your hands with soap and hot water, especially before and after milking. You wash the udder of the animal to be milked, too. People with big herds use a disinfectant, but we just use hot water, having only a few animals. A separate washcloth for each animal helps prevent mastitis from spreading if it should occur.

If you've never milked before, you can practice with a rubber glove full of water and a pinhole in the end of one finger. Curl your upper fingers around the top of the glove, to hold the water below, then squeeze with the lower fingers to press the milk out of the hole. Always strip all the milk an animal has; otherwise production will go down and the chance of mastitis increases.

Milk should be strained right after milking, and, unless you intend to work with it right away, it should be chilled at once. You may then allow milk to accumulate for up to three days before making milk products, but don't add warm milk to cold — it will give the milk an off taste.

Cleanliness in the Dairy

As long as your animals are healthy, you don't have to sterilize everything every day, but you should follow a special procedure in washing up milk and milk products. Because hot water cooks milk onto the surfaces of bottles, buckets, and all, you must first rinse them with cold water, then wash with soap and hot water, and rinse with hot. Some people prefer to use bleach because detergent is said to leave a soapy film. Others swear by washing soda. If you haven't got time or hot water to wash right away, leave milk product containers and tools soaking in cold water.

Ordinarily this process is adequate, but every once in a while (usually early summer) you get a bacteria in the milking bucket that just won't quit. The containers look clean and smell clean after washing, but they're really harboring germs that make the milk taste "goaty" or "cowey." To get rid of "milk stones," fill the container half-full with boiling water, then top it off with vinegar. Let sit overnight. Rinse with boiling water in the morning, and declare it clean.

Chilling the Milk

It's important to chill milk as soon as possible after milking. When we first moved here, we used to immerse it in the fast-flowing mountain stream that runs alongside our driveway. This was only good until the children got too big to send up to the stream for milk. Then my husband installed an old wringer washer in one corner of the pantry, with water from the mountain stream continually running through it. You can chill your milk this way by filling the sink half-full of cold water.

If you have a fridge, you may soon find it overfull of milk containers. You might install a second fridge just for milk — it need not be in the kitchen. I have friends who use their freezer for rapid chilling, but they are a whole lot more organized than I ever hope to be.

Separating Milk and Cream

The cream in cow's milk rises readily to the top of the milk container within 12 to 24 hours, unless it is homogenized; the cream from goat's milk comes less readily to the top. Although there is just as much cream (or butterfat) in goat's milk — sometimes more — the fat is enclosed in smaller sacs or globules, and stays mixed in with the milk for 2 or 3 days. If you wish to separate cow's milk, you may do a fair job by skimming after 12 to 24 hours, although you won't get all the cream out of the milk.

Separating in a Shotgun Can: In some old dairies or milk-producing farms you can find a special tall can with a spigot at the bottom and a glass tube running up the side. Whole milk was poured in after milking and left to separate; the amount of milk in the can and the proportion of cream could be seen in the glass tube. When they had separated, you let the milk out the bottom and left the cream in until needed. The shotgun can was kept in cold water to chill the milk. This method is pretty good, if you can find such a container. It isn't perfect, but it beats skimming with a ladle and doesn't have the mechanical complexities of a centrifugal separator.

The Centrifugal Separator: This is a very Victorian hand-crank machine with millions of parts and adjustments. On top is a wide bowl, into which you pour whole fresh milk; below are two spigots, for skim milk and for cream. Two factors are critical. One is temperature: the milk should be fresh and at 90°F to separate completely. If the machine is cold, and chills the milk, it won't work; you should run warm water through to heat it up in cold weather. The other factor is the exact speed at which the handle is turned. The one we have has a little bell, which rings every time you turn the crank until it gets to the right speed. When the separator roars like a jet plane ready for takeoff and the bell stops ringing, turn on the spigot and it should work.

To clean the separator, first remove the skim milk and cream buckets, replacing them with other containers. Run through several quarts of cold water. Then dismantle the working parts, being careful to keep the separating plates in exact order (our machine has a clip to string them on when washing). Wash with cold, then hot soapy water or bleach, then rinse. Dry everything at once to prevent rust. Cover until next use.

YOGURT

Yogurt is a traditional form of food in many parts of the world, particularly in the Mediterranean and Middle East. Without refrigeration, the daily milk quickly sours in the heat, so people eventually hit on a souring bacteria that makes milk thick and delicious. This type of bacteria also rendered the milk safe to drink, because (for various reasons) it kills off any other bacteria that might get into the milk, including those harmful to people.

The process of making this soured milk is as simple as its history implies. A little of the live culture from a previous batch is added to fresh milk, and kept between 90° and 118°F. (In the Mediterranean summer, it makes itself; on cooler days, it is set over the stove.) It takes about 4 to 6 hours — the amount of time from morning milking to supper, or from evening milking to the following day. If left unjiggled, it becomes the delicate, firm, custardlike product we call yogurt.

Food Value: Yogurt has all the food value of milk, but is more digestible, being partly broken down. Some yogurts (known as acidophilus) stay alive as they travel through the digestive system. As they go, they kill off any "unfriendly" bacteria in the intestines. In this way they act like an antibiotic; but unlike antibiotics, acidophilic yogurt doesn't destroy B vitamins. Instead, it goes to work making B vitamins for you.

Yogurt Culture: There are several different strains of yogurt-producing bacteria, which result in varying degrees of taste and thickness. When you buy a container of yogurt, you are purchasing a combination of these cultures. Provided it is unsweetened, unpreserved, and relatively fresh, you can use it as the culture for a batch of homemade yogurt, and continue using it until it gets contaminated or runs

out. If you're a regular yogurt eater, make up a batch of mother culture (*see p. 223*). Freeze-dried yogurt cultures, available in health food stores and through mail-order catalogs, are always stronger and better flavored; renew them every 6 months for best results.

Containers: The best containers I've come up with are brown glass pint-sized containers with wide-mouthed tops and screw lids. (The brown glass keeps light out — light destroys vitamin B_2.) In any case, glass is better than plastic, and easier to clean.

Cleanliness: As soon as the yogurt container is empty, soak it with cold water; then scrub with hot water and soak 15 minutes. Rinse with hot and let it drain; store the jars upside down. Just before you fill them with fresh yogurt, rinse them out again with hot water. Sterilize the jar used for the mother culture.

The Milk: Because raw milk (especially goat milk) has enzymes that kill the yogurt culture, you should first scald the milk to destroy the enzymes. Bring the milk to a soft boil, then reduce it to 185° for a few minutes. After that, reduce it to 95° to 105°F for incubating, which makes a thicker, less tart yogurt. Milk set at 110° to 115°F makes a thinner, more acidulated yogurt; 120° makes a sour, thin drink — good for salad dressings and marinades.

Keeping a Constant Temperature: To make yogurt successfully, keep the containers at a constant temperature for 4 to 6 hours. There are, of course, yogurt-making devices that will do that, but you can improvise by setting the jars in a large heavy pot, surrounding them with warm water, covering the top and wrapping it in your winter coat. I have a friend who started a whole dairy business based on yogurt made by this tried-and-true method. To keep track of things, insert a thermometer to keep an eye on the temperature. Another incubation option (albeit for a small amount): incubate in a scalded, warm, wide-mouthed thermos.

Warning

The process of making yogurt is very simple, but it is not, alas, very flexible. You can't vary the procedure much; for example, you can't add culture to scalding milk; you can't leave culture for a month in the fridge without renewing it; you can't incubate it for 2 days. If you stick to the hard and fast rules, though, you will find it easy to keep stocked up with as much yogurt as your household will eat.

Yogurt Recipe

Please read about yogurt, above.

Heat very gently to 105°F:
1 qt whole or **skim milk**
Mix in with a wire whisk:
2 Tbsp yogurt mother culture
Pour into clean jars. Cover and keep at 95° to 105°F for 4 to 6 hours. As soon as it becomes thick, refrigerate.

MAKES 4 CUPS

Yogurt Cheese

This isn't really a cheese, but neither is cream cheese, and this is a lot more useful. Yogurt cheese may be used to make a simple nonfattening cheesecake *(see p. 221)*, or it can be mixed with herbs as a spread for crackers or toast.

Line a bowl with:
butter muslin or **a cheesecloth**
Put in it:
1 pint yogurt
Tie up the ends of the cloth and let the bag drip over the bowl for 4 to 6 hours. Chill yogurt cheese until used. It takes 2 batches of yogurt cheese to make a cheesecake.

Meat Tenderizer

Yogurt whey is a tried and true meat tenderizer. Crush into **1 qt yogurt whey**:
1 clove garlic
1 tsp thyme
pinch of crushed rosemary
Submerge meat, then poke a fork into it 10 or 15 times. Let soak a few hours; the flavor will permeate to the bone!

CULTURED BUTTERMILK AND SOUR CREAM

Cultured buttermilk is not the same product as real buttermilk, although they have a similar taste. It is made by the same process as making yogurt, but you use a milder-tasting culture and incubate it at a lower temperature. Sour cream is made in the same way, except that you use cream instead of milk.

Cultured Buttermilk

Mix together with a whisk or egg beater:
1 qt whole or skim milk
1 pkg starter or **½ cup previously made buttermilk** or **store-bought cultured buttermilk**
Pour into clean, freshly rinsed jars. Incubate at 75° to 85°F for 5 to 7 hours. You can also incubate buttermilk at room temperature (65° to 75°F) for up to 24 hours. When the culture becomes thick, shake and refrigerate.

Sour Cream

Mix together with a whisk or egg beater:
2 cups whole cream
2 Tbsp previously made or **store-bought buttermilk**
Pour into a clean, freshly rinsed jar, and incubate at 75° to 85°F for 7 to 10 hours. You can also incubate sour cream at 65° to 75°F for up to 24 hours.

BUTTERMAKING

In many rural communities of the 19th century, buttermaking was a housewife's main means of barter — her "pin money." You could find more different sorts of churns than mousetraps at the turn of the century, and there are still quite a few around, as anybody discovers who whips cream a little too long (and suddenly has it separate into buttermilk and golden flecks of butter.)

Butter forms suddenly, but the preliminaries do sometimes go on for rather a long time. In the spring and summer, butter comes more easily than in midwinter. We churn butter at 57°F in summer, 62°F in winter. In winter we also add 2 Tbsp cultured buttermilk (or mesophilic mother culture) to cream 24 hours before churning and let it sit at 60° to 65°F (room temperature) overnight, or until it gets thick.

Churning should take 20 to 30 minutes by hand. If there is no sign at all of butter — simply gobs of whipped cream — it is probably too cold. Warm it up by placing the churn in a bucket of warm water for an hour or so; then try again. If, on the other hand, the cream is too warm, the butter will appear in tiny flecks instead of solid lumps. Cool it down for an hour or so, then churn 5 minutes to bring it together. Sometimes nothing works. If that happens to you, stir in a couple tablespoons of buttermilk; let it sit, covered overnight; and drain it through a cloth as crème fraîche.

Once made, butter must be thoroughly washed, either by filling the churn with water at 57° to 62°F repeatedly until it runs clean, or by kneading butter under water in a container. Then press and knead the water out of the final product. In the old days this was done with a pair of grooved paddles; the great trick was to make "curls" for the dinner table.

Butter is usually shaped into solid patties, about ½ cup each. You may work in salt at this point; I use:

1 pinch of salt per ½ cup patty

Store butter wrapped in waxed paper or plastic wrap. It will keep its fresh delicious flavor up to 2 weeks; past that, freeze it.

CHEESEMAKING

I must say, I envy the cheesemaking system traditionally practiced in mountain villages of Europe. As spring arrived and the upper pastures became green, the young people gathered all the cattle, goats, and sheep together and took them up into the hills; they gave over all their attention to the animals — to birthing and milking, and dairy work. For these purposes, they kept a rough dairy/bunkhouse by a fresh flowing stream; and they stayed there for some months, herding the animals to new pastures every day, while the fields in the village below ripened into hay for the next winter. There the baby animals were born and pan-fed (a demanding chore: babies must be babied). Butter was churned, and the milk soured for curds and cheeses, both fresh and aged. Once a week the packhorse would descend, carrying cheeses and returning with supplies from the main village below.

Not only was the task of milking and the production of cheeses on a large scale thus simplified, but the cheese itself was different stuff from "lowland cheese," which was thought to be rubbery and tasteless by comparison. The milk of an animal that forages spring pasture, wandering and choosing from a variety of herbs, shrubs, leaves, and grasses is thicker, less watery, and more flavorful than that of animals that stand around munching plain grass all day. There will be less milk than if the cows were on lowland pastures; but it will make better cheese.

Nor is it only a matter of milk, though the milk is the most important factor in making any kind of cheese. In the warmth and dampness of spring and early summer, the bacteria and molds that we introduce to produce certain flavors are most likely to grow and work well in the milk.

How Cheeses are Made: All cheese is made by the firming of casein, a substance in the milk. As this casein becomes firm, it gathers together the milk solids in its elastic webs; this is called the *curd*. The pale, yellowish liquid left over is called the *whey*.

There are two ways to firm casein. One is by bacterial action; the other is by rennet action. Fresh cheeses, such as cottage cheese, cream cheese, pot cheese, and farmer cheese, are made by firming casein with bacterial action alone. They are to be eaten fresh, within a week or two. Hard cheeses are made by combining the bacterial action with the added firming enzyme action of rennet. They are slowly heated and then pressed to expel whey and make a firm shape; these can be eaten within a few months. Alternatively they are sealed and aged, or inoculated with mold to make blue or Stilton-type cheeses. The aging of hard cheese takes months, sometimes years, depending on what you want.

Cheese Cultures: All fresh raw milk contains some level of bacteria in it. These friendly bacteria are what will sour the milk naturally, if you leave it long enough at room temperature. Traditionally, these bacteria were used to make cheese and other milk products without anybody having much idea how and why it happened. Some work better at higher temperature than others. Some have more power in curdling milk; others have delicate and delicious flavors. What dairy suppliers do is to isolate specific bacteria alone or in combination, and freeze-dry them. Most cheeses are made with the same mesophilic culture; the variations in taste or texture in most cheeses comes from differences in timing and temperature. You can buy a mesophilic culture from a cheese supply house, or you can use fresh cultured buttermilk from the store, which is made with the same culture. It will work just as well, as long as it doesn't get too old. To make multiple usage of it, make a bag of frozen "mother culture."

Making a Mother Culture: To make a batch of cheese culture starter with which to start regular cheeses, freeze fresh starter in molded plastic ice-cube trays. When frozen, empty them into a plastic freezer container labeled with contents and date. Mother culture should be renewed every 6 months or as needed. Signs of contamination include sour taste, fruity smell, or refusal of the culture to set a curd.

Rennet: Rennet, an enzyme taken from the fourth stomach (the abomasum) of an unweaned calf, is also available in a vegetable-derived form, which I have used; it works exactly the same as ordinary rennet. Rennet and imitation rennet are available both as liquids and as tablets. The liquid is easier to measure in small amounts, but doesn't last forever. The tablets last forever.
¼ rennet tablet = 1 tsp liquid rennet

Cheese Colorings: Cheeses have been colored since the Welsh used calendula blossoms bruised in the fresh milk. The West Indian annatto seed is the most frequently used butter and cheese coloring today.

Salt: Salt is used to retard mold and yeast growth in cheese. Use only non-iodized salt such as pickling salt, kosher salt or sea salt.

Milk: The quality of the milk has a great deal to do with the end product. If dairy animals get into a strongly flavored weed patch, for example, you will taste it in the cheese or butter made from that milk. Summer milk, from grass-fed animals, has more color, fat, and flavor than that of animals fed hay in winter. Even the breed of animal makes a difference. Vermont Cheddar is made with Jersey milk, which is the richest, most highly colored and flavored cow's milk. Pasteurization, which destroys many enzymes and bacteria, doesn't improve cheese flavor or texture, but is required by some commercial cheese operations.

Warning

Never use milk that isn't fit to drink. Milk from a sick animal, or one taking antibiotics, is of no use to the cheesemaker. Milk that has spoiled or soured already cannot be used either.

Soft Cheeses: When I first moved to Cape Breton, in 1971, many households still kept a cow and made butter and curds every week. I was fortunate enough to live next door to such a household, and Peggy Ryan's curds often found their way into our fridge, until I learned to make them myself.

Curds are most easily made with skimmed cow's milk. Peggy set 3 days' milk in an enameled pot behind the stove. When a thin, jellylike curd could be seen floating in a translucent whey, she would wrestle the pot up on the oil stove and cut the curd. Then it heated, slowly, until the curds were firm. Finally, Peggy washed them in a colander, under cold running water for 5 minutes. Her curds were firm, almost rubbery. More delicate curds cannot be so treated.

Soft cheeses such as cottage cheese, yogurt cheese, and cream cheese are made by firming casein with bacterial action alone. A more sophisticated form of soft cheese, the French Neufchâtel, is made by bacterial action and a very small amount of rennet to make a slightly firmer, but still spreadable cheese.

Incubating Soft Cheeses: Using a thermometer and a whisk, heat milk gradually to the right temperature. Milk, like wool, reacts poorly to being suddenly heated or cooled. Always stir while heating. At the right temperature, add the mother culture. Stir for at least 2 minutes to make sure the culture is evenly distributed.

Soft cheeses usually have a long incubation period. Make sure the temperature of the milk remains steady during this time.

Cutting the Curd: The purpose of cutting up the curd is to allow the whey to circulate freely. It is the whey that contains the acid as the bacteria change it. So after you cut the curd up into cubes, let it rest a while longer.

The traditional way to cut curd is to take a long, sharp knife, and cut through the curd all the way to the bottom of the pot in parallel lines. Then cut them in the other direction. This gives you an attractive but deceptive pattern of cuts; the cubes are all as deep as the curd. So you cut them again, this time at slanted angles, all around the pot, until they seem pretty well chopped up to you. Take your time. Curd made by lactic acid alone is weak and delicate, yet oddly elastic; it should be cut slowly.

A simpler, less professional method of cutting curd is to twist a whisk into the set curd in overlapping plunges.

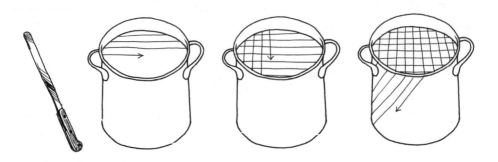

Heating the Curd: For all this, curd formed by lactic acid alone is too fragile to hold its shape when you try to separate it from the whey. It must be heated, and heated gently. Heat will cause the webs of casein to shrink, expelling whey and making the curds small and firm. If you heat it too fast, the casein will shrink so quickly that they dump the milk solids back into the whey and toughen the casein, making "squeaky cheese."

There are two ways to raise the temperature of the curds and whey gradually enough so that milk solids are retained by the casein:
1. Set the pot in a sink of water; the water should be almost level with the milk and at the same temperature as the milk. Gradually raise the temperature of the water in the sink by adding hot water.
2. Ladle out a few cups of whey; heat it to around 100°F, and return it to the pot gradually.

Both these methods should be accompanied by a little gentle stirring of the curds, as soon as they are firm enough to be moved without falling apart. At first the curds will be pretty soft. Gradually they come to have more shape and the outer skin shrinks a little.

Whatever you do, don't heat it up suddenly in a fit of be-done-with-this. The casein will shrink like a snapped elastic, and you'll be stuck with a handful of rubbery "cheese" (95 percent casein) and a large pot of slightly sour, extremely nutritious whey.

Draining and Rinsing: Fresh cheeses containing cream are drained by hanging the curds in a bag to drip, and are not rinsed. The whey that comes out should be relatively clear after the first few minutes. If it isn't, you may try gently reheating, but generally it should be taken as a sign that you ought to be paying more attention to the thermometer and the clock during incubating and heating.

Fresh cheeses made with skim milk can be drained and rinsed in an open colander, if you have used a good lively culture and kept it warm through incubating and heating. The curds should be quite firm, and the whey should be clear. If your curds are too soft to drain and rinse, hang them to drain in a bag for 6 to 8 hours instead.

Salting: Salt helps to further firm and preserve curds. I add anywhere from a pinch to ½ teaspoon of salt per 1 cup of fresh cheese.

CHEESEMAKING EQUIPMENT

Curd Pot: For every 1 pound of hard cheese or 2 pounds of soft cheese you make, you will be starting with 1 gallon of milk, for which you need a stainless-steel pot.

Larger Pot: Any kind of pot will do, as long as the curd pot will fit into it, so you can surround the milk or curds with hot water and heat them gradually or you can use the sink.

Thermometer: To heat all milk products regularly, you will need a reliable thermometer ranging from 32° to 220°F. I have found it much easier to work in Fahrenheit, which has twice as many degrees as Celsius or centigrade; in milk work, a degree or two makes all the difference. Glass thermometers break, and are unreliable. What you want is a stainless steel dial on a bimetallic strip with a clip to fix it to the side of the pot. They are available from cheesemaking supply houses and photography places.

Cheesecloth: Ordinary cheesecloth works, but soon disintegrates. Equally temporary is the commercially available paper Handiwipe. Butter muslin, several layers of which are used to make baby diapers, lasts the longest; this is available from cheese-making supply houses. Used sheets and pillowcases also work very well.

Colander: Should be large, stainless steel, enamel, or plastic.

Timer: Cheesemaking is largely a matter of exact timing. Electronic timers last longer than spring-type devices.

Cheese Press: While you can separate milk and churn butter without special equipment, there is, believe me, no way to press hard cheese without a cheese press. I have tried: holes punched in ice cream containers, coffee cans, bricks balanced on top, rocks falling off in the middle of the night, triangular cheeses in the morning. Besides the matter of exact weight, there is cleanliness to be considered. I have friends who press cheeses in their cider press, but I fail to see how they can keep it clean. My friend, Ellen Wright, who helped edit this chapter and makes cheeses and yogurt much more professionally than I do, uses a PVC pipe with holes drilled in it, a plastic disc as a follower, and a coffee can full of pebbles as a press.

Two kinds of presses are available for small cheese makers. One is the lever press, for which parts and plans can be purchased, but which any carpenter with a slide rule can re-invent. By changing weights and balance points, you can vary pressure from 5 to 100 pounds, as long as you have room in your kitchen to hinge a piece of hardwood to the wall.

The screw press is more expensive, but portable, and does not require any calculations.

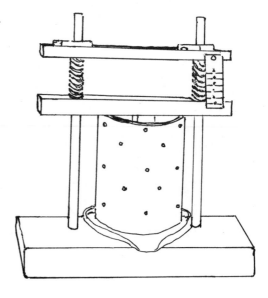

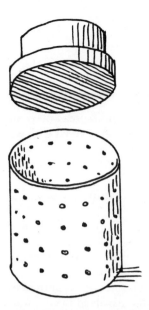

Cheese Mold and Follower: Hard cheese (and some soft cheeses) are pressed in a cylinder of food-grade plastic or stainless steel with both ends open and little holes drilled at intervals around the sides. The mold for a 1-pound cheese is about the size of a coffee can. Larger cheeses require larger molds, because cheeses press better if they are broader than their height. You will also need a follower — a flat, round piece that exactly fits into the mold and presses the curds with the weight of the press. Food-grade plastic or stainless steel is best; wood eventually rots.

Drainage Mats: The best thing I've found is the plastic canvas sold in craft stores. It can also be used to air-dry finished hard cheeses before waxing.

Miscellaneous: A stainless-steel whisk with a long handle; a stainless-steel, slotted spoon; and a long, straight knife for cutting curds.

Waxes: Beeswax works wonderfully well, but costs a lot, unless you have bees. Paraffin is too hard and cracks easily, but can be used if mixed half-and-half with cooking oil. Cheese waxes, both natural and plastic, are available from cheesemaking supply houses.

Cottage Cheese

Allow to set overnight (12 hours) at 68° to 75°F, covered:
1 gallon skim cow's milk
½ cup mesophilic cheese culture or **cultured buttermilk**
Cut curd into ½-inch cubes *(see pp. 234–35)*, but do not stir. Raise the temperature 1°F every minute to 104°F, stirring gently. Hold there for 10 minutes. Stir gently.

Raise the temperature again, at 1°F per minute, to 120°F and hold it there for 20 minutes. Stir gently every few minutes. If curds are not firm enough yet, hold them at 120°F until they are.

Empty curds into a colander and rinse gently twice with warm water. If stored at this point, they will be delicious for cooking, but a little tart for plain eating.

To cool them gradually and remove all whey, immerse them first in water at 80°F for 20 minutes, then at 65°F for 20 minutes, then in clean water at 45°F for the last 20 minutes.

Drain, salt to taste, and pack in containers.

2 POUNDS

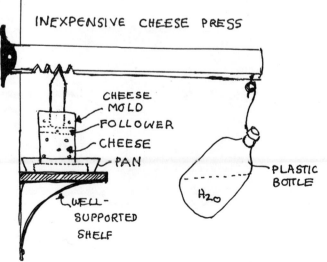

INEXPENSIVE CHEESE PRESS

CHEESE MOLD
FOLLOWER
CHEESE
PAN
WELL-SUPPORTED SHELF
PLASTIC BOTTLE
H₂O

Goat's Milk Cottage Cheese

Follow instructions for Cottage Cheese, using these ingredients:
1 gallon whole milk
½ cup buttermilk
5 drops rennet in 2 Tbsp water

2 POUNDS

Fromage Blanc

Also known as *queso blanco*, this light cheese is the very best thing for cheesecake or dips.
1 gallon whole goat's milk
½ cup cheese culture or **cultured buttermilk**
5 drops liquid rennet in 2 Tbsp water
Heat milk gradually to 185°F, then cool to 80°F by placing the pan in a sink of cool water. Stir in buttermilk and dissolved rennet for at least 1 minute. Cover and incubate at room temperature (65° to 80°F) overnight or until curd floats in whey. Spoon curd into a cloth-lined colander and let it drain until it reaches the desired density, from creamy to fairly dry. It gets drier if you tie up the cloth and let the bag hang for an hour or so.

Store in jars or plastic containers. Keeps up to a month in the fridge. It can be frozen (but it will not taste very good).

2 POUNDS

Neufchâtel

A soft fresh cheese, Neufchâtel is common in Europe, where it is spread on coarse bread or crackers and served with wine, olives, and green onions.

Mix together:
2 qts whole cow's milk
1 cup cream
Heat gently to 65°F. Add and stir in for 2 minutes:
½ cup mesophilic cheese culture or **cultured buttermilk**
1 drop liquid rennet or **1 crumb of a rennet tablet dissolved in cold water**
Cover the pot and set it in a warm place for 12 to 18 hours.

Line a colander with butter muslin or a cheesecloth. Ladle in curds and hang them up to drip for 2 to 4 hours, or until they stop dripping.

Scrape the curd out of the cloth into a bowl and mix in:
1½ tsp salt
You may also add any of the following:
2 Tbsp fresh chopped chives
2 Tbsp freshly chopped parsley
¼ tsp paprika
1 clove crushed garlic
1 Tbsp crushed onion
dash of ground pepper or **rubbed sage**
To expel more of the whey, press the curd at around 10 pounds for 6 to 8 hours. You may do this in a cheese press or without one: tie up the curd firmly in a cloth, place it in a colander over a drainage bowl, and set a small plate on top of the curds. Top with a 10-pound weight such as bricks, a rock, or flatirons. Set in a cool place until it stops dripping (about 4 hours).

1 TO 1½ CUPS

Liptauer Cheese

This is a soft, delicious spread that is good on dark bread and with soup or salad. Or you might just keep a pot of it for snacks. Some people like to flavor it with onion juice or chopped herbs, but it is also good just plain.

Measure out:
3 Tbsp butter
Let this sit in a dish until it becomes soft, for about 1 hour. Mash it up with a fork. Then mash in or buzz in blender:
1½ cups cottage cheese
You can use dry curds if you have them, or you can let the cottage cheese sit in a sieve for a while before adding it, to drain out the cream; but it is good made with cottage cheese just as it is. To flavor it, you can add:
2 Tbsp chopped parsley
1 Tbsp chopped chives
1 Tbsp onion juice *(see p. 10)*
1 Tbsp paprika

1½ CUPS

Panir

Commonly made in Asian kitchens, panir is virtually tasteless and can be cubed and marinated or flavored with garlic, chives, peppers, or herbs, fried, grated, sliced for sandwiches, or even smoked.
1 gallon milk
¼ cup vinegar or **very acidic lemon juice**
salt to taste
Bring milk gradually to almost boiling, from 205° to 210°F hr., stir in vinegar and remove from heat when the milk separates. Pour into a cloth-lined colander. Gently fork seasonings into curds while still hot. Wrap in cheesecloth and gently press with a plate and a 4 or 5-pound weight.

ABOUT 1 PINT

Pashka

Traditionally this was served in Eastern Europe, where Easter breakfast celebrated the end of winter and Lenten fasts. The Pashka mold was first decorated with slivers of almonds and dried or fresh fruit; then the cheese mixture was pressed into the mold. When unmolded, the letters XB were written on the side, in colored icing, to declare: Christ is Risen!

Soak overnight in ½ cup water:
¼ cup raisins
¼ cup currants
Combine in a food mill, blender, or food processor:
1½ cups cottage cheese
½ cup cream cheese at room temperature
Or you may use:
2 cups Neufchâtel or **fromage blanc**
Blend into the cheese:
2 Tbsp sugar or **honey**
1 tsp vanilla
1 tsp lemon juice
grated rind of 1 well-washed lemon
Turn the cheese into a bowl and stir in:
soaked raisins and currants
½ cup sliced fresh fruit
Rinse a mold or clean flowerpot in cold water and pack with cheese. Chill overnight. Unmold by dipping mold carefully in a pan of hot water, not allowing hot water to come into contact with cheese. Invert molded cheese on serving dish and decorate with almonds, dried and fresh fruit, or icing. Surround with sliced, fresh fruit.

2 TO 2 ½ CUPS

MAKING HARD CHEESES

Always keep records in a notebook of how you actually made each cheese. It will be weeks or months before you sample the cheese; your notes are the only thing that makes it possible to improve quality next time. To number cheeses, use a paper tag until the cheese is waxed; then paint the number on with hot crayon wax.

Bacterial Action in Hard Cheese: Bacterial action is a form of acid coagulation in making milk products. The bacteria eat lactose (milk sugar) and produce lactic acid; this acid activates the casein in milk, and also causes the end product to have good texture and flavor. Bacterial culture, such as that in cultured buttermilk, is usually stirred into the milk an hour or more before rennet is added, to give the bacteria a chance to work.

Setting the Curd: Rennet coagulates milk into a firm curd. It is available in tablets or liquid form *(see p. 233)*. Rennet tablets must be crushed and dissolved in a little cold (never warm) water before adding it to the milk. It takes about 45 minutes for rennet and culture together to coagulate the milk. The exact time is not as crucial as the right consistency. To test it, insert a thermometer in the curd, then lift it at a slight angle. If it's still a little soft, like yogurt, leave it. You are looking for a "clean break," something like gelatin or custard. In making most cheeses it is important to cut the curd as soon as this point is reached. Eventually the curd begins to get flaky, and loses strength.

Cutting the Curd: Curd is cut into little cubes, anywhere from ⅛ to ½ inch, by cutting parallel lines first in one direction, then at right angles, then through to the "four sides" at gradually increasing angles. This is done so the acidic whey will penetrate evenly to all the milk. After cutting, allow it to rest for a few minutes, then stir up the big curds left on the bottom and cut them smaller. This is especially important when making dense cheeses, such as Romano or Cheddar.

Heating Curd: Always heat and cool curd gradually: 2°F every 5 minutes. The internal temperature of the pot must be monitored constantly. Gently stir curds as they heat, to keep them from matting on the bottom. If curd overheats, rescue the cheese by adding cold water.

If you find the stove unreliable, try immersing the pot in hot water in the sink, where it's much easier to control temperature. You can also dip out whey and dip in hot or cold water, directly in the cheese pot; this is in fact a procedure in making Goudas and other "washed curd" cheeses.

Pressing Cheeses: To press cheese, you need a good cheese press *(see pp. 236–37),* a mold, follower, mat, and cheesecloth, all freshly sterilized by sitting in live steam or boiling water for 5 or 10 minutes. Presumably all this is ready by the time you drain and salt your curds, so you can pack them in the mold and press while they are still warm and elastic.

Most pressing is done with gradually increasing weight. A cheese starts off at 10 or 15 pounds, but is soon up to 50 or more pounds pressure. Periodically the cheese is taken out, turned over, and sometimes "redressed" or rewrapped in clean cheesecloth. This is all so that the curds won't break under high pressure, but will be gently squeezed, and the whey expelled without losing milk solids.

Drying: After pressing, the cheese is unwrapped and any loose fragments are pared off. Then the cheese is set to air-dry in a cool dark place. Freshly pressed cheese should be turned every 2 hours the first day, then twice daily until the rind dries. They are then ready to be waxed.

Waxing: Cheeses are waxed to keep airborne molds at bay. *(See p. 237 for types of waxes.)* Heat wax slowly, and use it with care; it is terribly flammable. Apply wax hot to kill surface mold or bacteria. Apply 2 or 3 coats with a soft brush; then paint on the cheese number with a small paintbrush and a little hot melted crayon.

Aging Cheeses: Cheese takes months to develop flavor. During that time it should be stored in a clean, dry, well-ventilated and mouseproof cheese cupboard. The cheeses should sit on a plastic or stainless steel rack, and should be turned once a week.

Cape Breton Cheese

This is a good basic cheese recipe. It takes about 6 weeks to ripen, but is better at 8, dry at 10, and tart after that. Good for sandwiches, cooking, and snacks.

You will need:
1 gallon whole cow's milk
2 Tbsp cheese culture
⅛ rennet tablet dissolved in ¼ cup cold water
1 Tbsp coarse salt
Warm the milk to 90°F. Add cheese culture and stir for 2 minutes. Hold 1 hour at 90°F.

Dissolve rennet in cold water for 2 minutes. Stir into milk for 2 minutes. Cover and hold 45 minutes at 90°F.

Cut curd into ⅜-inch cubes. Raise temperature very gradually, no more than 2°F per 5 minutes, from 90° to 100°F over 30 minutes. Stir to prevent matting. Cover and hold at 100°F for 30 minutes. Stir often; drain through a colander. Sprinkle a scant tablespoon of coarse salt over the curds. Line mold with cheesecloth and crumble in curds. Press:
- **10 lb for 10 minutes**
- **Turn and press 20 lb for 10 minutes**
- **Turn, rewrap and press 30 lb for 10 minutes**
- **Turn and press at 40 lb for 30 minutes**
- **Turn, rewrap and press at 50 lb for 12 hours**

Remove cheese from mold and air-dry 3 to 5 days on a rack. Coat with wax and label. Store 6 to 8 weeks.

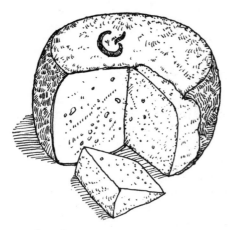

Gouda Cheese

Gouda is a Dutch washed-curd cheese. The high quality for which it is famous comes from fresh, unpasteurized milk from Jersey cows or others which has a high butterfat content. It has a very smooth texture, and after 2 months has a delicious tangy flavor.

You will need:
1 gallon whole cow's milk
4 Tbsp cheese culture
⅛ rennet tablet dissolved in ¼ cup cold water
1 lb coarse salt dissolved in 2 quarts cold water
Warm the milk gradually to 90°F. Add cheese culture and stir well. Hold 15 minutes at 90°F. Dissolve the rennet in water, mashing it up for 2 minutes. Stir it into the milk for 2 minutes. Cover and let the curd set for 1 hour at 90°F.

Cut curd into ½-inch cubes. Gently stir up and cut bottom cubes. Hold 5 to 7 minutes at 90°F. Then very gradually raise the temperature from 90° to 100°F over the course of 30 minutes. Stir to prevent matting.

To "wash the curd," dip out around a quart of whey and replace with a quart of water at 100°F, 3 times or every 10 minutes over the next 30 minutes. Continue to stir gently now and again.

Line a mold with cheesecloth. Drain curd through a colander, then pack quickly into the mold, breaking the matted curd as little as possible.

Press the cheese at 20 lb for 20 minutes
Turn and press 30 lb for 30 minutes
Turn and press 40 lb for 3 hours

Remove cheese from mold and unwrap. Pare off any uneven bits, but don't cut into the cheese. Dissolve the salt in water. Immerse the cheese in this brine for 3 to 4 hours. Then pat the cheese dry and place it on a wooden or plastic rack to dry for 1 week. Turn cheese several times the first day and once a day thereafter, until it is dry all over.

Red wax is traditional on Gouda cheese. Turn daily for 8 to 12 weeks before serving.

1 POUND

Variations
Flavorings may be added to Gouda cheeses to make specialty cheeses.

Caraway Gouda

Before starting the cheese, simmer together for 15 minutes:
½ cup milk
1 Tbsp caraway seeds
Strain this milk, reserving the seeds, and use as part of the milk to start your cheese. Add the seeds to the curds as they drain, before they mat.

Jalapeño Gouda

Before starting the cheese, crush or grind into small pieces:
1 tsp jalapeño peppers
Add the peppers to:
½ cup boiling water
Boil for 10 minutes. Strain out peppers, reserving them for later use, and add the water to the milk before you start the cheese. Add the peppers to the curds as they drain, mixing them in well.

Colby Cheese

Colby is a bland, mild, fresh-tasting cheese. It melts nicely and makes good pizza cheese. It is ready to eat in 4 weeks, and better after 6.

You will need:
1 gallon whole cow's milk
3 Tbsp cheese culture
⅛ rennet tablet dissolved in ¼ cup cold water
1 Tbsp coarse salt
Warm the milk gradually to 86°F. Add cheese culture and stir in for 2 minutes. Cover and hold 1 hour at 86°F. Dissolve rennet in water for 2 minutes, then add to milk, stirring for 2 minutes. Hold for another 45 minutes, covered, at 86°F.

Cut the curd into ½-inch cubes. Hold 5 minutes at 86°F. Gradually raise the temperature from 86° to 102°F over 35 minutes. Stir now and then. Hold at 102°F for 30 minutes, being careful not to let temperature drop.

Drain off about 2 cups of whey, down to the level of the curds, by tipping the pot. Pour in cool water until the temperature reaches 80°F. Cover and hold temperature at 80°F for 30 minutes.

Drain curds through a colander, and sprinkle a scant tablespoon of salt on them. Line a mold with cheesecloth and crumble in the curds, packing them in with your knuckles.
- **Press at 20 lb for 20 minutes**
- **Turn and press 30 lb for 20 minutes**
- **Turn, rewrap and press 40 lb for 60 minutes**
- **Turn, rewrap and press 50 lb for 24 hours**

Remove and set cheese on a rack to air-dry for 2 to 4 days. Turn until completely dry. Wax, label, and store 4 to 8 weeks.

1 POUND

Goat's Milk Feta

Feta was originally made from sheep's milk, which is richer than goat's or cow's milk and makes a more crumbly cheese. It requires very light pressing, which can be done without a cheese press. Feta is delicious crumbled into salad, and also good in omelets and other cookery.

You will need:
1 gallon fresh goat's milk
4 Tbsp cheese culture or **cultured buttermilk**
¼ tablet dried rennet dissolved in ¼ cup cold water
½ cup coarse salt
Preheat milk to 185°F, then cool to 85°F. Stir cheese culture or buttermilk in for 2 minutes, then allow to ripen, covered, at 85°F for 1 hour.

Crush rennet into water for 2 minutes, then stir into the milk for 2 minutes. Cover, and allow curd to set for 30 minutes at 85°F. Sinks are great for this.

Cut the curd into ¼- to ½-inch cubes or use a large whisk. Gradually raise temperature to 95°F over 1 hour, stirring occasionally. Curds will shrink a bit. Cut oversized curds as necessary. Drain curds through a colander, stirring gently for 2 or 3 minutes. A straight-sided pasta cooker colander works well for draining feta. Drain for 1 hour, then turn curds over and drain another 30 minutes.

Remove from the colander, cut into wedges or chunks, and submerge in a mixture of:
1 qt water
¼ cup coarse salt
Refrigerate for at least 2 weeks. Stored in the brine, it will be good for up to 2 months.

1 POUND

Cheddar Cheese

Cheddar is a very strong, rich cheese, made by a special cheddaring process, using whole Jersey milk at the height of summer. Supermarkets sell something called Cheddar, but it is made from the milk of a Holstein cow, which is about twice the size of a Jersey cow and gives at least 4 times as much (inferior) milk. The difference in milk quality is nowhere more evident than in the making of Cheddar cheese.

Cheddar is also one cheese for which it is preferable to use raw milk and a real cheese culture, rather than cultured buttermilk. The culture used for buttermilk has a tendency to produce carbon dioxide and a "green" flavor in long storage.

In making Cheddar, the heating of the curd goes one step further than in most cheesemaking. After cutting and heating the curd, it is further heated and held at 100°F. This version is a "stirred" Cheddar, in which the curd is kept from matting by agitation.

You will need:
1 gallon whole Jersey or Guernsey milk
2 Tbsp cheese culture
⅛ rennet tablet dissolved in ¼ cup cool
     water or ½ tsp liquid rennet
1 Tbsp coarse salt
Warm the milk gradually to 86°F. Add cheese culture and stir it in for 1 minute. Cover and hold at 86°F for 45 minutes. Dissolve the rennet in water for 2 minutes; then add to milk, stirring for 2 minutes. Cover and hold 45 minutes at 86°F.

When the curd is absolutely rigid, cut into ¼-inch cubes. Use a whisk and knife to get at the ones on bottom. Hold 15 minutes at 86°F.

Raise the temperature very gradually, especially at first, from 86° to 100°F over 30 minutes. Stir to prevent matting. Cover and hold 30 minutes at 100°F.

Drain the curds through a colander; then return them to the pot, in the colander, so that they drain but stay warm. Let them sit 1 hour at 100°F.

With a knife, crumble or "mill" the curds, which will have matted together, into walnut-sized pieces. Sprinkle with salt. Line a mold with cheesecloth and pack in the curds. Press at:
- **10 lb for 15 minutes**
- **Turn and press 20 lb for 30 minutes**
- **Turn, rewrap, and press 40 lb for 2 hours**
- **Turn, rewrap, and press 50 lb for 24 hours**

Remove from the mold, unwrap, and air-dry for 1 week, turning every couple hours at first, then 2 or 3 times a day. When dry, coat with wax and label. Store for a minimum of 3 months. As a young cheese, Cheddar has almost no flavor; but it improves with age, becoming sharper and finally more mellow.

1 POUND

Romano Cheese

This is a hard, Italian grating cheese, like Parmesan, but a little richer and smoother. It is more piquant if made with part goat's and part cow's milk, but you may use either alone. Romano should be aged at least 3 months, but only begins to get really good after a year.

Many Italian cheeses, such as Parmesan, Romano, and mozzarella make use of a thermophilic rather than a mesophilic cheese culture. You can use yogurt, which is almost exactly the same thing.

You need:
1 gallon skim milk
⅓ cup cream
4 Tbsp fresh pure yogurt
⅛ tablet rennet dissolved in ¼ cup cold water
2 lb coarse salt dissolved in 1 qt warm water

Warm the milk gradually, and hold for 10 minutes at 88°F. Stir crushed rennet into milk and yogurt for 2 minutes. Cover and let curd set for 45 minutes at 88°F. When the curd is very stiff, cut it into ¼-inch cubes. Raise the temperature very slowly from 88° to 113°F. Hold at 113°F for 30 minutes. Stir to prevent matting.

Drain curds in a colander. Line cheese mold with cheesecloth and pack in curds.
- **Press at 10 lb for 10 minutes**
- **Turn and press 10 lb for 30 minutes**
- **Turn, rewrap, and press 20 lb for 2 hours**
- **Turn, rewrap, and press 40 lb for 12 hours**

Stir salt in warm water until it dissolves, then add 3 qts cold water. Soak the cheese in this brine for 24 hours, weighted by a plate to keep it submerged.

Romanos and Parmesans are air-dried for 2 or 3 weeks. They should be turned daily, and may be lightly oiled. If any whitish patches of mold show up, wipe them often for several days with a vinegar-soaked rag. Once dry, they are stored without waxing, usually for a year — sometimes more.

1 POUND

Suppliers
A & L Feed
Feed and Garden Supplies
Box 2068
2308 Central Avenue
McKinleyville, CA 95521

Lehman Hardware and Appliances
One Lehman Circle, P.O. Box 41
Kidron, OH 44636

New England Cheesemaking Supply Co.
Box 85, Maine Street
Ashfield, MA 01330

Tel (413) 628-3808

Home Brewing

BEER

To some people, brewing beer is an art. The finest ingredients, the fanciest equipment, and the closest attention to detail go into producing ales and lagers that are sampled, savored, and shared by brewers and their friends. Cost is not a consideration. Time is irrelevant. The important things are flavor, body, and head. Although I can appreciate the genre, I am not one of these people. They make wonderful brews: thick, rich, creamy ales, light sparkling lagers.

To others among us, beer is something you make to avoid having to buy it at the liquor store, with accompanying taxes. The low cost of home brewing has always been and continues to be a very attractive angle of beer-making. With little more than a bucket or two and a lot of beer bottles (you can re-use bottles with screw-on tops, or even pop bottles) and a small collection of groceries, you can make almost any kind of beer.

How Beer Works

Basically, you mix a can of hop-flavored malt with sugar, a little yeast and around 5 gallons of water. You cover it with a sheet of plastic to keep out airborne bacteria, but allow for the escape of carbon dioxide, which is produced as the yeast eats up sugar and makes alcohol. It takes about 4 or 5 days for the beer to foam up and subside, but it's still working slowly as you siphon it off into a bucket equipped with a fermentation lock. You let it sit 2 or 3 days, or until the lock stops bubbling. Then you add a little more sweetness and bottle the beer. The yeast wakes up and eats the new sugar, releasing more carbon dioxide, but there's no way for the gas to escape, because the bottle's sealed. That's what makes beer fizzy. Store bottles in a cool place for at least 3 weeks before testing.

BEER MAKING EQUIPMENT

1. *A 6- or 7-gallon* pail for primary fermentation. It should be at least 20 percent larger than the amount of beer you are brewing, to allow for foaming, and should be made of food-grade plastic. Cover with a plastic sheet secured with elastic or with a tight lid and a fermentation lock.

2. *A 5-foot clear, plastic siphon hose, ¼-inch inside diameter.* It helps if the open end fits into your kitchen tap, enabling you to easily rinse out large buckets.

3. *Lots of carbonated-drink bottles, glass or plastic.* Pint-sized bottles are more convenient than larger sizes.

4. *Bottle caps* appropriate to your bottles. New caps, both press-on and screw-on, are available in supermarkets and brewery stores. Bottle cappers are needed for press-on caps. You may re-use old screw-on caps, provided they are not damaged.

5. *A pair of sterile plastic gloves,* like nurses wear in the operating room. These can make the difference between good and skunky beer.

Cleanliness

To keep beermaking equipment such as bottles, buckets, carboys and thermometers clean, rinse them thoroughly with lots of hot water right away and let them drip-dry before storage. Soap is bad for beer — makes it taste soapy, with no head; and chlorine bleach is bad for everything else.

INGREDIENTS

1. *Hop-flavored malt extract:* Malt extract has, in the can, the density of 90-weight engine oil. I put the unopened can in a 3- or 4-quart pan, open both top and bottom

with a can opener, and press it through. Eventually, when the stuff dissolves in hot water, I retrieve the lids, wearing my gloves and using clean tongs.

2. *Beer yeast:* Most malt extracts come with a little package of beer yeast attached to the can. Before adding it to the mixture, make sure it works.

To proof yeast; mix together:
1 Tbsp beer yeast
½ cup tepid water (not hot)
pinch of sugar
If it doesn't begin to bubble within 10 minutes, it's not much good. (You may also use bread-making yeast, but the beer won't taste very good, because so much yeast sediment will be left in it.) It's a good idea to keep extra beer yeast on hand.

3. *Sugar:* Most brewers recommend dextrose, also known as invert or corn sugar, which has a simpler molecular structure that yeast prefers. Some beermakers say that you can convert white sugar into invert sugar by adding to the batch of beer:
1 tsp lemon juice or **1 tablet vitamin C**

4. *Good-quality water:* If your water tastes good, your beer has a better chance of tasting good. If your water is chlorinated, you can evaporate some of it by letting it sit, or boiling it, but it will never be as good as good-quality water.

PROCESS

1. Rinse out a 6- to 7-gallon food-grade plastic bucket with boiling water.

2. To make the wort, mix in a 4-quart stainless steel pot:
2 qts good quality water
1 3-lb can hop-flavored malt extract
6 cups dextrose sugar
Stir and cook over very low heat until the malt extract and sugar dissolve. Measure 4½ gallons of good-quality water into your plastic bucket. Add the dissolved malt mixture. Check the temperature; it should be 70° to 75°F. (To alter temperature, dip out liquid and heat or cool it.)

3. Proof the yeast *(p. 248),* and stir it into the wort.

4. During this primary fermentation stage, you can either cover the bucket with a piece of plastic, secured with string or elastic, as I do, or you can seal the bucket with a tight lid and put the fermentation lock in place, with water in the lock so that carbon dioxide can escape but air can't get

in. The wort will sit quietly for a day or so and then work madly for about 2 days. If you have the fermentation lock in place it'll bubble and pop all the time; it may even pop the cap off the lock.

5. On the fourth or fifth day, all beer-makers agree, it is a good idea to siphon the beer into another container, put a fermentation lock on it, and allow it to work more slowly for 2 or 3 days. This is known as secondary fermentation.

6. Then siphon the beer into a new container. This second siphoning clears yeast sediments and improves flavor. Measure into each bottle:
¼ tsp sugar
This is called priming.

7. To bottle the beer, use the siphon hose and fill the bottles to within 1 to 1½ inches of the top. It is important to leave this air space. Seal on lids tightly.

8. Store bottles in a cool place for at least 3 weeks; 3 months is better.

State-of-the-Art Brewing
Brewing in the '90s is taking on a whole new look. In many places, nowadays, you can go into a beer store, select the components, and have 5 gallons of beer brewed for you within the week. As long as you break the yeast into it yourself, legally it's your batch — and it doesn't take 3 weeks or 3 months to age.

The shorter period of production is part of the CO_2 revolution. Carbon dioxide under pressure, stored in a compression tank, puts bubbles in the beer even better and faster than the sugar-in-the-bottle method. That, in fact, is how breweries make beer, and it's a good part of the reason that home brew tastes different from commercial beer.

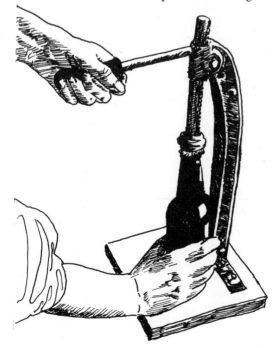

You can even keep a tank of carbon dioxide under pressure and carbonate beer after the secondary fermentation; and by using stainless-steel kegs you can eliminate the need for bottling altogether and just draw as much or as little as you want at a time. To take beer to a party, you draw it into a bottle and screw the top on.

WINE

These recipes are from our friends Brian Coady and Maria Peters, who make exceptionally fine wines out of fruits that grow in Cape Breton.

When they brew wine, Brian and Maria put the huge jug of wine in the middle of the house, up off the floor, where it keeps warm and they can keep an eye on it. The carboy, as the jug is called, is exceptionally lovely, and the little glug. . . glug. . . it makes, every once in a while, is not unpleasant. It's easy to keep an eye on the fermentation lock, which has to be kept full of water to work. And, of course, when they notice the bubbles have stopped, it's handily in the middle of the room for siphoning and bottling. Five gallons of wine is something you don't want to have to carry up and down stairs.

I think the success of these wines is also due in part to the special ingredients — the pectic enzyme and acid blend, which put in things that are missing from non-grape wines.

Keep a notebook on all your wines, adjusting sweetness and body with the various components. Remember, some fruits are sweeter than others, and fruits can also be combined. Wines can be blended, too.

The Basic Process of Making Wine

First, you gather a whole bunch of fruit. As soon as possible, mash it a bit, to get the juices running, and add sugar, water, and a little wine yeast. The yeast goes to work converting the sugar into alcohol and giving off carbon dioxide. This is called primary fermentation, and takes 4 or 5 days. The fruit mixture starts slowly to bubble, then froths furiously. When it stops working, you siphon, or rack it off, into another container for secondary fermentation, this time with a fermentation lock on it. As the wine continues to work slowly, bubbles of carbon dioxide will come up in the lock. When they stop coming, in 2 to 4 weeks, you again rack and then bottle your wine. Most wines are aged a minimum of 3 months, but they improve with age. Corked wines should be stored on their sides in a cool place.

There are two important things to look after in winemaking. The first is that wine yeasts are fussy about temperature. Excessive heat, over 100°F, will kill them. And if it isn't warm enough, under 65°F, they become inactive. With a reliable thermometer, see if you can find a good place for a 7-gallon bucket that will stay at 70° to 75°F. If not, devise a gentle stove by hooking up a 40-watt lightbulb in a shallow bucket and using it to heat your fermentation bucket.

The second essential thing is keeping airborne wild yeasts, fungi, and bacteria out of your wine. At the same time, you have to let out carbon dioxide. This used to be a big hassle in home winemaking, unless you had some chemist friends, but fermentation locks are now available in most larger supermarkets and brewery stores. The fermentation lock only works if it is full of water; periodically the water must be renewed.

WINEMAKING EQUIPMENT

1. *Primary fermentation bucket.* This should be about 20 percent larger than the amount of wine you intend to make, to allow for the giant frothing and bubbling that goes on in some of the more robust wines. To make 5 gallons of wine, use a 7-gallon bucket. Cover this with a plastic sheet, tied in place with sewing elastic.

2. *Secondary fermentation bucket or carboy.* This should have a fermentation lock. The carboy, or large bottle, is better than the bucket because it has a narrow neck, thus excluding air; the bucket, on the other hand, has the advantage of opacity. Light is thought to darken wine.

3. *A 4-foot flexible transparent siphon hose.*

4. *Twenty quart-sized wine bottles and fresh, new corks.* You may find it convenient to use a corker, not an expensive device. Soak corks in water for 1 to 2 hours before using them.

Cleanliness
Soap does terrible things to wine. Bleach does terrible things, period. Baking soda is good to help soak out old crud, but the best way to keep winemaking equipment clean is to rinse it out with lots and lots of hot water as soon as you're through using it.

INGREDIENTS

Water: Good-tasting water is important to good brewing. Chlorine can be partly evaporated by letting water sit in a container for 10 hours, then boiling it; but the water still won't taste great.

Fruit: Fruits such as berries and rhubarb can be frozen and later defrosted for brewing. Though the flavor will not be quite as fresh, this technique is handy to know, because some people find it easier to brew in the winter, when there are no rows to weed or warm beaches to go to.

Acid Blend: Grape wines are naturally acid enough, but other fruit wines taste better with this mixture of citric, tartaric, and malic acids. It also helps break down the sugar.

Pectic Enzyme (pectinol, pectolase): Occurring naturally in grape wine, this breaks down pectins, which hold fruit flavor suspended in them. Without pectic enzymes, your wine will be less tasty and more cloudy.

Yeast: Yeast is a single-celled organism, dormant when you buy it, which wakes up when you mix it with tepid water. If you give it a little sugar, it eats the sugar, gives off alcohol, and divides and multiplies, swelling its population until it runs out of sugar and is killed by the alcohol or by excessive heat.

To "proof" or test the yeast before adding it to the wine; mix:
1 Tbsp (1 packet) wine yeast
½ cup tepid water
pinch of sugar
Allow to sit for 10 minutes. It should bubble slightly; if it does not, the yeast isn't very strong. Allow it to sit for another 10 or 20 minutes. If it still doesn't become foamy, it's dead. It's wise to keep extra yeast packets on hand.

Yeast Nutrient: This nutrient helps complete fermentation. There is also a super-nutrient, known as *Yeast Energizer*, which has vitamins that encourage wine yeast to work even in the presence of alcohol.

Strawberry Wine

A delicate rosé, not overly sweet, with a wonderful strawberry bouquet. Our friends proudly served it with roast chicken and vegetables — all home-produced.

Crush in a stainless steel pot:
18 lb fresh strawberries
Add:
2 qts boiling water
9 lb sugar
1¼ tsp grape tannin
2½ tsp pectic enzyme powder
5 tsp acid blend
Stir for several minutes, until the sugar dissolves. Then add this to:
4½ gallons water
Make sure the temperature is between 70° and 75°F before you add:
1 Tbsp wine yeast
Cover with a plastic sheet secured with an elastic, and let it sit in a cozy place at 75°F for 5 or 6 days. It will foam up and settle down. Strain out the pulp and siphon the wine into a container with a fermentation lock. Add water as needed to make 5 gallons liquid. Allow to sit for 3 weeks at 70° to 75°F, then siphon again and let sit overnight, covered, before bottling the wine. Fill bottles to within 1 inch of the cork. Age at least 3 months.

5 GALLONS

Blueberry Wine

This is a dark, purplish red wine, with a good red wine flavor and a hint of blueberry but no sweetness about it. Best after 3 months.

Crush in a large stainless steel pot:
10 lb fresh or frozen blueberries
Add:
8 lb sugar
5 lb raisins
5 tsp acid blend
2½ tsp pectin enzyme powder
2 qts boiling water
Stir until sugar dissolves; then add:

4½ gallons water
Stir thoroughly for 2 minutes. Make sure the temperature is between 70° and 75°F before adding:
1 Tbsp wine yeast
Cover with a plastic sheet tied with elastic, and let it sit in a warm place at 70° to 75°F for 5 to 6 days, or until the yeast stops working. Strain out the pulp and siphon the wine into a container with a fermentation lock. Add water as needed to make 5 gallons liquid. Allow to sit for 3 weeks at 75°F, then siphon again before bottling the wine. Fill bottles to within 1 inch of the cork. Age at least 3 months.

5 GALLONS

Saskatoon Berry Wine

Saskatoons, or serviceberries, are a little bigger and even sweeter than blueberries, and grow on small trees all over Canada and parts of the United States. They make excellent wine.

Crush in a large stainless steel pot:
15 lb saskatoons
Add:
7 lb sugar
5 lb raisins
2 qts boiling water
Stir until sugar dissolves. Then add:
2½ tsp yeast energizer
2½ tsp pectin enzyme powder
5 tsp acid blend
3½ gallons water
Stir thoroughly. Make sure the temperature is around 72°F before adding:
2 Tbsp wine yeast
Cover with a plastic sheet tied with an elastic, and brew at 70° to 75°F for 5 to 6 days, or until the wine stops working. Strain out the pulp and siphon wine into a container with a fermentation lock. Add water as needed to make 5 gallons liquid. Allow to sit for 3 weeks, then siphon again before bottling. Fill bottles to within 1 inch of the cork. Age 3 to 6 months.

5 GALLONS

Dry Rhubarb Wine

This balance of ingredients produces a nice white table wine.

Chop and place in a clean 7-gallon bucket:
13 lb rhubarb
Pour over the rhubarb:
8 lb sugar
Let this sit, covered, for 24 hours. Add:
1 gallon boiling water
Stir to dissolve sugar. Then add:
4 gallons cold water
1¼ tsp grape tannin
Allow mixture to cool to 75°F. Then mix together:
½ cup water at 75°F
1 Tbsp wine yeast
Add dissolved yeast to the mixture. Stir and cover. Let sit 48 hours.

Strain out fruit and siphon the wine into a container with a fermentation lock. Add water as needed to make up 5 gallons liquid. Allow to sit at 70° to 75°F for 2 to 4 weeks, or until the fermentation lock stops bubbling. Rack and clarify if necessary. To prevent cloudiness, drop in a slightly beaten egg white. In 2 days all the sediment in the bottle will have collected in the egg white, and can easily be strained out. Bottle and age at least 3 months.

5 GALLONS

APPLE CIDER

To make real cider, you can use any kind of apple, the sweeter (and riper) the better. You need a chopper and a press. The chopper chops the raw apples up into what's called a "cheese." Then with the press, you extract juice. People I know have experimented with all kinds of jacks, levers, and so forth; one couple succeeded in raising their barn a couple of feet with a homemade device that was meant to press down the apples — but nobody seems to have had any luck making cider without a screw-type apple press.

Cider will keep, in a cool place, for a couple of months at the most. After that it starts going hard, and the released carbon dioxide blows corks, or breaks bottles, or turns to cider vinegar, if unsealed. Cider freezes well; remember to leave air space in the container, as all liquids expand about 10 percent when frozen.

If you wish you can fit it with a fermentation lock *(see p. 250)* and have hard cider. When bubbles stop rising, it'll keep for years if sealed: a substance of terrible potency.

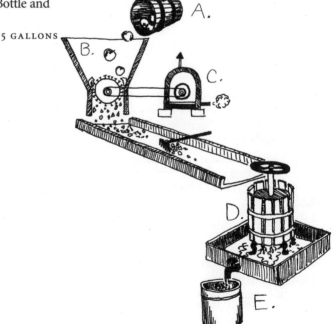

Food Storage

Food can be stored in various ways, depending on the climate and conditions you live with.

Plain Keeping (root cellar and attic storage): Some foods, such as roots, seeds, nuts, and certain fruits and vegetables, naturally keep out the air, and they can be stored over most of a winter just as they are, as long as the right temperature and humidity is maintained *(see p. 254).*

Drying Fruits and Vegetables: Many fruits, all herbs, and some vegetables can be dried, in small quantities, to be eaten later as snacks or revived in a soup or stew. The process is best done in a food drier; drying outdoors can be a little tricky in a damp, northern climate but can be done in drier places quite easily *(see p. 258).*

Canning: Hot water-bath canning is suitable for canning fruits, pickles, jams, and tomatoes, all of which have a certain amount of acid in them *(see p. 262).*

Jellies, Jams, and Pickles: Many fruits and vegetables may be used to make an astonishing array of bottled condiments to liven up the bored old winter-farmhouse supper table *(see pp. 266–68, 271–74).*

Freezing: Almost anything can be stored in a freezer, and many foods (such as fresh meats and green vegetables) can be stored only in a freezer. It's easier than canning, and the food is better for you than if stored by any other method. As a practical device, it has no equal; but it does require electricity *(see p. 275).*

PLAIN KEEPING

Husks, skins, and shells on some foods keep air out, and they can be stored over most of the winter just as they are, if you maintain the right temperature and humidity and are careful not to let them freeze.

Root Cellar (cool and damp)
apples
beets
Brussels sprouts*
cabbages*
carrots
cauliflower*
celery*
Chinese cabbage*
head lettuce*
Jerusalem artichokes*
kohlrabi*
leeks*
oranges, lemons, grapefruit*
parsnips and salsify*
pears*
potatoes
turnips and rutabagas

Attic (cool and dry)
beans, peas, seeds
dried fruits and vegetables
garlic
grains
onions
winter squash and pumpkins*

* These foods will keep only for a limited time, 1 to 3 months.

Root Cellar Storage
To store roots for any length of time, you must have a damp, cool root cellar. The temperature should be constant, just above freezing, no lower than 32°F and never much over 40°F. The humidity should be from 90 to 95 percent, or the roots will shrivel after a few months.

There are various ways to make root cellars. The most common is in the cellar of your house, where it will be handy. However, in that case, you should install rodent-proof bins or cans. You can make one big bin, if you'd rather — but be careful to keep the apples away from the vegetables, as apples give off a gas that hastens the decay of most roots.

If your house or cabin doesn't have a cellar, you can build one outside. Choose a well-drained slope where snow will pile up (snow insulates). In southern places, it need not be deep; two feet will do. Farther north you should go down below the frost line, but the storage area doesn't have to be entirely below it; the packing material and snow will serve to insulate it. Remove any nearby rocks; stone transmits frost.

The food may be packed in boxes or clean barrels. Some people don't use containers, but this seems risky to me; rodents might discover your cache. If the climate is mild, you can set the containers directly in the earth, but in Nova Scotia we pack sawdust around them. Some roots such as carrots and beets should be packed in some insulating material — sawdust, sand, leaves, or straw; this also helps keep rot from spreading. Build a close-fitting lid that will be easy to remove, with a wooden handle, and provide a ventilation pipe with a cap on top to keep out moisture. Bank with plenty of leaves or straw, and top with earth. Finally, dig a V-shaped drainage ditch to divert the water in case of a rainy spell or January thaw.

Keeping Roots

Don't try to store anything until cold weather ensures that the cellar will be cool enough to keep them. As you bring in each box of vegetables, trim off the tops to within ½ to 1½ inches of the crowns. Gently wipe off excess dirt and check for damage or disease. Sort the roots into three categories:

1. Undersized or damaged roots to be used within a month; you need not pack these in sand, just store them loose in a cardboard or wooden box

2. Medium-sized, blemished, or odd-shaped roots (such as multirooted carrots) to be used within 3 months; store in leaves, fresh sand, or sawdust in wooden crates and label as such

3. Large, perfect roots to be used in late winter; store roots in clean sawdust or fresh sand in wooden crates and label as such

Beets: 32° to 40°F; 90 to 95% humidity; store loose or pack in fresh sand or sawdust. Pull beets as the hard frosts commence. Trim tops to within 1 inch; you may freeze or dry beet tops. Large beets will keep very well all winter.

Carrots: 32° to 40°F; 90 to 95% humidity; store packed in fresh sand or sawdust. Keep an eye on your carrots after the first light frosts; sometimes rodents chew the tops off ones that are sticking out of the ground, making them unfit for long storage. Otherwise pull as the hard frosts commence. Trim tops ½ to 1 inch. Sort carefully and pack into graded boxes with damp sand. Use fresh sand each year. Keep carrots in a rodent-proof bin. Carrots will begin to wither and sprout new greens as the cellar warms up. If you want to have really great carrots in the early spring, leave a row in the garden, well-hilled and mulched with leaves or straw. Dig as needed, after the ground thaws; these carrots will not keep well.

Jerusalem Artichokes: 32° to 40°F; 90 to 95% humidity; store well packed in fresh damp sand. It is better, to my mind, however, to leave them on the plant until spring *(see Spring Vegetables, pp. 30–31).*

Parsnips and Salsify: 32° to 40°F; 90 to 95% humidity; store packed in sawdust or sand. These do not really keep well; a couple of months is the maximum. They keep very well in the garden, however; hill the tops slightly and mulch well with leaves or straw. Dig as needed in the spring; they will not keep more than a few days.

Turnips and Rutabagas: 32° to 40°F; 90 to 95% humidity; store loose. Turnips keep very well into late spring.

Potatoes: 32° to 40°F; 85 to 90% humidity; store loose. Dig potatoes after the first light frosts and harden them for a few days by spreading them out in a warm, dry, dark place (about 70°F). Sort into three categories:

1. The largest, most perfect potatoes for seed next year

2. Very small, damaged, or imperfect potatoes, for immediate use

3. Just ordinary potatoes

Store potatoes loose in a dark, rodent-proof bin. It is not necessary to pack potatoes in sand or sawdust; you can just pile them loose. If possible, it is better to spread them out over a large area than to pile them up in barrels or cans as they will rot without ventilation. Nothing smells or looks as terrible as a rotten potato.

Keeping Vegetables

Celery, leeks, and members of the cabbage family may be kept for several months, with care. In general they store better with a little less humidity than roots (85 to 90% is optimum) and about the same temperature (32° to 40°F). Some people store them in dry leaves or straw; I find it easier to hang them up by their roots, or root them in a bin of sand on the cellar floor. They will not, however, keep all winter, so use them up.

Cabbage: 32° to 40°F; 85% humidity; store loose or in dry leaves or straw for 1 to 3 months. Pull cabbages after the first few light frosts, leaving on all leaves and roots. Pick out any worms or insects. If you have a lot of cabbage, you may store it by hanging it on nails or ropes suspended from the rafters, upside down. The big danger in storing cabbages is rot from too much humidity, so keep an eye on them. The firmer, larger heads of winter cabbage variety will keep the longest.

Cauliflower: 32° to 40°F; 85 to 90% humidity; store rooted in moist sand. Pull cauliflower after the first light frosts, roots and all. I have kept cauliflower this way, rooted, until Christmas. They may also be pickled with very good results.

Brussels Sprouts: 32° to 40°F; 85% humidity; store rooted in moist sand. Pull plants after the first light frosts, roots and all; pull off the leaves and root them in sand in a very dark spot. They may last as long as the end of December if your cellar is not too damp.

Kohlrabi: 32° to 40°F; 85 to 90% humidity; store rooted in moist sand. Pull off the outer leaves and pull plant, roots and all, after the first frosts. Kohlrabi will keep for a couple of months this way; you may also pickle it.

Chinese Cabbage: 32° to 40°F; 85 to 90% humidity; store rooted in moist sand. A moderately good keeper, lasting for several months.

Celery: 32° to 40°F; 85 to 90% humidity; store rooted in moist sand. Will keep into January or about 3 months.

Head Lettuce: 32° to 40°F; 85 to 90% humidity; store rooted in moist sand. Large, firm heads will last from 1 to 2 months.

Leeks: 32° to 40°F; 85 to 90% humidity; store rooted in moist sand. Leeks will last all winter, even if very small.

Keeping Fruits

Fruits and vegetables should not be stored close to one another. Fruits will absorb odors from turnips, cabbages, etc; and apples give off a mild gas that makes potatoes and carrots rot. If all you have is one dark hole, store apples separately.

Apples: Some apples will keep all winter. Some won't last 3 weeks. The names of good keepers are Winesap, Spy, Golden Delicious, and some of the newer kinds of McIntoshes, Cortland, Jonathan: the crisp, dense apples with thick skins. Wrap perfect fruit in newspaper or get a stack of pressed-paper fruit racks from your local supermarket. Store at 32°F, 80 to 90% humidity.

Oranges, Lemons, Grapefruit: Citrus fruit will keep quite well in the root cellar for a couple of months. Optimum: 32°F, 80 to 90% humidity.

Pears: Pick pears when full grown but still hard and green. You never know. Sometimes they will take months and months and months to ripen, but mostly they're all gone long before Christmas. Pack as for apples, *see above*. Store at 32°F, 85 to 95% humidity.

Attic Storage

Winter squash, pumpkins, onions, dried beans and peas, and dried vegetables should not be kept in a root cellar, as it is much too damp and they will rot. An attic or room in the house or barn is the best place for them. The temperature should be around 40° to 50°F, and there should be plenty of ventilation or room for the air to circulate.

Winter Squash and Pumpkins: After the first light frost, cut mature squash from the vine and leave outside on a bed of straw or hay to cure the shells as they harden in the sun. Handle carefully to avoid bruising. Store on dry shelves, separated from one another, and check them every few weeks for moldy spots. You may stop the mold by wiping it off, but if dark spots develop, use the squash or pumpkin immediately. Unripe squash should be brought in and used within a couple weeks.

Onions: Onions with thick stalks won't keep well. In short growing seasons, you may hasten the decay of the stalk by bending it over at the end of the summer, a few weeks before harvest. At the first good frosts, pull the onions and let them sit for a week in a barn or dry shed; turn them over now and then to let all sides dry. If you wish to braid them, they may be kept in the attic or in any dry, cool room of the house; or you may trim the tops and keep them in a mesh bag. Use those with thick tops first; save the largest and best-formed for longest storage. Onions will keep until the weather gets warm and damp; usually they start to sprout in May. The green tops make very good salad material.

Garlic: Treat as for onions. They may be hung in the kitchen or, for longer storage, in the attic or an upstairs room.

Beans, Peas, and Other Seeds: All such things should be kept in clean, dry glass jars, sealed plastic containers, or tins. You can often get good wide-mouthed jars from restaurants. If you are drying and storing your own seeds, you should first store them in a very warm place. After 12 hours, see if any condensation has formed inside the jar; this will warn you that they are not completely dried and will rot in long storage.

Besides the moisture problem, there is also the rodent problem. It's no use saying, "But we *never* have mice"; if you keep seeds and peas and stuff around, you soon will.

Grains: Grains may be kept at any temperature under 65°F. It doesn't matter if they freeze; the main problem is rodents. Lids should be tight to keep out grain moths. One solution is to keep them in galvanized garbage pails; they have nice tight lids and are just the right size for 50 to 100 pounds of grain. However, they cost. There are also Mennonite lard tins that hold 50 pounds. You might make bins of your own, out of wood, and line them with sheet metal around cracks and corners, where rodents usually chew holes. Grains kept in such a bin should be in burlap sacks. For short storage, you can use plastic garbage pails with tight lids, but they aren't proof against a determined rodent.

DRYING FRUITS AND VEGETABLES

Drying is a wonderfully compact way to store certain fruits and vegetables. Eighty to 90 percent of the water in dried foods is removed. Some vitamins are lost in the process, but minerals and other nutrients are concentrated. Dried fruits and vegetables taste sweeter, not because sugar is added but because liquid is subtracted. Dried fruits make good travelling food, not only for hikers and backpackers, but also for those far from home in cars, buses, trains, planes, or boats, who prefer to avoid fast-food snacking.

Drying is remarkably simple. It can be done outside under the sun, or inside with a mild heat source such as a lightbulb. Driers of all kinds are on the market, or you can make your own without much difficulty.

As a result of living in one of the world's dampest climates, I haven't done anywhere near as much drying as some. You can find reams more advice in Rodale's *Stocking Up.* I dry herbs, apples, plums, tomatoes, blueberries, rose hips, and chanterelle mushrooms. In some parts of the world you can slice a pumpkin and leave it on a stone wall in the morning and pick up dried pumpkin as you go to bed, but this does not happen in Cape Breton. What works here is a wooden box with 1 x 3-foot frames on which removable cheesecloth is stretched. Underneath is a heat lamp, and in the side is a small fan to blow air up and around and out. You can also make experimental driers using cardboard boxes, with pegs holding the cloth.

The temperature should be from 95° to 145°F, optimum being around 110°F. If your drier doesn't have a thermometer, get one. Indoor heated driers need some form of air circulation built into them, but outdoor solar driers can rely on natural air movement, as long as it is not too strong. The solar drier can have glass or plastic on top to trap the heat of the sun, but sides should be open or partly open to let air through. At night, as the dew falls, the solar drier should be covered, and it should be emptied or brought in when it's rainy out.

NOTE: when drying, don't put stuff too close together on rack.

How long does it take for things to dry? It can be 2 days or 2 weeks, depending on air circulation and temperature. The sooner the better — better texture, flavor, and color. Drying is finished when the fruit or vegetable feels leathery — dry, but still pliable. Seeds, on the other hand, should be hard as rocks, and leaves should be absolutely brittle. Check trays every day, and remove pieces as they are finished. Put them in a glass jar in a warm place for 24 hours; if moisture condenses inside the jar, something is still losing moisture rapidly.

It is often recommended that you steam-blanch all vegetables, and some fruits, before drying. Some driers also treat their driables with ascorbic acid or sulphur, and after drying, they may be *pasteurized,* or heated to 175°F briefly to kill any mold spores that might have taken up residence. But I should just mention in passing that it is not absolutely necessary to do any of that. Your dried goods will be a little darker, and not so reliably mold-free, but lots of people, myself included, have dried lots of food without any preparations whatever.

Fruits for Drying
apples
apricots
peaches
plums
round berries*
cherries
grapes
pears
bananas
rose hips
tomatoes

* Blueberries, cranberries, and other kinds of berries

Vegetables for Drying
mushrooms
string beans
shell beans
broccoli
sweet peppers
hot chili peppers
herbs
pumpkin
summer squash
greens
turnips

Things should in general be no thicker than ¼-inch, but you may, for example, quarter small pears and tomatoes. Round berries, cherries, and grapes should be pierced before drying. This can be done manually or by blanching, which is recommended to preserve vitamin C in berries.

Things that brown easily, such as apples, bananas, pears, will stay lighter in color if dipped in a solution of 500 mg vitamin C (ascorbic acid) dissolved in 1 cup cold water.

To *steam-blanch* fruits or vegetables, pile them 2 or 3 layers deep in a perforated steamer or rack over boiling water. Cover tightly and boil rapidly for 2 to 3 minutes. Don't confuse steam with water vapor, which is cloudy-looking; steam is hot enough to burn your hand or run a nuclear power plant. Cool steam-blanched food at once, laying it on a damp cloth over a layer of ice, or submerging it in ice water.

Dried Fruits
Apples: Use large, firm, sweet apples with good keeping qualities, such as Baldwin, Northern Spy, Winesap, Jonathan, Golden Delicious, Russet. Some people peel them; I don't, but I do like to core them. Then slice them about ⅛-inch or so thick and dip them in ascorbic acid solution. Steam-blanch 2 to 3 minutes. Dry until leathery (like suede).

To use, pour boiling water over them, just to cover. Let sit 1 hour or until soft; use in pies or baking as you would fresh apples. Our favorite use of dried apples is on long car trips; a pile of them on the dashboard has sustained many a weary mile.

Blueberries, Huckleberries, Cranberries: Set a cup or two at a time in a wire strainer and dip them into boiling water for 15 seconds to crack the skins; then dip in cold water to cool them. Spread on a cloth rack or nonmetal screen and dry in the sun, or overhead in the kitchen or attic, for 2 or 3 days, until quite hard. Pasteurize them by spreading them on a cookie sheet and setting them in a 175°F-oven for 3 minutes. To use, pour boiling water over to just cover, and soak 1 hour. Use in muffins, cakes, or cooked with other fruits.

Cherries: Spread on cloth racks and set racks in the sun or overhead in the kitchen or attic; dry until leathery and sticky. To use, pour boiling water over to just cover and soak 1 hour or until soft.

Peaches, Pears: Choose just-ripe, sweet fruits. Cut in half and remove pits and cores. Dip in ascorbic acid. Steam-blanch 2 minutes, then place cut-side-up on cloth racks and dry inside or out; be careful to cover them against flies. They will take up to a week to dry out completely, until leathery. Turn several times a day during drying. To use, pour boiling water over to just cover, and soak 2 hours or until soft; cook with other fruits for compote, or chop into small pieces for use in cakes, cookies, etc. These are very good eaten dried.

Plums: Cut in half and stone them. Steam-blanch 2 to 3 minutes; spread, cut-side-up, on cloth racks. Dry indoors or in the sun until leathery; turn several times while drying, and be careful to cover them against flies. Set on cookie trays and pasteurize them (set in a 175°F-oven) 2 minutes; cool and store. To use, pour boiling water over to cover and let sit ½ an hour or until soft. Cook in mixed fruits or use as you would raisins or store-bought prunes.

Fruit Leather

Squish out seeds from raw plums (peels or no peels), blend with sliced apple, sugar to taste and lemon peel.

Spread on plastic wrap just thin enough.
2 cups plums, peaches, pears, or **apricots**
½ cup sugar (or to taste)
1 sliced apple or **pear**
grated lemon rind

To prevent insect infestations, put fruit leather in freezer for 3 days. The freezer is a good way to store dried fruit leather anyway.

DRIED VEGETABLES

Since vegetables do not have the quantity of acids and sugars that act as natural preservatives in fruits, it is much more important to steam-blanch before drying and to pasteurize after drying; otherwise they may develop mold in storage.

Leather Britches Green Beans: Use small, tender beans. Nip off the ends and steam-blanch 15 minutes; cool over ice. Lay on cloth racks or string on knotted cord; dry indoors overhead in the kitchen or attic, or outside on a clear, windy day.

When they are leathery, stick them in the oven at 175°F for 5 minutes. To use, soak in cold water for 2 or 3 hours and then cook them in that water (it may take 1 hour or longer to tenderize them enough to eat).

Shell Beans, Limas, Peas: When pods are fully ripe but not yet brown, pick and shell them; spread to dry in the sun on cloth racks until hard. Another method, not so foolproof but easier, is to pull whole plants when the pods are ripe and hang them in the barn for a week or two; then bring them in and shell as needed. I used to know some people in Vermont who put their dried beans, plants and all, in a barrel next to the woodstove to dry; when they wanted to use them, they put a kid in there to flail and stamp around as a "chore." Then the contents of the barrel were dumped out on a sheet and sorted. *(See p. 89 for cooking times of various dried peas and beans.)*

Corn: Corn is dried on the cob, either with the husks on, or peeled back. When dry, rub from the cob. *(To use, see pp. 166–67 on corn in the Grains chapter.)*

Greens, Daylilies: Choose young, tender leaves, daylily buds, or withered flowers. Set a handful (no more) loosely in a steamer and steam for 5 minutes or until wilted. Spread on cloth racks, singly, to dry. Greens will take 2 to 3 days, daylilies up to a week. To use, just add dried greens to whatever soup, stew, etc., you are cooking, or boil directly in water. To use daylilies, soak first for 1 hour in cold water, then use as you would fresh. They are best in soups and stews.

Mushrooms: Use only fresh, young mushrooms for the best flavor; at any rate, don't use any that have begun to rot. Spread on cloth racks and dry until leathery, almost crisp. (Pasteurize for 10 minutes in a 175°F-oven to prevent mold.) To use, soak in cold water for 1 hour; use in stews, soups, and Chinese foods.

Peppers (Hot or Green): Thread hot peppers, whole, on knotted cord; hang in the sun until crisp, or store in the attic. Green peppers should be split, cored, and cut into strips or quarters. Spread on cloth racks. Dry in the sun or indoors, on racks or knotted string, until quite crisp. To use, soak in cold water for ½ hour, then cook for use in rice or other grain dishes, stews, tomato sauces, etc. These are also quite good dried, as snacks.

Pumpkin, Winter Squash, and Summer Squash: Use squash fresh from the garden. Slice quite thin; spread on cloth racks. Dry on racks outdoors or in, or on knotted cord. The denser the squash, the longer it will take to dry until quite crisp. Pasteurize for 10 minutes in a 175°F-oven. To use, eat zucchini chips like potato chips; or soak all squashes in cold water to cover until soft, then cook in the water you soaked them in.

Tomatoes: Sundried tomatoes (or any kind of dried tomatoes) are nice little things to have around the kitchen. Good to gnaw on while you consider what there is to cook. Nice with cheese and crackers and a cup of herbal tisane *(see p. 64)*.

My cousin June, who lives on the West Coast, sent me a Ziploc bag of dried tomatoes through the mail. She recommends plum tomatoes, quartered, spread on racks and dried by either solar or indoor heat. Dried tomatoes can also be used in cooking; first soaked 2 hours in hot water, then added to rice or pasta. Dried tomatoes have a sweet flavor and a texture something like that of raisins, even when they have been soaked and cooked. Very tasty.

DRIED ROOTS

Some roots are dried and ground, such as chicory, comfrey, ginseng, and sassafras. To get the most out of roots, dig them up in the late fall, when the strength of such a plant goes to the roots. To dry them completely, scrub them well and trim off any root hairs. Slice them into strips or diagonals, about ¼-inch thick, trying to keep the pieces more or less the same size and thickness. Dry them in a 100° to 150°F-oven for 2 or 3 hours; when you see some edges go brown, keep a close eye on them. They should be bottled, or ground and bottled, at once or they will absorb moisture again.

meat and soups and certain vegetables: peas, beans, carrots, corn, and pumpkin come to mind. To pressure can, a large pressure cooker is filled with jars of food and some water; the lid is sealed on, the pressure raised by heat to a measured point, and then the food is cooked in heat and pressure anywhere from 20 minutes to 2 hours.

The reason for all this hassle is to eliminate the possibility of botulism, rare but extremely dangerous bacteria that, once in a while, develop in the top of a jar of nonacidic food (usually fish) that hasn't been pressure canned properly. Botulism toxin cannot be seen, smelled, or tasted, and it doesn't turn silver spoons black, but it is so toxic that a tiny amount can kill, and there isn't any known antidote.

CANNING

When I first moved to Cape Breton in 1971, Margie Kirkham and I got into canning together. We were largely ignorant and wholly unprepared. She knew a little more than I did, from her mother, and I had a book about how to do it properly. We had no equipment; we barely had enough pots and pans to cook meals with — we had no jars, and in fact we didn't even have a garden, having just landed in Cape Breton. But we had tremendous amounts of energy, and went at it with that. We bought jars. We begged vegetables. We borrowed a pressure cooker from a local fast-food place called Lick-a-Chick. The pressure cooker was not needed for all our canning efforts, but we wanted to try everything.

There are basically two kinds of canning. In one, you fill a hot canning jar with hot food and seal it with a rubberized lid. This method is only used for fruits, tomatoes, and pickles that are sour enough to discourage the growth of bacteria in a canning jar. The other kind of canning is called pressure canning, and it is used for nonacidic foods. These include fish and

We were doing our cooking, that summer, on Margie's leaky old wood-burning stove. It worked quite well with the dry wood that was there when we first arrived, but when that was gone, we ordered a load of slabs and a pile of hardwood. The slabs turned out to be freshly cut, and the hardwood was mostly birch. After one awful day in which we filled the house with smoke, and still never got the pressure canner up to 20 pounds, we almost gave up. But we were nothing if not persistent. We decided to make one last try, using her Coleman camp stove. We balanced the pressure cooker, full of jars and food and water, on the tippy little green stove, and fired it up. It was so obviously dangerous that we declared the kitchen off-limits to kids, dogs, and husbands. And we canned. We pressure canned peas and beans and corn and carrots. We also, without pressure, canned tomatoes and applesauce and all kinds of pickles: dill, sweet-and-sour, mustard, relish, and green tomato chow. We canned raspberries and blackberries, and, one sunny day, organized an enormous expedition to Cape Smokey for blueberries. On the way, we ran out of gas and had a flat tire, but we persevered, got gas, fixed the tire, picked 10 gallons of blueberries, and canned them all. We put the shining jars, red and blue and green and yellow, into our root cellars. We were proud of ourselves.

That winter, whenever we went down to the root cellar for potatoes, we brought up our shining jars of canned goods, and we had something special. At least, some of it was special.

The stuff we'd canned without pressure cooking — the tomatoes, apples, blueberries and pickles — was wonderful. But the food that had taken so much effort, the pressure-canned peas and beans and carrots and corn, tasted just like canned stuff from the store. Insipid. Boring. Tasteless.

Which is the reason I haven't bothered again with pressure canning, in my life or in this book. The next year, we planted our own garden and got an 18-cubic-foot deep freeze, for peas and beans and other nonacidic foods. It's also possible to freeze many of the things I like to can, such as applesauce and blueberries and tomatoes. I don't know why I do it. Pride, I guess, and those rows of shining jars.

Preparations

Canning, more than any other kitchen endeavor, requires preparation and forethought. You have to lay in supplies, get organized, and set aside a day for it. If you plunge in willy nilly, you'll soon find yourself amid more chaos than you ever believed possible. But a properly planned and executed canning day can be a great delight.

Supplies

Jars: There are 4 sizes of canning jars available today, in hardware stores, supermarkets, and direct from Ball Mason Jar: two-quart, quart, pint and half-pint.

Lids: There are two parts to the lids:
1. a flat metal disk with a rubber ring inset in the bottom, where the lid meets the jar, and

2. a screw-type ring that holds the disk in place. The lid seals because the air in the airspace left in the top of the jar expands when hot, forcing some air out, and contracts when it cools, sucking the heat-softened rubber down around the rim of the jar, just enough to make an effective air seal.

Rings and flat lids are sold both separately and together. There are also one-piece plastic lids available in the same size, so that you can replace the seal of a jar of pickles or jelly, as soon as you open it, with a one-piece lid.

Containers: To heat acidic foods, use stainless-steel or enamel pans only; aluminum, cast-iron and copper can leach into the food and darken or spoil the quality and flavor of the food. The enamel on cheap enameled pots chips easily; after buying and discarding half a dozen of them, I have found it more economical to invest in stainless steel. For temporary storage, you may also use stainless steel, glass, or food-grade plastic.

Canning Kettle: This can be of any material, but should be deep enough so that you can set a quart bottle in it and cover with boiling water.

Miscellaneous: You'll need tongs to pull bottles and lids out of boiling water; clean dishcloths to wipe rims; and plenty of hot water to wash jars. I've also found that a good pair of rubber gloves makes canning much easier.

Sealing Jars
The two methods I have used successfully to seal jars are:

Hot Pack, in which hot food is packed in hot jars, after which the lids seal by themselves, and

Boiling Water Bath, in which hot food is packed in hot jars, covered with lids, and then the jars are submerged in boiling water until they seal.

In both methods, the lids seal because the hot air molecules in the airspace shrink as they cool, pulling the soft rubber of the lid around the neck of the jar. The airspace is important. In 2-quart jars it's 1¼ inch, in 1-quart jars it's 1 inch, and in 1-pint and half-pint jars it's ¾ inch.

Hot Pack
1. Prepare jars by washing and rinsing them in hot water. Then submerge them in boiling water for at least 5 minutes, or until you are ready to seal in the food.

2. Boil lids at least 5 minutes, separate from jars.

3. Heat food to the boiling point.

4. Remove each jar with tongs, fill exactly to its shoulder and wipe the rim with a clean cloth. Place lid on top and screw down the lids firmly but not tightly.

5. Place jar in a draft-free place and allow to cool for 2 hours before testing.

6. To test, remove the rings and see if the lids are tight.

Boiling Water Bath
1. Prepare jars by washing and rinsing them in hot water. Then keep warm or submerge them in boiling water until you are ready to seal in the food.

2. Boil lids at least 5 minutes, separate from jars.

3. Heat food to the boiling point.

4. Remove each jar with tongs, fill exactly to its shoulder and wipe the rim with a clean cloth. Place lid on top and screw it down firmly but not tightly.

5. Submerge jar in boiling water for the prescribed length of time. Remove from water with tongs and allow to cool in a draft-free place for 2 hours before testing.

6. To test, remove the rings and see if the lids are tight.

Bottled Tomatoes

If you can grow them, or buy them cut-rate in season, tomatoes are pretty easy to can, and very rewarding. If you eat a lot of dried beans, you need a lot of tomatoes (to make beans tasty).

Most tomatoes are acidic enough to rule out the possibility of botulism, so they can be hot water–canned. The exceptions are yellow tomatoes, or those big, bland, overripe beefsteak tomatoes we all love to eat raw. Always be sure to cut any bad or soft spots out of tomatoes before cooking them for canning. You may remove skins, or not, as you choose; to do so, scald them in hot water, then dip in cold and rub off the skins.

You should not can other vegetables with tomatoes (such as onions, peppers, etc.) by the hot water bath method; the sweetness of them will reduce the acidity of the tomatoes too much for safety.

Tomato Juice

Use the good parts of imperfect, half-rotten, or spotty **tomatoes.** Simmer until soft in an enameled or stainless-steel pot; stir often. Put through the fine sieve of a food mill. For every quart of juice, add 1 teaspoon of salt. Store in a cool place up to 1 week. When you have accumulated enough juice, use for canning whole tomatoes, or:

Pour boiling hot **tomato juice** to within ¾ inch of the tops of pints, 1 inch below tops of quarts. Adjust caps; process pints 10 minutes and quarts 15 minutes, under boiling water. Cool 2 hours; test lids.

Tomatoes in Juice

This is my favorite way to can tomatoes; you can even serve them, quartered, in salads. I use small, whole tomatoes. If you use large ones, you should quarter, halve, or core them. Peel if you like:
7 to 10 perfect tomatoes per quart
Pack them into canning jars; pour over, leaving ¾- to 1-inch head room:
boiling tomato juice
Adjust caps; process pints 35 minutes, quarts 45 minutes, under boiling water. Cool 2 hours; test lids.

Bottled Tomatoes, Hot Pack

Skin, if you like, and core, if large:
7 to 10 tomatoes per quart
Put them in an enameled or stainless steel pot along with:
1 cup boiling water
Cook them for 5 to 10 minutes, stirring and turning so they heat through. Lift them into the jars, pack tight, to within ¾ to 1 inch of top. Adjust lids; process pints 10 minutes, quarts 15 minutes. Cool 2 hours; test lids.

Ketchup

As you might guess, ketchup is not too hard to make. The great thing about doing it yourself is that you are in control of the ingredients; you can make it without salt, sugar, or any preservatives.

Heat in a stainless steel pot:
10 lb fresh or canned tomatoes
1 cup chopped onion
1 chopped carrot
2 stalks chopped celery
Tie in a bit of cloth and submerge in the pot:
½ cinnamon stick
1 clove garlic
3 bay leaves
1 tsp paprika
2 whole cloves
2 tsp mustard seed
2 tsp celery seed
½ tsp allspice berries
Cover and simmer 1 to 2 hours. Remove cloth bag and put the vegetables through a sieve. Add:
⅓ cup brown sugar or **sugar to taste**
1 cup cider vinegar
1 tsp salt or to taste
Cook down further, uncovered, to desired consistency.

Stir frequently as ketchup thickens. Pour into sterile hot half-pint jars, leaving the top ¾-inch airspace. Adjust lids, submerge jars in boiling water and boil 5 minutes.

2 TO 3 QUARTS

Bread and Butter Pickles

Pick fresh and slice evenly into rounds:
30 pickling cucumbers
Slice thinly:
10 medium-sized onions
In a large crock or plastic container, dissolve together:
1 cup pickling salt
4 quarts water
Keep cool and covered overnight.

Wash in hot water and sterilize in boiling water:
10 pint jars
Boil separately:
10 canning jar lids
In a stainless steel or enamel pot, boil:
10 cups vinegar
7 cups white sugar
2 tsp turmeric
1 Tbsp freshly grated ginger
1 Tbsp celery seed
1 Tbsp mixed pickling spices
Drain off the brine and add the cucumbers and onions to the hot pickle. Bring to a boil again, for 5 minutes; then commence filling jars. Leave ¾- to 1-inch airspace and carefully wipe the rims. Adjust lids and allow to cool in a draft-free place. If done quickly, no further sealing will be necessary.

10 PINTS

Vegetable Pickles

When the garden is at its height, everything coming in at once, I generally make a batch of mixed vegetable pickles. You may use any one of these vegetables alone in this pickle; but I find the contrast of a good mixture makes all of them much more interesting. Even after a year they will all be crisp and tart, but not too sour or strong-flavored. The mixture looks glorious and makes a good present for a friend.

In a large crock, bowl, or plastic bucket, dissolve:

1 cup pickling salt (also called kosher)
1 gallon water
Chop into this brine:
2 cups small carrots, cut into 1-inch sticks of ½-inch diameter
2 cups tiny gherkin cucumbers or **larger cukes, cut in slices or sticks**
2 cups celery, cut in 1½-inch sticks
2 cups small, fresh green beans
2 green peppers, cut in small strips or diamonds
1 medium-sized cauliflower, cut in florets
2 cups small, round pickling onions or **onions, cut in chunks**
2 cups small, green tomatoes, quartered
Set a plate over these, weighted down with a quart jar of water. Leave in brine overnight. Next day, drain off the brine. Boil 8 pint jars; in another pan boil 8 lids and rings. Keep bottles as hot as possible when filling them. Heat in a big enameled or stainless steel pot:
4 quarts (16 cups) water
6 cups distilled white vinegar
½ cup mustard seeds
2 Tbsp dill seeds
4 cups sugar
Add the vegetables and simmer until they are hot, about 20 minutes; distribute in hot jars and pour over the pickle, leaving ¾-inch headroom; do not allow vegetables to protrude above the liquid. Adjust lids and screw down tops. Set in a draft-free place and do not disturb lids until jars have cooled completely — 2 or 3 hours.

8 PINTS

Mustard Bean Pickles

Margaret Gillis gave me this recipe just after I wrote my first cookbook; I wrote it in the back of the book and used it until that copy of the book wore out.

Pick freshly, wash, trim, and chop into 1-inch lengths:
15 cups green beans
Steam the beans until tender (10 to 15 minutes).

Meanwhile, bring to a boil a large pot of water. Wash and sterilize:
7 pint jars
In another pot, boil:
7 jar lids
In a large stainless-steel saucepan, combine:
2½ cups sugar
1 Tbsp turmeric
2 tsp salt
½ cup dry mustard powder
½ cup flour
Blend in:
½ cup vinegar
Heat in a saucepan:
2½ cups vinegar
1 Tbsp celery seeds
Gradually stir the hot vinegar into the mustard mixture. Simmer 5 minutes, then add vegetables. Bring to a boil. Ladle into jars, leaving ¾- to 1-inch airspace in the necks, and adjust lids.

6 PINTS

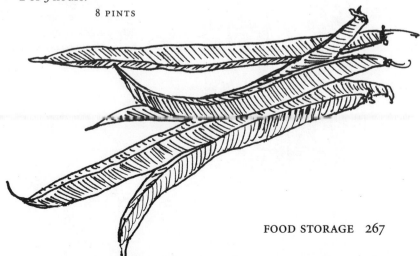

Proper Dill Pickles

These pickles are lightly fermented, making them both milder and more tasty than pickles that are simply bottled in a mixture of water, vinegar, and spices. In the interests of crispness, always use slender, freshly picked, pickling cucumbers. You may quarter them if you like; I do them whole. The advantage of slicing cucumbers is that you can pack more in the jar; the advantage of whole cucumbers is the crisper quality of the product.

In a clean crock or plastic container, combine:
⅔ cup pickling salt
1½ cups cider vinegar or **white vinegar**
5 quarts water
1 large bunch fresh dill
5 large cloves whole garlic
20 to 30 whole cucumbers
Cover the cucumbers with a plate weighted down with a jar of water to keep the cucumbers under the liquid.

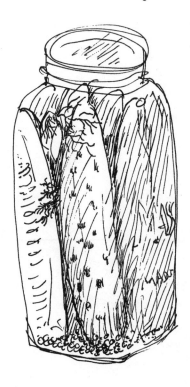

Cover the container with a lid and leave it in a cool place for 2 weeks.

After about a week, these are very good. Keep a sharp eye out for pickle filchers.

By the end of 2 weeks, or whenever you get around to bottling them, there may be some white scum on the surface of the liquid. Don't worry about it. You are going to throw out the brine anyway; rinse off the cucumbers under cold water.

Prepare and sterilize 5 to 7 jars, fresh lids and rings *(see p. 264).*

Dill pickles are of varying lengths; select quart bottles for long ones and pints for short.

In a stainless-steel pan, heat together:
2½ quarts water
¾ cup cider or **vinegar**
⅓ cup pickling salt
While this is heating to a boil, place the drained cucumbers in the jars.
Poke in each jar:
1 dill blossom and several dill leaves
1 large clove peeled garlic
1 tsp mixed pickling spices
Fill each quart to within 1 inch, and each pint to within ¾ to 1 inch of the top. Wipe rims, close lids tightly, and pop them into boiling water. The water will instantly stop boiling, but no matter. Cover and cook 15 minutes from the moment you put the jar in the pot. You will likely hear the lids pop lightly as they seal, and can test by pressing down lightly on a lid (after it's out of the pot). Allow to cool in a draft-free place.

4 QUARTS

Bottled Applesauce

Generally I like to put up about 30 quarts of applesauce in 5-quart batches. It's very easy, and it makes a versatile commodity. You can serve it as dessert, or on pancakes, or with dinner (very nice with cornbread, or beans, or pork, or all three). Kids especially like it. It's instant food, of a kind in big demand and short supply in the winter.

The best apples for applesauce are very sweet ones; they can be a little on the soft side, or a little overripe. Throw in 1 or 2 tart apples now and then to keep up the flavor.

Halve into a large enameled or stainless-steel pot:
½ bucket of apples
Add:
½ cup water or so
cover, and stew until apples are soft. Put them through a food mill. Add sugar or honey as needed. Don't add any spices. Store in the refrigerator up to 1 week.

When you have stewed up and accumulated around 2 gallons of applesauce, it's time to can. Heat the applesauce very slowly, adding water if necessary to keep it liquid enough so it doesn't stick in the pans.

Fill bottles to the shoulder of the jar, poking down each side with a knife to make sure there aren't any air bubbles. The level of applesauce should be ¾ to 1 inch below the rim of the jar. Wipe rims of jars with extra care, and adjust lids.

Process pints and quarts 20 minutes under boiling water; let cool 3 to 4 hours, and test lids.

Bottled Blueberries

Blueberries are the wild grapes of the North; from the middle of August until the frost, they're everywhere, and everybody likes to pick them. They need no sugar, but hold their shape a little better if you add per quart of blueberries:
2 to 4 Tbsp sugar
½ tsp lemon juice
There's no need to add water; blueberries make their own juice if you mash a few as you put them in the pot to heat up.

For every 2 quarts of fresh blueberries, figure on 1 quart bottled.

Measure blueberries into stainless-steel or enameled pots; cover, and bring to a boil.

Wash an appropriate number of bottles; set lids and canning kettle of water to boil. Fill bottles with boiling blueberries ¾ to 1 inch below tops of jars. Wipe rims and adjust lids. Set bottles in boiling water bath.

Time from the moment you put the last bottle in; boil the bottles for 20 minutes. Cool for 2 to 3 hours. Remove rings and test lids. Store in cool dark place.

Bottled Peaches or Pears

Pick Bartlett, or sweet pears when ripe but not soft. Store in a cool dark place until tender.

Choose peaches that are ripe but still firm and a little tart. If you wish to remove the skins, dip for a minute in boiling water; then halve, pit, and peel them.

As you cut up pears or peaches, dip in a solution of:
1 cup water
½ tsp ascorbic acid or **1 tsp citric acid** or **2 Tbsp lemon juice**
For every 4 quarts sliced peaches or pears, boil together:
4 cups water
1 cup sugar or **½ cup honey**
Bring bottles to a boil in a canning kettle; boil lids separately.

Keep the bottles boiling hot until the moment you fill them.

When the syrup boils, add the fruit and let it simmer for 5 minutes. Pack the fruit in hot jars and cover with boiling syrup to within ¾ to 1 inch of the rims. Wipe and adjust lids. If you manage to keep everything hot enough, you won't have to process the jars; they will seal as they cool. If they don't seal, submerge them in the boiling water bath and process 10 minutes. Cool and check lids.

FRUIT JUICES

While I have never gotten my life so organized that I could bottle rows and rows of fruit juices, sufficient to have some every morning for breakfast, I do usually manage to put up a few pints of juice in case somebody comes down with an awful cold. My juices are very thick and bitter; they are really unsweetened concentrates, meant to be mixed with honey and water and drunk very hot. Besides doing wonders for a sore throat or stuffed sinus, they're very high in vitamin C. If you like, these juices may be spiced, while they simmer, with cinnamon sticks, cloves, or allspice berries, in a bag .

Blackberry Cordial

In an enameled or stainless-steel pot, mash and heat:
a quantity of blackberries
When the berries lose color, hang them to drip overnight in a cloth bag. In the morning, wring out the bag and return juice to the pan; for every quart, add:
½ cup honey
Boil until thick, and pour into pint-sized canning jars, leaving ¾-inch headroom. Adjust lids. Cool 2 hours; test lids.

Elderberry Rob or Cranberry Juice

If you can get both kinds of berries at once, you should try mixing them; they go together very well.

Boil together in an enameled or stainless-steel pot:
equal amounts of berries and **water**
When the elderberries lose their color, or the cranberries burst, strain through cloth bag, hang overnight; wring out bag in the morning. To each quart of juice, add:
1 cup sugar
Boil and pour into pint canning jars, leaving ¾-inch headroom.

JELLIES AND JAMS

The canning of fruits and making of jams, jellies, and such are, to me, a rather special art, a jewel-like link between summer and winter. We seldom eat our jellies in the summer, but space them out over the long cold months. I like to label them with care, as:

Raspberry Jam
From the Ryan's pasture
or
Strawberry Jelly
Made the day Chris came to tea

That way, in the taste, we remember summer in more ways than one.

After discovering that crab apple peels contain enough pectin to jell almost anything, I just use crab apple jelly, half and half with syrup or stewed berries or fruit pulp, to make jellies and jams of all kinds. (You have to save a little crab apple jelly for the spring and early summer berries — not always easy to do.) Later in the season I just stew the apples and whatever else is around (rose hips, plums, blackberries) together in the same pot, strain it, and make jelly out of it.

What You Need for Making Jams and Jellies

1. One or two medium-sized heavy enameled or stainless steel pots

2. Cheesecloth (a couple of yards per season will do) and a place — you may have to devise something — where you can hang a bag of fruit to drip without it's getting in anybody's way for 3 or 4 hours

3. A tin can half full of paraffin wax (for sealing jelly)

4. Lots and lots of sugar — at least 10 pounds per season. You can use honey if you don't mind everything tasting a little like honey.

5. Bottles. Jelly makers collect all sizes and shapes, even colors, of bottles; anything will do as long as it has a wide-mouthed top and a decent lid (to keep the mice out). You especially need some very small bottles for gifts, or for bits of leftover jelly. Keep an eye peeled for good ones.

6. A candy thermometer.

Homemade Pectin

All apples, and many other fruits, contain pectin, an enzyme that causes the juice of the fruit to jell after it has been cooked for a while and cooled. Apples have a great deal of pectin, and although they are often quite tart and make good jelly by themselves, theirs is a flavor that is easy to alter by the addition of juices and syrups made from other fruits that have a little pectin of their own. By using an equal amount of apple syrup, you may make jellies of juice from strawberries, raspberries, blackberries, peaches, elderberries, cherries, hawthorn berries, rosehips, and mint

Or you may use apple syrup in combination with fruit pulp, to make a slightly jelled jam.

Add:
1 part apple syrup *(see p. 272)*
to:
3 parts strawberries, raspberries, peaches, cherries, plums, blueberries, oranges

Sweetening

All jams, jellies, conserves, and the like take quite a bit of sweetening. You can use honey, if you like, but honey does have a slightly acid tang that flavors all jams and jellies made with it. Certainly if you use honey it should be very mild, such as light clover, wildflower, or orange blossom honey — something without too much taste of its own. The *Ball Blue Book* recommends using no more than half honey, the other half white sugar. I have always used only sugar, but I use less than most recipes call for; my system is to cut the given amount of sugar in half, then add more as needed, to taste.

Spices

If you wish to flavor jelly with spices, such as cinnamon, cloves, allspice, and ginger, don't add powdered spices; they taste weird after long storage. Instead, buy whole spices, tie them in a cloth bag (with a string trailing over one side of the pot) and simmer along with the fruit or syrup. Remove bag and dry out the spices; you can reuse them a couple of times.

Steps in Making Jelly

1. Never try to work with more than 4 cups of fruit syrup at a time when making jelly. For some reason, more than 4 cups just won't jell. So mix up your syrup, out of whatever, in an enamel or stainless-steel pot, and add:

2. Sweetening: for every 4 cups syrup:
2 cups sugar or **1 cup sugar and 1 cup honey** or **1½ cups honey**

3. Bring to a rapid boil. Continue boiling rapidly for the entire time you cook the jelly. Meanwhile set your can of paraffin in a pot of water to heat.

4. As "scum" forms on top, skim it off with a slotted spoon or ladle. (It's perfectly good stuff to smear on bread but it makes cloudy jelly.)

5. When the syrup has been boiling for about 20 to 30 minutes and has reduced by about a third, it is probably jelly. If you have a candy thermometer, *jelly jells at 220° to 223°F.* If you don't have a candy thermometer, it's not easy to tell.

There is much glib talk about syrup "sheeting off a spoon" when it's ready. I have made gallons of jelly and I have yet to see it sheet off a spoon. (I keep trying: maybe it's a wet spoon? A cold spoon?) What I do is this: Take a spoonful of hot syrup out and pour it on one side of a cool dish and set it on the windowsill for a few minutes. If it forms a thick skin within 2 or 3 minutes, it's likely jelly. After you have made a few batches of jelly successfully, you will come to recognize the thickness of syrup ready to jell.

6. Pour the syrup into clean jars, recently rinsed. (Pour a little into a small glass for breakfast — and to find out if it really was jelly. Wait until you find out to label the jars. If it wasn't, and you really want jelly, pour it back in the pot, reheat, and cook some more.) Pour paraffin immediately over hot syrup in the jars, forming a very thin seal. Allow paraffin and jelly to cool for an hour or so; then pour on a second, thicker layer of paraffin.

7. Next morning, label jar, screw on lid, and store in a cool, dark place.

Apple Syrup

Use crab apples when possible. Red crabs make the brightest color jelly. Eight quarts chopped apples and 4 cups water will yield about 1 quart syrup.

Chop apples in half (skins, cores, and all) into a large enamel or stainless-steel pot with:

1 cup water for every 3 cups apples (roughly)

Stew over moderate heat until apples disintegrate, 1 to 2 hours. Stir the mixture; it should be liquid, like a cream soup; add water if necessary and cook a little longer to mix it in.

Line a number of ceramic or plastic containers with coarsely woven cloth, a cheesecloth or 3 layers of cheesecloth. Ladle 2 cups apple glop into each and tie up the bag with strong cord; hang to drip over the bowl. Do not press or squeeze, but allow to drip 3 to 4 hours or overnight.

This is Apple Syrup, unsweetened. To sweeten it, add 1 cup white sugar or ¾ cup honey for every 2 cups syrup, and simmer until mixed.

You may then use it on desserts or pancakes, can or freeze it, use it to make apple jelly, or mix with other fruit syrups to jell them.

It will keep up to 2 months in the refrigerator; store in a lidded jar.

Apple Jelly

Homemade apple jelly has a wonderfully tart and fragrant flavor, quite a bit like currant jelly. If you use bright apples, it's quite red. You can make it ot any sort ot apples, but crab apples are best.

In an enameled pot, heat:
4 cups apple syrup *(see above)*

2 cups sugar

Boil 20 minutes, skimming off scum that forms as needed; at 223°F, remove from heat and pour into hot sterile jars. Seal at once.

2 CUPS

Spiced Apple Jelly

Put any or all of these:
2 whole cloves, 1 stick cinnamon, a piece of ginger root, or **3 whole allspice berries**
in a cloth bag; tie and cook in with apple syrup *(see p. 272)* for the first 20 minutes. Remove before bottling.

Strawberry Jelly

Mash in a ceramic or enameled container:
2 cups wild strawberries
1 cup sugar
Hang in a bag to drip for 3 hours. Add an equal amount of apple syrup and sugar to taste (about a cup, but it varies; usually I have already sweetened the syrup, since it's canned or frozen). Bring to a rolling boil, skim, and boil until thick.

At 223°F, remove from heat and pour into hot sterile jars. Seal at once.

2 CUPS

Raspberry Jelly

Bring to a boil in an enameled or stainless-steel pot:
4 cups crushed raspberries
When the berries are soft, hang them in a cloth bag for 4 hours; squeeze out the remaining liquid. Mix:
2 cups raspberry juice
2 cups apple syrup *(see p. 272)*
1 cup sugar (if needed)
Bring to a rolling boil, skim, and boil until thick.

At 223°F, remove from heat and pour into hot sterile jars. Seal at once.

2 CUPS

Blackberry Jelly

Bring to a boil in an enameled or stainless-steel pot:
4 cups crushed blackberries
2 cups water
When the berries are soft, hang them in a cloth bag for 4 hours; squeeze out any remaining liquid. Mix:
2 cups blackberry juice
2 cups apple syrup *(see p. 272)*
1 to 2 cups sugar (as needed)
Bring to a rolling boil, skim, and boil until thick.

At 223°F, remove from heat and pour into hot sterile jars. Seal at once.

2 CUPS

Peach or Cherry Jelly

Mix in an enameled or stainless-steel pot:
4 cups sliced peaches or **4 cups whole pie (sour) cherries**
1 cup water
Simmer until soft. Hang in a cloth bag for 4 hours. Take:
2 cups peach or **cherry juice**
2 cups apple syrup *(see p. 272)*
1 cup sugar (if needed)
Boil rapidly, skimming as needed, until thick.

At 223°F, remove from heat and pour into hot sterile jars. Seal at once.

2 CUPS

Elderberry Jelly

Mix in an enameled or stainless-steel pot:
a quantity of elderberries (some stems are okay)
1 cup water
Stew until elderberries lose their color. Strain through a sieve. To:
2 cups elderberry juice
add:
2 cups apple syrup *(see p. 272)*
2 cups sugar

Boil rapidly, skimming as needed, until thick.

At 223°F, remove from heat and pour into hot sterile jars. Seal at once.

2 CUPS

Mint Jelly

Pour:
1 cup boiling water
over:
1 cup mint leaves (firmly packed in measuring)
Let stand for an hour or two; empty into a cloth and wring them out to extract juice. To each:
½ cup mint juice
mix in and bring to a rapid boil:
1 cup sugar
Skim as necessary; boil until thick.

At 223°F, remove from heat and pour into hot sterile jars. Seal at once.

2 TO 3 CUPS

Grape Jelly

Grapes have their own natural pectin, and grape jelly is wonderfully easy to make.

Wash, stem, and partly crush:
8 cups Concord grapes
Put them in a stainless-steel or enamel pot with **2 cups water** to boil until soft, about ½ hour. Hang them in a cloth bag to drip for 2 hours.
Bring to a boil:
4 cups grape juice
2 cups sugar
At 223°F, remove from heat and pour into hot sterile jars. Seal at once.

2 TO 3 CUPS

FREEZING

I have always been a major fan of freezers. When I was growing up, we had this great big old army-surplus freezer in our basement, left behind by a previous owner of our house. It was a chest-type freezer with three compartments, each with a separate hatch lid. In one, my mother kept frozen vegetables from the garden. In the second we kept frozen chickens, annual products of my 4-H activities. The third was, for the most part, empty. On the back of the freezer, on top of the compressor, was a large stack of *Life* magazines from the years 1940 to 1945: the War. Drawn to the basement because it was cool and quiet on the hottest day, I discovered that I could just fit in the empty compartment, with the lid off, and there was enough light from the window to read by. I was well aware of the energy waste of this activity, but as I recall I found the heat so debilitating that I just didn't care. It was bliss. And so I became a lifelong fan of freezers.

There are all kinds of freezers. Look around before you buy one. First of all, make sure it's large enough. You just look in there and figure out for yourself how much will fit; don't take anybody's word for it. Think ahead. Are you planting a garden? How about buying a side of meat? Or, say, a case of broccoli in season, to last all year?

You may be able to get a freezer secondhand. The world is filled with people who bought the wrong size, or are moving next month, or are getting on in years and can't take the freezer to that condominium flat in town. Ask around for a month or two, maybe tune in to your local radio's early morning swap shop. There are stand-up freezers and chest-type freezers. Chest freezers are marginally more efficient.

A freezer, any freezer, works best if it is kept in a room where the temperature is between 50° and 60°F. For some inscrutable reason known only to manufacturers, they do not work as efficiently in very cold places (like outdoors, or in a subzero outbuilding). They should not be subjected to dampness (they will rust). They should be placed well away from the wall so you can periodically clean away lint, a fire hazard, around the motor.

Maintaining a Freezer: Periodically, a freezer has to be defrosted and cleaned. Most people do it once a year, in June, when the freezer is at its emptiest.

Unplug the freezer, first of all, and move all the food into the fridge, which you can set at the coldest setting. A vacuum cleaner is a very good tool for defrosting freezers rapidly. Hook up the hose of the blower end, so that it blows hot air out instead of sucking air in, and direct the hose at the ice — which will rapidly melt. Sponge the melt into a bucket. To clean the freezer, use a solution of baking soda and hot water. Wipe once, then rinse, using clean water. Dry with a clean cloth before plugging it in again.

Power Failures: If the power goes off, don't open the freezer. The temperature will stay constant for at least 24 hours. After that it varies; the larger (and fuller) your freezer is, the colder it will stay.

When the power is restored, check the contents at once. Partly thawed and then refrozen foods will be tougher and less flavorful, even if they aren't a total loss. Completely thawed foods must be used at once, except for high-acid fruits (for example, applesauce) or baked goods, such as bread, cake, and biscuits. You should be particularly fussy about the things that have a short lifespan in the freezer anyway, such as fish, shellfish, and organ meats; use them right up. As long as they stay hard, meats will probably be okay, but you must not, on any account, refreeze completely thawed meats, poultry, or fish. The bacteria that were arrested in freezing commence their activities at a terrific rate as they thaw; in 24 hours at 70°F, a thawed steak was found to have over a million bacteria in it. You might, I suppose, control the population explosion by cooking and refreezing thawed meats. They won't be gourmet items, but as least they would be safe to eat.

After a power failure in which some of your stored foods were partly thawed, you should go through and mark all the labels with a red marking pen to remind yourself that these must be used up within the month. (A curt and furious slash will do.)

Quality Freezing

The most important thing about keeping frozen foods is the maintenance of a constant temperature of 0° to 5°F. The second most important thing is the freshness of the food you put in the freezer. Fish, shellfish, and vegetables must be absolutely fresh. Fruits are less perishable. The third factor is the packaging. If you are planning to keep the food longer than a few weeks, special freezer wrap is necessary to exclude air and keep in moisture. The food must be wrapped tightly and sealed carefully. Meats and milk products should be double-wrapped.

Some fruits and vegetables (or meats) are liquid and will freeze in a solid brick if the filled bag is placed in a small container. Then the bag can be removed and the container reused.

To seal plastic bags, twist the top 2 inches of the bag, bend it back on itself, and tie with a wire twisty (or string, in a pinch). This is known as a gooseneck seal.

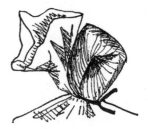

Freezing Grains and Nuts

As long as the protective husk or shell of a grain or nut is left intact, there is no need to freeze grains, seeds, or nuts. Once you crack the shells or grind them, however, you are faced with a storage problem. After 2 weeks at room temperature, such foods as wheat germ, nuts, and shelled seeds lose their flavor. After a month they may begin to go rancid.

Fortunately for those who prefer to buy flour preground and nuts without shells, these may be kept very easily in the freezer for a year or longer.

Freezing Fruits

Fruits are very easy to freeze, and keep very well in the freezer. Fruits that have been frozen are very good in all kinds of cooking and baking. To eat them raw, do not allow them to thaw completely; eat them frozen or half-frozen.

You will find that, in general, I try to use as little sugar of any kind as possible, much less than other cooks who offer freezing instructions. We eat our raw fruit without sugar; why add so much to frozen fruits? If you always add only as much as your taste dictates, you will soon find yourself using much less. And some fruits (such as blueberries or peaches) don't need any, or very little.

If you are going to add sugar or honey anyway, when you thaw and cook the fruit, then you might as well add it before freezing — sugars do help to preserve things. Just don't add any more than you need to. Don't overlook the possibilities of combining sweet and tart fruits, too, such as cranberry-orange relish, or blueberry-apple pie.

Preparations

1. *Washing:* If your fruit comes from commercial growers, chances are it has been sprayed for various diseases, fungi, or insects; better wash it under cold running water. If you grew it or picked it wild, there's no need to wash it unless it's dirty.

2. *Slicing:* As soon as you slice into most fruits, the vitamin C in them begins to oxidize and turn into tannin. There's nothing "bad" about brown fruit, but it does have less vitamin C, and it doesn't look as pretty. The best way to prevent this is to slice it directly into a mixture of:
1 tsp ascorbic acid to 1 cup cold water
Ascorbic acid is just pure vitamin C. As far as I know there's nothing wrong with it, nutritionally speaking, but if you prefer you can use:
2 tsp citric acid to 1 cup cold water
Or if you really prefer to be very organic and don't mind the lemon flavor, you can use:
1 Tbsp lemon juice to 1 cup cold water

Sliced Apples

Apples turn brown when sliced, so if you wish to retain the light color and vitamin C in them, slice them into ascorbic acid, citric acid, or lemon juice solution *(see above).*

Unsweetened Dry Pack: For use in pies, cobblers, and other baking. Choose firm, tart apples. Slice around the core, leaving skins on, into acid-water solution. Dry with paper or a towel; pack in plastic bags.

Syrup Pack: For use in pies, cobblers, other baking, dessert topping. Choose firm, tart apples. Make up a syrup by heating together until well mixed:
4 cups water
2 cups sugar or **1 cup honey**
Cool and add:
4 tsp ascorbic acid or **2½ Tbsp citric acid**
   or **juice of 1 lemon**
Slice apples directly into this mixture, tossing after each apple. When you have enough to fill a plastic container, pack apples in and cover with syrup. To keep apples submerged, wad cellophane or plastic under the lid. Leave 1 inch per quart airspace to allow for expansion of liquid when frozen.

Applesauce: Choose sweet apples; if bland, add a tart one for every 10 sweet apples to insure flavor. Quarter or slice whole apples (peel, core, and all) into:
2 cups water
2 tsp ascorbic acid or **1 Tbsp citric acid** or
   2 Tbsp lemon juice (optional)
Toss apples as you add them to coat them with liquid, and remove them into a large enameled or stainless-steel pot from time to time. When you have a potful, set on a tight lid and add 1 cup of the liquid; bring rapidly to a boil and cook apples until quite soft, ½ to 1 hour. Put through a food mill. Add water if needed; add sugar or honey if needed, but leave out spices. Cool and pack in plastic or coated cardboard containers (you can staple shut milk cartons); leave 1 inch per quart to allow for expansion. If you're short on stiff containers, line them with plastic bags; fill them, freeze until solid, remove the bag of applesauce, and reuse containers.

Cider: Homemade, or unpasteurized, unpreserved cider may be frozen like any juice. When we have room, we freeze gallons of cider in the fall. Remember to leave 1-inch airspace per quart to allow for expansion of liquid when frozen. Thawed in midwinter, it has a terrific fresh flavor. Commercial ciders usually have preservative chemicals in them that sour in freezing.

Soft Berries

By which is meant, blackberries, boysenberries, raspberries, and the like. Any of these berries, seedy when raw, are going to be twice as seedy after freezing. Moreover, the texture of the berry is utterly destroyed when it thaws. Pick over berries before freezing.

For use in syrups, sauce, ice cream, and baking
Heat together:
1 cup water or **berry juice**
½ cup sugar or **¼ cup honey**
Submerge fruit in cooled syrup in pint-sized plastic containers.

For use as separate fruit
To use as a garnish in whipped frozen desserts, ice creams, or Sponge Cake *(see p. 204)*, scatter berries on a cookie sheet and freeze; when hard, pack together in plastic bags or plastic containers.

Hard Berries

By which is meant blueberries, huckleberries, elderberries, saskatoon, or serviceberries. These can be bagged just as they are; you don't even have to pick over them if you don't have time. Frozen raw blueberries are an exceptionally wonderful thing to have on hand; they are excellent on cold or hot cereal, yogurt, or custard-type desserts; you can throw a handful in a cake or muffin or pancake batter, or just hand them out to instantly quiet even the most aggravated child. . . .

Tart Berries

Such as gooseberries, cranberries, and currants. More than likely, you will mix these with sugar or some other sweetener, so you might as well do it before freezing:
1 cup to the quart
Or you may pack them in a sweet syrup:
2 cups sugar cooked with 4 cups water (and cooled)
In the case of cranberries, try packing some chopped together with an equal quantity of chopped oranges (skins, pits, and all). This makes an excellent relish for fatty meats such as pork, moose, duck, or goose — as well as the traditional turkey.

Never use coated cardboard containers for packing these berries in wet form; their extreme acidity sometimes prevents them from completely freezing, and the container won't last forever.

Tart Cherries

Pie cherries come ripe but once a year, and they are among the most rewarding things to have in the freezer. Before setting down to the laborious business of pitting them, you may firm them up by soaking them for an hour in ice water.

For pies and baking
Pack raw, dry, and pitted, or rolled in:
½ cup sugar to 2 cups cherries

For dessert toppings
Mix and heat:
1 cup sugar to 4 cups water
until sugar dissolves; cool. Pack cherries in plastic (never coated cardboard) containers; cover with syrup, leaving ½-inch headroom per pint for expansion.

Peaches

Peaches are among the fruits that oxidize, or turn brown, most rapidly. There are two separate and distinct methods for dealing with peaches, depending on whether you like peaches yellow or peaches brown. Needless to say, it takes at least twice as long to freeze peaches yellow. I am a personal fan of peaches brown, but I will take them any way I can get them in Nova Scotia.

Peaches (Brown): If you want to skin them, immerse them in boiling water for 1 minute (using a wire basket for speed and convenience). Peel quickly, slice and pit, and pop into a light syrup or plain water to cover. Freeze packed in liquid in waterproof plastic containers.

Peaches (Yellow): Before cutting into the peaches, fill a large container with:
2 quarts of ice water
and add:
1 tablespoon ascorbic or **citric acid**
Also prepare sugar or honey syrup:
2 cups honey or **3 cups sugar to 4 cups hot water**
Stir and cook until mixed, then cool. Have ready your pint- or quart-sized plastic freezing containers, each about ⅓ full of syrup. Ready? Peel a peach under cold running water. Slice or halve it directly into the acid-water bath. Before starting on your next peach, put a plate on top of the water bath to keep the peaches from floating. When you have sliced up enough peaches to fill a container, pack them in, cover with syrup, and crumple a piece of plastic or cellophane in the top to completely submerge them. Seal, and freeze. On to the next.

Defrost peaches (yellow) in the refrigerator until almost, but not quite, completely thawed. Serve still frosty, or use in cooking immediately, to prevent browning. Whew!

Pears

The oxidation or browning, which in other fruits is mostly a matter of looks is, in pears, a more vital matter, affecting the delicate flavor and texture as well as the color. So pack pears as you would peaches (yellow) — *see above.*

Plums

Soak plums in ice water to firm them before gently pitting them. Pack whole, in plastic bags. If you wish to serve them peeled, drop whole frozen plums in ice water and they will peel easily within a few seconds.

For mashed plums, run them through the food mill and add:
½ teaspoon ascorbic acid per quart
Stir well and pack in rigid containers, leaving ½-inch per pint headroom.

Rhubarb

Imagine my delight to discover that the freezing process somehow changes the chemistry of rhubarb so that it requires less sugar to sweeten a pie than one ordinarily needs!

For Pies: Pack raw, sliced in 2-inch chunks and bagged.

For Desserts: Cook and sweeten with sugar or honey as you would for the table. Pack in pint or quart containers (plastic only) leaving ½- to 1-inch headroom.

Strawberries

To avoid having them freeze together, spread strawberries thinly on a baking sheet and quick-freeze until solid; then package them together. To serve, do not allow them to thaw completely. If you are freezing strawberries to use in a cooked sauce, treat as for soft berries (see p. 278).

FREEZING MEATS

Hanging, Chilling, and Subdividing: Before freezing, freshly butchered beef is ordinarily hung, to age, refrigerated, for 12 or more days. If you buy your beef ready-cut, you may assume that it has been hung and is ready to freeze after 24 hours of chilling.

Pork, lamb, veal, venison, and other game, however, can be frozen within 1 to 3 days after killing, and need only be chilled for 24 hours before freezing.

Rabbit and other small game are chilled 24 hours.

Poultry is frozen after 24 hours of chilling; but game birds, such as partridge, are hung for 3 days in a cool place.

If you are planning to buy sides of meat, ready-butchered and cut up to your specifications, you will do well to sit down for an hour with a diagram and figure out just how you want the meat cut up; make a few notes or take the diagram with you. Some cuts have different names in different localities. In any case, butchers are notoriously fast with the knife, and in seconds your Christmas roast will lie in slices if you don't speak up. Have your meat cut (or cut it yourself) to the size you will need, and no larger; you have no idea, unless you've tried to cut it, how hard frozen meat really is. (See meat diagram, p. 143.)

Thawing Frozen Meats: The more slowly meat defrosts, the tenderer and juicier it will be. Thus, the best way to defrost it is in a refrigerator, wrapped in its freezer wrapping. The larger (and tougher) the piece, the longer it will take to defrost. Plan ahead when you decide to use meat from the freezer, basing your calculations on the following guide:

	Per Pound
large roasts (beef rib or rump, leg of lamb or pork)	7 to 10 hours
small roasts (veal, lamb shoulder, etc.)	6 to 9 hours
steaks, chops, sliced liver, kidneys	6 to 8 hours
stewing meat	10 to 12 hours
ground meat	10 hours
hamburger or sausage patties	4 to 6 hours
bacon or fatback	1 to 2 hours

If you feel confident about the tenderness of your meat, you may defrost it (in its original wrap) at room temperature, and cut the time in half.

Poultry has such a tendency to dry out when thawed at room temperature that I really cannot recommend it. It should always be thawed in its wrappings, in the refrigerator, for the following periods of time:

	Per Pound
whole birds (depending on size)	6 to 8 hours
split broilers	3 hours
pieces	2 hours

All thawed meats, poultry, and fish should be cooked within a few hours of being thawed.

Cooking Frozen Meats and Poultry: There are times when even the most foresighted and conscientious of cooks may suddenly be faced with the necessity of cooking frozen meats. To cook solidly frozen meat, use low temperatures and cook it longer than usual. How much longer depends on the size, thickness, and type of meat. For example, a frozen beef pot roast should be cooked twice as long; this means 50 minutes to the pound instead of 25. A frozen beef steak, rare, would be cooked 1¼ times as long as if it were fresh or completely thawed. The tenderer, thinner, and smaller the piece, the quicker it will thaw and cook through.

Packaging

Meat must be wrapped up very carefully to keep it from drying out or going rancid in the freezer. These are two separate and distinct problems that should be taken very seriously.

Drying Out or Dehydration: Sometimes referred to as "freezer burn," dehydration occurs fairly quickly if the meat is unwrapped. Meat wrapped in plain butcher paper will dry out in about 3 weeks. The result is a dry, gray, tasteless flesh that even your dog won't want, unless he's a teething puppy with a taste for old leather. To prevent this, you must surround the meat as closely as possible with a moisture-proof material, and seal it.

Rancidity: Oxygen in the freezer combines with fat cells in your meat, causing the fat to change to highly unpalatable fatty acids. The more fatty the meat (such as pork, salmon, duck, etc.), the more likely this is to happen; hence fatty meats have a shorter maximum storage length in the freezer. You must be sure to seal the meat in a kind of wrap that does not let air through, such as freezer-grade plastic bags. Ordinary sandwich wrap, aluminum foil, and butcher paper are too porous.

To wrap ordinary, geometric-shaped cuts of meat (such as roasts), fold freezer paper closely around it as illustrated:

Odd-Shaped Pieces: Poultry or standing rib roasts, which have bones protruding, must be packaged with extra care to keep the wrap from tearing when they are moved around by somebody hastily hunting for the ice cream. You can ball up plastic or waxed paper around the sharp bone ends within the package. Wrap them in something flexible — freezer-weight plastic or aluminum foil. Birds, ribs, and whole fish go well in big freezer bags; to seal them closely, dip the bags in a pot of cold water and twist the end before sealing with a wire twisty. To be absolutely proofed against breakage, encase the piece in a net bag, stockinet, or an old sock.

Hamburgers, Steaks, and Chops: May be packaged accordion-style between two layers of freezer wrap so that you can take out just what you need, when you need it.

Bones: If you are short on freezer space, consider boning your meats, and tying the roasts into rounds. These and other bones may be used to make soup stocks, which you can freeze in pint- or quart-sized plastic containers. This stuff is very useful for gravies and sauces as well as soups. Be sure to leave an inch or so of expansion space at the top of the containers.

Storage Times

The amount of time you may keep a given piece of meat in your freezer varies, according to the type of meat, how large it is, and how cold your freezer is. Lean meats keep longer than fatty meats because there is less fat to oxidize. Large pieces keep longer than small pieces because less surface area is exposed.

Here is a list of the maximum storage times for certain cuts of meat. Remember, too, that many states have maximum legal storage times for game meats, and some require licenses for you to keep them frozen.

Maximum storage times for meats, poultry, and fish	Months at 0°

MEAT

Beef & Venison

Roasts, steaks	14
Stewing chunks	12
Ground meat, oxtails	8
Liver, heart, tongue, kidneys	4

Veal

Roasts, chops, steaks	12
Thin cutlets, cubes	10
Ground meat	6
Liver, heart	3

Pork (fresh), Moose, Elk

Roasts, chops, steaks	12
Cubes	6
Ground	4
Ground and seasoned	2
Liver, heart	2

	Months at 0°
Pork (cured)	
Ham and shoulder	6
Bacon, small pieces	3
Lamb	
Roasts, chops	14
Cubes, thin cuts	12
Ground meat	8
Chicken, Turkey, Duck, Goose, Game Birds	
Whole	12
Halved or cut up	10
Sliced or boned	6
FISH, SHELLFISH	
Lean whole fish	12
Lean fillets	8
Fat whole fish	8
Fat fillets	6
Cooked shrimp, lobster	3
Shellfish in liquid	10

FREEZING FISH

First of all, be sure your fish or shellfish is fresh. If you're not sure, see if it will float. One that has been frozen and thawed won't float.

If you wish to remove the fish head, take it off just above the shoulder bone around the gills, leaving the large bone to give it structure while cooking. Leave the tail on, if possible, for the same reason.

Small Fish: Very small fish, such as smelt or 9-inch trout, are best frozen whole, guts and all, in liquid — either water or fish broth. Pack them in a suitable plastic container or a bag-lined can. Chill overnight, making sure they are completely covered by liquid, and freeze the next day.

Clean and cook small fish before they are completely thawed. Use within 3 months.

Medium-Sized Fish: Ordinary-sized fish (around 9 to 15 inches) may be frozen whole, cleaned, and well wrapped twice in plastic with the air forced out. Be very careful to seal fish packages by folding the edges of the inner wrap together. The outer wrap is important, as it keeps the inner wrap from breaking (frozen fish tails are sharp). A medium-sized fish may also be filleted. Use within 6 months.

Large Fish: Large fish may be cut into fish steaks and stacked as you would stack hamburgers.

To save a large fish whole, such as for a party 6 weeks down the line, put fish in the freezer, unwrapped, and freeze it solid for 24 hours in a quick-freeze compartment or against the coldest wall of the freezer. When it is hard through, take it out and dip in cold water. Refreeze until the glaze is hard. Continue to dip and freeze until you have built up a glaze of about ¼ inch. No other wrapping is needed, but you should renew the dip every 3 weeks or so. Use within 6 to 8 weeks.

Fresh Fish with Vitamin C: Fish with a relatively high fat content such as mackerel, lake trout, and salmon do not keep as well as the leaner fish such as cod, haddock, or sole. To improve storage chances, mix 1 teaspoon ascorbic acid to 1 pint cold water. Dip in the fish for 30 seconds, drain, wrap, seal and overwrap.

Lobster and Crab: Lobster and crab are best cooked whole, chilled 24 hours, wrapped double, and frozen. In addition to conserving the internal moisture, the double wrap will help keep your freezer from smelling like a fish market.

Shrimp: Remove shrimp heads but leave on shells and back veins until after freezing. Shrimp should be tightly wrapped, or frozen in chilled liquid.

Clams, Oysters, Mussels: The only mollusk you can be sure of being fresh is a tightly closed mollusk, which means it is alive. You can steam them open and freeze them in the steaming liquid, to keep for only 2 or 3 months; or pry them open *(see pp. 122–23)* and freeze in their own liquid for up to 10 months.

To Thaw Fish: Thaw fish and shellfish in their wrappers, in a refrigerator. Allow large fish 24 hours to thaw, fillets 4 to 6 hours, and fish or shellfish in liquid 12 hours.

FREEZING VEGETABLES

Freezing vegetables is not quite as simple as freezing meats, fruits, and grains, because you don't freeze them raw. They must be blanched first, to destroy enzymes that will otherwise wipe out most of their vitamin content and toughen them slightly. Vegetables frozen raw look the same, and some of them taste the same; but their food value and texture are radically different.

Blanching: There are two ways to blanch: in boiling water or in steam. Since the vitamin you are most commonly trying to preserve is vitamin C, and since vitamin C is water soluble, I used to do everything in steam. The results were various, especially with beans and broccoli. Sometimes they were great, and sometimes nobody would eat them. The reason is that it is very difficult to keep a full head of steam going in a pot with a steamer rack when you are continually removing the lid and taking out or putting in more vegetables. It is easy to mistake water vapor, which rises out of any pot of hot water, for steam, the stuff that burns your hands and runs steam engines. Frozen vegetables that have been exposed to several minutes of water vapor taste just like untreated vegetables: terrible. Not worth your time. Which is

why I have switched to boiling-water blanching. It is easy to tell when a pot of water is boiling.

After blanching the vegetables for a couple minutes, they must be chilled at once, to stop the cooking process. The best way to do this is to plunge them directly into a sink or pot full of ice water. As soon as they are cooled, they should be dried, bagged, and frozen. The speed with which all this is accomplished has direct bearing on the quality of the frozen vegetables in your freezer.

The Process: Most of the work of blanching is in setting up — finding appropriate containers for blanching, draining, and bagging. It is more efficient to process a lot of something at once than to do a little bit every day. It also requires some concentration, and is more easily done without people in the kitchen, animals underfoot or constant interruption of any kind. The sink and stove should be relatively tidy; you will need them both. Make sure you have plenty of freezer bags, which are heavier quality than sandwich or bread bags. Freezer bags can be washed, dried and re-used for years. Other things you might need: paper towels (also recyclable) and plastic gloves.

All set? Bring a large pot of water to a full rolling boil. Immerse chopped vegetables for the prescribed length of time *(see pp. 285–87)*. Then pull them out, drain briefly and immerse at once in ice water. Move them around so they get properly chilled. Drain them — either on a rack, on paper towels, or in a spin-drier (very good for greens). Bag, seal, and freeze at once.

Each type of vegetable you blanch and freeze will present a slightly different situation. With some you might use a wire basket or vegetable steamer; others can be managed with a slotted spoon or tongs.

Asparagus: Asparagus may be frozen as Asparagus Bisque *(see p. 19)* up to 6 months. As for fresh asparagus, if you have more than you can eat, give it away.

Lima Beans: Lima beans freeze well, as long as they are young and green. Boil 1 minute, chill 1 minute.

String Beans: A most prolific crop. For freezing, pick them before they are fully swollen. Sort, chop, and blanch 2 minutes in boiling water, then chill 4 minutes. Dry on paper, bag, and freeze. To defrost, pour the frozen beans into a small, heavy pan, cover tightly and put over moderate heat for about 4 minutes. Poke and stir after 2 minutes and replace the lid. When fully defrosted and heated, they will be done. (If by chance you are freezing overripe beans, add a minute to your timing.)

Broccoli: Freeze only underripe dark green heads and florets, very freshly picked. Split or quarter the large heads; use small florets whole. Peel tough stems and slice stem pieces into equal lengths. To eliminate the possibility of cabbage worms, soak heads and florets in a sink full of cold water with ½ cup of pickling salt dissolved in it, for about 5 minutes. Worms (if any) will float to the top.

Boil stem pieces 5 minutes, halved heads 3 minutes, florets 2 minutes. Chill in ice water at once, then bag and freeze as soon as you can. To thaw: steam or boil 4 to 5 minutes.

Beets: Beets store very well, whole and unprocessed, in a root cellar *(see p. 255)*. They become rubbery when frozen; thus, I don't recommend freezing beets.

Beet Greens: See Greens, *p. 286.* Excellent.

Brussels Sprouts: Use the dark green parts only. Sort into large and small heads. Boil large heads 5 minutes, small heads 2 minutes. Chill at least 5 minutes in ice water. Bag and freeze at once. To thaw: steam or boil 4 to 5 minutes.

Cabbage: Cabbage does not freeze well. *(See Keeping Vegetables, p. 256).*

Carrots: Carrots freeze well; they also keep well in the root cellar *(see p. 255)*. To prepare for freezing, you may leave small carrots whole, but should slice larger carrots or at least cut them into fingers. Boil 4 minutes, chill 4 minutes. Drain, bag, and freeze. To thaw: steam, boil, or sauté about 4 minutes.

Cauliflower: People tell me that cauliflower can be frozen, but I think it loses too much of its firm texture and tender flavor. Maybe I just haven't learned how.

Chard: See Greens, *p. 286.*

Corn: Corn can be frozen various ways.

Corn on the Cob: Pick your own or buy it off the stalk. Pick only perfect ears. Toss them in the freezer, husk and all. Bag later. Use before Christmas.

Corn off the Cob: Boil a huge kettle of water. Pick, shuck, and boil corn on the cob 4 to 5 minutes. Remove and cool in ice water 15 minutes. Discard pale or unripe ears at this point, freezing only fully ripe, not overripe kernels. Slice corn from cobs and bag as needed. Freeze immediately.

Creamed Corn: This is a better method for dealing with slightly tougher corn. As usual, pick, husk, and prepare it as fast as possible. Blanch whole ears in boiling water and chill *(see above)*. With a very sharp knife, rapidly slice half-kernels off around each ear into a bowl; then turn your knife around and, with the dull edge, go down the rows again, squeezing out the milky juice. Refrigerate until chilled through. This stuff is easier to pack in plastic containers than in bags.

Eggplant: Eggplant will change color as you blanch it, but who cares, if it's going to wind up buried in a pot of tomato paste. Cut into ½-inch slices, and blanch a few at a time. Boil slices 2 minutes. Cool 2 minutes in ice water. Be careful to dry them enough. Package in plastic containers with sheets of paper between layers. Eggplant freezes moderately well, becoming slightly limp.

Fiddleheads: Gather ostrich fern fiddleheads when tightly curled. Pick off the papery brown husks at once and keep the heads cool until you blanch them 1 minute in boiling salted water. Chill in ice water 1 minute. Dry on paper; bag and freeze at once. To thaw: steam or boil 3 minutes. Serve at once.

Greens: Pick only the greenest, freshest, youngest greens; wash well. Boil tender greens (spinach, young chard, kale, beet greens, pigweed, poke shoots, etc.) 1 or 2 minutes. Boil strong greens (mustard, turnip, collards) 3 minutes. Chill in ice water 1 minute. Dry before packaging in bags within boxes or cans; remove later and stack. Be sure to label them! And freeze lots — they're good.

Herbs: Parsley, basil, and dill may be preserved in the freezer and used as garnish or as pot herbs. They should be finely chopped and their bags enclosed in a rigid plastic container.

Pesto (see p. 83) and *Salsa (see pp. 9, 83)* retain a great deal of freshness in the freezer. They may be frozen in an ice cube tray or similar small containers, then loosened with hot water and bagged or boxed together in a labeled container.

Kohlrabi: Kohlrabi freezes very well, but do be careful to choose only young ones that have no woody fibers — there's no way to cook those old ones so they're edible. Trim and slice ½-inch thick. Steam 1 minute. Chill 1 minute or until cold.

Milkweed Pods: Gather milkweed pods when young and tender; cut off stems, but leave whole. Immerse in boiling water; boil 1 minute, drain. Repeat process twice more. Chill 2 minutes.

Mushrooms: My preferred method of freezing mushrooms, both domestic and wild, is to sauté them in a pan with butter for 3 minutes, then cool them over ice before bagging and freezing. For best flavor, domestic and similar types of wild mushrooms (such as meadow mushrooms) should be defrosted as rapidly and cooked as briefly as possible.

Chanterelles are a bright orange funnel-shaped mushroom abundant in our northern coniferous woods. Cut them into similar-sized pieces and freeze raw. To defrost, they may be sautéed in butter and oil, or added to a stew or soup.

Peas: The prince of frozen vegetables, as long as you catch them young and sweet; sort older peas aside for immediate use in soups and casseroles. Peas change color as they blanch, so you may safely steam them, relying on your eye instead of the clock. Remove pods and steam peas about 1 minute, then chill in ice water 1 minute. Dry on paper and bag at once. To defrost, put them in a lightly oiled or buttered saucepan over moderate heat and cover with a good tight lid. It should take about 4 minutes to thaw and heat peas through.

Snow Peas: Flat edible-podded peas freeze well, and don't have to be podded. Choose best quality only for freezing. Slice diagonally or leave whole. Boil 1 minute, drain, and chill 1 minute in ice water. To defrost in a stir-fry or soup, simply include them just before cooking is finished. Cook 1 minute or longer.

Sugar Snaps: These edible-podded peas can be eaten when the pods are full, thus eliminating the tiresome chore of shelling. If they are large, string them before freezing. Boil 2 minutes, chill 3 minutes in ice water.

Peppers: The best peppers for freezing are the thickest-shelled types, such as the California Wonders. Slice or halve; remove cores. Boil halves 3 minutes. Boil slices 2 minutes. Chill 2 minutes; dry well, package, and freeze. As every freezer owner soon discovers, you can freeze peppers raw; they taste just the same, but have very few of the gazillions of vitamins left that they started out with.

Pigweed: See Greens, *p. 286.*

Potatoes: You can't freeze raw potatoes, and, believe me, everybody has tried. There are two ways you can freeze cooked potatoes. (1) French-fried. Consult some other cookbook if you want to freeze french-fried potatoes; I am not having any truck with them in this book. (2) Mashed potatoes. Not a gourmet item, but edible. Pack in plastic containers, allowing ½-inch airspace.

It's okay to freeze cooked stews and hashes with potatoes in them, although the defrosted end product will be a bit rubbery.

Pumpkin: See Winter Squash, *below.*

Rutabagas: See Turnips, *p. 288.*

Spinach: See Greens, *p. 286.*

Summer Squash: Summer squash and zucchini aren't ace freezers, but they're okay. They get a little limp and watery. Use only very young and small ones; slice and steam a few at a time. Steam slices 4 minutes. They may also be grated for baking. No boiling or cooking necessary.

Winter Squash: Winter squash and pumpkin may be frozen cooked and mashed, baked, or steamed in pieces. Steam slices 15 minutes. Put through a food mill or blender to mash. Chill well (24 hours) before freezing.

Tomatoes: First of all, sort them. Throw all the imperfect ones (minus their imperfections) in a juice pot, and simmer them for an hour or two; sieve or strain out seeds and skins.

Freeze juice as is or use it to pack whole tomatoes in.

To pack whole tomatoes, skin them by steaming or quickly immersing them in boiling water; then simmer 5 minutes in water or tomato juice. Cool; chill 24 hours in the refrigerator; pack in plastic bags within rigid containers. Freeze.

Another way to freeze tomatoes is to pack them whole and raw in bags and throw the bags in the freezer. When you want to cook with them, treat them as raw tomatoes, which they (almost) are. Tomatoes, remember, are a fruit.

Finally, there is the ever-popular home-made frozen tomato sauce, which can be thawed and used for literally hundreds of dishes. I have known people who made this stuff in 10-gallon batches, for efficiency *(for basic recipe, see p. 75).* Cool sauce before freezing, and freeze in bags lining rigid plastic containers. Later remove and re-use containers; the bags will retain their shape.

Turnips: Turnips and rutabagas keep fine in the root cellar, but if you want to freeze them, go ahead. Cut off tops and slice or cut in ½-inch cubes. Steam slices 4 minutes. Chill in ice water 4 minutes.

FREEZING COOKED FOODS

The dishes that make the most sense to freeze are those that take the most time and energy to prepare. Cook or bake them until almost, but not quite, done. Cool, chill, wrap, and freeze. To revive them, heat in a 400°F oven for ½ to 1 hour, covered.

You may freeze casseroles, especially those combining meats and vegetables and sauces such as cream sauce, tomato sauce, gravy, or cornstarch. Meatballs, stuffed vegetables, and meat pastries freeze well. Whole or mashed cooked beans freeze well. Soup broths of all kinds freeze well and are endlessly useful.

FREEZING BAKED GOODS

Yeasted and unyeasted breads, quickbreads, pies, cakes, and cookies all freeze well, with few exceptions. They are best if used within 4 months, but you can keep them up to a year. Baked goods do have a tendency to dry out, and you should plan to use them up within a few days of thawing.

Yeasted and Unyeasted Breads: The best breads for freezing are those made with oil and honey or molasses, and not overbaked. Herb and cinnamon breads tend to lose their flavor, alas. Rolls are a good thing to freeze; you can always thaw a few in a hurry to pad out a skimpy meal or welcome some unexpected company.

Quickbreads, Coffeecakes, Cookies: The richest and dampest do best; the dry ones get a little crumbly. Don't frost or fill cakes until after you thaw them. Spice cakes lose flavor, but fruity cakes are fine. To keep cookies from getting broken in storage, package them in plastic bag–lined containers.

Pies: You can freeze fruit pies, meat pies, or vegetable pies, either baked or unbaked. Don't, however, attempt to freeze custard pies, quiches, or anything else with eggs as a base.

The main problem in freezing pies is keeping the top crust from breaking in storage. Buy cheap aluminum pie plates; bake pies into half of them and invert the rest over the cooled pies. Wrap each in a plastic bag and stack them in one corner of your freezer.

To bake an unbaked frozen filled pie, set it unthawed in a 400°F oven for 1 hour; to reheat a baked frozen pie, bake at 400°F for 30 minutes.

Meat pastries and pies with potatoes in them should be baked before freezing.

Cookie and Biscuit Dough: While any dough or batter may be frozen, the only ones that really make life easier, instead of more complicated, are cookie and biscuit doughs. Wrap well and freeze the dough in flat lumps, to roll out, or in bars, to slice.

FREEZING EGGS AND DAIRY FOODS

Eggs: Eggs frozen in their shells will expand and the shells will crack. You may freeze eggs as follows:

Whole Eggs: Mix with a fork and add (to keep yolks from congealing):
¼ tsp salt or **1 tsp sugar per 4 eggs**
Pack in plastic containers or pour into divisions of ice cube tray (try to find egg-sized dividers) and later remove and package together in a plastic bag for individual use.

Egg Yolks: Mix together egg yolks and add:
½ tsp salt or **1 tsp sugar per 3 egg yolks**
Be careful not to incorporate air into the egg yolks. Freeze in small ice cube containers; empty out cubes and wrap in plastic before packaging together in a plastic bag.

Egg Whites: Mix together egg whites, being careful not to beat in air, and package in ice trays or plastic containers.

Label all eggs well. Eggs will keep from 1 to 2 years. Defrost eggs in a cool place if possible, unopened; use at once.

Milk and Cream: Both should be pasteurized before freezing. It is said that cream will whip after freezing, but I haven't had much success with this. Milk tastes funny after freezing but it's perfectly good for you. Remember to leave an airspace — 1 inch per quart — and freeze in plastic rather than glass containers, which can break as the fluid expands.

Milk and cream may be kept up to 4 months. Allow 2 hours per quart to defrost at room temperature.

Butter: Butters, lards, and all fats freeze easily, keep up to a year, and are unchanged. You should rewrap store-bought lard and butter in plastic bags, as the paper wrappers will not keep them from going rancid.

Cheese: Cheese does not keep its smooth texture, but has very much the same flavor in cooking after freezing. If you plan to grate it, you can do so before freezing. Wrap in plastic bags, excluding air.

Cottage Cheese: Cottage and other fresh cheeses are said to freeze well, up to 4 months — but I find that dry curds, frozen and thawed, have the texture of finely ground bubble gum. I used up quite a lot of this stuff one time in spinach pie, but I can't say that I'd do it again. It probably would have been better if I had added cream or milk to the curds. Freeze in plastic containers, leaving ½-inch airspace per pint.

FREEZING TOFU

Freezing is not only a method of preserving tofu, it is also used to make the tofu drier, spongier and more absorbent. Some darkening also occurs. Before freezing, cut tofu in slabs or crumble it by wringing in a clean cloth. Bag in plastic, excluding air. To defrost: pour boiling water over it and let stand 10 to 15 minutes.

WHAT YOU CAN'T FREEZE

• Foods that rely on eggs as a basis for texture really don't hold up in the freezer.

• Cooked grains become watery and tough, even if frozen in a soup or casserole.

• Raw, baked, and boiled potatoes become rubbery and lose their flaky texture — but mashed potatoes are fine.

Kitchen & Tools

KITCHEN

What you want in a kitchen is ease of function; two steps or less from stove to counter to fridge to sink. You also want to be out of the main stream of traffic; the table and the door shouldn't be in the middle of your work space.

Beyond that, a kitchen tends to be personal. It's important to me, for example, to have spare space for projects like brewing, cheese-making, bread-baking, dripping bags of cheese and fruit, and a lot of space around the sink for the piles of pots and tools needing to be washed. I also like a kitchen in which two people can work comfortably. Make a list of the functions you want out of your kitchen, in order of top priority. Does it change seasonally? Look at other people's kitchens, at plans in magazines. Review the list in a week or a month. Make it your own kitchen.

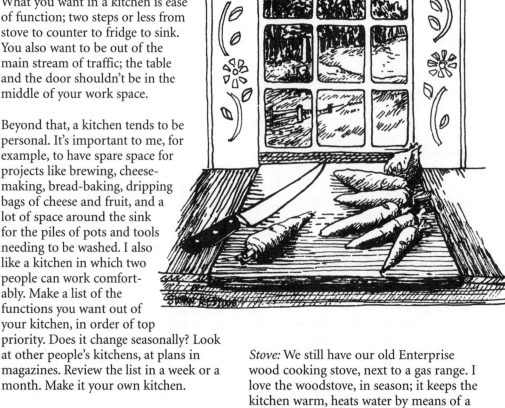

Appliances

Sink: A double sink is handy; you can fill one up with hot soapy water and rinse or pour things down the drain in the other. There's a neat European design for a double sink with an attached drainboard, available in England and Switzerland.

Stove: We still have our old Enterprise wood cooking stove, next to a gas range. I love the woodstove, in season; it keeps the kitchen warm, heats water by means of a pipe that runs through the firebox, and makes it possible to simmer and bake half a dozen things with the same fuel. I also love the gas stove, especially in the summer, when the woodstove will cook you out of house and home. It's also a lot speedier, in any season, than the woodstove.

I have seldom cooked on electric stoves, and perhaps have been slow to get used to them — but every time I try to cook on electric burners, I burn the butter.

Oven: Woodstove ovens work better because heat surrounds the baked goods. Some ovens heat only from the bottom and food tends to burn before it cooks through, especially if you open the door a lot to "see what's happening." However, I have a 110-volt electric oven, which works perfectly. In all types of ovens, it's important to preheat the oven before baking bread, cakes, pies, and cookies.

The best function of microwave ovens is to heat precooked foods and defrost frozen foods. Everybody who has them says they are no good for real cooking.

Refrigerator: Some refrigerators use ammonia instead of ozone-destroying Freon, and they're great. Keeps things cool. Somebody should make them for the mass American market.

Freezer: For long storage, it's important that the temperature in a freezer remain at 0°F. Little freezers attached to refrigerators seldom stay below 5°F, especially if they get opened all the time, so it's best not to rely on them for more than a few weeks.

Deep freezer chests last practically forever. We used an 18-cubic-foot freezer for a family of four, completely filling and emptying it annually. We're presently in the market for a smaller model. Freezers are one thing you can easily buy second-hand, because they almost never wear out — and eventually, farmhouse cooks do.

Crockpot: The crockpot is the answer to a working person's dream: fill it up, plug it in, and come home to a tenderly stewed pot of nice hot dinner. Most crocks have two settings:

Low (200° F) 8 to 9 hours
High (300°F) 4 to 5 hours

If you don't have time to slice onions or peel carrots in the morning, you can prepare your food in the evening and refrigerate it overnight. In the morning empty it in the pot, set the dial, cover, and plug it in. Crockpot favorites:

Chowder *(p. 19)*
Pork Roast Carbonnade *(p. 146)*
Minestrone Soup *(p. 20)*
Boeuf Bourguignon *(p. 147)*
Stone Soup*(p. 21)*
Cocido *(p. 146)*
Chicken Soup *(p. 16)*
Coq au Vin *(p. 139)*
Spareribs *(p. 150)*
Spaghetti Sauce *(p. 75)*
Baked Beans *(p. 90)*

There are many more, but you get the general idea. The heat of the crockpot is lower than that used for ordinary cooking, so food should be cooked longer. The result will be more tender — and, if you're tired and in a hurry, more delicious.

KNIVES

A selection of good knives is worth having. Knives should be kept very sharp. A dull knife is dangerous, because it can slip sideways and cut the wrong thing before you know it. Knives can be sharpened and honed by hand, but benefit tremendously from an annual trip to be professionally sharpened on a diamond belt. If you don't know where to go, ask a butcher.

Sharpening Knives: To sharpen a blade by hand, you will need a fine, flat stone and a piece of old newspaper. Set the stone on the folded newspaper against a wall, hold the blade at an almost flat 20° angle, and move the blade in one direction, as if you were slicing off a thin slab of stone. If you rub it the other way, a "burr" or rough edge may develop.

There is no need to lubricate with oil or water, but you may if you prefer to. Move the knife back and forth so that all parts of the blade are sharpened equally and evenly, on both sides. When the blade is sharp it will easily cut through two layers of newspaper. This will take much longer with stainless than with carbon steel.

Carbon Steel is softer than stainless; easy to sharpen, easy to dull. It can be readily identified because it tarnishes easily, especially in the presence of acid foods like tomatoes and apples.

Stainless Steel is shiny and hard, but seldom is of high enough quality to keep a good edge. Quality stainless steel knives are made, however, and are available from small companies the world over.

To hone, or align, the blade after sharpening, you need a butcher's steel. These are usually chrome plated and should be about as long, or longer than your longest knife blade. Hold the steel firmly. Lay the blade of the knife along it

at a very slight (20°) angle. Bring the blade around and back as you pull it down the steel, so that at the end of the stroke you are firmly pressing the side of the knife tip against the end of the steel. Lay the blade on the other side of the steel and repeat the gesture in reverse. Do each side of a thin knife 4 or 5 times; a thicker blade will need 10 strokes.

To keep knives sharp and safe, always wash and store them separate from other tools. Never store them in a drawer where their edges can be bashed and bent by metal, plastic, or ceramic. Always cut against wood, which does not dull the blade.

Butcher's Knife: A good butchering knife has a broad, somewhat heavy, curved blade, which cuts large pieces of meat smoothly in even strokes. It helps to have a blade a few inches longer than the width of the meat. A reasonable job can be done with smaller knives, but it takes more time and energy.

Butchering knives are often made of carbon steel, because it's easier to keep them very sharp. Many people keep them separate from other knives, so nobody inadvertently dulls it or gets cut. They frequently have a thumb depression in the handle to prevent slippage.

Boning Knife: The boning knife is a thin, curved blade, rigid and very sharp. It is used for tight jobs such as removing meat from the bone, getting between vertebrae or joints, and trimming odd bits off the meat. Be careful not to dull the blade by accidentally trying to cut bone itself;

instead, find the bone with the tip and then cut alongside it.

Chef's Knife: The tip of this long, triangular blade is often kept on the board, with the handle raised and lowered like a guillotine. This gives you extra control so that you can safely move vegetables, like onions, carrots, and celery, around with your other hand. A slight curve close to the tip of the blade gives the swing down a slight rocking motion.

Cleaver: The cleaver has a rectangular, heavy blade with a steeply beveled edge. It is used to cut meat and vegetables into small bits, and is thus especially useful in Eastern cooking. In many parts of the world, the cleaver is the only knife in the kitchen, and is used for all types of chopping and slicing. It has the advantage of its broad surface, which is handy for picking up all the chopped goodies and moving them into the pan.

Paring Knife: Paring knives are small blades, about 3 inches long, used for peeling, scraping, and paring. Often, they're used as practice knives for children. People tend to hold them so that they cut towards, rather than always away from their hands. For these reasons it's just as well not to keep paring knives too sharp. It's not necessary, anyway; you don't need a really sharp knife to peel a potato or trim a cabbage.

Serrated Knife: Serrated knives are really small saws, with a series of small depressions ground into the blades. By sliding the serrated knife blade back and forth, without bearing down, you can often cut difficult things like tomatoes, bread, and steaks. Serrated blades don't cut as clean a line as straight-bladed carving knives, but they also don't have to be kept as sharp, which is an advantage.

Slicing Knife: A long, straight blade with a very sharp edge is best for slicing meat; it's also good for bread and cheese. The blade should be well sharpened and honed just before slicing meat or poultry.

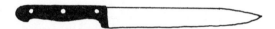

Utility Knife: The utility, or fillet, knife has a thin, somewhat flexible blade, 6 or 7 inches long. Unlike the boning knife, the blade is fairly straight. If it's to be used for filleting, it should be kept razor-sharp and out of the reach of children and people who use knives to pry lids off cans.

TOOLS

It certainly helps to have a good collection of kitchen tools. They aren't really expensive, but good ones may seem expensive because cheap versions are available at many chain stores. For half the price, you can get a garlic crusher that wastes garlic; enamelware that chips the first time you burn the rice in it; bowls that crack, and all sorts of spoons and spatulas and things with plastic handles that come off.

Where do you get good tools? Try a restaurant supply house, or a kitchenware store in a big town or city. Some mail-order places are less expensive. Many of my favorite tools are secondhand — things like a sausage grinder, pea sheller, or grain mill. Keep an eye out for the things you want at yard sales, or on secondhand exchange flyers. You never know.

Here are some things to consider essential:

Food Mill: Resembling a pot with holes in the bottom, this device purées soft food while leaving behind things like apple skins. For making puréed pumpkin, applesauce, mashed potatoes, baby food, there's nothing like it.

Grain Mill: Freshly ground wheat and other grains are much better tasting and better for you than yesterday's flour. When we were young and brimming over with energy, we ground all our own flour one day, and baked bread the next. Electric grinders are interesting, but remember that grinding flour is messy — so put the operation in an appropriate place.

Pots and Pans: Stainless-steel or enameled pans are the only safe kinds; aluminum is risky. A couple of cast-iron frying pans are great for frying, sautéeing, and lots of other things. New cast iron should be "seasoned," the pores of the iron impreg-

nated with oil: rub vegetable oil on all surfaces, then set it in a 250°F oven for an hour. Continue to rub in oil and cook it in until the metal can be safely washed without getting rusty.

Mixing Bowls: A good collection of stainless-steel bowls will do anything, but there's nothing like a big ceramic bowl for making bread.

Buckets: Create a good collection of plastic buckets for kitchen use only. Good for gathering, processing, and taking out the garbage.

Food Processor: I have lived most of my life without one, but they are very useful, for chopping, slicing, mixing, shredding, and grinding, especially in quantity.

Blender: There isn't anything a blender can do that you can't do without one, but once you get one, it's surprising how many things it can do. Pulverize basil. Grind fresh coffee. Make frappés.

Bread Baker: A nifty little machine now exists into which you pour ingredients, set the timer, and, later, or the next day, remove your own freshly baked bread. The machine mixes, kneads, times, and bakes the bread. It is not more fun than making it the old-fashioned way, but if you have to spend the day doing something else, and want your own kind of bread, this is for you. Comes highly recommended by those who use it.

Electric Mixer: Mixers range from the very small whirling whisk that runs on a rechargeable battery to heavy-duty mixers with a bread hook that will knead bread dough. There isn't anything in this book that you can't do without one, because I've never had one.

The Woodstove

A woodstove is a great thing. On a winter day, there is nothing like it. There is always a kettle boiling, bread rising, soup simmering, and boots drying around it. The steady warmth helps to grow sprouts, make cheese and yogurt, dry herbs and fruits, or brew beer and wine. And when you come in from the chores, it's wonderful to stand by the stove and soak up the heat. We have other stoves in the house — principally, a large Ashley chunk stove, which runs 24 hours a day, September through May — but the kitchen stove is the heart and soul of our existence, and we love it.

My first wood cookstove was a warped old Kitchen Queen, some years ago. When I think back on those days, and my ignorance, it's a wonder I didn't burn the house down. I did in fact burn several large batches of bread, cakes, sauces, stews, and several times, my hands. In time, though, I discovered the oven controls, the drafts, and the ashes in the interior; I learned which woods to burn, and when to cut them. The day came when we could bank down the stove (which is very small, as stoves go, and not too tight on top) and find three inches of hot embers there in the morning.

These days, many people are moving out to old farmhouses and rural areas. Many call it a simpler way of living, and there's no question that its joys are simpler. Long walks and visits now and then replace movies and television. Music is mostly homemade; clothes are individual, so to speak, to the wearer. Seasons change, children grow, and the steady rhythm of chores fills days that were once tense and uncertain. We grow closer to the earth, and life seems good, most days.

However, though our lives are less complicated, our roles in this world are not necessarily easier. An outhouse, for example, is a very straightforward sort of thing. But it takes more than the turning of a handle to keep it clean, safe, and useful. Kerosene lamps are cheap and lovely things, but they need to be cleaned and trimmed and filled. So it is with a woodstove; you need to know a little about it to enjoy living with it. What little I have gleaned from trial and error, I gladly pass on, in the hope that your rice never burn, your bread never fall, and your house be safe and warm.

WORKING PARTS OF THE WOODSTOVE

As far as I know, most woodstoves are constructed inside roughly like this:

The Firebox and Plates: The first consideration, naturally, is the firebox. This is the compartment in which the fire is built. The firebox should be lined with either cast iron or stove brick cut in special shapes to fit, so the heat doesn't spread out in all directions.

Stove designs vary. Some load from the side, some from the front, and in some the top of the firebox lifts up in one unit on a hinge.

Under the firebox is a grate for ashes to sift down through. In many stoves, this grate can be turned slightly by a removable handle. Turned one way, the grate is suitable for wood; the other, more open way, is for coal. When such a grate is set for coal, it has wider spaces between the cross pieces, because coal tends to build up a very solid bed of clinkers and ash; you always want there to be some draft. The wood grate is tighter, to prevent the embers (which are necessary for a good fire) from continually falling through. It is impossible to really bank a wood fire over a coal grate. Coal grates and coal/wood grates are more common in coal country. Sometimes grates are built so that they can be turned, slightly, in order to allow you to sift down ashes without getting your wrist black. If the handle is missing, or the grate doesn't turn, use a poker — or, if the stove is cold, a small stiff brush is handy.

The ashes underneath must be removed every so often, for which purpose it is handy to have a removable metal box under the firebox. Deposit these ashes outdoors, far from anything flammable. If your ashes are all from hard wood, you may use them to make soap. Ashes are also very useful in the garden mulch pile. If you have an outhouse, you can dump a scoop of ashes down the hole once a day to keep it from getting smelly, but set them aside first for 24 hours to make sure they contain no live embers.

On the side (and sometimes the front) of the stove, you will find various sliding or hinged doors, called drafts. When opened, they let in a draft of air, making the fire burn hotter. When closed, the fire will be banked — it will burn more slowly and for a longer time.

The equipment for your stove should include a handle for lifting the top pieces out and moving them around. When you use it, hold the circle of cast iron at an angle, so it won't slip off and go clattering on the floor, your foot, or small creatures below.

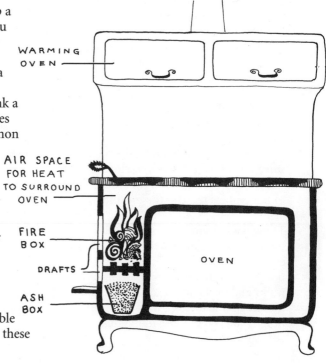

WARMING OVEN

AIR SPACE FOR HEAT TO SURROUND OVEN

FIRE BOX

DRAFTS

ASH BOX

OVEN

The Oven: In order to look at the oven closely, change into your least perishable clothes, and arm yourself with a flashlight, a dustpan, a brush, and wads of newspaper. Dismantle the top of the stove and take a look inside.

At the center back, where the stove is hooked up to the stovepipe, you will find a small sliding door. This has a control that enables the door to be opened and closed without opening the top of the stove. When the door is open, the oven is off. The heat and smoke from the fire will simply go through the open door and up the chimney. Any attempt to bake with the oven off will result in food baked on the top and one side, if at all.

Slide the door shut. The heat and smoke should go across the top of the stove, down the side, along the bottom, up the back, and out the chimney, through a passage up the back. In some models, it goes down a divided side, around the bottom in a U-shaped passage, back up the side and out through a passage in the top. Heat will surround the oven and bake your goodies from all sides. It will, of course, be hottest on the top, since the top is nearest the source of heat. For this reason I like to leave a light layer of ashes on top of the oven when I clean it.

Stovepipes: Most stoves are hooked up to the chimney with lengths of stovepipe. If you are putting in the connections yourself, keep the system as simple as possible. The more elbows and/or horizontal footage you have, the harder it will be for the smoke to be drawn up the chimney. If you have more than one stove using the same chimney, they shouldn't be connected to the chimney at the same level.

A stovepipe must be fastened together with sheet-metal screws, so it won't fall apart. The vibration of woodstoves is slow but sure, and sooner or later the pipes will

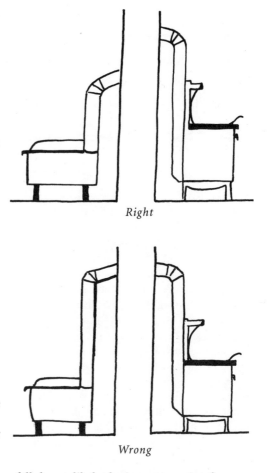

Right

Wrong

fall down, likely during a stovepipe fire. Properly fitting pipes do not need cement.

Periodically (once or twice a year) you ought to pull down the stovepipes and clean them out with a wire brush. Creosote will not collect in it as much as in stovepipes from heating stoves, but it has been known to accumulate and catch fire in houses where much softwood is used.

Your stovepipe should have one or more handles on it. These are dampers, and they control the speed at which hot air is sucked up the chimney. Inside the pipe is a flat circle of light metal that can close off, open, or partly open the stovepipe.

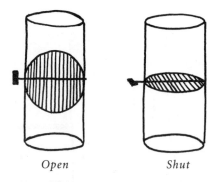

Open   *Shut*

When the damper is all the way open, the fire may burn too fast. Experiment with the drafts and dampers to find the combinations that provide the right amounts of heat for your purposes.

If your stovepipe doesn't have dampers, you certainly ought to get at least one, and install it high on the pipe. Better yet, get two, and set them about 18 inches apart. With one, you will be able to keep a fire going for hours and, since it keeps the heat from shooting up the chimney, the oven will stay hot for much longer. With two dampers, you will probably be able to bank down a fire so tightly at night that there will be hot coals in the ashes in the morning to start a new fire. All you do to install them is drill or punch two small holes in the pipe.

Periodically, the inner workings of the stove become clogged with ashes, and you should clean them out. A simple tool has been designed for this that makes the job very easy; it consists of a length of stiff wire about 2 feet long with a small square of iron attached to the end at a right angle, like a hoe.

With it, or some such device, you first sweep the ashes off the top of the oven into the firebox and shake them down into the ash box. Then, under the oven (either on the front or side of the stove) you will find a small removable panel that enables you to get at the ashes under the oven.

Scrape the ashes out carefully onto a newspaper, inspecting from all angles with a flashlight to make sure all the passages are clear. Replace the panel tightly.

You should not have to clean ashes out of the oven liner very often. In the winter, when I run the stove every day, I do it about once a month. In the summer, I do it maybe once. A lot depends on what you burn; the great stove-clogger isn't wood ashes at all but paper ashes. If you dispose of your paper garbage elsewhere, your stove will stay clean a lot longer.

While you're at it, you might as well invest in a bottle or can of stove polish and blacken the cast-iron parts of the stove. Remember to oil or polish the stove thoroughly if you are going off on a long trip, since more moisture will be in the air while you're gone.

USING THE STOVE

How To Start a Fire
So it's time to light the fire. Make sure that:
• the drafts and dampers are open
• the oven is off (little sliding door is open)
• the ash box isn't open
• the grate isn't clogged with ashes
Crumple into the firebox:
3 or 4 pieces of newspaper
Or distribute loosely, so air can get through:
3 or 4 large handfuls of sticks, dry bark, dry moss, or **wood shavings**
Add:
a crisscross stack of finger-thick, dry, softwood kindling
Light this as near the bottom of the pile as you can and be sure that the *front* of it is on fire. Then close down the wood feeding door, and hover around collecting or

splitting more finger-thick kindling. Don't get distracted. Within 3 minutes, the kindling in the firebox should be on fire. Add more, in a crisscross pattern. Don't just throw in handfuls; they will block out the air circulation. When the whole firebox is full of flaming, crackling kindling, add:

a couple of 2-inch-thick splits (pieces of split wood)

In another 5 minutes add:

a couple more 2-inch splits

a couple of 4-inch splits

If the fire is going well, turn on the oven (close the sliding door) to make the fire burn more evenly, and half-close the chimney damper to keep the heat down.

For the first 8 to 10 minutes, the left rear plate will be the hottest, since the oven is off and thus the heat is going back, over, and up the chimney. By the end of 10 minutes, the hottest plate will be the back middle one. If you want a cup of tea or coffee, that's where to put the kettle.

After you turn on the oven, the emphasis will shift. The two left plates will become much hotter, since all their heat isn't roaring up the chimney; also, the larger pieces of wood will be burning at a higher temperature. By the end of 20 minutes, your kettle of water ought to be boiling, and you can sit down. If you haven't done so already, turn the damper and draft down, and the oven on. Fill up the firebox and relax. It won't go out.

If Your Kindling Doesn't Work: If you are having a struggle every morning, it is most likely that your kindling is wet, or green, or both. The solution is to split it up very fine the night before and dry it out in the oven — with the door open, so the moisture can evaporate.

Whatever you do, don't mess with kerosene or gasoline. It takes eyebrows a long time to grow in again. You can, in a pinch, use waste oil to get green kindling started. Fill up an old dishsoap container and keep it handy (but not too close to the fire).

In Vermont, at the turn of the century, lack of dry kindling was legal grounds for a woman to get a divorce.

GENERAL COOKING

For most cooking, I want part of the stove to be hot enough to sauté, and part of it to be slow enough to simmer. The combination that works best on my stove is to have the oven on, the bottom draft open, and the stovepipe damper set at a diagonal, or half on. I use 2-inch to 4-inch splits and check the fire every 15 or 20 minutes. I try to keep the firebox full and a light bed of embers on the bottom — with enough air space for circulation.

If the stove is going well, the most convenient hot plate is the left front one. That's where I sauté and do most of my hot cooking — either with the plates on or off. The next best is the one just behind it, the left rear. I usually keep a kettle boiling on it, for two reasons. One, I always have hot water for boiling, steaming, or steeping things in a hurry. Two, I can tell from the steady racket it makes how the fire is doing below. The back middle plate is very hot and good for boiling as well.

For simmering, the front middle plate and the right back plate are about the same temperature. The front right gets the lowest heat on the stove — a good place to keep a sauce or a pot of tea warm, or the only place cool enough to simmer something when the stove is running full blast.

Of course, as the wood and weather vary, all of this may change. The best way to find out the temperature of a plate is to toast a piece of bread on it. If it burns before toasting, the plate is hot enough to sauté, fry, make pancakes, or boil a big pot of water fast. If it toasts nicely, it's about right for cooking eggs, simmering, stewing, and steaming. If it takes forever and dries out, the plate is right for keeping warm a pot of tea — or time to dry out some wood.

To Raise the Temperature of the Oven

Supposing you have had a good fire going all day, and you decide to bake some cornbread. You want to raise the temperature of the oven from its chronic 200°F to 450°F. Open the draft under the firebox, and poke down any dead ashes. Stir the coals if they have built up. Fill the firebox with very dry wood 2 to 4 inches thick. Leave the oven on, but adjust the chimney damper to half on. Pay attention to the fire; since it is running hot, you will have to put in a couple of sticks every 15 minutes. When the oven is up to the desired temperature, close the chimney damper and the draft under the fire. The oven should hold, if you keep the firebox full — and you won't have to fill it often. If the temperature starts to go down quickly, open the chimney draft and the draft under the firebox, and fill up the firebox with 2-inch splits.

A word about birch and rainy days. White birch absorbs moisture like magic. On wet days it won't dry out no matter what. It is a fine wood for slow fires, but if you try to run a fast fire with it on a wet day it will drive you crazy. You may have trouble getting the oven very hot on damp or rainy days anyway; the chimney has a hard time drawing fast. You can usually get it up to 350°F without much trouble, but I wouldn't plan anything that requires a really hot oven.

If the stove top is cracked or warped, you may get smoke seeping out through the top as soon as you turn on the oven. In that event, close the draft under the fire and keep the chimney damper open. Some stoves have a draft about the middle of the firebox on the left-hand side; this is handy if the top leaks. You can bake with a leaky stove, and bake successfully, but you really have to watch the fire. Use the smallest and driest pieces of wood you can find, supplement them with softwood, and experiment with the drafts from time to time. And by all means see if you can find a supplier who can provide you with replacement parts for the faulty pieces. There really is no need to put up with such an inconvenience.

To Lower the Temperature of the Oven

First of all, turn off the oven and open the chimney draft all the way, to let your heat go up the chimney. Leave the lower drafts closed around the firebox and throw in a big old piece of damp hardwood, if there's room.

If what's in the oven doesn't mind (like meat) you can always open the oven door. It might take as long as 15 minutes to bring the temperature really down; cast-iron ovens really hold their heat.

To Bank the Fire

A good deal of the time, you will simply want to keep the woodstove running banked — in other words, as slowly as possible. You will need, first of all, a good bed of embers in there. So run the fire hot, with the draft open, the oven on, and the damper half on, and check it every 15 minutes. In an hour or less there will be a 2- to 4-inch layer of embers. Don't stir them down. Simply fill the firebox with large pieces — 4- to 6-inch splits and limb-wood. It needn't be dry. Shut down everything as much as you can: close the chimney damper, close the drafts, and leave the oven on. With luck and a tight stove, the fire won't go out for 3 hours. It will burn down considerably though, so if you're going to be around, refuel it every hour or so. If your firebox is really tight and you're burning wood with a dense grain (like oak, sugar maple, or beech), a good bed of hot embers will be left from a banked fire 7 or 8 hours later.

If Your Fires Keep Going Out

If you have a terrible time keeping a fire going, there are two possible causes. One is that your wood is too heavy and wet. The big chunks will just sit there, steaming and smoking. If you have a wood heating stove running, you can keep them going with shovelfuls of hot embers from the other stove. If not — well, maybe some kindling can be stuffed under the wet wood, although that's a pretty smoky situation and one to be avoided. If it happens more than once, you had better get into splitting the wood finer and drying it out in the oven first.

More commonly, fires go out because they are burning too fast. Typically, it happens when company arrives. Suddenly you remember the stove, and too late — there's a handful of tiny embers winking at you. If the stove is running hot, you have to refuel it every 15 minutes. So if you want to do anything that is going to take longer than that, you had better bank down the fire. If you haven't got a stovepipe damper, install one and use it. Check the firebox for leaks and patch them if necessary with stovepipe cement. And remember to close the drafts and dampers when you aren't going to be near the stove.

Coal

Coal has its good points and its bad points. It burns much hotter and more slowly than wood. A fire banked with coal is much more efficient. There are different kinds of coal; the cheapest, and softest, leaves great big clinkers that won't sift down through the grates and that have to be picked out by hand when the stove is cold. The intense heat of coal warps the tops of many wood cooking stoves. I don't like to use coal because it also costs money, smells dreary, and makes the snow around the house sort of gray.

ACCESSORIES

Warming Ovens: Personally, I'm fond of those old cast-iron stoves with nothing but a curlicued shelf above the cooking surface. But I have to admit that the warming oven is an incredibly useful invention. Not only can it be used to keep food warm (without cooking it further) but it is also invaluable as a place to make

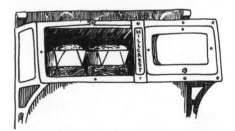

yogurt, raise bread dough, warm plates, and dry mittens. It maintains a constant, draft-free temperature of 90° to 120°F.

A Note of Warning: Whether your stove has a warming oven or a shelf, the bottom surface of it probably gets much too hot for living organisms (such as yeasts and bacteria). Unless the container you're using is very thick ceramic or wood, it's best to slip a heavy tile or a bit of board end under the container to ensure the safety of the contents.

Oven Thermometers: Most woodstoves were built with an oven thermometer on the door, and a good many of these thermometers are broken. If yours isn't working, it's worth every penny to go downtown and buy one to set inside. It's very difficult to bake without one. Bread, for example, comes out dense and soggy at 200°F; at 450°F it burns on the top long before it cooks on the bottom.

Miscellaneous: Keep a good supply of potholders. They will get unspeakably filthy in about 6 months. When they do, you can cover them with a nice dark wool material.

If you don't have a side shelf or hot water heater on the side, it's handy to invert a seldom used baking or frying pan on the right front plate. This is a useful place to put pots full of cooked grain, a sauce, or a bowl of pancake batter that you need close at hand but don't want to cook.

If you spill something like milk or oil on the stove while it's going, sprinkle the surface thoroughly with salt or baking soda. This will eliminate the smell and the fire hazard. I always keep a big box of baking soda on top of the stove anyway, just in case of grease fire. But I've never had to use it.

Measure & Conversion

TRICKS OF THE TRADE

It's good to have a measuring cup and spoons. But you don't need to use them all the time. They're not always around — the cup's in the sink, baby's got the spoons. Learn how to cook without them, because you can save a lot of time. Here's how you do it:

Pour a teaspoon of salt in your hand. Look at it. Now dump it back into the box and, guessing, pour about a teaspoon into your hand. Measure it. Pretty close, weren't you?

Set the teaspoon in a cake pan so it's level. Using the cap of the vanilla bottle, see how many capfuls equal one teaspoon. Now you know.

Take down your measuring cup and one each of whatever cups you keep around (ours are all different). Pour a measuring cup of water into each one. See how far up on the cup it comes; then try this with ½ and ¼ cup. You begin to get a pretty clear idea of what each one contains after a while.

Cut a pound of butter into quarters; then with a wet, sharp knife, cut 1 quarter into 8 equal pieces. Each of these is a tablespoon; save them for cooking.

Memorize:
3 tsp = 1 Tbsp
4 Tbsp = ¼ cup
½ pound shortening = 1 cup shortening
¼ lb cheese = 1 cup grated cheese

When you cook grain, the eventual volume will be the same as the amount of water you put in. For example, 1 cup rice plus 2 cups water equals 2 cups cooked rice; 1 cup rice plus 3 cups water equals 3 cups cooked (mushy) rice.

What's in a Pound?
A pint's a pound, the world around — unfortunately this only applies to water. Here are some other quantities that weigh a pound (lb):

1 lb butter or lard = 2 cups

1 lb cooking oil = 2⅛ cups

1 lb sugar = 2 cups

1 lb confectioner's sugar = 3½ cups

1 lb flour = roughly 4 cups

1 lb oatmeal = 2⅔ cups dry, 5⅓ cups cooked

1 lb rice = 2½ cups dry, 5 cups cooked

1 lb raw potatoes = 2 cups mashed

1 lb noodles = 4 cups dry, 9 cups cooked

1 lb cornmeal = 3 cups dry, 12 cups cooked

1 lb dry beans = 2¼ cups dry, 6 cups cooked

1 lb kidney beans = 4 cups dry, 12 cups cooked

1 lb hamburger = about 2 cups

1 lb Cheddar cheese = 5 cups grated

1 lb Parmesan cheese = 4 cups grated

1 lb mushrooms = 5 cups sliced raw

1 lb raisins = about 3 cups

1 lb bananas = 3 or 4 whole, 2 cups mashed

SUBSTITUTIONS

1 tsp baking powder = ½ tsp baking soda + ½ tsp cream of tartar

2 tsp baking powder = ¼ tsp baking soda + ½ cup buttermilk

1 pkg dried baker's yeast = 1 Tbsp dried yeast or 1 cake moist yeast

1 cup butter = ½ lb butter

1 cup butter = ⅞ cup oil, and decrease liquid in recipe by ½ cup

1 cup sugar = 1 cup molasses and decrease liquid in recipe by ½ cup

1 cup sugar = ½ cup honey and decrease liquid in recipe by ¼ cup

1 cup sugar = ¾ cup maple syrup and decrease liquid in recipe by ½ cup

1 gal maple syrup = 40 gal maple sap

1 oz unsweetened solid chocolate = 3 Tbsp unsweetened cocoa + 1 Tbsp butter

1 lb coffee = 35 cups of coffee

1 Tbsp fresh herbs = ½ tsp dried, or ¼ tsp powdered

1 whole lemon = 3 Tbsp lemon juice

1 cup uncooked noodles = 2⅓ cups cooked noodles

1 cup uncooked oatmeal = 2 cups cooked oatmeal

1 cup uncooked rice = 2 cups cooked rice

1 cup uncooked cornmeal = 4 cups cooked cornmeal

1 cup dried beans = almost 3 cups cooked beans

3 lb whole chicken = 4 cups cooked, chopped chicken

¼ lb cheese = 1¼ cups grated cheese

5 large eggs = 1 cup eggs

METRIC VOLUME MEASURE

In the metric system, there is one volume measure for both dry and liquid: the liter (L). Anything smaller is measured in a milliliter (mL).

1,000 milliliter (mL) = 1 liter (L)

AMERICAN STANDARD DRY MEASURE

3 teaspoon (tsp) = 1 Tablespoon (Tbsp)
4 Tbsp = ¼ cup
16 Tbsp = 1 cup
2 cups = 1 pint
4 cups = 1 quart
4 qts = 1 gallon

METRIC-TO-STANDARD DRY MEASURE CONVERSION

A liter is approximately a quart, or 4 cups. A milliliter is approximately ¼ teaspoon. The following conversion is approximate, not absolutely accurate. The metric amounts are a little larger in most instances, than the standard. You can, however, use these equivalencies for making your own conversions.

Milliliter (mL)	Approximate Standard Measurement
1 mL	¼ tsp
2 mL	½ tsp
5 mL	1 tsp
10 mL	2 tsp
15 mL	1 Tbsp
30 mL	2 Tbsp or ⅛ cup
60 mL	¼ cup
125 mL	½ cup
250 mL	1 cup
500 mL	2 cups or 1 pint
1 liter	4 cups or 1 quart
4 liters	1 gallon

Accurate Equivalencies
946 mL or .946 L = exactly 1 quart

AMERICAN STANDARD FLUID MEASURE

2 Tbsp = 1 ounce (oz)
¼ cup = 2 oz
1 cup = 8 oz
1 pint (pt) = 16 oz or 1 pound (lb)
1 quart = 32 oz or 2 lb
1 gallon = 128 oz or 8 lb

TEMPERATURE CONVERSION

The Fahrenheit scale of temperature measurement is roughly (but not exactly) twice the size of the Celsius scale. Here are a few familiar temperatures:

Deep freeze	0°F	⁻17°C
Freezing	32°F	0°C
Body temperature	98.6°F	37°C
Boiling water	212°F	100°C
Oven temperature	350°F	177°C

To convert Fahrenheit to Celsius, subtract 32, multiply by 5, and divide by 9.

To convert Celsius to Fahrenheit, multiply by 9, divide by 5, and add 32.

METRIC WEIGHT CONVERSION

The basic unit of weight in metric is the gram, which is a very tiny amount:
28.3 grams (g) = 1 ounce (oz)
Larger things are measured in kilograms.
1 kilogram (kg) = 1,000 grams (g)
To find accurate equivalencies in the standard system, use these figures:
1 lb = 453.59 g
1 kg = 2.2046 lb

METRIC-TO-STANDARD WEIGHT CONVERSION

This is an approximate chart.

¼ ounce (oz)			=	7 gram (g)		
1 oz	=		=	30 g		
2 oz	=		=	60 g		
4 oz	=	¼ lb	=	115 g		
8 oz	=	½ lb	=	225 g		
16 oz	=	1 lb	=	450 g		
24 oz	=	1½ lbs	=	675 g		
35.2 oz	=	2.2 lbs	=	1000 g	=	1 kg

PRESSURE CONVERSION

Pressure for pressure cookers and canners is measured in kilopascals (kPa) or pounds per square inch (PSI)

35 kPa	=	about 5 PSI
70 kPa	=	about 10 PSI
100 kPa	=	about 15 PSI

FAHRENHEIT TO CELSIUS CONVERSION SCALE

0° = –17°C	89°–90°F = 32°C	**212°F = 100°C**
31°–32°F = 0°C	**98°–99°F = 37°C**	300°F = 149°C
50°–51°F = 10°C	100°–101°F = 38°C	400°F = 204°C
68°–69°F = 20°C	102°–103°F = 39°C	500°F = 260°C
77°–78°F = 25°C	104°–105°F = 40°C	
86°–87°F = 30°C	122°–123°F = 50°C	

Index

Credits

EDITOR
Lloyd Kahn

DESIGN
David Wills
and
Susan Restino
Christina Reski
Damian Klaus
Lloyd Kahn

ADDITIONAL ILLUSTRATIONS
David Wills

PROJECT MANAGER
Christina Reski

COVER DESIGN
Rick Gordon

TYPESETTING & SCANNING
Christina Reski

PRODUCTION CONSULTANT
Rick Gordon

TYPE CONSULTANT
Alvin Eisenman

EDITORIAL CONSULTANT
Lesley Kahn

PROOFREADING
Kirsten Barendsen
Frances Bowles

INDEXING
Frances Bowles

WORD PROCESSING
Joan Creed

PRODUCTION HARDWARE
PowerMac 8100/80, 40MB/500HD; Quadra
950 64MB/1 GB; Fujitsu 128 Magneto
Optical drive; Agfa Arcus II scanner;
Laserwriter Pro 600

SOFTWARE
QuarkXpress 3.31, Adobe Photoshop 3.0.5

TYPEFACES
Adobe Minion, Adobe Minion Expert

PAPER
50 lb Cornwall Book recycled

PRINTER
Best Book Manufacturers, Petersborough,
Ontario, Canada

PRESS
Timson T32 Web

SPECIAL THANKS TO
Charley Restino for good ideas and lots of
dry kindling

AND TO
Joan Creed
Mike Davies
Page Dickinson
Hal Hershey
MacAuley's Garage,
    Baddeck, Nova Scotia
Marianne Rogoff
Maureen Watts
George Young

COVER WOODCUT AND LETTERING: Mary Azarian